FIDUCIARY ACCOUNTING HANDBOOK

2015

Authors
Margaret M. Hand
Heather Hamilton
Don Edward Green

CEB Attorney Editor
Beth Trittipo
David Peyerwold

CONTINUING EDUCATION OF THE BAR ▪ CALIFORNIA
Oakland, California

For update information call 1-800-232-3444
Website: ceb.com

ES-30020

Library of Congress Control Number: 2015931886

©2015
by The Regents of the University of California
Printed in the United States of America
ISBN 978-0-7626-2217-7

ES-30020

CEB

CONTINUING EDUCATION OF THE BAR • CALIFORNIA

By agreement between the Board of Governors of the State Bar of California and The Regents of the University of California, Continuing Education of the Bar—California (CEB) offers an educational program for the benefit of practicing lawyers. This program is administered by a Governing Committee whose members include representatives of the State Bar and the University of California.

Practice books are published as part of this program. Authors are given full opportunity to express their individual legal interpretations and opinions; these opinions are not intended to reflect the position of the State Bar of California or of the University of California. Materials written by employees of state or federal agencies are not to be considered statements of governmental policies.

CEB is self-supporting. CEB receives no subsidy from State Bar dues or from any other source. CEB's only financial support comes from the sale of CEB publications, programs, and other products. CEB's publications and programs are intended to provide current and accurate information and are designed to help attorneys maintain their professional competence. Publications are distributed and oral programs presented with the understanding that CEB does not render any legal, accounting, or other professional service. Attorneys using CEB publications or orally conveyed information in dealing with a specific legal matter should also research original sources of authority. CEB's publications and programs are not intended to describe the standard of care for attorneys in any community, but rather to be of assistance to attorneys in providing high quality service to their clients and in protecting their own interests.

CEB considers the publication of any CEB practice book the beginning of a dialogue with our readers. The periodic updates to this book will give us the opportunity to make corrections or additions you suggest. If you are aware of an omission or error in this book, please share your knowledge with other California lawyers. Send your comments to:

    Update Editor
    Continuing Education of the Bar—California
    2100 Franklin St., Suite 500
    Oakland, CA 94612
    customer_service@ceb.ucla.edu

CEB Governing Committee 2015

Wayne Smutz (Chairperson)
Dean, Continuing Education and UCLA Extension
University Of California Los Angeles

Marilyn D. Anticouni (Vice Chairperson)
The Law Offices of Marilyn D. Anticouni
Santa Barbara

Susan T. House
Hahn & Hahn LLP
Pasadena

The Honorable David B. Flinn
Judge of the Contra Costa County Superior Court
Martinez

Rex Bossert
Chief Executive for Communications
The State Bar of California

Michael Klein
Klein & Weisz
Los Angeles

Sanford M. Skaggs
Bingham McCutchen LLP
San Francisco

Erwin Chemerinsky
Dean & Distinguished Professor of Law
University of California, Irvine

Scott Monatlik
Senior Director, Corporate Financial Services
University of California
Los Angeles

Contents

Preface ix
About the Authors xi
Cutoff Dates and CEB Citation xiii

1   Introduction and Sample Accountings 1

2   Types of Fiduciaries and the Various Duties
     to Account 47

3   Preparing the Accounting, Step by Step 101

4   Assets on Hand—Beginning of Period 157

5   Additional Property Received During Period
     of Account 187

6   Receipts 193

7   Gains and Losses 237

8   Disbursements 251

9   Distributions 281

10 Assets on Hand—End of Period 319

11 Auxiliary Schedules 329

12 Summary of Account, Reconciliation 343

13 Adjustments Between Principal and Income 351

14 Conflicts and Litigation 369

15 Project Management; Useful Miscellanea;
     a Word to CPAs 403

Table of Statutes, Regulations, and Rules 439
Table of Cases 447
Table of Forms 449
Index 451

Preface

The California Probate Code imposes a duty to account on fiduciaries governed by the Code. Most of those fiduciaries—guardians, conservators, and personal representatives—must file their accountings with the court and therefore must prepare their accountings in the particular manner described in Prob C §§1060-1064. Those fiduciaries who are not required to use this format—trustees and agents under powers of attorney—may nevertheless find that this format best protects their interests. Yet, until the publication of this book, there has been no comprehensive guide to the preparation of those accountings described in Prob C §§1060-1064.

This book aims to demystify Probate Code accountings and describe a set of best practices for their preparation. The book is written for fiduciaries, their accountants, and their attorneys. It also is written for those para-professionals who prepare fiduciary accountings relying on the expertise gleaned from individual experience. Finally, it is written for judges, probate examiners, and court investigators, both those new to this topic and the experienced few. The purpose of this book is to help achieve greater uniformity in the preparation of fiduciary accountings and to increase the number of people who can prepare them competently.

The primary authority for this endeavor is the Probate Code, but often the code defines only the minimally sufficient standards and offers nothing for the practitioner who aspires to something more. In this book, readers can distinguish between the Code's minimal requirements and the book's higher standards by considering the citations. Any proclamation for which no authority is offered is likely just the author's opinion. These opinions are the product of many years of preparing fiduciary accountings, teaching about their preparation, and litigating their sufficiency, but they are, in the end, just the author's opinions. However, until California's Courts of Appeal say more about this topic, opinion will be the only authority we have.

Throughout this book, the term "accountant" refers not only to professionals entitled to call themselves Certified Public Accountants, but also to the broad group of people, including fiduciaries themselves, who sometimes or frequently prepare fiduciary accountings.

CEB owes a debt of gratitude to the attorneys who served as authors of this book: Margaret M. Hand, with Hand & Little, PC, in Oakland, who wrote 13 of its 15 chapters; Heather Hamilton, with Fiduciary Accounting Services, LLC, in Moraga; and Don Edward Green, a former Probate Commissioner for the Contra Costa County Superior Court.

CEB Attorney Editors Beth Trittipo and David Peyerwold and Legal Editors Kate Sheppard and Kristin Schwaighart contributed to this title. Administrative support was provided by Debby Harrison and Nila Kanzaria. The cover was designed by Amy Feldman. Darma DeMarco handled copyediting and production. Kathryn Te Selle prepared the index. Composition was performed by CEB's Electronic Publishing staff.

Michael Fenger
Practice Group Manager
Estate Planning &
Business Law

Pamela J. Jester
Executive Director

About the Authors

MARGARET M. HAND (Chapters 1, 2, 4–13, and 15) is a founder of the firm Hand & Little, PC, in Oakland. She is a certified specialist in estate planning, trust, and probate law, and is a fellow of the American College of Trust and Estate Counsel (ACTEC). She specializes in probate and trust administration, as well as conservatorships and guardianships. In addition, she teaches fiduciary accounting for the CalCPA Education Foundation. Ms. Hand received her undergraduate degree from the University of California at San Diego, and her J.D. from the University of California, Berkeley, School of Law.

HEATHER HAMILTON (Chapter 3, "Preparing the Accounting, Step by Step") is a principal of Fiduciary Accounting Services, LLC in Moraga. Prior to co-founding the firm in 2007, she had a 15-year career in banking, primarily serving privately held and family-owned businesses and technology companies. She is a graduate of the California State University at Chico, with a degree in Finance. She is a member of the Diablo Valley Estate Planning Council, and has served on the board of the Junior League of Oakland-East Bay, the Cancer Support Community, and the Contra Costa Ballet Foundation. She specializes in preparing accountings for trusts, estates, and conservatorships, and is widely regarded as one of the Bay Area's most knowledgeable and skillful practitioners of this type of accounting.

DON EDWARD GREEN (Chapter 14, "Conflicts and Litigation") received his B.A. in 1973 from California State University, Long Beach, and his J.D. in 1976 and LL.M. (Taxation) in 1983 from McGeorge Law School. He retired in 2010, having served as the Probate Commissioner, Contra Costa Superior Court, and formerly having served as probate staff attorney, Sacramento Superior Courts, from 1989 to 1998. Before working for the court, Mr. Green practiced law as a certified specialist in estate planning, trust, and probate law (suspended while serving as a judicial officer). He is a former chair of the California State Bar Trusts and Estates Section, served as an Executive Committee member for 10 years, and served as Judicial Liaison to that section. He also served as a member of the Judicial Council of California Probate and Mental Health Advisory Committee. Mr. Green is a frequent lecturer and speaker for CEB, PLI, CJER, sections of the State Bar of California, county bar associations, and various community groups and charities. He was named Pro Bono Judge of the Year 2003 by the Contra Costa County Bar Association.

Cutoff Dates and CEB Citation

Cuffoff Dates

We completed legal editing and analysis of authorities cited in this publication as of December 12, 2014, and monitored developments through January 26, 2015.

CEB Citation

Cite this publication as Fiduciary Accounting Handbook (Cal CEB).

1
Introduction and Sample Accountings

I. ORGANIZATION OF THIS BOOK §1.1

II. EXAMPLES §1.2
   A. The April Cash Trust §1.3
      1. The Settlor April Cash; Her Family and Her Assets §1.4
      2. A Rare Negative Number: Account Beginning Date Bisects Settlement of Securities Purchase §1.5
      3. Late Acquired Assets, Receipt From Fiduciary Accounting for Principal and Income §1.6
      4. Another Rare Negative Number: Purchase of Bond With Accrued Interest §1.7
      5. Dividend Reinvestment §1.8
      6. Distributions in Breach of Trust §1.9
      7. Miscellaneous and Routine Receipts and Disbursements §1.10
      8. Sales and Exchanges: Gains, Losses, and Sales Without Gains or Losses §1.11
      9. Trustee Fee, as a Liability §1.12
     10. Sample Accounting of the April Cash Trust §1.13
        a. Summary of Account §1.14
        b. Assets on Hand—Beginning of Period §1.15
        c. Additions to Trust §1.16
        d. Receipts §1.17
        e. Gains on Sales §1.18
        f. Disbursements §1.19
        g. Losses on Sales §1.20
        h. Distributions §1.21
        i. Assets on Hand—End of Period §1.22
        j. Changes in Form of Assets §1.23
        k. Liabilities §1.24

B. The Real Estate Trust §1.25
  1. The Settlor David Jones; His Family and His Assets §1.26
  2. Rents and Security Deposits §1.27
  3. Receipt in Escrow §1.28
  4. Gains and Losses on Sale §1.29
  5. Funeral Expenses and Debts of a Decedent §1.30
  6. Sale Without Gain or Loss: Sale for a Note §1.31
  7. The Short Sale §1.32
  8. Repairs and Capital Improvements §1.33
  9. Mortgage Payments §1.34
  10. Disbursements in Escrow §1.35
  11. Cancellation of Indebtedness Income §1.36
  12. Trustee's "Loans" to Trust §1.37
  13. Absconding Beneficiary and the Proposed Distribution §1.38
  14. Sample Accounting of the David Jones Trust §1.39
     a. Summary of Account §1.40
     b. Assets on Hand—Beginning of Period §1.41
     c. Receipts §1.42
     d. Gains on Sales §1.43
     e. Disbursements §1.44
     f. Losses on Sales §1.45
     g. Distributions §1.46
     h. Assets on Hand—End of Period §1.47
     i. Changes in Form of Assets §1.48
     j. Liabilities §1.49
     k. Proposed Distributions §1.50

§1.1   I. ORGANIZATION OF THIS BOOK

This chapter introduces the reader to the topic of fiduciary accounting, and includes two complete sample accountings for the reader to review. Chapter 2 describes each type of Probate Code fiduciary and for each, the particular duty to account. Chapter 3 provides a detailed description of how to gather and examine the fiduciary's data. By following the steps in Chapter 3, the accountant can be assured that he or she is working with a full data set and that the accounting will balance.

Beginning with Chapter 4, the authors devote one chapter apiece to each of the schedules of a fiduciary accounting. Beginning with assets on hand at the beginning of the account period, the authors describe the role each schedule plays in the story told by a fiduciary accounting. Each provision of the Uniform Principal and Income Act (UPAIA) (Prob C §§16320-16375) that affects the preparation of a schedule has been integrated into the discussion of the schedule implicated by the provision. For example, the rules governing when an income interest begins and ends (Prob C §16345) are discussed in Chapter 4, because it is in the preparation of this schedule that the accountant must grapple with the questions answered in this statute. Similarly, the rules that govern allocation of receipts between principal and income are discussed in Chapter 6, but those sections of the UPAIA that discuss "receipts," while really referring to sales proceeds, are discussed in the chapter on gains and losses, Chapter 7. Auxiliary schedules are the topic of Chapter 11, and the schedule-by-schedule approach to preparation of the fiduciary's account ends in Chapter 12.

The schedule-by-schedule chapters are illustrated with short one-event accountings. For example, Chapter 7 shows how one would account for the sale of a real property if that sale were the only transaction to occur during the account period. By modeling a transaction in isolation from all other transactions, the authors hope to teach readers about the fundamental truth of fiduciary accounting: charges must equal credits. Prob C §1061(c). The one-event accountings are later aggregated into two large model accounts, one for the Cash Trust and one for the Real Estate Trust. The story behind these two trust administrations is told in §1.4 and the sections that follow.

Chapter 13 discusses those provisions of the UPAIA that do not dictate how the accountant presents the fiduciary's data in a court accounting. In Chapter 13, one finds a discussion of accounting separately for a trade or business, Prob C §16336 adjustments between income and principal, increasing income to preserve the marital deduction, depreciation reserves, transfers between income and principal in anticipation of a large disbursement, and the mandatory and discretionary adjustments of Prob C §16375.

Chapter 14 addresses court accountings from the perspective of the judge. This chapter, written by Commissioner Don Green (Ret'd), addresses the role of the court in fiduciary accounting, including a discussion of ethics, discovery, alternative dispute resolution, and remedies.

Chapter 15 is a collection of ideas from accountants who regularly prepare fiduciary accountings. In this chapter, the reader will find a sample engagement letter, suggestions for project management, a brief discussion of software, a quick reference guide to the UPAIA, and other useful information.

§1.2 II. EXAMPLES

The lucky trustee has a boring life and his accounting does not make a good teaching tool. The authors therefore illustrate this text with two tales of unusually beleaguered trustees. These trustees have more problems with their siblings than is typical, but they also have remarkably modest attorney fees and unrealistically good returns on their investments. Their insurance companies pay with alacrity. And most unusual of all, the trustees account only 6 months into their administrations.

§1.3 A. The April Cash Trust

In the example of the April Cash Trust, the authors illustrate many common financial transactions, as well as several of the problems lay trustees often create for themselves. In this example, readers will find the following:

- Two of the rare instances in which a negative number appears in a fiduciary accounting:
  - The beginning date of accounting bisects the settlement period for the purchase of securities; and
  - The purchase of a bond that has accrued interest;
- An estate in which life insurance is an asset on hand at the beginning and the fiduciary receives interest on the policy proceeds;
- The receipt of property from a fiduciary who must account for income and principal, *i.e.*, receipts from a distributing estate or trust;
- Accounting for receipts of income and principal;
- Accounting for automatic reinvestment of dividends, sometimes called a DRIP ("dividend reinvestment program") accounting;
- Accounting for distributions of income and principal;

- Sales for a gain, sales at a loss, and sales for which there is no gain or loss;
- A sale for which a commission is paid; and
- Treatment of trustee fees that have been earned but not disbursed.

§1.4 1. The Settlor April Cash; Her Family and Her Assets

April Cash survived her own father, Carson Cash, by only a few months. April herself was the mother of four children: Sally Cash, Rachel Cash, Mike Cash, and Damien Cash.

While living, April established the April Cash Trust, which she funded with all of her assets. April also assigned to the trust her expectancy in her father's estate. April died debt free. She owned no real property. At the time of her death, April was employed at Acme Plumbing Supply and had not collected her last paycheck.

April served as trustee until the date of her death, January 1, 2013, at which time Sally Cash succeeded to the office. Once Sally had assumed the office of trustee, she persuaded April's employer to make the paycheck payable to the trust.

April was a limited partner in Widget Supplier LP, but otherwise owned nothing unusual. She had cash in two Wells Fargo accounts and in a Charles Schwab securities account. In the Schwab account, she also held stocks, a corporate bond, a U.S. Treasury bond, and some mutual funds. She had a small life insurance policy, a little jewelry, and the furnishings in her apartment. See §1.15.

§1.5 2. A Rare Negative Number: Account Beginning Date Bisects Settlement of Securities Purchase

April participated in an automatic dividend reinvestment program offered by Franklin California Tax-Free Income Fund A. On December 31, 2012, the day before she died, Fund A paid her a $383.46 dividend. Fund A then automatically reinvested the dividend into more shares of the fund. That reinvestment is accounted for as a purchase and such purchases typically take 2 days to settle. Because April died before her new shares settled in her account, on the date of April's death, her Charles Schwab statement showed a negative cash balance, representing the dividend that had been spent to purchase those shares which had not yet settled in the account. Consequently, in the trustee's accounting, the schedule Assets on Hand—Beginning of Period shows a negative cash balance in the Schwab account. The newly purchased additional shares can be found on the Changes in Form of Assets schedule, on the settlement date, January 2, 2013. Fiduciaries rarely use negative numbers in their accountings, but this is one of the situations in which a negative number is appropriate. See §§1.15, 1.23.

On the schedule Assets on Hand—Beginning of Period, another example of the appropriate use of a negative number would be the bank account that is overdrawn on the date an accounting begins. Although the overdrawn account is a liability, if it will be on hand for some portion of the account period, identifying it as on hand at the beginning eliminates confusion about how the fiduciary came to be responsible for the account.

3. Late Acquired Assets, Receipt From Fiduciary Accounting for Principal and Income

Sally accounts for two assets as late acquired assets. She found $5000 cash in her mother's apartment and because she wanted her schedule of Assets on Hand—Beginning of Period to tie directly to the bank and brokerage account statements, Sally lists the cash as an Addition to Trust. See §1.16. It would have been equally appropriate for Sally to put this cash on the schedule Assets on Hand—Beginning of Period.

Sally's other addition to trust is a consequence of the order of final distribution in the probate of the estate of her grandfather, Carson Cash. Sally received the final distribution from the probate on June 25, 2013, and because the receipt was from a fiduciary who was accounting for income and principal, Sally characterized the receipt as part income and part principal. See §1.17.

4. Another Rare Negative Number: Purchase of Bond With Accrued Interest

On March 1, 2013, Sally purchased a $24,000 bond, for which she paid $24,000. The bond was issued by J.P. Morgan Chase many years ago and Sally purchased it from a third party. On the date of purchase, two-thirds of the first financial quarter had passed, and the selling party was therefore entitled to two-thirds of the quarterly interest payment. To purchase the bond, Sally therefore had to pay not only for the bond itself, but also for the accrued interest of $608.12. Thus, Sally paid $24,000 for the bond, plus $608.12 for the interest, for a total of $24,608.12. This sum is not the purchase price of the bond; it is the purchase price of the bond plus the interest. As explained below, Sally should always distinguish between these items. The amount paid for the bond is a change in form of asset and the amount paid for the interest is a *negative* receipt. See §1.17.

To understand this approach to accrued interest, consider what would happen to Sally's accounting if she did otherwise. If Sally treated the bond as if it cost $24,608.12, she would use this figure as the carry value of the bond and, because that value would be inflated, a later sale might appear to be a sale at a loss when in fact it was not. Additionally, when Sally eventually receives the quarterly dividend of $948, the entire amount would be treated as a receipt, increasing the value of the estate accounted for. If the trust allows trustee fees to be calculated on the basis of the trustee's receipts, as some trusts do, this treatment would inflate the basis of Sally's fee. Indeed, in a probate, such would be the case. See Prob C §10800(b).

The same logic prevents Sally from treating the purchase of interest as a disbursement. If Sally accounted for the $608.12 she paid to purchase the accrued interest as a disbursement, when she received the quarterly interest of $948 she would treat the entire amount as a receipt. In fact, Sally is receiving only the difference between the sum, $948, and the amount she paid to purchase that sum. In other words, Sally's actual receipt is $948 − $608.12 = $339.88. The figure $339.88 does not appear in Sally's accounting, but because she states the purchased interest as a negative number, the figure is implied.

Fiduciaries should state the purchase of interest on a bond as a negative receipt because, by so doing, they accurately state the receipt of interest when the interest is received.

§1.8   5. Dividend Reinvestment

April participated in a dividend reinvestment program offered by

Franklin California Tax-Free Income Fund A. Each time April received a dividend, Franklin automatically used it to purchase for April more shares of the fund. In a fiduciary accounting, the dividend is a receipt from an entity, the purchase of additional shares is a change in form of asset, and the result of the reinvestment is that the number of shares carried, and the carry value, increases—an increase shown on the schedule Assets on Hand—End of Period. This topic is discussed at some length in §6.44, and is illustrated in the Cash Trust accounting on the schedules of Receipts, Changes in Form of Assets, and Assets on Hand—End of Period. See §§1.17, 1.22–1.23.

§1.9   6. Distributions in Breach of Trust

Sally is accounting for a 6-month period because her brother, the beneficiary Damien Cash, is angry about several things Sally has done and he has demanded an accounting. Four months into her trust administration, and frightened by her brother's anger, Sally finally sought the advice of an attorney. A few weeks earlier, Sally had given $1000 to April's grandson, Jake, as a birthday present. About the same time, Sally had distributed some cash and securities to two of the beneficiaries, but nothing to herself and Damien. Explaining these actions to her lawyer, Sally said that she gave Jake $1000 "because my mother would have wanted me to," but also admitted that Jake was her son. Sally explained the large distributions to her siblings, Rachel and Mike, by reference to their lifelong dependence on handouts from their mother.

Sally's attorney gave Sally some advice that is reflected in the accounting. The attorney explained that making a gift to one who is not a trust beneficiary is a breach of the duty to administer the trust according to its terms (Prob C §16000), and making a gift to one's own son is a violation of the duty of impartiality (Prob C §16003). Sally's attorney therefore recommended that Sally treat the gift to Jake as a distribution to herself, which Sally has done. See §1.21.

Sally cannot so easily rectify the problems created when she distributed cash and securities to only two of the four beneficiaries. Damien is angry because Sally favored Rachel and Mike with early distributions. Rachel is angry because she received stock that has declined in value since Sally distributed it. Mike is angry because

Sally distributed all the Bank of America and Chevron stock to him and Rachel, meaning Sally now must distribute something different to herself and Damien. Mike thinks that Sally will give herself and Damien something more valuable than the stock he got, and Mike is angry that Sally is now spending money on an attorney to straighten this out. Sally's attorney adds to Sally's woe by pointing out that Sally's failure to make equal distributions to all four beneficiaries is a breach of her duty of impartiality. Prob C §16003. The attorney also explains that Sally now appears to be commingling her and Damien's distributive shares with the assets of the trust estate, which may be a breach of Sally's duty to separately identify trust property. Prob C §16009. Sally cannot remedy these problems with an accounting entry, but she can reveal the problem in her accounting and get the statute of limitations running on actions against her for breaches of trust (see discussion in §§14.24, 15.12, 15.25); thus the attorney's recommendation that Sally account for a period shorter than the usual 1-year period (see discussion of period of account in §§2.11–2.15).

§1.10   7. Miscellaneous and Routine Receipts and Disbursements

The accounting for the Cash Trust also introduces the reader to receipts of income and principal, as well as distributions of income and principal. "Income" in trust accounting parlance means something different than when used in a tax accounting, and the examples in the Cash Trust acquaint the reader with some of these differences. The differences are discussed throughout chaps 6 and 7.

§1.11   8. Sales and Exchanges: Gains, Losses, and Sales Without Gains or Losses

Sally sold her mother's investment in Franklin Universal Trust at a small gain. See §1.18.

Sally sold her mother's furniture at a loss, perhaps because she overestimated its value in the first place and carried it at $5000. See §§1.15, 1.20. Sally paid a commission to Ally's Auction House, which conducted the sale. See §1.19.

Sally also sold a U.S. Treasury Bond at no gain or loss and exchanged the life insurance policy for the policy proceeds. See the schedule Changes in Form of Assets, §1.23.

§1.12   9. Trustee Fee, as a Liability

Sally told her siblings that she would serve as trustee without charging a fee, but Sally now resents working so hard and thinks her siblings' anger at her is unfair. Facing the possibility of liability for breaches of trust, and on the advice of her attorney, Sally states on the schedule of Liabilities a trustee fee of 1 percent of the date of death value of the trust estate, including the additions to trust. Sally tells herself she will forego her fee if her siblings will stop complaining.

§1.13   10. Sample Accounting of the April Cash Trust

The following is a complete accounting of the April Cash Trust, described above.

§1.14   a. Summary of Account

APRIL CASH TRUST
SALLY CASH, TRUSTEE

FIRST ACCOUNTING
FOR THE PERIOD JANUARY 1, 2013 THRU JUNE 30, 2013
SUMMARY OF ACCOUNT

CHARGES

		CARRY VALUE
ASSETS ON HAND - BEGINNING OF PERIOD		$ 1,798,991.47
ADDITIONS TO TRUST		$ 107,000.00
INCOME	$ 2,000.00	
PRINCIPAL	$ 105,000.00	
RECEIPTS - SCHEDULE A		$ 31,729.76
INCOME	$ 25,361.76	
PRINCIPAL	$ 6,368.00	
GAINS ON SALES - SCHEDULE B		$ 429.06
TOTAL CHARGES		$ 1,938,150.29

CREDITS

DISBURSEMENTS - SCHEDULE C				$	14,052.80
INCOME		$	5,790.22		
PRINCIPAL		$	8,262.58		
LOSSES ON SALES - SCHEDULE D				$	2,168.16
DISTRIBUTIONS - SCHEDULE E				$	304,973.12
ASSETS ON HAND - SCHEDULE F				$	1,616,956.21
INCOME		$	21,571.54		
PRINCIPAL		$	1,595,384.67		
	TOTAL CREDITS			$	1,938,150.29

ADDITIONAL SCHEDULES
    CHANGES IN FORM OF ASSETS
    LIABILITIES

§1.15 b. Assets on Hand—Beginning of Period

APRIL CASH TRUST

SALLY CASH, TRUSTEE

FIRST ACCOUNTING

FOR THE PERIOD JANUARY 1, 2013 THRU JUNE 30, 2013

ASSETS ON HAND - BEGINNING OF PERIOD

SHARES / PAR VALUE	DESCRIPTION		CARRY VALUE
CASH AND CASH EQUIVALENTS			
	WELLS FARGO BANK CHECKING A/C #XXXXXX9876	$	16,575.00
	WELLS FARGO BANK SAVINGS A/C #XXXXXX4321	$	280,567.25
	CHARLES SCHWAB CASH INVESTMENT A/C #XXXX-6549	$	(383.46)
	CHARLES SCHWAB SCHWAB PREMIER MONEY FUND INVESTMENT A/C #XXXX-6549	$	30,890.46
	TOTAL CASH AND CASH EQUIVALENTS	$	327,649.25
EQUITIES			
2,200.000	BANK OF AMERICA CORP	$	26,466.00
1,608.000	CHEVRON CORP	$	177,507.12
1,940.000	CISCO SYS INC	$	39,459.60
4,800.000	EXXON MOBIL CORP	$	425,808.00
1,200.000	MERCK & CO INC	$	49,608.00
2,400.000	ORACLE CORP	$	83,256.00
1,440.000	PEPSICO INC	$	99,835.20
7,200.000	WELLS FARGO & CO NEW	$	252,360.00
	TOTAL EQUITIES	$	1,154,299.92

SHARES / PAR VALUE	DESCRIPTION	CARRY VALUE
CORPORATE BONDS		
24,000.000	BANK OF AMERICA CORP 8.125% MAY/NOV 15 DUE 12/31/48 CALLABLE $100.00 ON 05/15/18	$ 23,428.52
	TOTAL CORPORATE BONDS	$ 23,428.52
GOVERNMENT BONDS		
	US TREASURY 3.5% DUE 05/31/11	$ 20,000.00
	TOTAL GOVERNMENT BONDS	$ 20,000.00
MUTUAL FUNDS		
14,202.081	FRANKLIN CA TAX-FREE INCOME FUND A	$ 95,722.03
1,000.000	FRANKLIN UNIVERSAL TRUST	$ 6,343.75
1,000.000	NUVEEN CA INVT QUALITY MUN FUND	$ 12,315.00
1,000.000	NUVEEN CA MUN MKT OPPORTUNITY	$ 12,490.00
	TOTAL MUTUAL FUNDS	$ 126,870.78
LIMITED PARTNERSHIPS		
5.000	WIDGET SUPPLIER LP	$ 82,000.00
	TOTAL LIMITED PARTNERSHIPS	$ 82,000.00
LIFE INSURANCE		
	METLIFE POLICY #XXXX4587 DTD 07/01/05	$ 57,243.00
	TOTAL LIFE INSURANCE	$ 57,243.00
PERSONAL PROPERTY		
	FURNITURE AND FURNISHINGS	$ 5,000.00
	JEWELRY	$ 2,500.00
	TOTAL PERSONAL PROPERTY	$ 7,500.00
	TOTAL ASSETS	**$ 1,798,991.47**

§1.16   c. Additions to Trust

APRIL CASH TRUST

SALLY CASH, TRUSTEE

FIRST ACCOUNTING

FOR THE PERIOD JANUARY 1, 2013 THRU JUNE 30, 2013

ADDITIONS TO TRUST

DATE	DESCRIPTION	INCOME	PRINCIPAL
02/20/13	CASH FOUND IN SETTLORS RESIDENCE APARTMENT 2A		$ 5,000.00
06/25/13	CERTIFICATE OF DEPOSIT RECEIVED FROM ESTATE OF CARSON CASH, FATHER OF DECEDENT (INCLUDES INCOME FROM 12/31/12)	$ 2,000.00	$ 100,000.00
	TOTAL INCOME AND PRINCIPAL	$ 2,000.00	$ 105,000.00
	TOTAL ADDITIONS TO TRUST	**$ 107,000.00**	

§1.17   d. Receipts

APRIL CASH TRUST
SALLY CASH, TRUSTEE

FIRST ACCOUNTING
FOR THE PERIOD JANUARY 1, 2013 THRU JUNE 30, 2013
RECEIPTS
SCHEDULE A

DATE	DESCRIPTION	INCOME	PRINCIPAL
DIVIDENDS			
03/25/13	BANK OF AMERICA CORP	$ 22.00	
03/10/13	CHEVRON CORP	$ 4,642.56	
04/20/13	CISCO SYS INC	$ 116.40	
03/10/13	EXXON MOBIL CORP	$ 2,112.00	
06/10/13	EXXON MOBIL CORP	$ 2,256.00	
01/05/13	FRANKLIN CA TAX-FREE INCOME A	$ 383.46	
02/02/13	FRANKLIN CA TAX-FREE INCOME A	$ 385.00	
03/02/13	FRANKLIN CA TAX-FREE INCOME A	$ 405.20	
04/04/13	FRANKLIN CA TAX-FREE INCOME A	$ 406.93	
05/03/13	FRANKLIN CA TAX-FREE INCOME A	$ 408.70	
06/02/13	FRANKLIN CA TAX-FREE INCOME A	$ 409.64	
01/14/13	FRANKLIN UNIVERSAL TRUST	$ 38.00	
02/15/13	FRANKLIN UNIVERSAL TRUST	$ 38.00	
03/15/13	FRANKLIN UNIVERSAL TRUST	$ 38.00	
04/15/13	FRANKLIN UNIVERSAL TRUST	$ 38.00	
01/07/13	MERCK & CO	$ 456.00	

DATE	DESCRIPTION	INCOME	PRINCIPAL
04/07/13	MERCK & CO	$ 456.00	
02/28/13	ML MONEY MARKET FUND	$ 0.85	
03/31/13	ML MONEY MARKET FUND	$ 4.52	
04/30/13	ML MONEY MARKET FUND	$ 7.59	
05/31/13	ML MONEY MARKET FUND	$ 7.89	
06/30/13	ML MONEY MARKET FUND	$ 9.09	
02/01/13	NUVEEN CA INVT QUALITY MUN FD	$ 76.00	
03/01/13	NUVEEN CA INVT QUALITY MUN FD	$ 76.00	
04/01/13	NUVEEN CA INVT QUALITY MUN FD	$ 76.00	
05/02/13	NUVEEN CA INVT QUALITY MUN FD	$ 76.00	
02/01/13	NUVEEN CA MUNICIPAL MKT OPP FD	$ 78.00	
03/01/13	NUVEEN CA MUNICIPAL MKT OPP FD	$ 78.00	
04/01/13	NUVEEN CA MUNICIPAL MKT OPP FD	$ 78.00	
05/02/13	NUVEEN CA MUNICIPAL MKT OPP FD	$ 78.00	
02/09/13	ORACLE CORP	$ 120.00	
05/04/13	ORACLE CORP	$ 144.00	
01/03/13	PEPSICO INC	$ 691.20	
03/31/13	PEPSICO INC	$ 691.20	
06/30/13	PEPSICO INC	$ 741.60	
01/28/13	SCHWAB PREMIER MONEY FUND	$ 0.69	
03/01/13	WELLS FARGO & CO NEW	$ 864.00	
06/01/13	WELLS FARGO & CO NEW	$ 864.00	
	TOTAL DIVIDENDS	$ 17,374.52	$ -

DATE	DESCRIPTION	INCOME	PRINCIPAL
SHORT TERM CAPITAL GAINS			
03/01/13	NUVEEN CA INVT QUALITY MUN FD	$ 12.00	
03/01/13	NUVEEN CA MUNICIPAL MKT OPP FD	$ 14.00	
	TOTAL SHORT TERM CAPITAL GAINS	$ 26.00	$ -
LONG TERM CAPITAL GAINS			
03/01/13	NUVEEN CA INVT QUALITY MUN FD		$ 82.00
03/01/13	NUVEEN CA MUNICIPAL MKT OPP FD		$ 86.00
	TOTAL LONG TERM CAPITAL GAINS	$ -	$ 168.00
INTEREST			
05/16/13	BANK OF AMERICA CORP 8.125% MAY/NOV 15 DUE 12/31/48	$ 975.00	
04/30/13	JP MORGAN CHASE & CO 7.900% APR/OCT 30 DUE 12/31/48	$ 948.00	
01/15/13	METLIFE POLICY #XXXX4587 DTD 07/01/05	$ 21.92	
01/31/13	WELLS FARGO BANK SAVINGS A/C #XXXXXX4321	$ 281.51	
02/28/13	WELLS FARGO BANK SAVINGS A/C #XXXXXX4321	$ 285.91	
03/31/13	WELLS FARGO BANK SAVINGS A/C #XXXXXX4321	$ 286.15	
04/30/13	WELLS FARGO BANK SAVINGS A/C #XXXXXX4321	$ 186.39	
05/31/13	WELLS FARGO BANK SAVINGS A/C #XXXXXX4321	$ 186.54	
06/30/13	WELLS FARGO BANK SAVINGS A/C #XXXXXX4321	$ 197.94	
	TOTAL INTEREST	$ 3,369.36	$ -

DATE	DESCRIPTION	INCOME	PRINCIPAL
ACCRUED INTEREST ON PURCHASES			
03/01/13	JP MORGAN CHASE & CO 7.900% APR/OCT 30 DUE 12/31/48	$ (608.12)	
	TOTAL ACCRUED INTEREST ON PURCHASES	$ *(608.12)* $	-
PARTNERSHIP INCOME			
06/30/13	WIDGET SUPPLIER LP	$ 5,200.00	
	TOTAL PARTNERSHIP INCOME	$ *5,200.00* $	-
OTHER RECEIPTS			
01/02/13	ACME PLUMBING SUPPLY - WAGES 12/15/10 TO 12/31/10		$ 3,200.00
03/15/13	ACME PLUMBING SUPPLY - UNION DEATH BENEFIT		$ 3,000.00
	TOTAL OTHER RECEIPTS	$ -	$ *6,200.00*
	TOTAL INCOME AND PRINCIPAL	$ 25,361.76	$ 6,368.00
	TOTAL RECEIPTS	$ **31,729.76**	

§1.18 e. Gains on Sales

APRIL CASH TRUST
SALLY CASH, TRUSTEE

FIRST ACCOUNTING
FOR THE PERIOD JANUARY 1, 2013 THRU JUNE 30, 2013
GAINS ON SALES
SCHEDULE B

DATE	SHARES	DESCRIPTION	CARRY VALUE	PROCEEDS	GAINS
05/05/13	475.000	FRANKLIN UNIVERSAL TRUST	$ 3,013.28	$ 3,442.34	$ 429.06
		TOTALS	$ 3,013.28	$ 3,442.34	$ **429.06**

§1.19 f. Disbursements

APRIL CASH TRUST
SALLY CASH, TRUSTEE

FIRST ACCOUNTING
FOR THE PERIOD JANUARY 1, 2013 THRU JUNE 30, 2013
DISBURSEMENTS
SCHEDULE C

DATE	PAID TO	CHK #	FOR	INCOME	PRINCIPAL
ADMINISTRATIVE EXPENSES					
01/05/13	MARGARET'S RESTAURANT	204	MEMORIAL DINNER		$ 722.36
01/05/13	FRED'S FUNERAL HOME	205	MEMORIAL SERVICE		$ 1,750.00
03/01/13	BEST BUY	206	LAPTOP	$ 300.00	$ 300.00
04/07/13	LAW OFFICES OF LUCY LAWYER	208	LEGAL FEES	$ 250.00	$ 250.00
06/01/13	ALLY'S AUCTION HOUSE		CONSIGNMENT COMMISSION ON FURNITURE SALE	$ 750.00	$ 750.00
06/28/13	WELLS FARGO BANK	AUTO	WIRE TRANSFER FEE	$ 15.00	$ 15.00
06/28/13	WELLS FARGO BANK	AUTO	WIRE TRANSFER FEE	$ 15.00	$ 15.00
06/30/13	SALLY CASH	209	TRUSTEE FEE	$ 4,460.22	$ 4,460.22
			TOTAL ADMINISTRATIVE EXPENSES $	5,790.22	$ 8,262.58
			TOTAL INCOME AND PRINCIPAL $	5,790.22	$ 8,262.58
			TOTAL DISBURSEMENTS $	**14,052.80**	

§1.20 g. Losses on Sales

APRIL CASH TRUST
SALLY CASH, TRUSTEE

FIRST ACCOUNTING
FOR THE PERIOD JANUARY 1, 2013 THRU JUNE 30, 2013
LOSSES ON SALES
SCHEDULE D

DATE	SHARES	DESCRIPTION	CARRY VALUE	PROCEEDS	LOSSES
04/15/13	475.000	FRANKLIN UNIVERSAL TRUST	$ 3,013.28	$ 2,932.02	$ 81.26
05/05/13	700.000	NUVEEN CA MUNICIPAL MKT OPP FD	$ 8,743.00	$ 8,684.35	58.65
05/05/13	1,000.000	NUVEEN CA INVT QUALITY MUN FD	$ 12,315.00	$ 12,286.75	28.25
06/01/13		FURNITURE AND FURNISHINGS	$ 5,000.00	$ 3,000.00	2,000.00
		TOTALS	$ 29,071.28	$ 26,903.12	**2,168.16**

§1.21

h. Distributions

APRIL CASH TRUST
SALLY CASH, TRUSTEE

FIRST ACCOUNTING
FOR THE PERIOD JANUARY 1, 2013 THRU JUNE 30, 2013
DISTRIBUTIONS
SCHEDULE E

DATE	CK #	SHARES	DESCRIPTION		AMOUNT/CARRY VALUE
RACHEL CASH					
03/15/13	WIRE		CASH DISTRIBUTION	$	50,000.00
03/15/13		1,100.000	BANK OF AMERICA CORP	$	13,233.00
03/15/13		804.000	CHEVRON CORP	$	88,753.56
			TOTAL DISTRIBUTION TO RACHEL CASH	$	*151,986.56*
MIKE CASH					
03/15/13	WIRE		CASH DISTRIBUTION	$	50,000.00
03/15/13		1,100.000	BANK OF AMERICA CORP	$	13,233.00
03/15/13		804.000	CHEVRON CORP	$	88,753.56
			TOTAL DISTRIBUTION TO MIKE CASH	$	*151,986.56*
SALLY CASH					
03/15/13	207		BIRTHDAY GIFT TO GRANDSON, JAKE CASH	$	1,000.00
			TOTAL DISTRIBUTIONS TO SALLY CASH	$	*1,000.00*
			TOTAL DISTRIBUTIONS	$	**304,973.12**

§1.22 i. Assets on Hand—End of Period

APRIL CASH TRUST

SALLY CASH, TRUSTEE

FIRST ACCOUNTING

FOR THE PERIOD JANUARY 1, 2013 THRU JUNE 30, 2013

ASSETS ON HAND - END OF PERIOD

SCHEDULE F

SHARES / PAR VALUE	DESCRIPTION	CARRY VALUE	MARKET VALUE
CASH AND CASH EQUIVALENTS			
	WELLS FARGO BANK CHECKING A/C #XXXXXX9876	$ 22,449.92	$ 22,449.92
	WELLS FARGO BANK SAVINGS A/C #XXXXX4321	$ 237,728.89	$ 237,728.89
	WELLS FARGO BANK CERTIFICATE OF DEPOSIT	$ 102,000.00	$ 102,000.00
	MERRILL LYNCH CASH INVESTMENT A/C #XXXX-2222	$ 4,477.11	$ 4,477.11
	MERRILL LYNCH ML MONEY MARKET FUND INVESTMENT A/C #XXXX-2222	$ 65,859.82	$ 65,859.82
	TOTAL CASH AND CASH EQUIVALENTS	$ 432,515.74	$ 432,515.74
EQUITIES			
1,940.000	CISCO SYS INC	$ 39,459.60	$ 47,219.60
4,800.000	EXXON MOBIL CORP	$ 425,808.00	$ 433,680.00
2,400.000	MERCK & CO INC	$ 49,608.00	$ 111,480.00
2,400.000	ORACLE CORP	$ 83,256.00	$ 73,704.00
1,440.000	PEPSICO INC	$ 99,835.20	$ 117,777.60
7,200.000	WELLS FARGO & CO NEW	$ 252,360.00	$ 297,144.00
	TOTAL EQUITIES	$ 950,326.80	$ 1,081,005.20

SHARES / PAR VALUE	DESCRIPTION	CARRY VALUE	MARKET VALUE
CORPORATE BONDS			
24,000.000	BANK OF AMERICA CORP 8.125% MAY/NOV 15 DUE 12/31/48	$ 23,428.52	$ 23,150.00
24,000.000	JP MORGAN CHASE & CO 7.900% APR/OCT 30 DUE 12/31/48	$ 24,000.00	$ 24,125.00
	TOTAL CORPORATE BONDS	$ 47,428.52	$ 47,275.00
MUTUAL FUNDS			
14,565.205	FRANKLIN CA TAX-FREE INCOME FUND A	$ 98,120.96	$ 104,578.17
50.000	FRANKLIN UNIVERSAL TRUST	$ 317.19	$ 341.50
300.000	NUVEEN CA MUN MKT OPPORTUNITY	$ 3,747.00	$ 3,909.00
	TOTAL MUTUAL FUNDS	$ 102,185.15	$ 108,828.67
LIMITED PARTNERSHIPS			
5.000	WIDGET SUPPLIER LP	$ 82,000.00	$ 82,000.00
	TOTAL LIMITED PARTNERSHIPS	$ 82,000.00	$ 82,000.00
PERSONAL PROPERTY			
	JEWELRY	$ 2,500.00	$ 2,500.00
	TOTAL PERSONAL PROPERTY	$ 2,500.00	$ 2,500.00
	TOTAL ASSETS	**$ 1,616,956.21**	**$ 1,754,124.61**

§1.23   j. Changes in Form of Assets

APRIL CASH TRUST
SALLY CASH, TRUSTEE

FIRST ACCOUNTING
FOR THE PERIOD JANUARY 1, 2013 THRU JUNE 30, 2013
CHANGES IN FORM OF ASSETS

DATE		DESCRIPTION	CASH	CARRY VALUE
ACCOUNTS OPENED				
01/28/13		MERRILL LYNCH INVESTMENT A/C #XXXX-2222		
ACCOUNTS CLOSED				
01/28/13		CHARLES SCHWAB INVESTMENT A/C #XXXX-6549		
COLLECTION OF LIFE INSURANCE				
01/15/13		METLIFE POLICY #XXXX4587 DTD 07/01/05	$ 57,243.00	$ (57,243.00)
SALES W/O GAIN OR LOSS				
05/31/13		US TREASURY 3.5% DUE 05/31/11	$ 20,000.00	$ (20,000.00)
PURCHASES				
03/01/13	24,000.000	JP MORGAN CHASE & CO 7.900% APR/OCT 30 DUE 12/31/48 CALLABLE $100.00 ON 04/30/18	$ (24,000.00)	$ 24,000.00

01/01/13	14,202.081	BALANCE				$	95,722.03
01/02/13	57.063	FRANKLIN CA TAX-FREE INCOME A	$	(383.46)	$		383.46
02/02/13	58.959	FRANKLIN CA TAX-FREE INCOME A	$	(385.00)	$		385.00
03/02/13	61.116	FRANKLIN CA TAX-FREE INCOME A	$	(405.20)	$		405.20
04/04/13	62.413	FRANKLIN CA TAX-FREE INCOME A	$	(406.93)	$		406.93
05/03/13	61.551	FRANKLIN CA TAX-FREE INCOME A	$	(408.70)	$		408.70
06/02/13	62.022	FRANKLIN CA TAX-FREE INCOME A	$	(409.64)	$		409.64
	14,565.205					$	98,120.96

STOCK SPLITS

01/15/13	1,200.000	MERCK & CO (2:1 SPLIT)	

§1.24 k. Liabilities

APRIL CASH TRUST

SALLY CASH, TRUSTEE

FIRST ACCOUNTING

FOR THE PERIOD JANUARY 1, 2013 THRU JUNE 30, 2013

LIABILITIES

DATE	DESCRIPTION	INCREASE	DECREASE	BALANCE
DUE TO SALLY CASH, TRUSTEE				
06/30/13	TRUSTEE FEE (1% PER ANNUM, BASED UPON DATE OF DEATH VALUES PLUS ADDITIONS TO TRUST)	$ 9,529.96		$ 9,529.96

§1.25 B. The Real Estate Trust

In the example of a Real Estate Trust, the authors illustrate the problem-ridden administration of trustee Thomas Jones. In the accounting, readers will find examples of all of the following:

- The allocation between income and principal of payments received from the debtor on a trust-owned note receivable;
- Accounting for rents paid by tenants of trust-owned properties;
- The sale of real property at a gain, the receipt in escrow of a property-tax refund, and the disbursement in escrow of commissions, fees, and other expenses of sale;
- Mortgage payments;

- Disbursement of the expenses of carrying real property;
- Casualty losses (a trust-owned vehicle was totaled, and the insurer paid less than its carry value);
- Distribution to a beneficiary of the debt she owes to the trust;
- Loss to foreclosure; and
- Confiscation by a beneficiary.

§1.26 1. The Settlor David Jones; His Family and His Assets

David Jones lost his wife when he was in his 70s. She left her entire estate to David, outright, and he promised that on his death he would leave everything to their two children, Thomas and Rebecca. For the most part, David kept his promise.

After his wife's death, David remained in the family home on Sunnyside Street for several years, then moved to Retirement Lane. Shortly after this move, David accidentally knocked his lit cigarette into the laundry hamper. Absent-minded by nature and in a rush to finish some chores, David gave the missing cigarette no thought. He lit another, finished writing his grocery list, and went out. Meanwhile, the fire that started in the hamper grew, igniting some cleaning products which exploded in a conflagration that consumed the entire home.

David was not hurt in the fire, but died not long after, on January 1, 2012. By the time of his death, he had sold the Retirement Lane property without rebuilding. Escrow had closed on the sale, but David had yet to cash the check he received at the close of escrow. While living, David made a claim on his State Farm insurance policy, but he died before the insurance company settled the claim.

David's estate plan consisted of a revocable trust to which he had transferred all of his assets. At David's death, the trust owned five real properties: the two houses on Sunnyside Street and Foreclosure Way, a fourplex apartment building at 111 Management Ave., commercial rental property at 321 Franchise Row, and an unimproved lot. The trust also owned a Mercedes, a speed boat, the State Farm insurance claim, an uncashed check from the sale of Retirement Lane, and about $80,000 in cash. In his trust, David left $75,000 to Animal Rescue Fund and left the balance of his trust estate equally to Thomas and Rebecca. Thomas succeeded David as trustee of the trust.

At the time of David's death, Rebecca was living in the trust-owned property on Foreclosure Way. When she first moved in, Rebecca had paid her father $2000 each month for rent, money David had used to make his mortgage payments on the property. The mortgage exceeded the property's fair market value, however, and eventually David stopped making payments. Rebecca used this as an excuse to discontinue paying rent, something David complained about to Thomas, though he never confronted Rebecca. As a result, when David died, Thomas believed Rebecca owed the trust $24,000 for 1 year of unpaid rent, and Rebecca believed that their father had agreed she could occupy Foreclosure Way rent free.

Rebecca was accustomed to receiving financial assistance from her parents, but after her father died, Thomas warned her that she would receive nothing for some time. He did not have enough cash to pay the general pecuniary devise and administer the estate; thus he would have to sell some real properties before he and Rebecca could receive their distributions. Thomas also told Rebecca that he was letting the bank foreclose on her home.

Reacting to this news, Rebecca hitched her father's speedboat to his Mercedes and drove off. She will not tell Thomas what she did with the boat. As for the Mercedes, it was totaled, Rebecca says, by an unidentified motorist, while parked outside Rebecca's home on Foreclosure Way.

§1.27   2. Rents and Security Deposits

The tenants of the trust's two rental properties pay rent, which Thomas accounts for as trust-accounting income. Prob C §16356; see §6.17. By contrast, when a new tenant gives a security deposit, that receipt is a receipt of principal (see §1.42) and the security deposit creates a liability (see §1.49). When Thomas sells the two properties, he transfers the security deposits to the buyers, thereby eliminating the liabilities.

§1.28   3. Receipt in Escrow

Most of the money received in the escrow of a sale of real property is accounted for as a gain, a loss, or as a change in form. See discussion in chap 7. Occasionally, however, a fiduciary will receive in escrow money that must be accounted for as a receipt. Thomas received one such receipt, on the sale of Franchise Row, when he received a $2500 refund of prepaid property taxes. See §1.42.

§1.29   4. Gains and Losses on Sale

Thomas sold one property for a gain (see §1.43) and sold another for a loss (see §1.45). Thomas also had a casualty loss: the Mercedes. See §1.45.

§1.30   5. Funeral Expenses and Debts of a Decedent

Thomas's accounting illustrates that payment of funeral expenses and the debts of a decedent is a disbursement of principal. Like the expense of a burial or cremation, the expense of a family allowance, and certain other expenses incurred as a consequence of a death, the fiduciary has no discretion to allocate these expenses to income. Prob C §16340(c)(2)-(3). This rule is discussed in chap 8, where it is contrasted with those Uniform Principal and Income Act (UPAIA) provisions that grant fiduciaries the discretion to allocate other similar expenses either to principal or income. See Prob C §16340(c)(2).

§1.31   6. Sale Without Gain or Loss: Sale for a Note

David had long tried to sell the trust's undeveloped real property and Thomas listed the property for sale again, shortly after his father died. Thomas could not find a buyer willing to pay cash and therefore agreed to sell the property to a developer in exchange for a $200,000 promissory note. Thomas had never been confident of the property's date-of-death value and so carried it in his accounting at the sales price of $200,000. See §1.41. Consequently, the sale produced no gain or loss and Thomas reports it as a change in form of assets. See §1.48.

During the period of the account, Thomas received one payment from the developer; he accounts for the interest portion as a receipt (see §1.42) and for the principal portion of the payment as a change in the form of a principal asset (see §1.48).

§1.32   7. The Short Sale

On the date of David's death, the balance due on the Foreclosure Way mortgage was $289,500, but the fair market value of the property was less than this. Three months after David's death, the bank sold Foreclosure Way for $275,000, and David adopted this value as the date-of-death value for the property. Thus, David accounts for the property as a sale for no gain or loss, and his disbursement for the mortgage payoff (a credit) balances the carry value of the property (a charge). See §1.44.

§1.33   8. Repairs and Capital Improvements

After moving to Retirement Lane, David had begun rehabilitating the old family home on Sunnyside Street. He died in the midst of adding a second bathroom to the home and, because no bank would lend on the property until the City of Anytown had given final approval of the work, Thomas had to complete the project. Thomas accounts for the $23,000 he spent on the addition as a change in form of assets. See §1.48. This work increased the carry value of the home from $750,000 to $773,000, but only increased the market value of the home by $5000. (Compare the Assets on Hand—Beginning of Period schedule (§1.41) with the market values stated on the Assets on Hand—End of Period schedule (§1.47).)

In addition to the capital improvements to Sunnyside Street, Thomas paid for repairs to the property, for gardening, for utilities, and for pest control. These expenses are disbursements (see §1.44) that do not affect the property's carry value.

§1.34   9. Mortgage Payments

Thomas also paid the mortgage on Sunnyside Street. With each payment, the amount allocated to interest (hence, paid from trust accounting income) decreased, and the amount allocated to principal (and paid from trust accounting principal) increased. See §1.44. Additionally, the principal payments reduced the amount due on the mortgage—reductions which are accounted for on the Liabilities schedule. See §1.49.

§1.35   10. Disbursements in Escrow

Thomas sold three of the trust's real properties during the period of his account. In the sale of the vacant lot, there were no expenses paid in escrow, but for both Management Avenue and Franchise Row, there were. Thomas categorizes these expenses separately from the expenses of carrying each property. See §1.44.

§1.36   11. Cancellation of Indebtedness Income

By contrast, Thomas did not pay the mortgage on Foreclosure Way. As a result, the balance due on that mortgage increased with each unpaid interest payment and late fee, as well as with the fees charged in the foreclosure. See the Liabilities schedule (§1.49). Under tax law, the trustee may be treated as receiving income from cancellation of indebtedness, but this is not the type of receipt a trustee would include on the fiduciary accounting. The trustee might mention the looming tax liability in a note or a report, but the accounting will not reflect the phenomenon of income from cancellation of indebtedness until the trustee actually pays some tax on that phantom income. Then the tax payment will be reported as a disbursement.

§1.37   12. Trustee's "Loans" to Trust

Thomas paid out of pocket for his father's obituary and for the meal following his father's memorial service, and believes he should be reimbursed this expense. He lists this debt on the Liabilities schedule as a way of alerting Rebecca that he intends to repay himself.

§1.38   13. Absconding Beneficiary and the Proposed Distribution

Thomas proposes distributing $1 million apiece to himself and Rebecca, but he wants to treat Rebecca as if she has received a portion of her $1 million already. He will charge her share with three items (see §1.50):

- The speedboat;
- The difference between the date-of-death value of the Mercedes and the amount he received from the insurance company when the car was totaled; and
- Rebecca's debt for unpaid rent.

§1.39   14. Sample Accounting of the David Jones Trust

The following is a complete sample accounting of the David Jones Trust, described above.

§1.40   a. Summary of Account

DAVID JONES TRUST

THOMAS JONES, TRUSTEE

FIRST ACCOUNTING

FOR THE PERIOD JANUARY 1, 2012 THRU JUNE 30, 2012

SUMMARY OF ACCOUNT

CHARGES

			CARRY VALUE
ASSETS ON HAND - BEGINNING OF PERIOD		$	4,199,811.68
RECEIPTS - SCHEDULE A		$	47,862.53
INCOME	$ 43,362.53		
PRINCIPAL	$ 4,500.00		
GAINS ON SALES - SCHEDULE B		$	175,000.00
TOTAL CHARGES		$	4,422,674.21

CREDITS

DISBURSEMENTS - SCHEDULE C		$	318,239.77
INCOME	$ 35,491.65		
PRINCIPAL	$ 282,748.12		
LOSSES ON SALES - SCHEDULE D		$	154,650.00
DISTRIBUTIONS - SCHEDULE E		$	90,000.00
ASSETS ON HAND - SCHEDULE F		$	3,859,784.44
TOTAL CREDITS		$	4,422,674.21

ADDITIONAL SCHEDULES

    CHANGES IN FORM OF ASSETS
    LIABILITIES
    PROPOSED DISTRIBUTIONS

§1.41 b. Assets on Hand—Beginning of Period

DAVID JONES TRUST

THOMAS JONES, TRUSTEE

FIRST ACCOUNTING

FOR THE PERIOD JANUARY 1, 2012 THRU JUNE 30, 2012

ASSETS ON HAND - BEGINNING OF PERIOD

SHARES / PAR VALUE	DESCRIPTION	CARRY VALUE
CASH AND CASH EQUIVALENTS		
	BANK OF AMERICA CHECKING A/C #XXXXXX6789	$ 5,279.53
	BANK OF AMERICA SAVINGS A/C #XXXXXX6789	$ 75,002.15
	PROPERTY MANAGEMENT COMPANY	$ 1,000.00
	UNCASHED CHECK FROM OLD REPUBLIC TITLE PROCEEDS OF 555 RETIREMENT LANE, ANYTOWN SALE CLOSED PRIOR TO DATE OF DEATH	$ 22,530.00
	TOTAL CASH AND CASH EQUIVALENTS	*$ 103,811.68*
REAL ESTATE		
	SINGLE FAMILY HOME 987 SUNNYSIDE STREET, ANYTOWN, CALIFORNIA	$ 750,000.00
	SINGLE FAMILY HOME 654 FORECLOSURE WAY, ANYTOWN, CALIFORNIA	$ 275,000.00
	COMMERICAL PROPERTY 321 FRANCHISE ROW, ANYTOWN, CALIFORNIA	$ 1,500,000.00
	APARTMENT BUILDING 111 MANAGEMENT AVE, ANYTOWN, CALIFORNIA	$ 1,200,000.00
	LAND (UNIMPROVED) ANYTOWN, CALIFORNIA	$ 200,000.00
	TOTAL REAL ESTATE	*$ 3,925,000.00*

SHARES / PAR VALUE	DESCRIPTION		CARRY VALUE
RECEIVABLES			
	DUE FROM REBECCA JONES (12 MOS RENT ON FORECLOSURE WAY)	$	24,000.00
	TOTAL RECEIVABLES	$	*24,000.00*
OTHER ASSETS			
	STATE FARM INSURANCE CO CLAIM PENDING RE: FIRE AT 555 RETIREMENT LANE, ANYTOWN, CA	$	125,000.00
	2010 MERCEDES C230 VIN K47834N923498M	$	7,000.00
	2007 MALIBU SPEEDBOAT VIN B987345H0934	$	15,000.00
	OTHER ASSETS	$	*147,000.00*
	TOTAL ASSETS	$	**4,199,811.68**

§1.42 c. Receipts

DAVID JONES TRUST
THOMAS JONES, TRUSTEE

FIRST ACCOUNTING
FOR THE PERIOD JANUARY 1, 2012 THRU JUNE 30, 2012
RECEIPTS
SCHEDULE A

DATE	DESCRIPTION	INCOME	PRINCIPAL
INTEREST			
01/31/12	BANK OF AMERICA SAVINGS A/C #XXXXXX6789	$ 64.59	
02/29/12	BANK OF AMERICA SAVINGS A/C #XXXXXX6789	$ 60.42	
03/31/12	BANK OF AMERICA SAVINGS A/C #XXXXXX6789	$ 64.59	
04/30/12	BANK OF AMERICA SAVINGS A/C #XXXXXX6789	$ 62.50	
05/31/12	BANK OF AMERICA SAVINGS A/C #XXXXXX6789	$ 64.59	
06/30/12	BANK OF AMERICA SAVINGS A/C #XXXXXX6789	$ 62.50	
05/31/12	NOTE RECEIVABLE FROM LAND INVESTORS LLC	$ 666.67	
06/30/12	NOTE RECEIVABLE FROM LAND INVESTORS LLC	$ 666.67	
	TOTAL INTEREST	$ 1,712.53	$ -
RENTAL INCOME - 321 FRANCHISE ROW			
01/02/12	BETTY'S BARGAIN BOUTIQUE, FRANCHISE ROW	$ 2,000.00	
02/01/12	BETTY'S BARGAIN BOUTIQUE, FRANCHISE ROW	$ 2,000.00	
03/01/12	BETTY'S BARGAIN BOUTIQUE, FRANCHISE ROW	$ 2,000.00	

DATE	DESCRIPTION	INCOME	PRINCIPAL
04/01/12	BETTY'S BARGAIN BOUTIQUE, FRANCHISE ROW	$ 2,000.00	
05/01/12	BETTY'S BARGAIN BOUTIQUE, FRANCHISE ROW	$ 2,000.00	
01/02/12	CHERYL'S CHEESESTEAKS, FRANCHISE ROW	$ 750.00	
02/01/12	CHERYL'S CHEESESTEAKS, FRANCHISE ROW	$ 750.00	
03/01/12	CHERYL'S CHEESESTEAKS, FRANCHISE ROW	$ 750.00	
04/01/12	CHERYL'S CHEESESTEAKS, FRANCHISE ROW	$ 750.00	
05/01/12	CHERYL'S CHEESESTEAKS, FRANCHISE ROW	$ 750.00	
01/02/12	ERNIE'S ELECTRONICS, FRANCHISE ROW	$ 3,500.00	
02/01/12	ERNIE'S ELECTRONICS, FRANCHISE ROW	$ 3,500.00	
03/01/12	ERNIE'S ELECTRONICS, FRANCHISE ROW	$ 3,500.00	
04/01/12	ERNIE'S ELECTRONICS, FRANCHISE ROW	$ 3,500.00	
05/01/12	ERNIE'S ELECTRONICS, FRANCHISE ROW	$ 3,500.00	
	TOTAL RENTAL INCOME - 321 FRANCHISE ROW	$ 31,250.00	$
RENTAL INCOME - 111 MANAGEMENT AVE			
01/05/12	111 MANAGEMENT AVE, APT A	$ 700.00	
02/05/12	111 MANAGEMENT AVE, APT A	$ 700.00	
03/05/12	111 MANAGEMENT AVE, APT A	$ 700.00	
01/05/12	111 MANAGEMENT AVE, APT B	$ 800.00	
02/05/12	111 MANAGEMENT AVE, APT B	$ 800.00	
03/05/12	111 MANAGEMENT AVE, APT B	$ 800.00	
01/05/12	111 MANAGEMENT AVE, APT C	$ 900.00	

§1.43

DATE	DESCRIPTION	INCOME	PRINCIPAL
02/05/12	111 MANAGEMENT AVE, APT C	$ 900.00	
03/05/12	111 MANAGEMENT AVE, APT C	$ 900.00	
02/01/12	111 MANAGEMENT AVE, APT D - SECURITY DEPOSIT		$ 2,000.00
02/05/12	111 MANAGEMENT AVE, APT D	$ 1,000.00	
03/05/12	111 MANAGEMENT AVE, APT D	$ 1,000.00	
	TOTAL RENTAL INCOME - 111 MANAGEMENT AVE	$ 9,200.00	$ 2,000.00
OTHER INCOME			
03/31/12	EXPLORERS OIL LEASE INCOME ON LAND (UNIMPROVED) ANYTOWN, CA	$ 1,000.00	
	TOTAL OTHER INCOME	$ 1,000.00	$ -
REFUNDS			
04/30/12	SAFE INSURANCE - REFUND OF AUTO INSURANCE UPON CANCELLATION OF POLICY	$ 200.00	
05/15/12	STEWART TITLE COMPANY - REFUND OF PREPAID PROPERTY TAX ON 321 FRANCHISE ROW, RECEIVED IN ESCROW		$ 2,500.00
	TOTAL REFUNDS	$ 200.00	$ 2,500.00
	TOTAL INCOME AND PRINCIPAL	$ 43,362.53	$ 4,500.00
	TOTAL RECEIPTS	$ 47,862.53	

§1.43   d. Gains on Sales

DAVID JONES TRUST
THOMAS JONES, TRUSTEE

FIRST ACCOUNTING
FOR THE PERIOD JANUARY 1, 2012 THRU JUNE 30, 2012
GAINS ON SALES
SCHEDULE B

DATE	SHARES	DESCRIPTION	CARRY VALUE	PROCEEDS	GAINS
05/15/12		COMMERICAL PROPERTY 321 FRANCHISE ROW, ANYTOWN, CALIFORNIA	$ 1,500,000.00	$ 1,675,000.00	175,000.00
		TOTALS	$ 1,500,000.00	$ 1,675,000.00	$ **175,000.00**

§1.44 e. Disbursements

DAVID JONES TRUST
THOMAS JONES, TRUSTEE

FIRST ACCOUNTING
FOR THE PERIOD JANUARY 1, 2012 THRU JUNE 30, 2012
DISBURSEMENTS
SCHEDULE C

DATE	PAID TO	CHK #	FOR	INCOME	PRINCIPAL
ADMINISTRATIVE EXPENSES					
01/03/12	FANCY FUNERAL HOME		MEMORIAL SERVICE		$ 1,200.00
01/04/12	FANCY FUNERAL HOME		BURIAL FEES		$ 8,000.00
01/29/12	LAW OFFICE OF DUDLEY SMITH		REIMBURSMENT FOR COSTS ADVANCED	$ 52.00	$ 52.00
01/31/12	BANK OF AMERICA		MONTHLY SERVICE FEE	$ 5.00	$ 5.00
01/31/12	DISCOVER CARD		CREDIT CARD - DEBT OF DECEDENT		$ 521.34
02/15/12	ANYTOWN HOSPITAL		DEBT OF DECEDENT		$ 600.00
02/15/12	ANYTOWN MEDICAL GROUP		DEBT OF DECEDENT		$ 230.00
02/28/12	BANK OF AMERICA		MONTHLY SERVICE FEE	$ 5.00	$ 5.00
03/31/12	BANK OF AMERICA		MONTHLY SERVICE FEE	$ 5.00	$ 5.00
04/16/12	LAW OFFICE OF DUDLEY SMITH		LEGAL FEES	$ 500.00	$ 500.00
04/20/12	INTERNAL REVENUE SERVICE		2011 FEDERAL TAX DUE		$ 5,230.00
04/20/12	FRANCHISE TAX BOARD		2011 STATE TAX DUE		$ 2,140.00
04/30/12	BANK OF AMERICA		MONTHLY SERVICE FEE	$ 5.00	$ 5.00
05/05/12	LOUIE & LOUIE, CPA		TAX PREPARATION	$ 250.00	$ 250.00
05/31/12	BANK OF AMERICA		MONTHLY SERVICE FEE	$ 5.00	$ 5.00
06/30/12	BANK OF AMERICA		MONTHLY SERVICE FEE	$ 5.00	$ 5.00
			TOTAL ADMINISTRATIVE EXPENSES	$ 832.00	$ 16,753.34

DATE	PAID TO	CHK #	FOR	INCOME		PRINCIPAL
REAL ESTATE EXPENSES - 987 SUNNYSIDE STREET						
01/05/12	QUALITY MORTGAGE COMPANY		MORTGAGE PAYMENT	$ 787.50	$	712.50
01/17/12	PACIFIC GAS & ELECTRIC		UTILITIES	$ 52.75		
01/28/12	EBMUD		WATER SERVICE	$ 62.45		
01/28/12	KILLER PEST CONTROL		EXTERMINATOR	$ 150.00		
01/30/12	WASTE MANAGEMENT COMPANY		GARBAGE SERVICE	$ 142.00		
01/30/12	COMCAST		CABLE AND TELEPHONE SERVICE	$ 160.80		
02/05/12	QUALITY MORTGAGE COMPANY		MORTGAGE PAYMENT	$ 784.53	$	715.47
02/15/12	PACIFIC GAS & ELECTRIC		UTILITIES	$ 53.21		
02/29/12	COMCAST		CABLE AND TELEPHONE SERVICE	$ 162.90		
03/05/12	QUALITY MORTGAGE COMPANY		MORTGAGE PAYMENT	$ 781.55	$	718.45
03/12/12	ROOTER ROOTER		PLUMBING REPAIR	$ 475.00		
03/15/12	GORGEOUS GARDENS		GARDENING SERVICE (3 MONTHS)	$ 300.00		
03/17/12	PACIFIC GAS & ELECTRIC		UTILITIES	$ 50.98		
03/27/12	EBMUD		WATER SERVICE	$ 65.01		
03/28/12	WASTE MANAGEMENT COMPANY		GARBAGE SERVICE	$ 142.00		
03/31/12	COMCAST		CABLE AND TELEPHONE SERVICE	$ 161.75		
04/05/12	QUALITY MORTGAGE COMPANY		MORTGAGE PAYMENT	$ 778.56	$	721.44
04/07/12	A-1 ROOFING		ROOF REPAIR	$ 3,600.00		
04/18/12	PACIFIC GAS & ELECTRIC		UTILITIES	$ 51.37		
04/30/12	COMCAST		CABLE AND TELEPHONE SERVICE	$ 160.90		
05/05/12	QUALITY MORTGAGE COMPANY		MORTGAGE PAYMENT	$ 775.55	$	724.45

DATE	PAID TO	CHK #	FOR	INCOME	PRINCIPAL
05/17/12	PACIFIC GAS & ELECTRIC		UTILITIES	$ 51.22	
05/31/12	EBMUD		WATER SERVICE	$ 61.98	
05/31/12	COMCAST		CABLE AND TELEPHONE SERVICE	$ 161.85	
06/01/12	WASTE MANAGEMENT COMPANY		GARBAGE SERVICE	$ 142.00	
06/05/12	QUALITY MORTGAGE COMPANY		MORTGAGE PAYMENT	$ 772.53	$ 727.47
06/15/12	PACIFIC GAS & ELECTRIC		UTILITIES	$ 53.01	
06/30/12	COMCAST		CABLE AND TELEPHONE SERVICE	$ 162.25	
	TOTAL REAL ESTATE EXPENSES - 987 SUNNYSIDE STREET			$ 11,103.65	$ 4,319.78
REAL ESTATE EXPENSES - 321 FRANCHISE ROW					
01/15/12	COUNTY TAX COLLECTOR		SECOND INSTALLMENT OF 2011-2012 PROPERTY TAX	$ 7,550.00	
01/18/12	JOE'S ELECTRICAL		INSTALLATION OF OUTDOOR LIGHTING	$ 1,200.00	
01/26/12	WASTE MANAGEMENT		GARBAGE SERVICE	$ 450.00	
02/08/12	PAT'S PAVING		PARKING LOT REPAVING	$ 4,500.00	
02/15/12	PAUL'S PAINTING		PARKING LOT PAINTING	$ 2,300.00	
02/25/12	WASTE MANAGEMENT		GARBAGE SERVICE	$ 450.00	
02/27/12	SAL'S PLUMBING		PLUMBING REPAIR	$ 752.00	
03/25/12	WASTE MANAGEMENT		GARBAGE SERVICE	$ 450.00	
04/25/12	WASTE MANAGEMENT		GARBAGE SERVICE	$ 450.00	
	TOTAL REAL ESTATE EXPENSES - 321 FRANCHISE ROW			$ 18,102.00	$ -
REAL ESTATE EXPENSES PAID IN ESCROW UPON SALE OF 321 FRANCHISE ROW					
05/15/12	BETTER HOMES REAL ESTATE COMPANY		BROKER COMMISSION		$ 47,265.00
05/15/12	PRUDENTIAL REAL ESTATE COMPANY		BROKER COMMISSION		$ 47,265.00
05/15/12	SELLER CREDIT		CREDIT FOR CLOSING COSTS		$ 25,000.00

DATE	PAID TO	CHK #	FOR	INCOME		PRINCIPAL
05/15/12	SUPER CONSTRUCTION		LOADING DOCK REPAIRS REQUIRED FOR SALE		$	40,000.00
05/15/12	ERNEST EVIRONMENTAL		INSPECTION FEE		$	750.00
05/15/12	STEWART TITLE CO		PRO-RATED RENT COLLECTED FOR MAY 2012		$	3,125.00
05/15/12	STEWART TITLE CO		SECURITY DEPOSITS		$	12,500.00
05/15/12	STEWART TITLE CO		ESCROW AND TITLE FEES		$	1,000.00
05/15/12	STEWART TITLE CO		DOCUMENTATION FEE		$	500.00
05/15/12	STEWART TITLE CO		NOTARY FEE		$	20.00
05/15/12	STEWART TITLE CO		COURIER FEE		$	100.00
			TOTAL REAL ESTATE EXPENSES PAID IN ESCROW	$ -	$	177,525.00
REAL ESTATE EXPENSES - 111 MANAGEMENT AVE						
01/02/12	MAGNIFICENT MANAGEMENT		PROPERTY MANAGEMENT FEE	$ 225.00		
01/15/12	FINE FENCES		FENCE REPAIR -- UNIT B	$ 1,500.00		
01/22/12	GUPPY GLASS		WINDOW REPAIR -- UNIT B	$ 250.00		
01/31/12	AMY'S APPLIANCES		WASHER / DRYER -- UNIT D	$ 600.00		
01/31/12	CAPPY'S CARPET		CARPET REPLACEMENT - UNIT D	$ 550.00		
01/31/12	DOLLY'S DECORATING		INTERIOR PAINTING - UNIT D	$ 750.00		
02/02/12	MAGNIFICENT MANAGEMENT		PROPERTY MANAGEMENT FEE	$ 225.00		
02/17/12	JOE'S ELECTRICAL		INTERCOM REPAIR	$ 325.00		
03/02/12	MAGNIFICENT MANAGEMENT		PROPERTY MANAGEMENT FEE	$ 225.00		
03/15/12	PAUL'S PAINTING		EXTERIOR PAINTING OF BUILDING IN PREPARATION FOR SALE		$	7,000.00
03/15/12	FANNIE'S FURNACE		FURNACE REPAIR IN PREPARATION FOR SALE		$	2,500.00
			TOTAL REAL ESTATE EXPENSES - 111 MANAGEMENT AVE	$ 4,650.00	$	9,500.00

DATE	PAID TO	CHK #	FOR	INCOME	PRINCIPAL
REAL ESTATE EXPENSES PAID IN ESCROW UPON SALE OF 111 MANAGEMENT AVE					
04/01/12	COLDWELL BANKER		BROKER COMMISSION		$ 31,500.00
04/01/12	ZEPHYER REAL ESTATE		BROKER COMMISSION		$ 31,500.00
04/01/12	DAN'S DISCLOSURES		HAZARD DISCLOSURES		$ 200.00
04/01/12	COUNTY TAX COLLECTOR		PRO-RATED PROPERTY TAX DUE		$ 3,650.00
04/01/12	OLD REPUBLIC TITLE		TITLE AND ESCROW FEES		$ 750.00
04/01/12	OLD REPUBLIC TITLE		DOCUMENTATION FEE		$ 250.00
04/01/12	OLD REPUBLIC TITLE		SECURITY DEPOSITS		$ 6,800.00
			TOTAL REAL ESTATE EXPENSES PAID IN ESCROW $	-	$ 74,650.00
OTHER DISBURSEMENTS					
01/17/12	MIKE MECHANIC		SMOG CHECK	$ 75.00	
01/31/12	DEPARTMENT OF MOTOR VEHICLES		AUTO REGISTRATION	$ 129.00	
01/31/12	SAFE INSURANCE		AUTO INSURANCE	$ 400.00	
02/16/12	TOWING SERVICE OF AMERICA		TOWING FEE TO REMOVE MERCEDES AT ACCIDENT SITE	$ 200.00	
			TOTAL OTHER DISBURSEMENTS $	804.00	$ -
			TOTAL INCOME AND PRINCIPAL $	35,491.65	$ 282,748.12
			TOTAL DISBURSEMENTS $	318,239.77	

§1.45   f. Losses on Sales

DAVID JONES TRUST
THOMAS JONES, TRUSTEE

FIRST ACCOUNTING
FOR THE PERIOD JANUARY 1, 2012 THRU JUNE 30, 2012
LOSSES ON SALES
SCHEDULE D

DATE	SHARES	DESCRIPTION	CARRY VALUE	PROCEEDS	LOSSES
04/01/12		APARTMENT BUILDING 111 MANAGEMENT AVE, ANYTOWN, CALIFORNIA	$ 1,200,000.00	$ 1,050,000.00	$ 150,000.00
04/03/12		2010 MERCEDES C230 VIN K47834N923498M (TOTALED IN ACCIDENT ON 02/15/12, PROCEEDS FROM SAFE INSURANCE CO)	$ 7,000.00	$ 2,350.00	$ 4,650.00
		TOTALS $	1,207,000.00	$ 1,052,350.00	$ **154,650.00**

§1.46   g. Distributions

DAVID JONES TRUST

THOMAS JONES, TRUSTEE

FIRST ACCOUNTING

FOR THE PERIOD JANUARY 1, 2012 THRU JUNE 30, 2012

DISTRIBUTIONS

SCHEDULE E

DATE	DESCRIPTION		AMOUNT/CARRY VALUE
ANIMAL RESCUE FOUNDATION			
	CASH DISTRIBUTION PECUNIARY GIFT	GENERAL	$ 75,000.00
		TOTAL ANIMAL RESCUE FOUNDATION $	*75,000.00*
REBECCA JONES			
01/05/12	2007 MALIBU SPEEDBOAT VIN B987345H0934		$ 15,000.00
		TOTAL REBECCA JONES $	*15,000.00*
		TOTAL DISTRIBUTIONS $	**90,000.00**

§1.47   h. Assets on Hand—End of Period

DAVID JONES TRUST

THOMAS JONES, TRUSTEE

FIRST ACCOUNTING

FOR THE PERIOD JANUARY 1, 2012 THRU JUNE 30, 2012

ASSETS ON HAND - END OF PERIOD

SCHEDULE F

SHARES / PAR VALUE	DESCRIPTION	CARRY VALUE	MARKET VALUE
CASH AND CASH EQUIVALENTS			
	BANK OF AMERICA CHECKING A/C #XXXXXX6789	$ 99,754.44	$ 99,754.44
	BANK OF AMERICA SAVINGS A/C #XXXXXX6789	$ 2,768,030.00	$ 2,768,030.00
	TOTAL CASH AND CASH EQUIVALENTS	$ 2,867,784.44	$ 2,867,784.44
REAL ESTATE			
	RESIDENCE 987 SUNNYSIDE STREET ANYTOWN, CALIFORNIA	$ 773,000.00	$ 755,000.00
	TOTAL REAL ESTATE	$ 773,000.00	$ 755,000.00
RECEIVABLES			
	DUE FROM REBECCA JONES (12 MOS RENT ON FORECLOSURE WAY)	$ 24,000.00	$ 24,000.00
	NOTE RECEIVABLE DUE FROM LAND INVESTORS LLC SECURED BY LAND (UNIMPROVED) ANYTOWN, CA	$ 195,000.00	$ 195,000.00
	TOTAL RECEIVABLES	$ 219,000.00	$ 219,000.00
	TOTAL ASSETS	$ 3,859,784.44	$ 3,622,784.44

§1.48 i. Changes in Form of Assets

DAVID JONES TRUST

THOMAS JONES, TRUSTEE

FIRST ACCOUNTING

FOR THE PERIOD JANUARY 1, 2012 THRU JUNE 30, 2012

CHANGES IN FORM OF ASSETS

DATE	DESCRIPTION		CASH	CARRY VALUE
CAPITAL IMPROVEMENTS - 987 SUNNYSIDE STREET				
01/01/12	CARRY VALUE ON HAND - BEGINNING OF PERIOD			$ 750,000.00
04/15/12	CREATIVE CONSTRUCTION	DEPOSIT FOR BATHROOM ADDITION	$ (5,000.00)	$ 5,000.00
04/30/12	CREATIVE CONSTRUCTION	BATHROOM ADDITION	$ (10,000.00)	$ 10,000.00
05/15/12	CREATIVE CONSTRUCTION	BATHROOM ADDITION FINAL PAYMENT	$ (8,000.00)	$ 8,000.00
06/30/12	CARRY VALUE ON HAND - END OF PERIOD			$ 773,000.00
SALES W/O GAIN OR LOSS				
03/30/12	RESIDENCE 654 FORECLOSURE WAY, ANYTOWN, CA	SOLD BY MORTGAGE COMPANY (SEE LIABILITIES)	$ 275,000.00	$ (275,000.00)
04/30/12	LAND (UNIMPROVED) ANYTOWN, CALIFORNIA	SOLD IN EXCHANGE FOR NOTE RECEIVABLE	$ 200,000.00	$ (200,000.00)
PURCHASES				
04/30/12	NOTE RECEIVABLE 10 YEARS, DUE 4/01/22 INT MONTHLY, 4% P.A. PRIN $5,000 QTR	DUE FROM LAND INVESTORS INC	$ (200,000.00)	$ 200,000.00
COLLECTION OF RECEIVABLES				
01/05/12	STATE FARM INSURANCE CO	CLAIM RECEIVED RE: FIRE AT 555 RETIREMENT LANE, ANYTOWN, CA	$ 125,000.00	$ (125,000.00)
06/30/12	LAND INVESTORS INC NOTE RECEIVABLE 10 YEARS, DUE 4/01/22 INT ONLY, 4% P.A.	PRINCIPAL PAYMENT	$ 5,000.00	$ (5,000.00)

COLLECTION OF RECEIVABLES

01/05/12	STATE FARM INSURANCE CO	CLAIM RECEIVED RE: FIRE AT 555 RETIREMENT LANE, ANYTOWN, CA	$	125,000.00	$ (125,000.00)
06/30/12	LAND INVESTORS INC NOTE RECEIVABLE 10 YEARS, DUE 4/01/22 INT ONLY, 4% P.A.	PRINCIPAL PAYMENT	$	5,000.00	$ (5,000.00)

§1.49 j. Liabilities

DAVID JONES TRUST
THOMAS JONES, TRUSTEE

FIRST ACCOUNTING
FOR THE PERIOD JANUARY 1, 2012 THRU JUNE 30, 2012
LIABILITIES

DATE	DESCRIPTION	INCREASE	DECREASE	BALANCE
DUE TO QUALITY MORTGAGE COMPANY				
SECURED BY PROPERTY LOCATED AT				
987 SUNNYSIDE STREET, ANYTOWN, CALIFORNIA				
01/01/12	BALANCE DUE			$ 189,000.00
01/05/12	PRINCIPAL PAYMENT		$ 712.50	$ 188,287.50
02/05/12	PRINCIPAL PAYMENT		$ 715.47	$ 187,572.03
03/05/12	PRINCIPAL PAYMENT		$ 718.45	$ 186,853.58
04/05/12	PRINCIPAL PAYMENT		$ 721.44	$ 186,132.14
05/05/12	PRINCIPAL PAYMENT		$ 724.45	$ 185,407.69
06/05/12	PRINCIPAL PAYMENT		$ 727.47	**$ 184,680.22**
DUE TO SECRET MORTGAGE COMPANY				
SECURED BY PROPERTY LOCATED AT				
654 FORECLOSURE WAY, ANYTOWN, CALIFORNIA				
01/01/12	BALANCE DUE			$ 289,500.00
01/15/12	LATE FEE	$ 250.00		$ 289,750.00
01/30/12	INTEREST DUE	$ 1,206.25		$ 290,956.25
02/15/12	LATE FEE	$ 250.00		$ 291,206.25
02/15/12	FORECLOSURE NOTICE FEE	$ 500.00		$ 291,706.25
02/15/12	MORTAGE BANK FEES	$ 300.00		$ 292,006.25
02/29/12	INTEREST DUE	$ 1,225.25		$ 293,231.50
03/15/12	LATE FEE	$ 250.00		$ 293,481.50
03/30/12	INTEREST DUE	$ 1,250.50		$ 294,732.00
03/30/12	FORECLOSURE, TRANSFER OF DEED		$ 275,000.00	$ 19,732.00
03/30/12	BANK WRITE OFF		$ 19,732.00	-

DATE	DESCRIPTION	INCREASE	DECREASE	BALANCE
DUE TO TENANTS /SECURITY DEPOSITS				
01/01/12	BETTY'S BARGAIN BOUTIQUE, FRANCHISE ROW			$ 4,000.00
05/15/12	SECURITY DEPOSIT TRANSFERRED IN ESCROW		$ 4,000.00	$ -
01/01/12	CHERYL'S CHEESESTEAKS, FRANCHISE ROW			$ 1,500.00
05/15/12	SECURITY DEPOSIT TRANSFERRED IN ESCROW		$ 1,500.00	$ -
01/01/12	ERNIE'S ELECTRONICS, FRANCHISE ROW			$ 7,000.00
05/15/12	SECURITY DEPOSIT TRANSFERRED IN ESCROW		$ 7,000.00	$ -
01/01/12	111 MANAGEMENT AVE, APT A			$ 1,400.00
04/01/12	SECURITY DEPOSIT TRANSFERRED IN ESCROW		$ 1,400.00	$ -
01/01/12	111 MANAGEMENT AVE, APT B			$ 1,600.00
04/01/12	SECURITY DEPOSIT TRANSFERRED IN ESCROW		$ 1,600.00	$ -
01/01/12	111 MANAGEMENT AVE, APT C			$ 1,800.00
04/01/12	SECURITY DEPOSIT TRANSFERRED IN ESCROW		$ 1,800.00	$ -
02/01/12	111 MANAGEMENT AVE, APT D	$ 2,000.00		$ 2,000.00
04/01/12	SECURITY DEPOSIT TRANSFERRED IN ESCROW		$ 2,000.00	$ -
DUE TO THOMAS JONES, TRUSTEE				
01/03/12	ADVANCE TO TRUST FOR MEMORIAL LUNCHEON AT SUNSET HILLS COUNTRY CLUB	$ 7,052.00		$ 7,052.00
01/04/12	ADVANCE TO TRUST FOR OBITUARY PAID TO NEWSPAPER ASSOCIATION	$ 400.00		$ 7,452.00
06/30/12	TRUSTEE FEE	$ 20,999.06		$ 28,451.06

§1.50 k. Proposed Distributions

DAVID JONES TRUST

THOMAS JONES, TRUSTEE

FIRST ACCOUNTING

FOR THE PERIOD JANUARY 1, 2012 THRU JUNE 30, 2012

PROPOSED DISTRIBUTIONS

DATE	DESCRIPTION	AMOUNT / CARRY VALUE	TOTAL
PROPOSED DISTRIBUTION TO REBECCA JONES			
01/05/12	2007 MALIBU SPEEDBOAT VIN B987345H0934 (ALREADY DISTRIBUTED)	$ 15,000.00	
03/30/12	DUE FROM REBECCA JONES (12 MOS RENT ON FORECLOSURE WAY)	$ 24,000.00	
04/03/12	2010 MERCEDES C230 VIN K47834N923498M (DIFFERENCE BETWEEN ASSET VALUE ON HAND BEGINNING AND AMOUNT RECEIVED BY TRUST AFTER ACCIDENT)	$ 4,650.00	
	PROPOSED CASH DISTRIBUTION	$ 956,350.00	
	TOTAL PROPOSED DISTRIBUTIONS TO REBECCA JONES		$ 1,000,000.00
PROPOSED DISTRIBUTION TO THOMAS JONES			
	PROPOSED CASH DISTRIBUTION	$ 1,000,000.00	
	TOTAL PROPOSED DISTRIBUTIONS TO THOMAS JONES		$ 1,000,000.00
	TOTAL PROPOSED DISTRIBUTIONS		**$ 2,000,000.00**

2
Types of Fiduciaries and the Various Duties to Account

I. INTRODUCTION §2.1

II. TYPES OF FIDUCIARIES, BRIEFLY
   A. Guardians §2.2
   B. Conservators §2.3
   C. Agents Under Powers of Attorney §2.4
   D. Personal Representatives
      1. Nature of the Fiduciary Relationship §2.5
      2. Types of Personal Representatives §2.6
   E. Trustees
      1. Brief History §2.7
      2. Modern Will-Substitute Trusts §2.8

III. ACCOUNTS REQUIRED OF GUARDIANS AND CONSERVATORS
   A. Start Here: Inventory and Appraisal
      1. Guardians and Conservators §2.9
      2. Temporary Guardians and Temporary Conservators §2.10
   B. Periodic Accounting
      1. First Account §2.11
      2. Frequency of Accountings §2.12
      3. Guardian or Conservator Dies or Absconds §2.13
      4. Temporary Conservators and Guardians §2.14
   C. Final Account §2.15
   D. Standard or Simplified Accounting? §2.16
      1. Judicial Council Account Forms §2.17
      2. Standard Accounting
         a. When to Perform a Standard (Categorized) Accounting §2.18
         b. When to Use Judicial Council Forms §2.19
         c. Presenting Data on the Mandatory Judicial Council Form §2.20

3. Simplified Accounting **§2.21**
4. All Accountings, Whether Standard or Simplified **§2.22**
E. Supporting Documents **§2.23**
F. Penalties for Late Accounts **§2.24**
G. The Guardian's or Conservator's Audience **§2.25**
H. Waiver of Account **§2.26**
I. Release of Guardian by Ward **§2.27**
J. Petitioning for Approval of Accounting
   1. Guardian's Petition for Approval of Accounting **§2.28**
   2. Conservator's Petition for Approval of Accounting **§2.29**

IV. ACCOUNTS REQUIRED OF PERSONAL REPRESENTATIVES
A. Start Here: Inventory and Appraisal
   1. Requirements for Filing an Inventory and Appraisal **§2.30**
   2. When Administration Follows a Guardianship or Conservatorship **§2.31**
B. Periodic Accounting
   1. Generally, at End of Administration **§2.32**
   2. Mid-Administration Accounting **§2.33**
C. Terminated Personal Representative **§2.34**
D. Deceased or Incapacitated Personal Representative **§2.35**
E. The Absconding Personal Representative **§2.36**
F. Documents That Support the Account **§2.37**
G. Penalties for Failure to Account **§2.38**
H. Waiver of Account **§2.39**
I. "Report" Instead of Account **§2.40**
J. Personal Representative's Audience **§2.41**
K. Petition to Approve Personal Representative's Account **§2.42**

V. ACCOUNTS REQUIRED OF TRUSTEES OF IRREVOCABLE TRUSTS
A. Why Distinguish Between Irrevocable and Revocable Trusts? **§2.43**
B. Duty to Account, Generally, to Report, and to Provide Information
   1. Beneficiaries Defined **§2.44**
   2. Duty to Account
      a. Duty Owed to Current Beneficiaries **§2.45**
      b. No Duty Owed to Remainder Beneficiaries **§2.46**
      c. Waivers
         (1) Waivers in the Trust Instrument **§2.47**
         (2) A Beneficiary's Written Waiver **§2.48**

            (3) Waiver Does Not Trigger the Running of the Statute of Limitations §2.49
        d. Frequency §2.50
     3. Duty to Report §2.51
     4. Duty to Keep Beneficiaries Reasonably Informed §2.52
     5. Trust Records and the Beneficiaries' Right of Inspection
        a. Beneficiaries Have a Right to Inspect Trust Records §2.53
        b. Records the Trustee Should Keep §2.54
        c. The "Personal" Records of the Trustee Who Commingles §2.55
  C. Accounting as a Preliminary Step to the Performance of Other Duties §2.56
  D. Accounting Protects the Trustee
     1. The 3-Year Statute of Limitations §2.57
     2. The 180-Day Statute of Limitations §2.58
     3. Petitions for Court Approval §2.59
     4. Release of Liability for Disclosures Made in Accounting §2.60
        a. Beneficiary Must Have Capacity §2.61
        b. Full Disclosure §2.62
        c. Not Induced by Improper Conduct §2.63
        d. No Unfair Advantage §2.64
  E. Serving the Accounting §2.65
  F. Petitioning for Court Approval of Trustee's Account §2.66

VI. ACCOUNTS REQUIRED OF TRUSTEES OF REVOCABLE TRUSTS
  A. Duties Owed to Whom? §2.67
  B. When Person Holding the Power to Revoke Is Not Competent §2.68
  C. Distinguishing Persons to Whom Duties Are Owed From Persons With Standing §2.69
  D. Safe Practices §2.70

VII. FORMAT OF TRUST ACCOUNTS
  A. Minimum Requirements §2.71
  B. Why Trustees Should Account as if Preparing for Court Review §2.72

§2.1 I. INTRODUCTION

Many relationships are fiduciary in nature. Marriage creates a fiduciary relationship, as does the formation of a partnership. This book discusses only those fiduciaries whose duties are codified in the Probate Code: guardians, conservators, agents under powers of attorney, personal representatives, and trustees. The purpose of this chapter is to introduce the reader to these types of fiduciaries, with the aim of distinguishing one from another. For a complete discussion of guardians, see California Guardianship Practice (Cal CEB). For a complete discussion of conservators, see California Conservatorship Practice (Cal CEB). For a complete discussion of agents under powers of attorney, see California Powers of Attorney and Health Care Directives (Cal CEB). For a complete discussion of personal representatives, see California Decedent Estate Practice (Cal CEB). For a complete discussion of trustees, see California Trust Administration (Cal CEB).

II. TYPES OF FIDUCIARIES, BRIEFLY

§2.2 A. Guardians

The court may appoint a guardian of the person of a minor, or of a minor's "estate," or of the person and estate of a minor. Prob C §1514. Only guardians of a minor's estate must account and whenever these materials refer to a guardian, it is a reference to the guardian of a minor's estate. Often, a minor's estate is the consequence of the minor receiving a gift, bequest, or devise. For these estates, the person who gives the gift, or who leaves the bequest or devise, may nominate a guardian. Prob C §1501. In such cases, the court will appoint the nominee as guardian, unless the person is unsuited for the responsibility. Prob C §1514(d).

A minor's estate also may be the consequence of the death of an intestate decedent—for example, the death of the minor's parent. For these minors, the court will appoint a guardian on the petition of an interested person (Prob C §1510) and will appoint as guardian that person nominated by the child's parent or parents, unless the court finds the nominee unsuitable. Prob C §§1500, 1514(c). Finally, a minor's estate may be the consequence of a personal injury suit, although the awards made and settlements reached in these suits are more often paid by a structured settlement that does not create a guardianship estate.

A guardian's duties begin on appointment and are said to end when the minor attains majority, *i.e.*, when the ward reaches age 18, or if the minor dies before reaching age 18, when the minor dies. In practice, however, the guardian's duties continue until the guardian has distributed the ward's estate to the ward, or to the ward's successor in interest, and the guardian has been discharged.

§2.3   B. Conservators

Similar to guardianships, the court may appoint a conservator of an adult, or of a married minor, or of a minor whose marriage has been dissolved. Prob C §1800.3. The court may appoint a conservator of the person, of the estate, or of both. Prob C §1800.3. Conservators are appointed only after the court has found by *clear and convincing evidence* that an adult (Prob C §1821):

- Is unable to properly provide for his or her own needs for physical health, food, clothing, and shelter;
- Is substantially unable to manage his or her own financial resources; or
- Is unable to resist fraud or undue influence.

Once the court makes this finding, the conservatee loses his or her rights to enter into contracts, sell or transfer property, borrow money, make gifts, delegate powers, and waive rights. Prob C §§1870–1871. After a conservator has been appointed, the conservator holds these rights, some of which the conservator may only exercise with prior court approval.

Only the conservator of the estate, and not the conservator of the person, is required to account. For a discussion of the accounting issues that may arise when one person is conservator of the estate and another is conservator of the person, see California Conservatorship Practice §19.7 (Cal CEB).

There is probably no fiduciary more powerful than a conservator, nor one more closely supervised in the use of that power. With letters of conservatorship, the conservator may administer all of the conservatee's assets, except those held in trust. Regarding trust assets, the conservator stands in the shoes of the conservatee. Typically, the conservator may amend and revoke trusts of which the conservatee is the settlor only after obtaining substituted judgment (Prob C §2580), but the conservator is otherwise entitled to exercise the conservatee's rights (Prob C §§850(a)(1)(D), 2462), including the right to demand accountings (Prob C §§2462, 17200).

With a few narrow exceptions, a conservator may exercise his or her powers only for the benefit of the conservatee. See Prob C §§2400-2595. Exceptions include:

- The repair and maintenance of a home or other dwelling of persons entitled to such from the conservatee (Prob C §2457);

- The renewal, modification, and termination of insurance for those legally entitled to support from conservatee (Prob C §2459); and, with a court order,

- Payment of excess income to persons entitled to support from the conservatee (Prob C §§2420-2423).

One might conclude from this, though no cases have so held, that a conservator owes duties only to the conservatee and, unlike trustees, is not required to weigh the conservatee's interests against those who might be the conservatee's heirs or beneficiaries. These people are entitled to notice of the hearing of the conservator's account (Prob C §2621), however, and their selfish interests therefore cannot be ignored. Occasionally, a conservatorship ends because the conservatee is restored to legal capacity. More often, the conservatorship ends at the conservatee's death. Thus, a conservatorship may be quite brief or quite long. The uncertain duration, coupled with the conservator's duty to provide the conservatee with comfortable and suitable support, suggests that conservators should invest conservatively and disburse funds sparingly.

§2.4   C. Agents Under Powers of Attorney

A power of attorney is a document whereby one person, the "principal," gives another person the power to make decisions or take action on behalf of the principal. The person who is given the power to act on behalf of the principal is called the "agent," or sometimes the "attorney-in-fact."

Unlike trustees, who have legal ownership of trust assets, an agent has only power: the power to administer another person's assets. Consider Prob C §4230, which defines the extent of the duties of an agent, and note that the agent who undertakes one transaction has no duty to participate in subsequent transactions.

Probate Code §4230 states:

> (a) Except as provided in subdivisions (b) and (c), a person who is designated as an attorney-in-fact has no duty to exercise the authority granted in the power of attorney and is not subject to the other duties of an attorney-in-fact, regardless of whether the principal has become incapacitated, is missing, or is otherwise unable to act.
>
> (b) Acting for the principal in one or more transactions does not obligate an attorney-in-fact to act for the principal in a subsequent transaction, but the attorney-in-fact has a duty to complete a transaction that the attorney-in-fact has commenced.
>
> (c) If an attorney-in-fact has expressly agreed in writing to act for the principal, the attorney-in-fact has a duty to act pursuant to the terms of the agreement. The agreement to act on behalf of the principal is enforceable against the attorney-in-fact as a fiduciary regardless of whether there is any consideration to support a contractual obligation.

Agents under powers of attorney have a duty to keep records of all their transactions with the principal's property and must make those records available for inspection by the principal, the principal's conservator, the personal representative of the principal's estate, and any other person given access pursuant to a court order. Prob C §4236. Unlike the other fiduciaries discussed in this chapter, however, agents have no affirmative duty to account periodically. Agents must account only under the following circumstances (Prob C §4236(b)):

- At any time the principal requests;
- When the power of attorney requires the agent to account and specifies to whom the account must be made;
- On request by the conservator of the estate of the principal while the principal is living;
- On request by the personal representative of the principal, after the principal has died; and
- Pursuant to court order.

Agents owe duties only to the principal and so, like guardians and conservators, they need not account for distributions of principal and income in the manner required by the Uniform Principal and Income Act (Prob C §§16320–16375). Additionally, unless ordered to account to the court or desiring court approval, the law of powers of attorney prescribes no particular format for the accounting. On the other hand, an agent ordered to account to a court, or one who seeks the court's approval, must prepare his or her accounting in the same manner as described in this book.

D. Personal Representatives

§2.5   1. Nature of the Fiduciary Relationship

The public policy of the State of California favors the speedy administration of a decedent's estate. *Estate of Beach* (1975) 15 C3d 623, 641. Though probate itself is a notoriously slow process, the statutes governing probate proceedings all embody this public policy. Personal representatives, the creatures of statute, thus have duties and powers meant to speed the distribution of the decedent's property to his or her heirs or beneficiaries. If the conservator's mandate is to conserve as if the conservatee might live forever, the personal representative's mandate is to get rid of the net estate as soon as the debts have been paid and the claims settled.

In a probate, the decedent's estate is subject to the rights of the estate's beneficiaries, the decedent's creditors, and any other person with rights provided by law. Prob C §7001. The personal representative is accountable to all of these people. Prob C §11000. By contrast, guardians and conservators administer the ward's or conservator's estate solely for the benefit of the ward or conservatee and account to others for the oversight they may provide. See, *e.g., Conservatorship of Lefkowitz* (1996) 50 CA4th 1310, 1314.

§2.6   2. Types of Personal Representatives

The term "personal representative" refers to any person or entity appointed by the court to administer a decedent's estate in a formal probate proceeding. Prob C §58. The term includes *executors,* meaning those named in the decedent's will, as well as *administrators,* meaning those appointed to administer the estate of one who dies intestate. Prob C §58. It also includes *administrators with will annexed,* meaning persons not named in the will who administers the estate of a testate decedent (Prob C §58), and *special administrators,* typically meaning those appointed by the court for a limited duration, pending the appointment of another fiduciary. Prob C §8540.

When discussing the personal representative's duty to account, it is important to distinguish between "personal representatives" and "general personal representatives," the difference lying with special administrators. Only a special administrator with general powers, *i.e.*, with all the "powers, duties, and obligations of a general personal representative under Section 8545," is a "general" personal representative. Prob C §58. There are important differences between special administrators who have general powers and those who do not, but for the purposes of this book, the difference that matters is the duty to file an inventory. The deadline for filing an inventory is 4 months after the appointment of a general personal representative (Prob C §8800(b)), which suggests that special administrators who lack general powers are either not required to inventory the estate, or have no deadline for doing so. Inventories and appraisals are further discussed at §2.9.

E. Trustees

§2.7   1. Brief History

A trust is established when a property owner entrusts his or her property to another person for the purpose of providing a benefit to the trust's beneficiaries. Historically, to create a trust there had to be an actual transfer of property from the property owner, called the "settlor," to another person, called the "trustee," for the benefit of yet a third person, the "beneficiary." Thus, for example, a wealthy landowner (the settlor) might entrust his real estate to a neighbor (the trustee) for the period of time necessary for the settlor's eldest son (the beneficiary) to reach maturity. During the term of the trust, the trustee would manage the estate, using the income from the land to pay the expenses of administration and to support the beneficiary. Under trust law, the attributes of property ownership were divided between the trustee, who had bare legal ownership, and the beneficiary, who owned all the beneficial interests in the property. As legal owner, the trustee had all the power an owner of property would have, but the trustee's exercise of that power was curtailed by the duties the trustee owed to the trust's beneficiaries.

§2.8   2. Modern Will-Substitute Trusts

Today, it is no longer necessary for the settlor, trustee, and beneficiary to be three different people. Prob C §15209. The law of trusts now allows one person (the settlor) to transfer the "estate" to oneself as trustee, for the settlor's own benefit. Prob C §15209.

The transfer of bare legal ownership from settlor to trustee remains important, however, because it is this transfer that makes the will-substitute trust a tool for avoiding probate. Generally speaking, a probate is necessary only if a decedent dies owning assets, the "estate," that would be subject to administration by the court. Decedents who, during their lifetime, transfer all of their estate to a trustee, die owning nothing. Similarly, decedents who, during their lifetime, declare that they themselves hold all of their estate in trust, die owning nothing. Consequently, there is nothing to administer in a probate. The property the decedent previously owned is now owned by the trustee and although the decedent's death may create a vacancy in the office of trustee, typically that vacancy can be filled without a lengthy court proceeding.

III. ACCOUNTS REQUIRED OF GUARDIANS AND CONSERVATORS

A. Start Here: Inventory and Appraisal

§2.9   1. Guardians and Conservators

The guardian's or conservator's Inventory and Appraisal will establish the beginning values used when accounting for the administration of the ward's or conservatee's property. Prob C §§1061(a)(1), 2610(a). Guardians of the estate and conservators of the estate must file an Inventory and Appraisal of the guardianship or conservatorship estate within 90 days of appointment. Prob C §2610. The inventory must include all of the ward's or conservatee's personal property and all real property located in California. Prob C §2600(b). Guardians and conservators need not inventory out-of-state real property, but they are required to account for these properties. Prob C §1063(h), codifying *Conservatorship of (Edward) Hume* (2006) 139 CA4th 393.

§2.10   2. Temporary Guardians and Temporary Conservators

Temporary guardians and temporary conservators need *not* file an Inventory and Appraisal, provided they file their final account within 90 days of appointment, in which case, they may inventory the estate in the account without appraising it. Prob C §2255(b). Temporary guardians and temporary conservators who cannot get their accountings filed this quickly (and most cannot) must file an

Inventory and Appraisal just like all other guardians and conservators. Prob C §2255(a).

B. Periodic Accounting

§2.11   1. First Account

Guardians and conservators must account at "the expiration of one year from the time of appointment." Prob C §2620(a). This mandate has been interpreted differently by various counties. For example, in Alameda County, the first account must be filed after the first anniversary of the establishment of the guardianship or conservatorship, but not later than 60 days after this anniversary. Alameda Ct R 7.780(a). By contrast, Contra Costa County requires guardians and conservators to file their first accounts on or before the first anniversary of appointment. Contra Costa Ct R 825.A. Thus, in Alameda County, guardians and conservators may file an account that ends on the anniversary of appointment, whereas in Contra Costa County, the fiduciary could not account for a full year without filing the accounting late.

§2.12   2. Frequency of Accountings

After the first accounting, guardians and conservators must account "biennially." Prob C §2620(a). The court may order guardians and conservators to account more frequently than statutes otherwise require (Prob C §2620(a)), but the courts rarely do. The guardian or conservator may wish to account more frequently than required, for reasons discussed in California Conservatorship Practice §19.1D (Cal CEB).

§2.13   3. Guardian or Conservator Dies or Absconds

If the *conservator* dies, his or her personal representative must account for the deceased conservator's administration of the conservatorship estate. Prob C §2632(b). If that person does not account, the court may order the attorney for the deceased conservator to do so. Prob C §2632(c). If the guardian or conservator absconds, the court may order the attorney for the absconding fiduciary to account. Prob C §2632(c).

§2.14 4. Temporary Conservators and Guardians

Temporary guardians and temporary conservators must account within 90 days after the appointment of a general guardian or conservator, or within some other time, as the court may allow. Prob C §2256. However, if the temporary guardian or temporary conservator is the one appointed general guardian or conservator, account for the period of temporary appointment may be included in the first account as general guardian or conservator. Prob C §2256.

§2.15 C. Final Account

If the ward or conservatee dies, the guardian or conservator must file a "final court accounting" that ends on the date of death. Prob C §2620(b). The guardian or conservator must also file a "separate accounting for the period subsequent to the date of death." Prob C §2620(b). This truly final account is often referred to as the "stub account."

PRACTICE TIP▶ To facilitate preparation of the stub accounting, the guardian or conservator should deliver assets to the successor fiduciary as soon as possible. In any case, after the ward's or conservatee's death, the guardian or conservator has almost no power to administer the assets. Prob C §§1600(a), 1860(a). (The fiduciary has ongoing duties of custody and conservation, but only such powers as are necessary for the performance of these duties. Prob C §2467.) Postponing this transfer is of benefit to no one.

PRACTICE TIP▶ If the conservatorship is followed by a probate, the personal representative should obtain control of the conservatorship estate using the letters testamentary. The personal representative need not, and should not, wait for the conservator to voluntarily hand things over.

§2.16 D. Standard or Simplified Accounting?

Guardians and conservators must account in the manner required by Prob C §§1060-1064. Additionally, they must determine whether their accounts are "standard accountings" or "simplified accountings," discussed in §§2.18-2.21.

§2.17 1. Judicial Council Account Forms

Charged by the legislature with the task of simplifying and standardizing the accountings guardians and conservators must file (Prob C §2620(a)), the Judicial Council created 34 forms and one worksheet to be used for standard (categorized) accountings and simplified (chronological) accountings. Only one of these forms is mandatory for all guardianship and conservatorship accountings: Summary of Account—Standard and Simplified Accounts (Judicial Council Form GC-400(SUM)/GC-405(SUM)). The use of this form is discussed in chap 12.

Professionals who regularly prepare accountings for guardians and conservators will rarely, if ever, use the 33 other Judicial Council forms or the worksheet. These forms and the worksheet were not a bad idea, but for practitioners who regularly prepare accountings, filling out the forms will be a deviation from standard procedures and therefore, their use would complicate, rather than simplify, the preparation of the accounting. Readers interested in a more thorough discussion of the forms should consult California Conservatorship Practice, chap 19 (Cal CEB).

2. Standard Accounting

§2.18 a. When to Perform a Standard (Categorized) Accounting

A conservator or guardian must use a standard accounting if (Cal Rules of Ct 7.575(b)):

- The estate contains income real property;
- The estate includes a whole or partial interest in a trade or business;
- The appraised value of the estate, exclusive of the conservatee's or guardian's personal residence, exceeds $500,000; or
- The court directs the conservator or guardian to file a standard accounting.

Additionally, if either the Receipts schedule or the Disbursements schedule, when prepared on the simplified form, would be more than five pages long, the conservator or guardian must use a standard accounting (although the balance of the accounting could be prepared as a simplified accounting, *i.e.*, using Judicial Council forms). Cal

Rules of Ct 7.575(b). A conservator or guardian *may* use a standard accounting for any accounting, even one that could be prepared on the "simplified" forms. Cal Rules of Ct 7.575(b). In other words, standard accountings are sometimes mandated, but simplified accountings never are.

§2.19   b. When to Use Judicial Council Forms

One could prepare a standard accounting using Judicial Council forms, but these forms are not spreadsheets and must be tallied by hand. Therefore, the authors recommend that practitioners prepare standard accountings by following the guidance given in this book, with one small exception. Instead of preparing a Summary of Account using the format found at §12.3 (*i.e.*, instead of using the practitioner-created Summary of Account), the practitioner must use the mandatory form Summary of Account—Standard and Simplified Accounts (Judicial Council Form GC-400(SUM)/GC-405(SUM)), discussed at §12.2. Again, for conservators and guardians, this form is mandatory for all accountings, whether they are standard or simplified, and this form is the only form mandated for every accounting. For a longer discussion of the optional Judicial Council forms one might use in a standard accounting, see California Conservatorship Practice §19.11F (Cal CEB).

§2.20   c. Presenting Data on the Mandatory Judicial Council Form

When using only the one mandatory Judicial Council form, care must be given to the presentation of the data. California Rules of Court 7.575(e)(2) specifies three rules.

First, the guardian or conservator "must state receipts and disbursements in the subject-matter categories specified in the optional Judicial Council forms for receipts and disbursements." Cal Rules of Ct 7.757(e)(2)(A). Those categories for receipts are (Summary of Account—Standard and Simplified Accounts (Judicial Council Form GC-400(SUM)/GC-405(SUM))):

- Dividends (GC-400(A)(1));
- Interest (GC-400(A)(2));
- Pensions, annuities, and other regular periodic payments (GC-400(A)(3));

- Rent (GC-400(A)(4));
- Social security, veterans benefits, and other public benefits (GC-400(A)(5)); and
- Other receipts (GC-400(A)(6)).

The categories for disbursements are:
- Conservatee's caregiver expenses (GC-400(C)(1));
- Conservatee's residential or long-term care facility expenses (GC-400(C)(2));
- Ward's education expenses (GC-400(C)(3));
- Fiduciary and attorney fees (GC-400(C)(4));
- General administration expenses (GC-400(C)(5));
- Investment expenses (GC-400(C)(6));
- Living expenses (GC-400(C)(7));
- Medical expenses (GC-400(C)(8));
- Property sale expenses (GC-400(C)(9));
- Rental property expenses (GC-400(C)(10)); and
- Other expenses (GC-400(C)(11)).

In the chapters devoted to the schedules of Receipts (chap 6) and Disbursements (chap 8), the authors also recommend using such categories, and guardians and conservators may rely on those chapters when preparing standard accountings.

Second, the guardian and conservator must "provide the same information about any asset, property, transaction, receipt, disbursement, or other matter that is required by the applicable Judicial Council accounting form." Cal Rules of Ct 7.757(e)(2)(B). Guardians and conservators who follow the guidance found in those chapters devoted to the preparation of individual schedules will meet this requirement, provided they also do the following:

- If reporting net income or net loss from a trade or business, provide all of the information disclosed on Schedule C or Schedule F of a business owner's federal income tax return. (GC-400(NI).)

- When property has been sold, include in the description of the sold asset the date the item was inventoried and its number on the Inventory and Appraisal. (GC-400(D)/GC-405(D).)

- For assets on hand, whether at the beginning, after-acquired, or at the end, and even cash assets, include in the asset's description the date the asset was inventoried, identify the type of inventory filed (for example, Partial No. 1, Final, Supplemental, Correcting, etc.), and state the number of the asset on the Inventory and Appraisal. ((GC-400(E)(1)/GC-405(E)(1); GC-400(PH)(1)/GC-405(PH)(1); GC-400(PH)(2)/GC-405(PH)(2); GC-400(E)(2)/GC-405(E)(2).) If an asset was appraised more than once, use the date and item number from the most recent appraisal. (GC-400(E)(2)/GC-405(E)(2).)

- For assets on hand at the end, list assets purchased during the account period, or acquired by trade or exchange, by the date of the acquisition. (GC-400(E)(2)/GC-405(E)(2).)

Finally, the guardian and conservator must present the information in the accounting using the same general layout as one finds in the Judicial Council forms, but may omit the instructional materials contained in these forms. Cal Rules of Ct 7.757(e)(2)(C). The presentation recommended in chaps 3-11 complies with this rule.

§2.21 3. Simplified Accounting

A simplified accounting differs from a standard accounting in two ways. First, a simplified accounting must be prepared on Judicial Council forms. Second, in a simplified accounting, one does not state receipts or disbursements categorically. In a simplified accounting, receipts and disbursements are listed chronologically.

A simplified account is never required: it is permitted when the guardianship or conservatorship estate is modest and owns no assets that might complicate the accounting. Specifically, guardians and conservators may file a simplified accounting only if the estate contains no income-producing real property, no interest in a trade or business, and the appraised value of the estate—exclusive of the conservatee's or ward's residence—is less than $500,000. See Cal Rules of Ct 7.575(b)(3). Additionally, if either the disbursement schedule or the receipt schedule would exceed five pages, a simplified accounting is prohibited. See Cal Rules of Ct 7.575(b)(4).

A simplified accounting must be prepared entirely on the mandatory Judicial Council forms. These Judicial Council forms can be distinguished from the optional forms used in a standard accounting by their numbers. The mandatory forms are numbered 405—for example, GC-405(C), which is the number of the form used for Schedule C, Disbursements—Simplified Account. For the simplified accounting, the mandatory forms are those listed below:

- GC-400(PH)(1)/GC-405(PH)(1): Cash Assets on Hand at Beginning of Account Period
- GC-400(PH)(2)/GC-405(PH)(2): Non-Cash Assets on Hand at Beginning of Account Period*
- GC-400(AP)/GC-405(AP): Additional Property Received During Period of Account*
- GC-405(A): Schedule A, Receipts—Simplified Account*
- GC-400(B)/GC-405(B): Gains on Sales*
- GC-400(OCH)/GC-405(OCH): Other Charges*
- GC-400(D)/GC-405(D): Losses on Sales*
- GC-400(DIST)/GC-405(DIST): Distributions to Conservatee*
- GC-400(OCR)/GC-405(OCR): Other Credits*
- GC-400(E)(1)/GC-405(E)(1): Cash Assets on Hand at End of Account Period
- GC-400(E)(2)/GC-405(E)(2): Non-Cash Assets on Hand at End of Account Period*
- GC-400(F)/GC-405(F): Changes in Form of Assets*
- GC-400(G)/GC-405(G): Liabilities at End of Account Period*

Of the forms listed above, those marked with asterisks may be omitted if the fiduciary is reporting no information that belongs on the particular form. For example, if there are no non-cash assets, no additional property received, no gains or losses on sales, no changes in form of assets, no other charges, no other credits, no distributions, or no liabilities at the end of the account period, the conservator can omit those schedules. See notation on the bottom of Summary of Account—Standard and Simplified Accounts (Judicial Council Form GC-400(SUM)/GC-405(SUM)).

PRACTICE TIP➤ The Judicial Council forms are available on the Judicial Council's website at http://www.courts.ca.gov/forms.htm.

For an example of a simplified accounting, see California Conservatorship Practice §§19.62A–19.62L (Cal CEB).

§2.22 4. All Accountings, Whether Standard or Simplified

When preparing an accounting, whether standard or simplified, the guardian or conservator must provide all the information required by Prob C §§1060–1063, and the guardian's or conservator's petition for approval of the account must contain all the information required by Prob C §1064. Cal Rules of Ct 7.575(f). The Judicial Council forms were created to standardize presentation of this required information and use of the forms does not reduce the amount of information that must be disclosed. In this book, the requirements of Prob C §§1060–1063 are discussed in the chapters devoted to the individual schedules of accounts. Probate Code §1064, which dictates what information conservators and guardians must provide in their petitions for approval of accounts, is discussed at length in California Conservatorship Practice, chap 19 (Cal CEB), where practitioners will find guidance on preparation of the petition.

§2.23 E. Supporting Documents

For their first account, conservators and guardians must file *original* account statements showing:

- The balance of every financial account for the period just prior to the date of appointment; and
- All account statements through the closing date of the first account.

Prob C §2620(c)(2). Private professional fiduciaries must file *original* account statements for all periods covered by all accounts. Prob C §2620(c)(3).

In addition to account statements, if real property is sold, the fiduciary must file *original* escrow closing statements and, if the conservatee is in a residential care facility (board and care, or long-term care), the original bills from the facility. Prob C §2620(c)(4)–(5).

If a statement that must be filed or lodged with the court contains personal information, such as a Social Security number, the fiduciary should either redact the personal information or file the information confidentially. See California Conservatorship Practice §19.18E (Cal CEB).

For a thorough discussion of the necessity of filing additional documents, and the implications of doing so, see Conserv Prac §§19.17-19.18.

§2.24　F. Penalties for Late Accounts

The court must issue a notice to any conservator or guardian who fails to file an accounting as required by Prob C §2620, and the court may allow the fiduciary no less than 30 days, but no more than 60 days, to file the accounting. Prob C §2620.2. Presumably, "failure" encompasses any defect in the accounting, whether it is tardy, in the wrong format, or unaccompanied by original documents.

If the fiduciary does not remedy the problem within the allowed time, he or she will be in contempt of court. Prob C §2620.2. The court may impose a whole list of penalties, including the appointment of a temporary conservator whose compensation "shall be treated as a surcharge against the conservator or guardian." Prob C §2620.2. See California Conservatorship Practice §§19.5-19.6 (Cal CEB).

§2.25　G. The Guardian's or Conservator's Audience

Conservators and guardians must obtain court approval of their accounts at a noticed hearing. Prob C §2620. As a consequence, the audience for the guardian's or conservator's account is potentially quite large. The persons entitled to notice of the hearing are (Prob C §§1460, 2621):

- The guardian or conservator;
- The ward or conservatee;
- The spouse (or registered domestic partner) of the ward or conservatee;
- Any person who has requested special notice of the matter; and
- Possibly the Director of Mental Health and/or the Director of Developmental Services.

These are also the people who may object to the accounting. Prob C §2622. Additionally, the court investigator, probate examiner, and the judge may object, as may any friend or relative of the ward or conservatee, any creditor, or other interested person. Prob C §2622.

§2.26 H. Waiver of Account

The court may waive an account in a guardianship or conservatorship if all of the below conditions are met (Prob C §2828(a)):

- The estate, at the beginning and end of the account period, is valued at less than $15,000, not counting the residence;
- Other than public benefits, the estate's monthly receipts are less than $2000; and
- All the estate's income is either spent on the conservatee or ward, or is retained.

Even after the court waives the accounting, the court may order the conservator or guardian to account on the court's own motion or on petition by the ward, the conservatee, or an interested person. Prob C §2628(b).

§2.27 I. Release of Guardian by Ward

On reaching majority, a ward may settle accounts with his or her guardian and may give the guardian a release, but the release is not effective until 1 year after the ward has reached majority. Cal Rules of Ct 7.1007. The court must find that the release was obtained fairly and without undue influence. Cal Rules of Ct 7.1007.

J. Petitioning for Approval of Accounting

§2.28 1. Guardian's Petition for Approval of Accounting

For a discussion of the contents of the guardian's petition to approve account, and for a sample petition, see California Guardianship Practice §§14.21–14.35 (Cal CEB).

For instructions on complying with the notice and hearing requirements for petitions to approve a guardian's account, see Guardian Prac §§14.57–14.59.

For instructions on objecting to a guardian's account, see Guardian Prac §§14.60–14.62.

For the contents of an order settling the guardian's account and approving of the guardian's report, see Guardian Prac §§14.63-14.64.

§2.29 2. Conservator's Petition for Approval of Accounting

For a discussion of the contents of the conservator's petition to approve account, see California Conservatorship Practice §§19.22-19.27 (Cal CEB).

For the form of a petition to approve a conservator's account, see Conserv Prac §§19.28-19.37.

For instructions on complying with the notice and hearing requirements for petitions to approve a conservator's account, see Conserv Prac §§19.63-19.67.

For instructions on objecting to a conservator's account, see Conserv Prac §§19.68-19.70.

For the contents of an order settling the conservator's account and approving of the conservator's report, see Conserv Prac §§19.71-19.72.

IV. ACCOUNTS REQUIRED OF PERSONAL REPRESENTATIVES

A. Start Here: Inventory and Appraisal

§2.30 1. Requirements for Filing an Inventory and Appraisal

Personal representatives must file an Inventory and Appraisal of "all the property to be administered in the decedent's estate" within 4 months of the appointment of a *general* personal representative. Prob C §§8800, 8850. This suggests that, in some circumstances, the special administrator not granted the powers of a general personal representative need not file an inventory. However, special administrators are required to account (Prob C §8546(c)), an undertaking that would be impossible without establishing a starting point, *i.e.*, without filing an Inventory and Appraisal.

The personal representative may file a partial inventory "where appropriate under the circumstances," but this does not extend the deadline for inventorying *everything*. Prob C §8800.

PRACTICE TIP▶ Attachment 1 of the inventory, listing the Prob C §8901 items, is prepared from financial statements—bank and brokerage account statements—and, typically, these statements arrive at the decedent's home just days after the date of death. Also typically, the attorney's first meeting with the personal representative follows the statements' arrival in the mail. If the attorney insists that the client bring the statements to the initial client meeting, the attorney may eliminate the possibility of the statements getting lost during the period of time between that first meeting and the date the court appoints a personal representative.

PRACTICE TIP➤ Though not always attainable, the attorney's goal should be to have the inventory prepared by the time the personal representative is appointed. In larger counties, there is often a 45-day delay between filing the petition and its hearing. During this interval, the would-be personal representative has no power, but often is eager to get started. Preparing the inventory (and the notice to creditors) is a good use of that enthusiasm. Remember, probate referees are entitled to 60 days to perform their task (Prob C §8940(b)), so at a minimum, the attorney should give the inventory to the probate referee no later than 60 days after the personal representative is appointed.

The personal representative's Inventory and Appraisal is the basis for the schedule of account, Assets on Hand—Beginning of Period. Prob C §§1060(a)(1), 8850(a). On this schedule, see chap 4.

§2.31   2. When Administration Follows a Guardianship or Conservatorship

When a personal representative receives assets from the conservator of a deceased conservatee, the personal representative may rely on the guardian's or conservator's accounting for the post-death period and has no duty to independently investigate the actions of the guardian or conservator. Prob C §10902. Moreover, the personal representative "may incorporate by reference any accounting provided by the conservator or guardian for the decedent for the period subsequent to the date of death." Prob C §10902.

At first glance, Prob C §10902 seems to reduce the personal representative's duty to account, but in practice, the accounting of a personal representative who receives assets from a guardian or conservator is little different from that of any other personal representative. The personal representative who follows on the heels of a conservator must nevertheless file an inventory that includes all the property to be administered. See Prob C §§8850-8873. Such an inventory is not only required by statute, but is necessary to establish new carry values and income tax bases for each of the decedent's assets (see discussion of carry value in §§4.12-4.14, 5.2). In short, although §10902 allows the personal representative to incorporate by reference transactions accounted for by the conservator, the personal representative must think through the implications of doing this.

B. Periodic Accounting

§2.32 1. Generally, at End of Administration

In most administrations, the personal representative need account only once, when the estate is in a condition to be closed. Then, the personal representative must file a final account and petition for an order of final distribution. Prob C §10951.

For a complete discussion of the purpose and timing of petitions for final distribution, see California Decedent Estate Practice §§31.1-31.5 (Cal CEB).

Petitions for final distribution must include a complete summary of the administration of the decedent's estate. For an overview of this requirement, see Decedent Estate Prac §39.1. For preparation of the account, report, and petition for final distribution, see Decedent Estate Prac §§31.16-31.96.

§2.33 2. Mid-Administration Accounting

In some administrations, the personal representative may wish, or be compelled, to account before the estate is in a condition to be closed. The court, on its own motion or on petition of an interested person, may order an account at any time. Prob C §10950. Additionally, on petition of an interested person, the court *must* order an account if either:

- It has been more than 1 year since the last account; or
- No prior accounts have been filed and it has been more than 1 year since the issuance of letters.

Prob C §10950.

For a complete discussion of status reports, see California Decedent Estate Practice §§31.6-31.8 (Cal CEB).

§2.34   C. Terminated Personal Representative

A resigning, removed, or "otherwise terminated" personal representative must file an account no later than 60 days after termination of his or her powers. Prob C §10952. If the personal representative fails to account, the court may compel an accounting. Prob C §10952.

§2.35   D. Deceased or Incapacitated Personal Representative

If the personal representative dies or becomes incapacitated and a "legal representative" (personal representative or conservator) is appointed for the deceased or incapacitated personal representative, that legal representative must file an account within 60 days of his or her appointment, unless the court extends the time. Prob C §10953(b). If no legal representative is appointed for the deceased or incapacitated personal representative, the court may compel the attorney for the personal representative to prepare the account. Prob C §10953(c).

§2.36   E. The Absconding Personal Representative

If the personal representative has absconded with assets, the court may compel the attorney for the personal representative to account for the personal representative. Prob C §10953(c).

PRACTICE TIP▶ In the initial client interview, schedule a few follow-up meetings with the client. Use one of the early meetings to gauge the personal representative's recordkeeping skills and trustworthiness. If concerns arise, communicate them in writing and suggest a better course of action. If the personal representative does not mend his or her ways, withdraw!

§2.37   F. Documents That Support the Account

It is surprisingly easy for an interested person to compel a personal representative to produce for inspection or audit the documents that support the personal representative's account. All the interested person need do is file a request with the clerk of the court and serve the request on the personal representative. Prob C §10901. On receipt of the request, the personal representative must produce the documents specified in the request. Prob C §10901. Alternatively, the court, on its own initiative, may order a personal representative to present for inspection and audit the documents specified in the order or request that support an account. Prob C §10901.

PRACTICE TIP▶ The threat of inspection provides additional motivation to keep good records. Consequently, counsel for the personal representative should warn the personal representative of Prob C §10901 early in the probate proceeding.

For a discussion of the importance of good recordkeeping, and for the form of a letter advising the personal representative to keep good records, see California Decedent Estate Practice §§24.1-24.4 (Cal CEB).

Personal representatives should keep the same types of records as trustees. See §2.54.

§2.38   G. Penalties for Failure to Account

If the personal representative does not account as required by law (Prob C §§10950-10954), the court must issue a citation and order requiring the personal representative to appear and show cause why he or she should not be punished for contempt. Prob C §11051(a). The personal representative who evades service of the citation must be removed. Prob C §11051(b).

§2.39   H. Waiver of Account

The personal representative need not file a final account if each person entitled to distribution of the estate gives either a written waiver of account or an acknowledgment that the person's interest has been satisfied. Prob C §10954. In practice, the courts will grant petitions for final distribution on waiver of account if waivers are given by all the residual beneficiaries, provided there are sufficient assets to satisfy the specific bequests.

PRACTICE TIP▶ The authors caution *trustees* against seeking waivers of account, but the personal representative who seeks a waiver of account does not run the same risks as does the trustee. The personal representative who obtains an order for final distribution on waiver of account is protected by that order from beneficiaries who might later accuse the personal representative of malfeasance. Trustees who obtain waivers of account have no such protection. See discussion below at §§2.47-2.49.

For a complete discussion of petitions for final distribution on waiver of account, see California Decedent Estate Practice §§31.11-31.15 (Cal CEB). For a list of persons who may execute a waiver, see Decedent Estate Prac §24.32.

§2.40 I. "Report" Instead of Account

The present book is about fiduciary *accounting* and readers interested in waivers of account are directed to the resources mentioned in §2.39. Just briefly, if a personal representative obtains waivers of account from each beneficiary entitled to an account, the personal representative nevertheless must "report" the basis of the calculation of the statutory fees payable to the personal representative and his or her attorney. Prob C §10954(c). This statutory requirement is interpreted differently by the counties in their local rules, but at a minimum the report must include the basis for determining the statutory fees. Prob C §10954(c)(1). The elements of the statutory fee are (Prob C §10810(b)):

- The inventoried assets; plus
- The gains on sales; plus
- The receipts; less
- The losses on sales.

PRACTICE TIP➤ Caution clients that, until the court orders final distribution on waiver of account, the personal representative should assume that an account will be required. Beneficiaries may demand an account, even after filing a waiver.

For a discussion of the additional information required in petitions for final distribution on waiver of account, see California Decedent Estate Practice §31.11 (Cal CEB).

§2.41 J. Personal Representative's Audience

The personal representative of a decedent's estate must obtain court approval of his or her accounts at a noticed hearing. Prob C §11000. The persons entitled to notice of the hearing are (Prob C §§1220, 11000):

- The personal representative;
- All persons who have requested special notice;
- Each known heir whose interest in the estate would be affected;
- Each known devisee whose interest in the estate would be affected;
- The Attorney General, if any portion of the estate will escheat; and
- If the estate is insolvent, each creditor who has filed a claim that has been allowed or approved but is unpaid.

§2.42 K. Petition to Approve Personal Representative's Account

For instructions on preparing the personal representative's petition to approve account, see California Decedent Estate Practice §§31.16-31.96 (Cal CEB).

For notice and hearing of a petition to approve personal representative's account, see Decedent Estate Prac §§31.97-31.102.

For objections to the account of a personal representative, see Decedent Estate Prac §31.102.

For the order settling the account of a personal representative, see Decedent Estate Prac §§31.103-31.154.

V. ACCOUNTS REQUIRED OF TRUSTEES OF IRREVOCABLE TRUSTS

§2.43 A. Why Distinguish Between Irrevocable and Revocable Trusts?

During the time that a trust is revocable and the person holding the power to revoke is competent, the trustee owes duties only to that person and that person has all the rights afforded by law to the trust's beneficiaries. Prob C §15800. Thus, the trustee of a revocable trust, when the person holding the power to revoke is competent, should have no trouble determining to whom his or her duties are owed. Identifying the persons to whom duties are owed once a trust becomes irrevocable, or on creation of the trust if it is irrevocable from inception, is only slightly more complicated. The trustee owes duties only to the trust's beneficiaries. Prob C §16002(a); *Arluk Med. Ctr. Indust. Group v Dobler* (2004) 116 CA4th 1324, 1335. The identity of those beneficiaries can be determined by examination of the trust instrument. See §§2.44-2.46.

It is far less clear to whom the trustee owes duties when a trust is *revocable* and the person holding the power to revoke is *not* competent. This is a significant problem for the trustee who would account, but the problem's significance becomes apparent only after one understands trust accountings more generally. Thus, this chapter first discusses trust accounting in the context of irrevocable trusts before accounting for the administration of revocable trusts in §§2.67-2.70.

B. Duty to Account, Generally, to Report, and to Provide Information

§2.44   1. Beneficiaries Defined

With regards to an irrevocable trust, when the Probate Code uses the word "beneficiary" without limitation, it is a reference to any person, now living or yet to be born, who has any beneficial interest, whether present or future and whether vested or contingent, in the trust. Prob C §24. To understand the breadth of this definition, consider the qualified terminable interest property (QTIP) trust established by Sam the settlor for his wife, Wendy the widow, which trust will be distributed to Sam's issue, by right of representation, on Wendy's death. Each of the following people would be a "beneficiary" of this QTIP trust:

- Wendy, who is the sole person entitled to current distributions of income or principal;
- Sam's children, even while Wendy is still alive and enjoying the trust's benefits (these children are contingent beneficiaries of future interests because their interests are contingent on surviving Wendy); and
- Sam's grandchildren, even those yet to be born, because a grandchild would take if:
  - The grandchild's parent who was a child of Sam's died before Wendy, and
  - The grandchild survived Wendy.

The word "beneficiary" has a narrower meaning, however, when found in the laws that codify the trustee's duty to account. The duty to account is owed only to "each beneficiary to whom income or principal is required or authorized in the trustee's discretion to be currently distributed." Prob C §16062(a). In the above example, the only person to whom the trustee owes the duty to account is Wendy. By contrast, the trustee has a duty to keep all the beneficiaries "informed of the trust and its administration" (Prob C §16060), and each beneficiary may demand and receive a report of information "relating to the administration of the trust relevant to the beneficiary's interest" (Prob C §16061). These three duties—the duty to account, the duty to provide reports, and the duty to keep beneficiaries informed—are discussed in §§2.45-2.52.

2. Duty to Account

§2.45 a. Duty Owed to Current Beneficiaries

As a general rule, trustees must account to each beneficiary to whom income or principal is required or authorized in the trustee's discretion to be currently distributed. Prob C §16062. Additionally, trustees must account to a broader class of beneficiaries, if required to do so by the trust instrument. Prob C §16000. For example, the trust might require the trustee to account to contingent remainder beneficiaries, or might require an accounting to a third party in the event of a beneficiary's incapacity.

NOTE▶ The trustee has no duty to account to a beneficiary when the beneficiary and the trustee are the same person. Prob C §16069(b).

The following provision is excerpted from a declaration of trust. Although it is prefaced by words suggesting a limitation on the duty to account, the provision actually requires the trustee to account to the broadest possible range of beneficiaries.

> Despite any provision of California Prob C §16062 to the contrary, the trustees are not required to render accounts or reports of the administration of the trust as long as the trustee renders an account or a report on the request of any successor trustee or any beneficiary, but not more frequently than once every six months, whether that beneficiary has a present or future interest, vested or contingent; and the trustee may render accounts or reports on the trustee's own initiative. The form, content and manner of delivery of an account or a report shall be in accordance with the provisions of California Probate Code sections 16060-16064.

Trustees owe the duty to account even to beneficiaries who passively await the trustee's performance. In other words, the trustee who fails to account cannot excuse his breach by pointing out that "no one ever asked." The duty to account, unlike the duty to "report" (see §2.51), must be performed as frequently as the law or the trust instrument requires, unless the beneficiaries or the trust instrument waive the performance of the duty. On waivers, see §§2.47–2.49.

Finally, "trustee" refers to the original, additional, and successor trustees, whether or not court appointed (Prob C §84), and all the codified accounting requirements merely refer to the "trustee."

§2.46 b. No Duty Owed to Remainder Beneficiaries

Remainder beneficiaries, *i.e.*, those beneficiaries with only future interests and no right to current distributions of income or principal, do not have the right to an accounting under Prob C §16062. Prob C §16062; see also *Esslinger v Cummins* (2006) 144 CA4th 517, 526.

Prior to 2010, however, remainder beneficiaries could obtain an accounting by:

- Demanding the report to which they were entitled (Prob C §16061; see §2.51); then

- Either:

    - Objecting to the report and demanding an accounting in that objection; or

    - Petitioning to compel an account if no report was forthcoming.

The court in *Esslinger* approved of this strategy by harmonizing the rule of Prob C §16062 with Prob C §16061 and a prior version of §17200(b)(7).

In 2010, the California State Legislature amended Prob C §17200(b)(7), effectively overruling that portion of *Esslinger* that approved of this strategy. Stats 2010, ch 621, §11. Now, a beneficiary who has demanded but not received a report under Prob C §16061 may petition for an order compelling the trustee to report. Prob C §17200(b)(7)(A). And a beneficiary who has demanded but not received an account, may petition for an order compelling the trustee to account. Prob C §17200(b)(7)(C). No longer may one entitled to only a report demand a report, and then, if unsatisfied, demand an accounting. But see §2.51.

c. Waivers

§2.47 (1) Waivers in the Trust Instrument

The trustee has no duty to account if the trust instrument waives the duty (Prob C §16064(a)), except that certain waivers found in the trust instrument are void as a matter of public policy. Specifically, waivers of account are void if the trustee is a "disqualified person" as that term was defined in now-repealed Prob C §21350.5, or if the trustee (Prob C §§16064(a) and 21380(a)(1)-(4)):

- Is the person who drafted the instrument;
- Was in a fiduciary relationship with the settlor and caused the instrument to be transcribed; or
- Was a care custodian for the settlor, who was a dependent adult, and the care custodian provided services to the settlor within 90 days before or after the time the instrument was drafted.

Additionally, waivers of account in the trust instrument are void if the trustee is related by blood or "affinity" to a person described in the previous sentence; or is a cohabitant or employee of such a person; or is a partner, shareholder, or employee of a law firm in which the drafter or the fiduciary has an ownership interest. Prob C §§16064(a), 21380(a)(1)-(a)(4).

Even if the trust instrument waives the trustee's duty to account, the court may compel the trustee to account on a showing that it is reasonably likely the trustee has committed a material breach of trust. Prob C §16064(a).

§2.48 (2) A Beneficiary's Written Waiver

The trustee has no duty to account to a beneficiary who has waived in writing the right to the accounting. Prob C §16064(b). Such waivers excuse the trustee's duty to account only for the period identified in the waiver, or for the period that ends on the date the beneficiary withdraws his or her waiver. Prob C §16064(b). And again, the court may order a trustee to account to a beneficiary who has waived his or her right to an account, if that beneficiary shows that it is reasonably likely the trustee has committed a material breach of trust. Prob C §16064(b).

The duty to account is only one of a trustee's many duties and a beneficiary's waiver of account waives the performance of only that one duty. The trustee who receives such a waiver nevertheless must administer the trust according to the trust instrument and, when the instrument is silent, according to trust law. Prob C §16000. Such a trustee will still owe the beneficiaries numerous duties, including a duty:

- Of loyalty (Prob C §16002);
- Of impartiality (Prob C §16003);
- To avoid conflicts of interest (Prob C §16004);
- To avoid the administration of adverse trusts (Prob C §16005);
- To take control and preserve trust property (Prob C §16006);
- To make trust property productive (Prob C §16007);
- To avoid commingling trust property with other property (Prob C §16009);
- To enforce the trust's claims (Prob C §16010);
- To defend the trust against actions that might result in a loss to the trust (Prob C §16011);
- Not to delegate, or to supervise the delegates (Prob C §16012);
- To apply the full extent of their skills to the administration of the trust (Prob C §16014);
- To administer the trust according to the Prudent Investor Act, unless the trust instrument provides otherwise (Prob C §§16045–16054); and
- To keep the beneficiaries informed of the trust and its administration (Prob C §16060).

The beneficiary who waives his or her right to an accounting does not waive any of the above-mentioned duties.

§2.49 (3) Waiver Does Not Trigger the Running of the Statute of Limitations

By relying on the waiver, the trustee may extend the period during which the trustee is liable for breaches of duties. This is because the beneficiary's waiver of account does not trigger the running of the statute of limitations that would shield the trustee from liability for other breaches. See §2.48. For this reason, in the authors' opinion, the trustee who relies on a waiver of account forgoes the most important protection the law affords trustees. Absent an accounting, the statute of limitations against the trustee will begin to run eventually, but that date will be a triable issue of fact not easily proven. Trustees who want to clearly mark the date their liability is cut off should prepare and serve an accounting and gather proof that each beneficiary has received it. See §§2.57–2.64.

§2.50 d. Frequency

Subject to the limitations discussed above, trustees must account at least annually, on a change of trustee, and at the termination of the trust. Prob C §16062(a). Trustees must account more frequently if the trust instrument so requires. Prob C §16000. Additionally, beneficiaries may demand more frequent accountings, which the court may compel, but it seems the court cannot compel a trustee to account more frequently than approximately once every 8 months. Prob C §17200(b)(7)(C).

> **NOTE▶** Probate Code §17200(b)(7)(C) allows a beneficiary to petition for an account before the trustee's duty to account arises under Prob C §16062. See *Esslinger v Cummins* (2006) 144 CA4th 517, 527.

Probate Code §17200(b)(7)(C) allows the court to compel the trustee to account "if the trustee has failed to submit a requested account within 60 days after written request of the beneficiary and no account has been made within six months preceding the request." In other words, if 6 months have elapsed since the trustee's last account, the beneficiary may demand another account, but then the beneficiary must give the trustee 60 days to comply with the demand. Only at the end of these two consecutive periods may a beneficiary seek an order compelling the trustee to account.

For a discussion of when the trustee might wish to account more frequently than minimally required, see California Trust Administration §7.56 (Cal CEB).

§2.51   3. Duty to Report

On the reasonable request of a beneficiary, the trustee must report to the beneficiary "by providing requested information to the beneficiary relating to the administration of the trust relevant to the beneficiary's interest." Prob C §16061. Section 16061 does not limit the definition of "beneficiary"; thus, unless the trust is revocable, trustees owe the duty to report to the broadest class of beneficiaries, *i.e.*, the duty is not owed only to those persons entitled to current mandatory or discretionary distributions. Similarly to demands for an accounting, a beneficiary may petition to compel a report if (Prob C §17200(a)(7)(B)):

- The trustee does not voluntarily provide the requested information within 60 days of the request; and

- The beneficiary has not received the requested information within the 6 months preceding the request.

The settlor cannot waive the duty to report in the trust instrument: any such waiver is void as against public policy. Prob C §16068(b). Finally, the information that must be provided in the trustee's report may be "more or different information" than required in an annual account (Comment to Prob C §16061), and although the trustee need reveal only that information "relevant to the beneficiary's interest" (Prob C §16061), the Law Revision Commission says that the information may be "a particular account under this section" (Comment to Prob C §16061).

Trustees concerned about providing sufficient information in a report must consider the beneficiary's relationship to the trust and the nature of the beneficiary's interests. To date, however, the court of appeal has not explained the parameters of this duty. The only case that has considered the question of how much information a trustee must report, primarily addressed the trial court's authority to order the trustee to account to a contingent remainder beneficiary. The court in *Esslinger* said, "a particular account might be narrow or might be as broad as an accounting for a full year, depending on the relief the probate court considers appropriate under the circumstances." *Esslinger v Cummins* (2006) 144 CA4th 517, 525. But the opinion offers no guidance to the trustee concerned with the question of how narrow a report may reasonably be.

§2.52   4. Duty to Keep Beneficiaries Reasonably Informed

In addition to the duties to account and report, the trustee has an affirmative duty "to keep the beneficiaries of the trust reasonably informed of the trust and its administration." Prob C §16060. Trustees must communicate "information that is reasonably necessary to enable the beneficiary to enforce the beneficiary's rights under the trust or to prevent or redress a breach of trust." Comment to Prob C §16060. The duty to provide information is in addition to the duty to account and is potentially broader. *Salter v Lerner* (2009) 176 CA4th 1184, 1188, citing with approval California Trust and Probate Litigation §13.1 (Cal CEB). Ordinarily, the trustee may satisfy the duty to provide information by accounting to the beneficiaries or providing information on demand, but if the trustee engages in transactions that affect the beneficiaries' rights during the intervals between accounts or reports, the trustee should communicate the material elements of these transactions to the beneficiaries.

5. Trust Records and the Beneficiaries' Right of Inspection

§2.53   a. Beneficiaries Have a Right to Inspect Trust Records

A trustee's records of the trust administration are part of the trust estate and beneficiaries have a right to inspect those records. *Strauss v Superior Court* (1950) 36 C2d 396, 402. In *Strauss,* a beneficiary attempted to subpoena documents from the bank/trustee in a proceeding to perpetuate testimony under former CCP §2084. The documents sought spanned a period of almost 15 years. The court granted the trustee's motion to quash the subpoena, and the beneficiary sought a writ of mandate to compel the court to vacate its order. Even though no suit had yet been filed, on review, the Supreme Court granted the writ. In other words, beneficiaries who want to inspect the trust's records have a right to do so *without filing suit or conducting formal discovery.* The right of inspection arises from the parties' common interests in the trust property. The right is not a creature of the Civil Discovery Act (CCP §§2016.010–2036.050), but of the ancient law of trusts. 2 Scott on Trusts §173; 4 Bogert on Trusts and Trustees §961; *Strauss v Superior Court* (1950) 36 C2d 396.

§2.54 b. Records the Trustee Should Keep

The trustee's records should be sufficient to allow the trustee to substantiate his or her authority, to prove the performance of his or her duties, to prepare accountings, and to file income tax returns. To achieve this, trustees should keep all of the following records:

To Substantiate the Trustee's Authority and Prove the Performance of Duties

- A copy of the trust instrument and all amendments thereto;
- A copy of any instrument exercising powers of appointment over the trust estate;
- All consents, releases, or waivers given by any beneficiary;
- Receipts for distributions to beneficiaries;
- All court orders affecting the trust administration;
- Copies of all notices served on the beneficiaries, with proofs of service;
- Copies of every accounting served on any beneficiary; and
- Trustee resignations, or acceptances of trust.

To Prepare Accountings or Tax Returns

- A copy of every appraisal or other record that establishes the carry value of each trust asset;
- A copy of any appraisal that establishes the current value of any trust asset;
- For marketable securities, periodic market valuations (brokerage account statements will supply this information);
- Records sufficient to track the basis of each capital asset;
- Documentation for each receipt and disbursement of income or principal, including:
  - Canceled checks;
  - Paid invoices;
  - Receipts for disbursements; and
  - Bank statements;

- Escrow closing documents and, for sales without an escrow, proof of the sale's receipts;
- All brokerage account statements;
- All income tax returns;
- Proof of quarterly payments of income tax;
- Audit reports from Internal Revenue Service audits;
- Evidence of every tax election, such as the Subchapter S election, and every request for extension to file returns;
- Records of any trust-owned business; and
- Reports to the Attorney General, if the trust is a charitable trust.

Regarding the Beneficiaries

- The name, current address, telephone number, and Social Security number of each beneficiary entitled to mandatory or discretionary distributions of income or principal;
- The name, current address, telephone number, and Social Security number of each person who would become a beneficiary on the termination of the current income interests;
- The name, current address, telephone number, and Social Security number of each person who, even though not one of the above, has a future interest in the trust;
- Copies of any written communication to any beneficiary and all correspondence from all beneficiaries; and
- Memoranda of telephone conversations and meetings.

Regarding Liabilities

- Information about all outstanding debts, whether secured or unsecured;
- Proof of payment;
- Information about potential unmatured liabilities, such as guarantees given by the settlor or damages for which the settlor's trust might be liable;
- Information about possible environmental contamination of trust-owned properties; and

- Pleadings in any case in which the trust may be liable for damages.

Regarding Trustee's Fees

- A log of all services performed by the trustee, including the date of performance and the time spent on the task.

Confidential Communications with Attorneys

- Copies of all confidential communications to or from attorneys. These copies should be kept in a file separate from the other trust records. Although any successor trustee may be entitled to these records, as to beneficiaries, they are confidential. *Wells Fargo Bank v Superior Court (Boltwood)* (2000) 22 C4th 201.

For additional information about liabilities, see California Trust Administration §7.32 (Cal CEB).

For a form that may be used to document the trustee's exercise of discretionary powers, such as the power to make adjustments between principal and income, see Trust Admin §7.34.

For a form of a letter advising trustees what records to keep, see Trust Admin §7.14.

As a quick reference, the trustee also may want to create a trust synopsis. See Trust Admin §7.19.

To document compliance with the Prudent Investor Act, see Trust Admin §7.37.

For advice on how long to maintain trust records, see Trust Admin §7.52.

§2.55 c. The "Personal" Records of the Trustee Who Commingles

"The rule is now settled in this state that when the money of the trustor can be traced into a particular fund, or deposit, though it be mingled with other money, the beneficiary may enforce the trust." *Kobida v Hinkelmann* (1942) 53 CA2d 186, 195 (trust beneficiary traced commingled trust funds to personal accounts of deceased trustee and established a trust in those accounts). And nearly 100 years earlier, the Supreme Court in *Gunter v Janes* (1858) 9 C 643 pointed out that a trustee cannot, by merely commingling, change his character to other than a trustee. The trustee's duties persist so long as he or she has trust assets in his or her possession. Prob

C §15644. These rules, combined with the beneficiaries' ownership interest in the trust's records (see *Strauss v Superior Court* (1950) 36 C2d 396), should entitle the beneficiaries to review the records of all accounts into which the trustee has commingled funds.

Commingling is a breach of trust. Prob C §§16009, 16400. The measure of the trustee's liability for the breach is measured by one of the following (Prob C §16440):

- The loss to the trust estate, plus interest;

- Any profit the trustee made as a result of the commingling; or

- The profit the trust lost as a result of the commingling.

Because the appropriate measure of liability cannot be determined without knowing whether the trustee profited from personal use of the commingled funds, inspection of trustee's records is also warranted under this argument.

§2.56   C. Accounting as a Preliminary Step to the Performance of Other Duties

In some circumstances, the trustee may be absolved of his or her *duty* to account, yet nevertheless find accounting an unavoidable necessity. Consider, for example, the following trust. On his death, grandfather established a generation-skipping trust. During her lifetime, grandfather's daughter is the sole beneficiary and she is entitled to the trust's net income. The trust instrument does not define "net income," which therefore is defined by California's Uniform Principal and Income Act (UPAIA) (Probate Code §§16320–16375). Prob C §16335(a)(3). During daughter's lifetime, she may not invade principal for her own benefit nor for the benefit of anyone else. The daughter is also the trustee.

During the daughter's lifetime, the daughter would not be *required* to account because she is the sole person to whom current distributions may or must be made and trustees are not required to account to themselves. Prob C §§16063(a), 16069. Yet, when calculating the amounts she must distribute to herself, the daughter could not simply subtract her disbursements from her receipts and claim the sum for herself. To calculate the net income to which the daughter would be entitled, she must subtract from "receipts allocated to income" those "disbursements made from income" during the "accounting period." Prob C §16328. See also Prob C §16322 (definition of "accounting period") and §16324 (definition of "income"). Often, the Act apportions receipts and disbursements between principal and income. This trustee could determine the amounts to which she is entitled only by preparing schedules of Receipts, Gains on Sales or Other Dispositions, Disbursements, Losses on Sales or Other Dispositions, and Distributions. Essentially, this trustee must prepare an account or risk distributing too much or too little. Wendy, in the QTIP example above (see §2.44), would be in the same position if she were the trustee and were entitled only to distributions of income.

D. Accounting Protects the Trustee

§2.57   **1. The 3-Year Statute of Limitations**

There is a 3-year statute of limitations on actions by beneficiaries against trustees for breach of trust. Prob C §16460. This statute begins running either when the beneficiary receives the trustee's account that "adequately discloses the existence of a claim against the trustee for breach of trust," or when the beneficiary discovers, or reasonably should discover, the "subject" of the claim. Prob C §16460. This statute of limitations is an absolute bar to claims against the trustee. *Estate of Bissinger* (1964) 60 C2d 756, 761; *Coberly v Superior Court* (1965) 231 CA2d 685. Nothing provides the trustee with greater protection—certainly not waivers of account.

A trust administration is not analogous to a probate, in which the personal representative's liability may be discharged even on waiver of account. In a trust administration, a waiver of account, whether provided in the trust instrument or given by an individual beneficiary (see §2.48), only waives the trustee's obligation to perform one rather narrow duty: the duty to account. Waivers do not trigger the running of the statute of limitations on actions alleging breaches of the trustee's many other duties. The only way a trustee may start the statute running is to provide an account.

PRACTICE TIP➤ When counseling a trustee who is reluctant to account, the practitioner may recount the following true story. Near the end of an uneventful trust administration, the trustee set aside a small reserve and distributed the remaining trust estate outright in five equal shares, as required by the trust instrument. The trustee later queried the trust's five beneficiaries and none had any complaints about the trustee's services. After allowing a few more months to pass, the trustee then distributed the reserve. Several years later, four of the beneficiaries still owned some of the property they had received from the trust. The fifth beneficiary, never good with money, was nearly bankrupt. She compared her situation to that of the other beneficiaries and reached the unsurprising conclusion that she had been shortchanged. Ten years after the trustee had fully distributed the trust, the spendthrift beneficiary sued for an accounting and for breach of trust. The trustee was forced to defend himself and had to pay for his defense himself. Had this trustee accounted to the beneficiary and served the accounting on her with the requisite warning under Prob C §16063(a)(6), he would have spared himself the expense and aggravation of the law suit.

NOTE▶ Trustees are entitled to indemnification out of the trust estate for expenses incurred in the administration of the trust, and the probate court may order a beneficiary to return trust assets as necessary for the trustee's indemnification. However, if a beneficiary has so changed position in reliance on distributions received that it would be inequitable for the court to compel the beneficiary to indemnify the trustee, indemnification may not occur. *Kasperbauer v Fairfield* (2009) 171 CA4th 229. In *Kasperbauer,* the beneficiaries were possessed of their distributions for only a short time before being ordered to return a portion, and the beneficiaries' counsel seemingly acquiesced to the court's order.

Accounting to a beneficiary only creates a limitation period as to that beneficiary and provides the trustee with no protection from, for example, contingent remainder beneficiaries who receive no accounting. For a discussion of how trustees might protect themselves from these beneficiaries, see California Trust Administration §7.65C (Cal CEB). For a discussion of minors and incompetent beneficiaries, see Trust Admin §7.65D.

§2.58 2. The 180-Day Statute of Limitations

The *settlor* can shorten the limitations period on actions against a trustee by including a provision to that effect in the trust instrument. Prob C §16461. Specifically, the trust instrument must say something to the effect that beneficiaries may not bring an action against the trustee for breaches of trust disclosed in the trustee's accounting, unless the action is brought no more than 180 days from the date the beneficiary receives the account. Prob C §16461(c). Additionally, when the trustee serves the accounting on the beneficiary, the trustee must give written notice in 12-point boldface type in the following form:

NOTICE TO BENEFICIARIES
YOU HAVE [insert "180 DAYS" or the period specified in the trust instrument, whichever is longer] FROM YOUR RECEIPT OF THIS ACCOUNT OR REPORT TO MAKE AN OBJECTION TO ANY ITEM SET FORTH IN THIS ACCOUNT OR REPORT. ANY OBJECTION YOU MAKE MUST BE IN WRITING; IT MUST BE DELIVERED TO THE TRUSTEE WITHIN THE PERIOD STATED ABOVE; AND IT MUST STATE YOUR OBJECTION. YOUR FAILURE TO DELIVER A WRITTEN OBJECTION TO THE TRUSTEE WITHIN THE PERIOD STATED ABOVE WILL PERMANENTLY PREVENT YOU FROM LATER ASSERTING THIS OBJECTION AGAINST THE TRUSTEE. IF YOU DO MAKE AN OBJECTION TO THE TRUSTEE, THE THREE-YEAR PERIOD PROVIDED IN SECTION 16460 OF THE PROBATE CODE FOR COMMENCEMENT OF LITIGATION WILL APPLY TO CLAIMS BASED ON YOUR OBJECTION AND WILL BEGIN TO RUN ON THE DATE THAT YOU RECEIVE THIS ACCOUNT OR REPORT.

If the trust instrument contains a provision that shortens a beneficiary's time to object to less than 180 days, that provision is invalid, but the trustee may elect to treat the provision as if the limitations period were 180 days. Prob C §16461(c)-(d). The trustee who so elects will be protected by the 180-day limitations period, provided the trustee follows the procedure of Prob C §16461(c). Prob C §16461(d).

§2.59 3. Petitions for Court Approval

If the trust does not want to rely for protection on the running of the 3-year or the 180-day limitations period, the trustee may petition for court approval of his or her account (Prob C §17200(b)(5)) and limit to 30 days the beneficiaries' time to object (Prob C §17203).

§2.60 4. Release of Liability for Disclosures Made in Accounting

A trustee also may extinguish potential liabilities by obtaining a release from a beneficiary. Prob C §16464. As discussed in §§2.61-2.64, a release precludes the beneficiary from suing for breach of trust, but only if the beneficiary is competent, fully informed of his or her rights, and cognizant of all the material facts relevant to the issue of the trustee's liability. Prob C §16464(b). It is the trustee's duty to provide the beneficiary with such facts. Prob C §16464(b)(2). Absent a full accounting of the trust administration, the beneficiary who regrets having waived his or her right to sue the trustee could argue that the waiver was given in ignorance of a material fact. The trustee's best protection is that afforded by providing beneficiaries with a complete account of the trust administration.

NOTE▶ Releases are of little value if they cannot be obtained from every beneficiary. For example, if the trustee seeks a release in order to make distributions terminating the trust, if even one beneficiary retains the right to sue for breaches of trust, the trustee cannot terminate the trust without being divested of the funds he or she might need for his or her defense.

§2.61   a. Beneficiary Must Have Capacity

Four criteria must be met before a release will be effective. First, each beneficiary who grants a release must have the capacity to do so. A release granted by a beneficiary who is incapacitated at the time the release was given is not effective. Prob C §16464(b)(1). Thus, the trustee should not seek a release from a minor, a conservatee, nor someone who would not meet the criteria of Prob C §812. At a minimum, the beneficiary must be able to communicate verbally, or by other means, that he or she appreciates and understands the following (Prob C §812):

- The effect the release may have on his or her rights, duties, and responsibilities;
- The probable consequences for the beneficiary, if he or she grants the release; and
- The significant risks and benefits of the release, and the reasonable alternatives to granting a release.

For evidentiary purposes, the release should be in writing and should fully describe each of the elements identified in Prob C §812.

PRACTICE TIP▶ A release should not say, for example, that the beneficiary "understands and appreciates the rights, duties, and responsibilities affected by the release." Instead, the release should explicitly describe the likely effect on the beneficiary by saying something such as, "the beneficiary understands that, absent this release, the beneficiary would have an additional 2 years to contemplate the trustee's accounting and consider whether the trustee had adequately performed every duty owed to the beneficiary."

§2.62 b. Full Disclosure

The second of the four criteria for an effective release is full disclosure. For a release to be effective, the trustee must inform each beneficiary of (Prob C §16464(b)(2)):

- The beneficiary's rights;
- All the material facts known to the trustee, or that the trustee reasonably should know; and
- Any material facts the trustee reasonably believes are unknown to the beneficiary.

Probate Code §16464(b)(2) affords beneficiaries who regret their releases great opportunity to recant them. Trustees who prepare releases should carefully recite all of the material facts that might affect a beneficiary's rights.

PRACTICE TIP▶ A trustee who accounts in conformance with Prob C §§1060–1064 can be relatively certain that he or she has disclosed all of the material facts necessary to fully inform the beneficiaries of their rights. A trustee who has accounted in a less formal fashion should consider whether the informal accounting makes adequate disclosures. Releases should not be sought for trustees who have not thoroughly accounted to the beneficiaries.

§2.63 c. Not Induced by Improper Conduct

Third, a release is ineffective if it is "induced by improper conduct of the trustee." Prob C §16464. Thus, the trustee must never condition distributions or payments to beneficiaries on the granting of a release. Prob C §16004.5. Trustees may maintain reserves for "reasonably anticipated expenses, including, but not limited to, taxes, debts, trustee and accounting fees, and costs and expenses of administration." Prob C §16004.5(b)(1). However, if the trustee is in possession of money or property due to a beneficiary, the trustee may wish to distribute that property before seeking a release. The trustee also should consider his or her other duties and question whether each has been adequately performed.

§2.64   d. No Unfair Advantage

Finally, a release is ineffective to shield a trustee from liability if the trustee has entered into a bargain with the beneficiary and thereby obtained an advantage that was not fair and reasonable. Prob C §16464(b)(4). Trustees must bear in mind that the beneficiary's release, if tested for enforceability, will be tested by a beneficiary who has become disgruntled with his or her bargain. Bargains that appear fair in the making, but that later turn to the trustee's advantage, may undermine the effectiveness of the beneficiary's release, exposing the trustee to liability.

§2.65   E. Serving the Accounting

Some of the information trustees are required to provide with their accountings is not readily apparent from the schedules of account, and the trustee should include this information with the accounting when it is served on the beneficiaries. This additional information is listed below:

- **Compensation.** The account must disclose the trustee's compensation for the last complete fiscal year of the trust, or since the last account. Prob C §16063(a)(3). This information may be apparent from the Disbursements schedule, if the trustee has been paying himself or herself currently, or the information may be set forth on the schedule of the trust's Liabilities, if the trustee fees have not been paid in full.

- **Liabilities.** The account must state the trust's liabilities as of the end of the account period. Prob C §16063(a)(2). Trustees who account in the manner recommended by this book will include this information as a matter of course, on their schedule of Liabilities. Trustees who account in a less formal fashion must not forget to include liabilities as part of their disclosures.

- **Agents.** The account must disclose the agents hired by the trustee. Prob C §16063(a)(4). This disclosure may be apparent from the Disbursements schedule, if the agents were paid during the account period. Additionally, the trustee must disclose the agent's "relationship to the trustee, if any." Prob C §16063(a)(4). Trust law does not specify which relationships must be disclosed and which are beneath mention, but the law views with suspicion those people identified in Prob C §21380. If the trustee has hired any of these people, the authors recommend that the trustee disclose that fact.

- **Notice of Right to Petition.** The trustee must provide a statement that "the recipient of the account may petition the court pursuant to §17200 to obtain a court review of the account and of the acts of the trustee." Prob C §16063(a)(5).

- **Notice of Statute of Limitations.** The account must include a statement that "claims against the trustee for breach of trust may not be made after the expiration of three years from the date the beneficiary receives an account or report disclosing facts giving rise to the claim." Prob C §16063(a)(6).

The statute of limitations on a beneficiary's action against a trustee begins to run when the beneficiary *receives* the trustee's accounting. Prob C §16063(a)(6). Thus the prudent trustee will obtain from each beneficiary signed proof that the beneficiary has received the accounting. Proof may be in the form of a signed receipt, or may be in the form of a proof of personal service on the beneficiary himself or herself.

For a sample letter to beneficiaries transmitting the trustee's account, see California Trust Administration §7.61 (Cal CEB).

§2.66 F. Petitioning for Court Approval of Trustee's Account

In general, trustees are not required to seek court approval of their accounts. They may do so if they wish (Prob C §17200(b)(5)), but the court may dismiss a trustee's petition for approval of account if it appears that the petition is not reasonably necessary to protect the interests of the trustee or a beneficiary. Prob C §17202. All accounts submitted by a trustee to the court for approval must be prepared in the manner required by Prob C §§1060–1064. Prob C §16063(b).

Trustees who submit their accounts to the court for approval necessarily subject their fees to the court's scrutiny. The trustee who has misbehaved risks removal by the court on its own motion. *Schwartz v Labow* (2008) 164 CA4th 417. For a discussion of the other considerations implicated in a petition to approve trustee's account, see California Trust Administration §7.65A (Cal CEB).

With some exceptions listed in the rule, Cal Rules of Ct 7.902 requires trustees who seek court approval of their accounts to list the names and last-known addresses of all vested or contingent beneficiaries. This rule does not say that all these beneficiaries are entitled to notice of the petition, and some would not be entitled to receive an account, but the rule implies that notice may be required.

For a discussion of venue, see Trust Admin §7.70. For a form of petition to approve trustee's account, see Trust Admin §7.114. For additional information on preparation of the petition, setting the petition for hearing, and notice requirements, see Trust Admin §§7.115-7.120. Regarding the hearing of the petition, see Trust Admin §7.121. For a form of order, see Trust Admin §§7.122-7.123.

VI. ACCOUNTS REQUIRED OF TRUSTEES OF REVOCABLE TRUSTS

§2.67   A. Duties Owed to Whom?

The duties owed by trustees to their beneficiaries are the same whether the trust is revocable or irrevocable. The difference between these two classes of trusts is to whom the duties are owed. The trustee of a revocable trust, during the period the trust is revocable and for so long as the person holding the power to revoke is competent, owes duties only to the person holding the power to revoke. Prob C §15800(b); *Estate of Giraldin* (2012) 55 C4th 1058. During this period, "'any interest that beneficiaries of a revocable trust have in trust property is "merely potential" and can "evaporate in a moment at the whim of the [settlor]."'" 55 C4th at 1066, citing *Johnson v Kotyck* (1999) 76 CA4th 83, 88. For so long as a trust is revocable and the person holding the power to revoke is competent, the trustee need only account to that person.

§2.68   B. When Person Holding the Power to Revoke Is Not Competent

It is an open question to whom the trustee should account if a trust is revocable and the person holding the power to revoke is not competent. It is equally problematic if the person holding the power to revoke insists that he or she *is* competent, but the trustee fears that the contrary is true. The statute of limitations on the trustee's liability to a beneficiary begins to run when the beneficiary receives an account or report that discloses the existence of a claim. Prob C §16460(a). But in the case of an adult who is "not reasonably capable of understanding the account and report," the statute does not begin to run unless the account or report is received "by the person's legal representative, including a guardian ad litem or other person appointed for this purpose." Prob C §16460(b)(2).

The following example illustrates the problem. Sam and Wendy had been married for 25 years when they established the Sam and Wendy Revocable Trust. During their joint lifetimes, Sam and Wendy were the sole beneficiaries of the trust and either could revoke it as to their community property. As to separate property, the trust was revocable by the spouse who had contributed the separate property. Initially, Sam and Wendy were cotrustees and the trust provided that one of them would be sole trustee, should the other fail to serve. Some years after creating the trust, Sam suffered a stroke from which he eventually recovered. During his rehabilitation, Wendy began paying all of the bills, without consulting with Sam. Sam's children from a prior marriage resented Wendy and mistrusted her power, but when Sam's abilities were restored, he told his children to leave Wendy alone. Sam later had a second stroke and Wendy became his full-time caregiver. Accustomed to managing their finances without Sam's help, she followed through on Sam's plan to sell his separate-property vacation home. Wendy invested the sales proceeds with the advice of Sam's financial planner, who because of Sam's cognitive deficits, began consulting only with Wendy. Already overburdened with responsibilities, Wendy never questioned whether she ought to be doing anything additional. She thought of herself as Sam's wife, not his trustee, and she certainly never questioned whether she should be accounting to Sam's children.

Had Wendy seen an attorney, what advice should the attorney have given her? Whether she recognizes it or not, Wendy is the trustee of a revocable trust. During the interval between strokes when Sam had all of his faculties, Wendy owed duties only to him (Prob C §15800(b)), including the duty to account (Prob C §16062). Wendy did not account to Sam, who never waived in writing her duty to do so. Prob C §§16062, 16064(b). Later, when Wendy sold Sam's vacation home, Sam was not competent to consent to the sale or waive Wendy's duty to account for it. Sam's children are not beneficiaries entitled to current distributions of income or principal, so Wendy is not duty bound to account to them. Prob C §16062(a). But on Sam's death, the children will have standing to sue Wendy for any breaches of trust she committed during Sam's lifetime. *Estate of Giraldin* (2012) 55 C4th 1058. If Wendy wants to limit her liability, she either must account to Sam's children or seek court approval of her accounts, two actions most wives would find egregiously distasteful. 199 CA4th at 598.

Estate planning attorneys who tout the benefits of plans built around revocable trusts often list planning for incapacity as one of the plan's virtues. On this list, one also finds mention of privacy. But the California Supreme Court decision in *Estate of Giraldin* has illuminated the risk fiduciaries may run when they privately administer a revocable trust on behalf of an incompetent person who holds the power to revoke.

§2.69   C. Distinguishing Persons to Whom Duties Are Owed From Persons With Standing

In *Estate of Giraldin* (2011) 199 CA4th 577, the settlor nominated his son Timothy as the initial trustee. The trust remained revocable during the settlor's lifetime, during which time the trustee invested heavily in a business he himself owned. At the settlor's death, this business had almost no value and several of Timothy's siblings sued him for breaches of trust. The trial court found Timothy liable for millions of dollars and Timothy appealed. The court of appeal opined that during the settlor's lifetime, the trustee owed duties to no one but the settlor and after the settlor's death, the contingent remainder beneficiaries lacked the standing to assert claims against the trustee for conduct during the settlor's lifetime. 199 CA4th at 598. California's Supreme Court, in a decision that surprised many, found quite the opposite. The court framed the question presented as follows (*Estate of Giraldin* (2012) 55 C4th 1058, 1065):

> When the settlor of a revocable inter vivos trust appoints, during his lifetime, someone other than himself to act as trustee, once the settlor dies and the trust becomes irrevocable, do the remainder beneficiaries have standing to sue the trustee for

breaches of fiduciary duty committed during the period of revocability?

The court answered the question with a resounding "yes," underscoring the dilemma of the trustee who serves an incompetent beneficiary who holds the power of revocation. During that person's lifetime, the trustee owes duties only to that person. Prob C §15800. But later, other people, people whose interests may not be aligned with those of the settlor, will have the power to sue. During the settlor's lifetime, the trustee has no duty to account to the contingent remainder beneficiaries, but perhaps the trustee should account to them anyway.

§2.70 D. Safe Practices

The Probate Code does not prohibit trustees from accounting to more than the statutorily defined minimum number of beneficiaries. In light of the protection an accounting provides the trustee, if the settlor of a revocable trust has become incompetent, it may be prudent for the trustee to account to the remainder beneficiaries. Trustees in this situation might also consider petitioning for the court's approval of their accounts, but those who do must be prepared to pay the fees of the guardian ad litem the court likely will appoint to protect the incompetent person's rights.

Private professional fiduciaries, however, must consider whether they have a duty to preserve the confidences of the people they serve and whether that duty allows the disclosure of a court petition.

NOTE▶ Professional fiduciaries who are members of the Professional Fiduciary Association of California (PFAC) agree that they owe a duty to preserve the confidences of their clients. See PFAC Mission Statement, http://www.pfac-pro.org.

It would be prudent for private professional fiduciaries to include in their contracts a provision that would allow disclosure to contingent remainder beneficiaries whenever the professional is concerned that the person holding the power to revoke is not competent.

When the person holding the power to revoke becomes incompetent and a conservatorship is established for that person, the trustee has a duty to account only to the conservator. *Johnson v Kotyck* (1999) 76 CA4th 83. However, this rule is based on the premise that the trust remains revocable because the conservator may revoke trusts through the process of substituted judgment. 76 CA4th at 89.

It is not clear what the rule would be if the trust instrument prohibited revocation by substituted judgment, or if the trust became irrevocable on the settlor's incapacity. Additionally, in *Johnson,* the conservator and the trustee were different people and, presumably, in the exercise of duties to the conservatee, the conservator provided the trustee with effective oversight. Had the conservator and the trustee been the same person, it is questionable whether the holding of *Johnson* would answer the question, "To whom must the trustee account?"

At a minimum, the trustee of a revocable trust should account to the person holding the power to revoke, even if that person might not be competent. The power-holder's incompetence may make it difficult to trigger the running of the Prob C §16460 statute of limitations, but the power-holder's incompetence is no justification for breaching the duty to account. That duty must be performed, unless waived by the trust instrument or by law.

VII. FORMAT OF TRUST ACCOUNTS

§2.71   A. Minimum Requirements

Unlike guardians, conservators, and personal representatives, whose accounts must comply with the statutory requirements for court accountings set forth in Prob C §§1060–1064, trustees who do not seek court approval of their accounts have great flexibility when choosing the manner and style of presenting information. The minimum requirements are set forth in Prob C §16063, which describes the substance, but not the format, of the trustee's account. Prob C §16063. If the trustee does not submit his or her account to the court for its approval, the account need only contain the following:

- A statement of receipts and disbursements of principal and income for the period of the account (Prob C §16063(a)(1));

- A statement of the trust's assets and liabilities "as of the end of the last complete fiscal year of the trust or as of the end of the period covered by the account" (Prob C §16063(a)(2));

- Disclosure of the trustee's compensation (Prob C §16063(a)(3));

- Disclosure of the agents hired by the trustee, their relationship to the trustee, and the compensation paid them during the period of the account (Prob C §16063(a)(4));

- A statement that "the recipient of the account may petition the court under §17200 to obtain a court review of the account and of the acts of the trustee" (Prob C §16063(a)(5)); and

- A statement that "claims against the trustee for breach of trust may not be made after the expiration of three years from the date the beneficiary receives an account or report disclosing facts giving rise to the claim" (Prob C §16063(a)(6)).

As an example of the difference between a court accounting and trust accounting that will not be submitted for court approval, consider the schedules of Receipts. In a court accounting, the schedule of Receipts must show the nature or purpose of each item, the source of the receipt, and the date. Prob C §1062(a). By contrast, trustees need provide only a Statement of Receipts of Income and Principal for the period of the account. Prob C §16063(a)(1). Trustees may meet this requirement by summarizing the trust's receipts and presenting them in the aggregate.

§2.72 B. Why Trustees Should Account as if Preparing for Court Review

The trustee who wishes to trigger the running of the statute of limitations on claims against trustees should question whether accounting in the summary fashion described in §2.71 would "adequately" disclose the existence of potential claims. Prob C §16460. More practically, if the trustee ever raised the statute of limitations as a defense, could the trustee persuade a judge of the adequacy of an account prepared in some manner other than that to which judges are accustomed? The trustee who hopes never to hear that question answered should account for his or her receipts with all the particularity required of personal representatives and other court-supervised fiduciaries.

The same holds true for each schedule of the trustee's account. Disbursements are best explained by a schedule prepared in the manner of Prob C §1062(b). Distributions to beneficiaries are best described in the manner of Prob C §1062(e). The trustee should provide auxiliary schedules that plainly state liabilities, changes in the form of principal assets, and all the other items described by Prob C §1063. The best format for these schedules is the format required in court accountings. Trustees are not *required* to account in this fashion, but those who worry about "adequate" disclosure should do so nevertheless.

PRACTICE TIP▶ Practitioners should discourage their trustee clients from that style of "accounting" in which the trustee merely sends the beneficiaries copies of bank and brokerage account statements. Though the statements may adequately disclose the source of some trust receipts, the statements will not categorize the receipts as principal or income as Prob C §§16063 and 16320-16375 require. Often, the source of a receipt will be unclear. Also, transactions that appear to be receipts may just be transfers from other trust accounts. Similarly, bank statements may not reveal much about the trustee's disbursements. The statements will not disclose the relationship between the trustee and the agents he or she has hired. Neither will the statements tell the beneficiaries that they have the right to seek the court's review and the right to sue for breach of trust.

In conclusion, the best practice is for trustees to prepare their accounts in the manner required by the Probate Code for accounts that will be filed with the court ("court accountings"), even though that level of detail is not required by trust law.

NOTE▶ All accounts to be filed with the court must be prepared as provided in Prob C §§1061-1064. Prob C §1060.

The trustee who accounts as if preparing for court review is most likely to make all the disclosures necessary to trigger the running of the statute of limitations. After preparing an account in this fashion, the trustee could seek court review at little additional expense and without risk that the court would disallow the cost of preparing the accounting a second time, in a different format. The cost of a court accounting is an expense of administration. Prob C §16247. Because court accountings are required of so many fiduciaries, including conservators and guardians (Prob C §2620) and personal representatives (Prob C §§10951-10953), the trustee should have no trouble finding a professional capable of putting the account in the proper format.

Chapters 3 through 13 discuss preparation of the fiduciary's account, schedule by schedule. Each section begins by contrasting the detailed presentation required in a court accounting with the less formal presentation permitted of trustees. The discussion then proceeds on the assumption that the practitioner will prepare a court accounting. For two reasons, the materials provide almost no guidance to the practitioner who presents a trust's beneficiaries with an account prepared in a less formal manner. First, the authors believe that the best practice is for the trustee to prepare an account he or she *could* defend in court. Second, statutes and rules of court provide *some* guidance to those who would prepare a court account, whereas there is no such guidance for those who would prepare something less formal.

3
Preparing the Accounting, Step by Step

I. SIX PASSES §3.1
   A. First Pass: Gathering and Organizing the Working Papers §3.2
   B. Second Pass: Reconciling the Cash
      1. Goals and Strategies §3.3
      2. Setting Up the Spreadsheets §3.4
      3. Checking Accounts §3.5
         a. The Description Columns §3.6
         b. The Receipts and Disbursements Columns §3.7
         c. Transfers Between Accounts §3.8
         d. Reconciliation §3.9
      4. Investment Accounts §3.10
         a. Entering the Data §3.11
         b. Assets §3.12
         c. Dividend Reinvestments §3.13
         d. Reconciling the Cash §3.14
         e. Money Market Funds §3.15
         f. Investment Accounts With No Cash §3.16
      5. Real Estate and Personal Property §3.17
      6. Final Review §3.18
   C. Third Pass: Reconciling the Assets §3.19
      1. Setting Up the Spreadsheet §3.20
      2. Entering the Data §3.21
      3. Reconciling the Assets §3.22
         a. The Steps §3.23
         b. Example: Purchases Only §3.24
         c. Example: When a Portion of the Asset Has Been Sold §3.25
         d. Example: When There Are Both Purchases and Sales of the Same Asset §3.26
         e. Example: Assets With No Activity §3.27
      4. Final Review §3.28

            5. When the Account Does Not Balance §3.29
        D. Fourth Pass: Reconciling the Whole Accounting §3.30
            1. Setting Up the Spreadsheet §3.31
            2. Entering the Data
                a. Cash Accounts §3.32
                b. Brokerage Cash Accounts §3.33
                c. Assets §3.34
                d. Special Assets §3.35
            3. Checking the Spreadsheet §3.36
        E. Fifth Pass: Preparing the Schedules §3.37
            1. Caption §3.38
            2. Receipts Schedule §3.39
            3. Additional Property Received During Period of Account Schedule §3.40
            4. Disbursements Schedule §3.41
            5. Distributions Schedule §3.42
            6. Gains and Losses §3.43
            7. Assets on Hand—End of Period §3.44
            8. Changes in Form of Assets §3.45
            9. Summary of Account §3.46
        F. Sixth Pass: Refining the Accounting §3.47
            1. Missing Descriptions §3.48
            2. Allocating Income and Principal §3.49
            3. Missing Information §3.50

II. EXHIBITS
    A. Form: Spreadsheet for a Checking Account §3.51
    B. Form: Spreadsheet for an Investment Account §3.52
    C. Form: Spreadsheet for Real Property §3.53
    D. Form: Spreadsheet for Personal Property §3.54
    E. Form: Third Pass Spreadsheet §3.55
    F. Form: Summary Reconciliation Spreadsheet §3.56
    G. Form: Summary of Account §3.57

§3.1 I. SIX PASSES

The goal of every fiduciary accounting is to balance charges and credits while presenting accurate and complete data. Working toward that goal, the accountant must gather the fiduciary's data, enter that data into the computer program he or she will use to prepare the fiduciary accounting, reconcile the data, and determine that it is complete and has been accurately entered into the computer. Only then can the accountant use the data to populate the schedules that comprise the fiduciary accounting. This chapter outlines the authors' recommended process for gathering, examining, entering, and formatting the fiduciary's raw data.

To depict these steps as clearly as possible, this chapter is written as if the person preparing the accounting (the accountant) is a person other than the fiduciary himself or herself. Each step is described as if the accountant is moving objects through the physical world, instead of manipulating electronic data visible only on a computer screen. Working on the premise that instructions must be concrete or they are useless, this chapter describes steps the accountant should take if he or she uses Microsoft Excel to prepare the accounting. Whether or not this is the case, most practitioners are comfortable enough with Excel to comprehend the actions intended by this chapter's Excel-specific instructions. Accountants new to fiduciary accounting should consider meticulously following the steps outlined below, at least for their first few projects, to avoid skipping a step meant to prevent incomplete or inaccurate data entry. The more experienced practitioner may decide for himself or herself whether skipping a step might increase the practitioner's efficiency.

In the authors' experience, the accountant must pass through the fiduciary's data six times before the fiduciary accounting is finished. If the fiduciary is represented by counsel, the attorney's examination of the completed accounting will constitute the seventh pass through the accounting data. When completed, a fiduciary accounting will consist of schedules of charges and credits, such as those discussed in chaps 4-13, but the accountant will not create the schedules until the fifth pass through the fiduciary's data. The fifth pass also is the first time the accountant will turn away from the fiduciary's account statements to look at records created by the fiduciary himself or herself. In other words, until the fifth pass, the accountant will focus only on that information that may be found in bank and brokerage account statements, escrow closing documents, and the like. Focusing on these records in isolation allows the fiduciary to input the numerical data undistracted by information irrelevant to the goal of balancing the accounting. Finally, it is not until the sixth pass that the accountant consults the fiduciary's checkbook register, QuickBooks file, shoe box full of receipts, or faulty recollections of transactions poorly recorded.

At each pass, the accountant's focus shifts to the information that was obscured in the prior pass. As a result, at each pass the accountant may identify missing data, the absence of which could not have been detected in an earlier pass. In the first pass, the accountant identifies any missing statements for known accounts. In the second pass, the accountant identifies accounts for which the fiduciary has provided no information whatsoever. (Often, these mystery accounts turn out to belong to the fiduciary, personally.) On the third pass, the accountant identifies distributions of assets or new assets that disappear or appear. Once the accounting is reconciled through the fourth pass and the schedules are prepared in the fifth pass, additional questions will arise in the sixth pass. At this point, the accountant has a draft account for the fiduciary's review and can request the details required to finalize the accounting.

The first step, of course, is to ask the fiduciary for the data needed to begin the accounting. The authors recommend making this request in writing (in the form of an "engagement letter"). (A sample letter can be found in chap 15.) The accountant should keep a copy of this letter for his or her file.

§3.2 A. First Pass: Gathering and Organizing the Working Papers

The goal of the first pass through the fiduciary's data is to discover whether the fiduciary has failed to deliver all the necessary account statements. Immediately after the fiduciary has delivered the financial records to the accountant, the accountant, or his or her assistant, should take the following steps.

Sort the financial records. Sort the financial records into piles: one pile for each bank account, one for each brokerage account, one for each statement from a mutual fund company, another for each escrow statement, and so on.

Organize the piles. Put each pile into its own file folder and label the file. For example, the accountant might create the following folders:

- Wells Fargo Bank checking account #XXXXXX-9876;
- Wells Fargo Bank savings account #XXXXXX-4321;
- Charles Schwab brokerage account #XXXX-6549; and
- Escrow, 321 Franchise Row, Anytown, CA.

At the end of this step, the accountant will have a file folder for each asset listed on the schedule Assets on Hand—Beginning of Period, with the exception of securities held in a brokerage account. Although each security is a separate asset and will be accounted for as such, the accountant will create only one file for each brokerage account. Note that sometimes two accounts are reported on the same statement. In this case, the accountant will create a file with the title of two accounts such as, "Wells Fargo Bank checking account #XXXXXX-9876 and Wells Fargo Bank savings account #XXXXXX-4321."

Put in chronological order. One folder at a time, put the account statements into chronological order. For each missing statement, create a placeholder—for example, a brightly colored piece of paper, clearly labeled with the date range of the missing statement. If two consecutive statements are missing, use two pieces of paper. At the end of this step, the accountant can easily identify every missing statement.

PRACTICE TIP➤ For bank accounts, savings accounts, and money market accounts, the first statement the accountant needs is the statement that includes the beginning date of the fiduciary's accounting. For brokerage statements, the accountant often needs the statement prior to this "first" statement. For escrow statements, the accountant will need the "final" closing escrow statement and should not rely on the estimated closing statement, which often is different from the "final" one.

List the missing statements. Prepare the Missing Statements List. At this point, it is a good idea to start identifying accounts with particularity, for example: "Charles Schwab, brokerage account, statement period: January 1, 2013 through January 30, 2013."

Ask for the missing statements. Send a copy of the Missing Statements List to the fiduciary. Ask the fiduciary to supply the missing statements and calendar a tickler to follow up with the fiduciary. If the accountant's engagement letter permits such a delay, the accountant may stop working on the accounting while waiting for the fiduciary to produce the missing statements.

Organize the newfound statements. Each time the fiduciary supplies a missing statement, place the statement in the folder where it belongs, remove the colorful placeholder, and cross the statement off the Missing Statements List. The accountant may wish to send the updated Missing Statements List to the fiduciary as a reminder of the statements that are still missing.

The accountant may begin the second pass of his or her work before completing the first pass, but the accountant cannot complete the second pass until the fiduciary has provided all the statements for each account, each escrow closing, and each individual security not held in a brokerage account.

PRACTICE TIP▶ In the engagement letter (see chap 15), the accountant may wish to say that he or she will not begin working until the fiduciary has delivered all of the statements necessary to finish the accounting. This statement does not prevent the accountant from beginning the second pass through the financial data, but provides the accountant with the excuse to postpone the second pass if other projects are more pressing.

B. Second Pass: Reconciling the Cash

§3.3 1. Goals and Strategies

The goal of the second pass is to reconcile the cash in each account to be included in the accounting. In the second pass, the accountant will also create a record of the source of information relied on, making it possible to later answer questions about each entry's reliability. The method outlined below ensures the data will be accurate and serves as the basis for reconciling the assets.

To begin, the accountant must distinguish between, on the one hand, cash and cash equivalents, and on the other hand, all other types of assets. In this book, a shorthand reference to "cash" means both cash—such as money in a checking account, savings account, or a brokerage account—and as cash equivalents, including money market funds with a fixed share price equal to $1.00. The term "assets" means non-cash items, including real estate, individual securities, or mutual funds. This is an important distinction because in the second pass, the accountant focuses only on reconciling the cash and cash equivalents.

Following the steps outlined below requires a basic understanding of the spreadsheet software program Microsoft Excel. Although the authors provide some tips on the efficient use of Excel, the words used when discussing calculations do not translate directly into Excel formulas. The accountant must know, for example, how to sum up a column of figures. Readers unfamiliar with the most basic Excel vocabulary and functions should seek preliminary guidance from the program manual and the program's help function. The entire accounting, from data entry to the production of the final schedules, will be completed in one Excel workbook. Each tab will be referred to as a new or separate spreadsheet within the workbook.

§3.4 2. Setting Up the Spreadsheets

In preparing to reconcile the cash, the transactions for each account will need to be entered into a spreadsheet. The accountant will set up a separate spreadsheet (a tab within a workbook) for each bank, brokerage, or escrow account.

Checking and savings accounts. For a checking or savings account, the spreadsheet should be set up with 9 columns, as shown below.

[Bank Name]								
[Full Account Number]								
[Title of Account as Listed on the Statement]								
Date	Description	Description	Check #	Receipts	Transfers In	Disbursements	Transfers Out	Balance

PRACTICE TIP➤ In Excel, the default title of each spreadsheet is found at the bottom of the spreadsheet, on what the authors call the "tabs." It is useful to change the title of these tabs from the default (typically Sheet1) to a shorthand version of the name of the bank account reflected on that spreadsheet. For example, the spreadsheet for the Wells Fargo checking account ending in number 9876, might be WFB 9876. Retitling the spreadsheets within the workbook makes it easier to find and reference the data, as required in subsequent passes.

Investment accounts. For an account that holds securities, mutual funds, or other investments, the spreadsheet should be set up with two additional columns—"Proceeds of Sale" and "Purchases"—as shown below. For more on investment accounts, see §§3.10-3.16.

	[Brokerage or Fund Name]								
	[Full Account Number]								
	[Title of Account as Listed on the Statement]								
Date	Description 1	Description 2	Shares	Receipts	Transfers In	Proceeds of Sale	Disbursements	Transfers Out	Purchases	Balance

Real estate and personal assets. Finally, for real estate or personal assets, the following simple spreadsheet will suffice. For more on real estate and personal property, see §3.17.

	[Property Address]					
	[Title Company Name]					
	[Name as Listed on the Closing Escrow Statement]					
Date	Description 1	Description 2	Receipts	Transfers In	Disbursements	Transfers Out

§3.5   3. Checking Accounts

Starting with the main operating account or main checking account (the checking account with the most activity), the accountant will begin entering the transactions into the spreadsheets he or she has created. The data entry steps are as follows.

Review the statement. Identify the opening balance on the first statement.

PRACTICE TIP▶ Always start and end with a statement balance, even if the accounting itself begins or ends on a date in the middle of the period covered by the statement. This eliminates the risk of misstating the starting balance—a mistake that can lead to countless hours spent trying to reconcile the accounting at the end. The extra transactions entered into the spreadsheet will be discussed later in this chapter.

Enter the starting balance. Enter the date of the starting balance in the first row of the Date column and enter the starting account balance in the first row of the Balance column. This initial entry in the Balance column is the only numeral the accountant will type into this column. All other cells in this column will be filled with a formula, discussed below.

Enter each transaction. Row by row on the spreadsheet, enter each transaction as it appears on the relevant account statement, including the following information in this order:

- The date;
- The description of the transaction;
- The check number; and
- The amount.

PRACTICE TIP▶ While doing this, pay particular attention to the description of the transaction found in the account statement, as well as to entering the dollar amount in the correct column.

§3.6   a. The Description Columns

There are two columns for descriptions. Information included in the columns depends on the nature of the transaction.

Deposits. If the transaction is a deposit, use the first column to identify the source of funds (payer) and the second column to identify the type of deposit. For example, the first column might say Widget Supplier LP, while the second column says Partnership Income.

Payments and checks. If the transaction is a payment or check, the first column should identify the payee and the second column the purpose of the payment. For example, the first column might say Margaret's Restaurant and the second Memorial Dinner.

Unknown transactions. When the statement provides no information about the transaction, enter a generic descriptor in the Description columns, such as "deposit" or "check." The missing descriptions will be reviewed and completed as part of the sixth pass, discussed in §§3.47–3.50.

§3.7   b. The Receipts and Disbursements Columns

When entering a transaction on the spreadsheet, it is essential to allocate each entry to the correct column. After entering the date and description, the accountant must decide in which column to enter the dollar amount.

The Receipts column. This column includes all deposits, income, refunds, and any other cash transactions that increase the account balance.

The Disbursements column. This column includes all payments, withdrawals, bank charges, and anything that decreases the account balance.

PRACTICE TIP➤ All transactions should be entered as a positive number.

§3.8   c. Transfers Between Accounts

Transfers between accounts, if both accounts are included in the project at hand, are neither receipts nor disbursements, and the fiduciary's final account need not disclose them. Prob C §1063(b). Indeed, treating transfers as if they were receipts and disbursements would inflate the fiduciary's charges and credits, which might have an effect on the fiduciary's fees. (Consider the statutory fee, which is based in part on receipts. Prob C §10810(b).) In the early passes through the fiduciary's data, however, the accountant must track such transfers, or the data entered into the initial spreadsheets will not reconcile with the fiduciary's bank and brokerage account statements.

To track transfers between accounts, both of which are being accounted for, deposits into an account should be entered in the column titled Transfers In and should be described by the deposit's source (for example, "Savings Account" or "Wells Fargo account #XXXXXX-4321"). Any disbursement from one of the fiduciary's accounts to another account should be entered on the spreadsheet in the column titled Transfers Out and should be described by reference to the account to which the disbursement was transferred, *i.e.,* the destination of the transfer.

§3.9   d. Reconciliation

Once the accountant has entered all the transactions into the spreadsheet and has entered each dollar amount in the column where it belongs, the accountant will enter a formula in each cell of the column titled Balance. Finally, the accountant will check the balance against the ending balance of the fiduciary's account statements, an action referred to as reconciling the accounting to the statements. The steps are described below.

Enter the formula. In the Balance column, directly below the hand-entered initial balance of the account, enter the following formula:

> Prior balance + Receipts + Transfers In − Disbursements − Transfers Out

This formula produces the new balance, *i.e.*, the balance in the account after the transaction in that row has been accounted for. The new balance is the prior balance, increased or decreased, as the case may be, by that row's transaction.

Determine the running balance. After checking that the formula is working, copy it into every cell in the Balance column, stopping at the last row of data. By so doing, the Balance column will show a new balance after each transaction: the running balance.

Double check. Check the last figure in the Balance column against the ending balance on the last statement consulted in the preparation of the spreadsheet. The two figures should match.

PRACTICE TIP▶ Compare the running balance at the end of each month and match it to the ending balance of each monthly statement. This will identify data entry errors as the transactions are entered, and allow them to be corrected before starting the next statement.

For a sample completed spreadsheet for a checking account, see §3.51.

§3.10 4. Investment Accounts

The data entry for investment accounts is similar to that of a checking or savings account described above. However, because the investment accounts or brokerage accounts hold assets that may be sold or purchased during the account period, the spreadsheet will have two additional columns: "Proceeds of Sales" and "Purchases." As a result of these two additional columns, the first three amount columns on the spreadsheet will hold those entries that represent cash coming into the account, while the second three amount columns will be used for the entries that show cash leaving the account.

§3.11 a. Entering the Data

Entering the data from the investment account statement into the spreadsheet, one starts as one did for the cash accounts, by entering the beginning date of the statement in the Date column and hand-entering the beginning cash balance by typing a numeral into the Balance column. Again, the beginning balance will be the only numeral typed into the Balance column. Every other cell in this column will contain a formula that produces a running balance.

After entering the beginning balance, begin entering each transaction reported on the account statement. When entering into the spreadsheet information about deposits, describe the source of funds (*e.g.*, Chevron Corp.) and type of deposit (*e.g.*, Dividend). Enter in the Receipts column all income, including interest, dividends, cash in place of partial shares, and class action settlements. When entering data about payments, describe the payee (*e.g.*, Charles Schwab) and the purpose (*e.g.*, Account Maintenance Fee). Enter in the Disbursements column all payments, including checks drawn on the account, investment management fees paid from the account, commissions paid, and foreign taxes. As with cash accounts, watch for transfers between two accounts, both of which are being accounted for. If a transaction is a transfer between two such accounts, enter the dollar amount of the transfer in the column Transfers In when the transfer increases the cash balance of the account, and enter the dollar amount of the transfer in the Transfers Out column when the cash balance is reduced.

§3.12 b. Assets

Assets in an account may be traded. Mutual fund and brokerage statements will often have a section listing assets sold and assets purchased. If an asset is sold, the transaction will be entered with the date in the Date column, a description of the asset in the Description 1 column, the word "Sold" in the Description 2 column, and the number of shares sold in the Shares column. The dollar amount will be allocated to Proceeds of Sale.

PRACTICE TIP► Just as the dollar amounts are always entered in the positive, so are the shares.

If an asset is purchased, the transaction will be entered with the date in the Date column, a description of the asset in the Description

1 column, the word "Purchase" in the Description 2 column, and the number of shares purchased in the Shares column. The dollar amount will be allocated to Purchases.

PRACTICE TIP▶ When entering transactions for trading assets, there may be both a "trade date" and a "settlement date." For the purposes of the accounting, use the settlement date. The risk of using the earlier trade date is that the transaction may not have cleared by the closing of the statement, resulting in accounting cash not balancing the statement cash.

§3.13   c. Dividend Reinvestments

Many brokerage accounts include dividend reinvestments. A dividend reinvestment has two components: a receipt and a purchase. More specifically, a dividend is a receipt that is immediately used to purchase more shares of the investment that paid the dividend. During the second pass of the account preparation, the transaction must be treated as if it were two transactions. Enter the dividend as a cash Receipt and the reinvestment as a cash Purchase. In most cases, the account statement also will describe the transaction as two separate events: the receipt of a dividend and a reinvestment of that receipt. Even when the statement does not represent the transaction in this fashion, the accountant must.

§3.14   d. Reconciling the Cash

Once every transaction on the brokerage account has been entered into the spreadsheet, to complete the cash reconciliation of the investment account, focus on the Balance column. In the cell just below the hand-entered beginning balance, enter a formula. As with the cash accounts, the formula is:

> Prior Balance + Receipts + Transfers In + Proceeds of Sales – Disbursements – Transfers Out – Purchases

Test the formula against one or two transactions and, once you are sure it is working, copy it into each cell in the Balance column. This will produce a running balance. The figure in the last row of the Balance column should match the cash and cash equivalents held in the investment account at the end of the period of the last statement.

The key to reconciling the cash in an investment account lies in understanding what to enter and what not to enter. During this second pass through the data, the objective is to reconcile the cash, not the assets. In other words, during this pass of the account preparation, sales matter because they increase the amount of cash in the brokerage account. Similarly, purchases matter because they deplete cash. Later, the accountant will use this data to calculate gains and losses, but in the second pass, it is immaterial whether an asset has sold for more or less than its carry value. It is also immaterial whether an asset has sold for more or less than its cost basis—a concept that has its place in tax accounting, but is not relevant to the type of accounting which is the subject of this book. With two exceptions, all that matters in the second pass are those transactions which increase or decrease the cash balance of the account.

The first exception is those non-cash transactions that increase or decrease the amount of an asset held in the account. Such transactions include stock splits, reverse splits, and spin-offs.

The second exception is those transactions that might obscure the identity of the asset, including exchanges of one company's stock for another's, the purchase of one entity by another, and name changes.

These transactions should be entered on the spreadsheet with the date, description, and shares. Do not enter any cost basis or tax basis that may be listed on the brokerage statement. In the completed spreadsheet for an investment or brokerage account set forth in §3.55, Merck & Co. had a 2-for-1 split. Since the account already had 1200 shares, the stock split reports the share increase of 1200 shares.

§3.15 e. Money Market Funds

A money market fund may have attributes of both a mutual fund (an asset) and a cash equivalent. Treat the fund as an asset if its per-share price is other than $1.00, and treat the fund as a cash equivalent if the fund has a per-share price of exactly $1.00. If the money market fund is a cash equivalent, enter disbursements from the fund and receipts as one would for a true cash account, but do not enter in the spreadsheet purchases and sales of interests in the asset.

PRACTICE TIP➤ Before entering any transactions on an investment or brokerage account, identify any mutual funds that are used as a daily investment "sweep." Often, these funds have a share price of $1.00 and must be treated as cash or a cash equivalent account.

§3.16   f. Investment Accounts With No Cash

The fiduciary may administer assets in an account that is 100 percent invested, *i.e.*, the account holds no cash. For such an account, although the starting balance and ending balance will both be zero, the accountant must make a spreadsheet to ensure that all of the transactions in every account have been captured. This information will be used in the third pass.

§3.17   5. Real Estate and Personal Property

While the data entry for real estate is relatively short compared to checking, savings, and investment accounts, the reconciliation is a little different. The objective is to make Receipts plus Transfers In equal to Disbursements plus Transfers Out, rather than to have a running balance. Account for real property as follows:

- Using the real estate spreadsheet and the final closing escrow statement, enter the contract sales price for the property as a transfer in.

- Enter each subsequent item on the escrow statement in a manner similar to the checking and savings account. Receipts may include refunds for property taxes or homeowners association dues while Disbursements includes all escrow fees, title fees, and loan payoffs, as well as any transfer of tenant security deposits from the old owner to the new. Again, the source of funds, payee, and purpose should be used for the descriptions.

- Enter the amount due to seller in the Transfers Out column.

To reconcile, total each column and confirm that the Receipts and Transfers In equal the Disbursements and Transfers Out.

For a sample real estate spreadsheet, see §3.53. The same spreadsheet can be used for personal property sold. In this case the gross sales price will be listed as a transfer in. The Disbursements may include commissions and related expenses, while the net amount transferred to the checking or investment account is allocated to the Transfers Out column. For a sample personal property spreadsheet, see §3.54.

§3.18 6. Final Review

As a final step in the second pass, review each of the cash reconciliation spreadsheets and, if the first statement beginning date is not identical to the fiduciary accounting beginning date, identify the true starting balance. Highlight this number, as it will be used later for the Assets on Hand—Beginning of Period schedule. Identify the true ending balance of the accounting period and highlight this number as well. It will be used later for the Assets on Hand—End of Period schedule.

PRACTICE TIP▶ If entered as recommended above, the transactions in the spreadsheet will appear in the same order as they appeared on the statements, and not necessarily in date order. But to determine the beginning or ending value for the fiduciary's accounting, it may be necessary to sort the first month's data or the last month's data chronologically. *Do not sort the whole spreadsheet by date.* In the event that the spreadsheet must be consulted months after its preparation, the spreadsheet will be a more useful reference point if its data can be cross-referenced against the account statements—something that would be impossible if one could not tell where one statement ended and another began.

Finally, total up each column between the accounting period starting balance and accounting period ending balance, only capturing the values of the transactions that occurred during the accounting period. These totals will be used in the third and fourth passes.

At this point, the second pass is complete and the accountant has a workbook with a tab for each account to be included in the accounting. Each spreadsheet matches the fiduciary's statements to the penny and all transactions have been allocated to the appropriate column. The cash is balanced for each account.

§3.19 C. Third Pass: Reconciling the Assets

The fiduciary's non-cash assets, called "assets" in this chapter to distinguish them from cash, are the focus of the third pass. The goal of the third pass is to reconcile each individual asset within the investment account and then reconcile the whole investment account. This means that the accountant will be establishing the starting carry value and then calculating the gains and losses and the ending carry value. The accountant also will reconcile the shares balances for each asset.

§3.20   1. Setting Up the Spreadsheet

Reconciling the assets requires the accountant to create a second, and different, spreadsheet for each investment account. This second spreadsheet will be filled with the transaction data entered in the first spreadsheet, during the second pass.

The spreadsheet should be set up as follows:

Date	Description	Description	Shares	Carry Value Beginning	Carry Value Changes	Carry Value End	Proceeds	Gain/Loss	Purchases

§3.21   2. Entering the Data

Once the spreadsheet is set up, copy into it the information already entered in the corresponding cash reconciliation spreadsheet by following the instructions below:

- For each account that holds assets, return to the spreadsheet created in the second pass and copy all the transactions entered in that spreadsheet. Paste these copied transactions into the spreadsheet created in the third pass.

- In the third-pass spreadsheet, sort the copied data by the column labeled Proceeds. The data may be sorted either high to low or low to high, it does not matter. The entries for which there is no figure in the Proceeds column will fall to the bottom of the sorted data.

- Focus now on those entries for which there is no numeral in the Proceeds column. Select these entries and sort again by Purchases. Again, high to low, low to high, it does not matter.

- Next, focus on those entries for which there is no numeral in the Proceeds or Purchases column. Select these entries and sort by Shares. This will capture the share changes that will be needed for the reconciliation of each asset.

- Focus now on all entries for which there is no numeral in the Proceeds, Purchases, or Shares columns. After the three sorts above, these entries will be found at the bottom of the spreadsheet. Delete these entries.

PRACTICE TIP➤ This is a good time to review the transactions to ensure that only transactions that occurred during the accounting period are listed. Remember, in the second pass (cash reconciliation), to reconcile two account statements, the accountant may have stated a beginning cash balance on a date prior to the beginning of the accounting period, and may have accounted for several transactions that occurred before the beginning of the account period or after the end of the account period. If any such transactions have been copied into the spreadsheet created in the third pass, simply delete them. This is also a good time to ensure that all the dollar values are in the correct column in the spreadsheet.

- For each account that holds assets once all of the purchases and sales are reflected in the assets reconciliation spreadsheet, copy into the spreadsheet the assets on hand at the beginning of the accounting period. Include only those assets that are held in the account currently being reconciled. For example, if the fiduciary has three brokerage accounts, when reconciling the first account, only copy into the third-pass spreadsheet those assets on hand that are held in that particular brokerage account. The assets should be listed individually, with the beginning date of the accounting, the name of the asset in the first description column, and the term "on hand" in the second description column. For each individual asset, enter the number of shares and the carry value as of the start of the accounting period. For a discussion on establishing carry value, see §§4.12–4.14.

- Sort all of the transactions first by asset name (column B), then by the description column (column C), and finally by date (column A).

- Finally, to make the spreadsheet easier to read while reconciling each asset, add a row or two between each asset grouping.

While this takes a few extra minutes, it provides room for calculations and notations, should the spreadsheet be referenced at a later date.

For a sample third-pass spreadsheet, see §3.55.

§3.22   3. Reconciling the Assets

The reconciliation is completed first by individual asset, then by account. During the fourth pass, each account will be reconciled with every other account accounted for. To ensure that the entire accounting will reconcile, start with the smallest reconciliation first: each asset.

The actively traded investment account may appear to be a tedious and overwhelming nightmare. Although the work may seem mind-numbing, if done incorrectly, hours and hours of time will be wasted trying to reconcile the accounting. Following the reconciliation steps in the following sections will limit errors and, if errors are made, they can be quickly identified.

§3.23   a. The Steps

To reconcile the assets, first confirm that all of the transactions within each asset grouping appear in date order. Failure to put the transactions in date order may result in the overstatement or understatement of gains and losses or ending carry value.

Once the transactions in a particular asset have been arranged in date order, the accountant can assess whether carry value has changed during the account period and, if it has changed, by how much. Carry value may change as the result of a purchase, in which case carry value will increase by the dollar amount expended on the purchase. Carry value may also change as the result of a sale, in which case carry value will decrease by the carry value of the asset sold. Note the difference: the sale of a portion of an asset decreases the carry value of the asset only in proportion to the portion sold. All such changes are tracked using the figures in the Carry Value (CV) Changes column. For example, if 100 shares of the Widget Company are purchased for $10,000, the carry value at the date of purchase would increase by $10,000.

PRACTICE TIP▶ Only enter data into the CV Changes column.

CV End will be a formula within the spreadsheet. The gains and losses will be a formula within the spreadsheet based on what is entered in the CV Changes column.

§3.24 b. Example: Purchases Only

The following is an example of the reconciliation of an asset for which there were only purchases from the Cash Trust described in chap 1. In this case, the Carry Value (CV) change is the purchase price. To calculate the CV End, simply add the CV Beginning to the CV Changes. Note that the Shares column is added as well.

Date	Description	Description	Shares	Carry Value Beginning	Carry Value Changes	Carry Value End	Proceeds	Gain/Loss	Purchases
1/1/13	On Hand — Beginning	Franklin CA Tax-Free Income Fund Cl. A	14,202.081	$95,722.03	$383.46				$383.46
1/2/13	Purchase	Franklin CA Tax-Free Income Fund Cl. A	57.063		$385.00				$385.00
2/2/13	Purchase	Franklin CA Tax-Free Income Fund Cl. A	58.959		$385.00				$385.00
3/2/13	Purchase	Franklin CA Tax-Free Income Fund Cl. A	61.116		$405.20				$405.20
4/4/13	Purchase	Franklin CA Tax-Free Income Fund Cl. A	62.413		$406.93				$406.93
5/3/13	Purchase	Franklin CA Tax-Free Income Fund Cl. A	61.551		$408.70				$408.70
6/2/13	Purchase	Franklin CA Tax-Free Income Fund Cl. A	62.022		$409.64				$409.64
	On Hand — End	Franklin CA Tax-Free Income Fund Cl. A	14,565.205			$98,120.96			

§3.25 c. Example: When a Portion of the Asset Has Been Sold

To reconcile an asset when a portion of the asset has been sold, the accountant takes an additional step. The beginning carry value is apportioned between the portion sold and the portion retained, in the following manner. The account statement for the period of the sale (*i.e.*, the data entered into the spreadsheet during the second pass) provides information about the cash proceeds of the sale, not the underlying carry value of the asset sold. To determine the change in carry value sold, first calculate the carry value of each share the moment before a portion of the asset was sold, then multiply the per-share carry value times the number of shares sold.

EXAMPLE➤ If the fiduciary has 25 shares of Widget Company stock with a carry value of $2500, the carry value will be $100 per share ($2500 divided by 25 equals $100). If the fiduciary sells five shares, the carry value of the shares sold is

$500 ($100 times the 5 shares sold). That $500 is also the amount by which the carry value of the remaining shares is reduced. In other words, the carry value of the remaining 20 shares is $2000. The carry value change is $500.

The following spreadsheet is an example of an asset sold from the Cash Trust. In this case, the carry value change was calculated by dividing the Carry Value (CV) Beginning, $6343.75, by 1000 (the number of shares on hand at the beginning). The result is a per-share carry value of $6.34. When this value is multiplied by the number of shares sold, 475, the product, $3013.28, is entered in CV Changes column.

Date	Description	Description	Shares	Carry Value Beginning	Carry Value Changes	Carry Value End	Proceeds	Gain/Loss	Purchases
1/1/13	On Hand— Beginning	Franklin Universal Trust	1,000.000	$6,343.75					
4/15/13	Sold	Franklin Universal Trust	475.000		$3,013.28		$2,932.02	$(81.26)	
5/5/13	Sold	Franklin Universal Trust	475.000		$3,013.28		$3,442.34	$429.06	
	On Hand— End	Franklin Universal Trust	50.000			$317.190			

To calculate the number of shares on hand at the end and the carry value of these shares, subtract the number of shares sold from the pre-sale number of shares and subtract the carry value of the shares sold from the pre-sale carry value.

The carry value change on an asset sold is compared to the proceeds to determine the gain or loss. If the carry value of the portion sold is less than the proceeds of the sale, the result is a gain. If the carry value of the portion sold is greater than the proceeds of the sale, the result is a loss. Note, this example reflects the same asset sold at both a gain and a loss, but the carry value change is the same for both entries because the entries are based upon the same CV Beginning.

§3.26   d. Example: When There Are Both Purchases and Sales of the Same Asset

When there are both purchases and sales of the same asset, it is critical that the transactions be in date order. The following illustrates this assertion. (This example is not found in chap 1.)

Date	Description	Description	Shares	Carry Value Beginning	Carry Value Changes	Carry Value End	Proceeds	Gain/Loss	Purchases
1/1/13	On Hand	Wells Fargo & Co New	7,200.000	$252,360.00					
2/15/13	Purchase	Wells Fargo & Co New	200.000		$8,000.00				$8,000.00
2/28/13	Sold	Wells Fargo & Co New	500.000		$17,591.89		$21,250.00	$3,658.11	
3/3/13	Purchase	Wells Fargo & Co New	1,000.000		$44,000.00				$44,000.00
		Wells Fargo & Co New	7,900.000			$286,768.11			

In the above example, the Carry Value Beginning was increased by adding the purchase made on 02/15/13, and then decreased by the sale made on 2/28/13. To trace the steps on the spreadsheet, the accountant may want to add a line on the spreadsheet for this calculation, as shown below. This provides a record of the calculations and the ability to review the work quickly.

Date	Description	Description	Shares	Carry Value Beginning	Carry Value Changes	Carry Value End	Proceeds	Gain/Loss	Purchases
1/1/13	On Hand	Wells Fargo & Co New	7,200.000	$252,360.00					
2/15/13	Purchase	Wells Fargo & Co New	200.000		$8,000.00				$8,000.00
		$35.18	7,400.00			$260,360.00			
2/28/13	Sold	Wells Fargo & Co New	500.000		$17,591.89		$21,250.00	$3,658.11	
3/3/13	Purchase	Wells Fargo & Co New	1,000.000		$44,000.00				$44,000.00
		Wells Fargo & Co New	7,900.000			$286,768.11			

§3.27 e. Example: Assets With No Activity

What about the assets where there was no activity at all? Simply copy the Carry Value Beginning to the Carry Value End column.

Non-cash transactions. There are a number of non-cash transactions that may be reported during the reconciliation of the individual assets. This includes stock splits, name changes, or transfers of assets. Stock splits or stock dividends will increase the number of shares carried, and a reverse split will decrease the number of shares carried, but none of these events have an impact on the asset's carry value. However, an increase or decrease in the number of shares will affect the per-share carry value. These changes will need to be accounted for on the date of the change to ensure that the carry value calculations are accurate.

Change of name. Name changes will be noted on the Changes in Form of Assets schedule (see chap 11) and will not affect the reconciliation; however, name changes will need to be identified to ensure that the carry value is moved from one name to the other. For example, if the Widget Company changed its name to the Data Company, the carry value of the Widget Company stock would become the carry value of the Data Company stock.

Sometimes, there is an exchange of shares with a name change. For example, 500 shares of Widget Company might become 250 shares of Data Company. When that happens, the per-share carry value increases in proportion to the decrease in the number of shares. In the prior example, each share of Data Company stock would have a carry value twice as high as the carry value of each share of the Widget Company. The carry value of the whole position would not change, but the per-share carry value would. In other words, the accountant will reconcile the asset by using the new name and the new number of shares, but the old carry value.

Transfers between accounts. Finally, when an asset is transferred from one account to another account that also is being accounted for, the accountant should note this event on the spreadsheet, but leave the old asset as an asset on hand. The asset has not left the fiduciary's hands, it was simply moved to another account and will be reconciled in the fourth pass: Reconciling the Whole Accounting.

§3.28   4. Final Review

Before completing the third pass, it is important to confirm that each asset reconciled, when added together, equals the total in the reconciled account. This will prove that all individual assets have been captured and reconciled, thereby eliminating the risk of not balancing the entire accounting in the fourth pass.

Check the share balances. For each asset, compare the number of shares identified on the spreadsheet with the number of shares reported on the final statements for the account period. Compare the share balance of each asset to the final statement. If they all match, move on to the second account reconciliation step below. If they do not match, review the transactions on the second pass or the statements to find the error. This is often a data entry error, as these numbers have not been confirmed until this step. If it is not a data entry error, look for stock splits or exchanges that may have been missed during the data entry. Again, these have no dollar value, so they have not been confirmed until this step.

Add the columns. When adding up each of the columns on the asset reconciliation spreadsheet, confirm the following:

- The Carry Value (CV) Beginning matches the Assets on Hand—Beginning of Period (see chap 4);
- The Proceeds column matches the total of the Proceeds column on the cash reconciliation spreadsheet created during the second pass; and
- The Purchases column matches the total of the Purchases column on the cash reconciliation spreadsheet created during the second pass.

Remember, you have already reconciled the cash, which means that you know that the cash in (proceeds of sale) and cash out (purchases) are correct. If the totals match, move on to the final step.

NOTE➤ In the final step of this third pass, it is important to remember that the assets are being reconciled, not the cash. As a result, a purchase is going to be an "asset in" and a sale is going to be an "asset out." The reconciliation is CV Beginning, plus total purchases, minus carry value of assets sold, equals CV End.

For a completed third pass spreadsheet, see §3.55.

§3.29 5. When the Account Does Not Balance

If the asset reconciliation result does not equal the Carry Value End, there is a calculation error in your Gain/Loss column. Again, you have already confirmed that purchases and proceeds are correct. The following reconciliation tips will help you discover the source of the error.

- Confirm that there is a calculated gain or loss in every row where there are Proceeds, and that there are no gains or losses in the rows where no proceeds are shown.
- Confirm that all values for Assets on Hand—End are in the correct column.
- Confirm that there are no stray calculations or numbers in your Assets on Hand—End column.
- Review the calculations, starting with the assets having the most activity.

§3.30 D. Fourth Pass: Reconciling the Whole Accounting

At this point, each account to be included in the accounting has a cash reconciliation spreadsheet that balances to the statements. Additionally, each account holding assets has an asset reconciliation spreadsheet, and each piece of real estate sold has a reconciliation spreadsheet.

The goal of the fourth pass is ensure that all accounts, when added together, reconcile as a whole. There is only one reason that the whole accounting would not balance at this point: transfers!

When cash or an asset is transferred between accounts, it has not left the fiduciary's hands, and therefore the transaction should not be included in the accounting. The accounting is a scale on which the fiduciary's responsibility is weighed. Treating a transfer in as a receipt would overstate the fiduciary's responsibility and perhaps inflate the basis of the fiduciary's fee. Treating a transfer out as a disbursement would understate the fiduciary's responsibility. Furthermore, if a transfer is treated as only a receipt, or only a disbursement, the overall accounting will not balance.

The objective is to have an accounting in which charges equal credits (see chap 12).

Assets on Hand—Beginning	$		Assets on Hand—End	$
Receipts			Disbursements/Distributions	
Gains			Losses	
Total	$	=	Total	$

To make the above statement true and exclude all transfers, transfers in must equal transfers out.

The accountant will check the reconciliation by using the summary above with the transfers included. Once the transfers balance, they can be removed and the accountant will be ready to move on to the fifth pass: Preparing the Schedules (see §3.37).

§3.31 1. Setting Up the Spreadsheet

Set up a Summary Reconciliation spreadsheet as follows:

Category	Total	Cash Acc't 1	Cash Acc't 2	Cash Acc't 3	Asset Acc't 3	Other Assets

The goal of this step is to compile on one spreadsheet the Summary Reconciliation and the conclusions reached on each spreadsheet created in the second and third pass. Before completing the Summary Reconciliation, refer back to the cash reconciliation spreadsheets created in the second pass to ensure that each column (Receipts, Transfers In, Disbursements, and Transfers Out) has a total at the bottom that includes only those transactions posted during the accounting period.

2. Entering the Data

§3.32   a. Cash Accounts

Enter the first cash account under Cash Account 1. Using the Assets on Hand—Beginning of Period schedule, enter the cash balance on hand at the beginning of the accounting period. Using the column totals from your cash reconciliation spreadsheet, enter the total Receipts, total Transfers In, total Disbursements, total Transfers Out, and the cash balance on hand at the end of the accounting period. In a cash account column, the gain or loss row will not be used.

PRACTICE TIP▶ The authors recommend changing the title of the column labeled Cash Account 1 to specifically identify the bank and the account number represented in the column. This will make it easier to follow the spreadsheet as it is populated with data.

Repeat the process for each cash account, including checking and savings accounts.

§3.33   b. Brokerage Cash Accounts

The brokerage account cash will be entered in a manner similar to the checking and savings accounts with two exceptions. First, the total of the Proceeds of Sales and Transfers In will be added together and entered in the Transfers In column. This represents cash transferred in to the account and cash transferred in from the sale of assets. Second, the total of Purchases and Transfers Out will be added together and entered in the Transfers Out column. This represents the cash transferred out of the account and the cash transferred to the broker to purchase additional assets.

§3.34   c. Assets

Once the sums have been copied from each cash account reconciliation spreadsheet to the Summary Reconciliation, the accountant must do the same for each asset reconciliation spreadsheet. Begin with the Assets on Hand—Beginning of Period. This is found on the asset reconciliation spreadsheet in the column total of Carry Value (CV) Beginning. Then enter the total gains or losses and the total CV End. At this point, the accountant must remember that he or she is entering the asset information. Therefore, using the asset reconciliation spreadsheet, the total purchases will be entered in the Transfers In column, and total Proceeds will be entered in the Transfers Out column. This is the opposite of the cash reconciliation. In the case of assets, each entry in the Transfers Out column represents a sale of an asset and therefore fewer assets held. An entry in the Transfers In column reflects the purchase of an asset, as more assets enter the account. Cash transfers are fairly straightforward, as cash out of one account will result in cash into another account. Asset transfers require a bit more attention. An asset that was transferred is listed under Assets on Hand—End on the asset reconciliation spreadsheet. The carry value of these assets will need to be added to the Transfers Out column, and will reduce the Assets on Hand—End. Subsequently, the asset account that received the asset will reflect an additional asset in and an increase in the CV End column.

For an example of a complete Summary Reconciliation, see §3.56.

§3.35   d. Special Assets

If the accountant is accounting for tangible property of a personal nature, such as jewelry, furniture, and furnishings, these items are listed as assets on hand, in their own column. It is useful to make a column for such items to reflect the complete activity of the accounting on the Summary Reconciliation.

If the tangible personal property is still on hand at the end of the account period, these assets will simply be listed on hand at the beginning and at the end with the same carry value.

If real estate or personal property is sold during the accounting, there will need to be a separate column established to reflect this activity. The carry value established at the beginning will be entered on the first row. Using the real estate reconciliation prepared in the second pass, enter the total receipts and total disbursements in the corresponding row. The total of the Transfers Out column will be entered on the Transfers Out.

PRACTICE TIP➤ While entering the Transfers Out, confirm that there is a corresponding Transfers In to one of the other accounts within the accounting. If not, check with the client. This may reveal a new account to be included in the accounting. It is also a good idea to review the escrow statement to ensure that the "final" closing escrow statement was used to prepare the real estate reconciliation.

Finally, the difference between the carry value and the transfer in will be listed as a gain or loss. This can be calculated directly on the Summary Reconciliation.

§3.36   3. Checking the Spreadsheet

Once the Summary Reconciliation spreadsheet is complete, add up the total of each row into the Total column on the left. Then total the Charges and the Credits separately. Total Charges equal total Credits.

Reconciliation tips:

- Review the column total on the cash reconciliation spreadsheets to ensure that only dates within the accounting period are included.

- Review the column totals for purchases and proceeds to ensure that the totals on the asset reconciliation match the cash reconciliation spreadsheet.

- Review cash transfers to ensure that Transfers In on one spreadsheet match Transfers Out on another spreadsheet.

- Review asset transfers to ensure that carry values were transferred accurately.

Once all accounts, including cash and assets, have been reconciled, and once the sums have been copied to the Summary Reconciliation spreadsheet, it is time to start the fifth pass: Preparing the Schedules (see §3.37).

§3.37   E. Fifth Pass: Preparing the Schedules

In a fiduciary accounting filed with the court, certain schedules are required. In the fifth pass, the accountant will prepare each of these required schedules from the data entered and groomed in the earlier passes. This section includes a discussion of the mechanics, or "how to," of preparing each schedule. To understand the "why" of each schedule, please see the schedule-by-schedule chapters elsewhere in this book.

At this point, the accountant will rely solely on those spreadsheets he or she has already completed. The fifth pass is not merely a giant copy and paste job, however, as care must be taken to ensure that each item is referenced to a particular account and spreadsheet.

The required schedules can be set up as a template for use time and time again. However, there is very little information in the initial setup. Every accounting presents a different story and no two accountings are exactly alike. Each accounting schedule will have unique subheadings, categories, and descriptions.

§3.38   1. Caption

Every schedule in the fiduciary accounting will have a caption. The following is an example of the schedule Assets on Hand—Beginning of Period, discussed in more detail in chap 4. Each schedule should have a caption like the one below, that includes the title of the accounting, the name of the trustee, executor, or administrator, the number of the accounting (see §§2.11–2.14), and the time period.

[TITLE]

[NAME OF TRUSTEE/EXECUTOR/ADMINISTRATOR]
[NUMBER OF ACCOUNTING]
[TIME PERIOD]

Assets on Hand—Beginning of Period

Shares/Par Value	Description	Carry Value

Shares/Par Value	Description	Carry Value

To prepare the schedule, label the categories of assets accounted for. These may include Cash and Cash Equivalents, Equities, Bonds, Annuities, Real Estate, Receivables, and Personal Property. Use these labels as subheadings on the schedule Assets on Hand—Beginning of Period. Each individual asset should be listed on this schedule under the appropriate category.

Each cash account must be listed separately, including separate cash equivalent mutual funds held in a single brokerage account. Similarly, each stock position, bond, or other individual asset must be listed separately. Brokerage accounts must be thought of as baskets that hold assets, not as assets in and of themselves.

Finally, the asset values will be listed under Carry Value. The sum of the figures in this column must equal that in the Summary Reconciliation prepared and balanced in the fourth pass.

See §1.15 for an example.

§3.39   2. Receipts Schedule

The Receipts schedule is where the fiduciary will report all deposits into every account. For more on the Receipts schedule, see chap 6. The schedule should be set up with the following headings:

Date	Description	Description	Income	Principal	Account

The Receipts schedule will include everything listed as a receipt on each of the cash reconciliation spreadsheets. To ensure that all transactions are captured, copy from each cash reconciliation spreadsheet and from each real estate reconciliation spreadsheet the entirety of each transaction in which an item appears in the Receipts column. Paste the copied data into the Receipts schedule. There, sort the copied data in the Receipts column and delete transactions that are not in fact receipts.

PRACTICE TIP➤ Before moving on, the accountant should add up the transactions moved from each account and confirm that the total matches that on the Summary Reconciliation. This will immediately alert the accountant to any transactions that failed to make it to the Receipts schedule.

Once the copied data has been pasted into the Receipts schedule, under the heading Account write the account number from which the transaction data was obtained. The Account column will not appear on the printed version of the schedules, but it will provide a reference point for future questions. Months after the accounting is finished, this column allows the accountant to easily research a particular transaction.

Sort the information by the type of transactions (Column C, *i.e.*, the second Description column). Once this is done, all dividends, interest, and refunds will be grouped together on the Receipts schedule. These groups of items—different types of deposits—will become the various categories required for the Receipts schedule. Use subheadings to set up the categories and allocate each transaction to a category. Categories may include dividends, interest, retirement income, annuity income, and refunds, to name a few.

Next, within each category sort the Receipts by asset name and then date. This sort forms groups of similar transactions (for example, receipts of Chevron dividends) and puts the receipt of these dividends into chronological order. At this point, the accountant can remove the category reference in the transaction description, as it is redundant to report "Chevron dividend" under the Dividend category heading. Finally, subtotal each of the categories on the schedule and create a grand total of all categories at the bottom of the schedule.

Once the transactions have been copied from the cash reconciliation spreadsheets into the Receipts schedule, the source account number has been added, and data has been categorized for every account included in the accounting, the total receipts will match the total receipts on the Summary Reconciliation. Receipts will be allocated between income and principal in the sixth pass: Refining the Accounting.

For a sample of the schedule, see §1.17.

§3.40 3. Additional Property Received During Period of Account Schedule

The Additional Property Received During Period of Account schedule reports all cash or assets that are added to the trust after the beginning of the account period. For more on this schedule, see chap 5. The schedule should appear as follows:

Date	Check #/ Shares	Description	Income	Principal	Account #

During the preparation of the Receipts schedule, there may have been deposits that are not income, refunds, or other credits generated within the normal account activity. These deposits are additions to the trust. These transactions should be copied from the Receipts schedule and pasted to the Additional Property Received During Period of Account schedule. Note, the source account number does not need to be added, as this step was completed with the preparation of the Receipts schedule.

Once copied to the Additional Property Received During Period of Account schedule, the transactions should be listed by date and described by the source of funds. In some cases, this may be a new account or an asset that has been added to the trust. In these cases, the accountant should list the source of funds as well as the title of the account or asset and number of shares, if applicable.

See §1.16 for a sample.

§3.41 4. Disbursements Schedule

The Disbursements schedule should report all payments made from the trust or estate. For more on the Disbursements schedule, see chap 8. The schedule should have the following headings:

Date	Description	Check #	Description	Income	Principal	Account

The Disbursements schedule will be prepared like the Receipts schedule:

- Start by copying from the cash reconciliation spreadsheet each transaction for which a numeral appears in the Disbursements column.

- Paste the copied transactions into the Disbursements schedule.

- Sort the information by the Disbursements column, deleting those transactions that are not in fact disbursements.

- Under the heading Account, add the reference account or source account of the information.

Unlike the Receipts schedule, where tidy categories were created during an earlier pass, the Disbursements schedule will be one long list of payees. To categorize the Disbursements schedule, sort the information by payee. Next, consider the particulars of the administration and group payees into reasonable categories. Categories will include administrative expenses, taxes, real estate expenses, expenses paid in escrow, etc. The number and type of categories depends on how many transactions are listed on the schedule and the type of activity within the trust. For example, in a very long accounting, administrative expenses may be broken down into subcategories such as legal expenses, investment expenses, etc. A trust with several pieces of real property will have a "real estate expenses" category for each property. However, real estate expenses paid in escrow are always their own category and are listed by property.

PRACTICE TIP▶ For Disbursements schedules with hundreds of transactions, it is useful to sort the transactions by payee, add a column outside of the print area, and then type in the category for each entry. Then the transactions can be sorted by category rather than placing each transaction into each category.

During the review and categorization, the accountant may find that some distributions to beneficiaries have been mischaracterized as disbursements. To understand the distinction, see §8.2. Once identified, the distributions should be moved into a category called Distributions. These transactions will be moved to the Distributions schedule when preparing that schedule.

The final step is to sort the transaction by date order within each of the categories and total each category. The total of all categories will match the Disbursements total in the Summary Reconciliation.

For a sample Disbursements schedule, see §1.19.

§3.42   5. Distributions Schedule

The Distributions schedule reports distributions of cash and other property to beneficiaries. For more details on this schedule, see chap 9. The schedule should be set up with the following headings:

Date	Check #/ Shares	Description	Account

To prepare the Distributions schedule, copy from the Disbursements schedule all those transactions identified as distributions and paste them into the Distributions schedule. The Distributions should be sorted by beneficiary and a category created for each beneficiary. Once the transactions are sorted by beneficiary, the description can be changed to the type of distribution. Types of distributions might include cash distributions, income distributions, a monthly allowance, or a settlement distribution. It is important to understand the trust or estate, or to confirm with the fiduciary or his or her attorney to ensure that distributions are properly described.

Assets may have been distributed, as well. Reference the asset reconciliation spreadsheets to identify any securities that were distributed. These should be categorized by recipient and listed with the name of the asset and number of shares.

WARNING➤ The fiduciary will seek credit for the *carry value* of the asset distributed and this value must appear on the Distributions schedule. If the market value is reported, that value should be for information only. Market value should not be used to calculate credits and charges or the accounting will not balance and will not accurately reflect the activity of the trust.

Assets on Hand—End will be reduced by the carry value of assets distributed.

For a sample Distributions schedule, see §1.21.

§3.43   6. Gains and Losses

The Gains schedule and the Losses schedule both report the carry value of the assets sold, the proceeds of the sale and the net gain or loss. For more details on these schedules, see chap 7. The Gains and Losses are reported on separate schedules because that is important to the final reconciliation. The schedules should be set up with the following headings:

Date	Shares	Description	Carry Value	Proceeds	Gain/Loss	Account

Referring to the asset reconciliation spreadsheets, copy all transactions from the Gain/Loss column and paste them to the Gains schedule. Losses will be identified and moved to the Losses schedule after it has been confirmed that the total Gains and Losses together match the Summary Reconciliation.

Once on the Gains schedule, sort the transactions by the Gain/Loss column and delete all transactions in which there was no gain or loss. .

PRACTICE TIP➤ To move information from the asset reconciliation spreadsheet, in which calculations are included to achieve the final reconciliation totals, the accountant must use the "paste special" function in Excel to retain the result of the formulas used to create the asset reconciliation spreadsheet.

The transactions will then be sorted by the Gain/Loss column. Total the Gain/Loss column to ensure that the sum of the gains and losses matches the sum of the gains and losses on the Summary Reconciliation.

PRACTICE TIP➤ If the sum of the Gain/Loss column does not match the sum of the Gain/Loss column on the Summary Reconciliation spreadsheet, the fault may be an omission of the sales of real property and tangible personal property. Remember, the reconciliation spreadsheets did not include the gain or loss. This was calculated by the accountant in the fourth pass.

Once the totals match the Summary Reconciliation, copy the transactions reporting losses to the Losses schedule.

There will be some final formatting to be done on the Gains and Losses schedules. The shares will need to be copied and pasted into the Shares column. Confirm that the carry value and the sales proceeds are reported in the correct columns, sort all transactions by date, and create a Total Gains and Total Losses row.

On the Gains schedule, confirm that the gains are calculated as Proceeds minus Carry Value to ensure a positive number in each row and a positive Total Gains.

Rearrange the data on the Losses schedule so that the Carry Value column is to the left of the Proceeds column, and the calculation in the Gain/Loss column subtracts the sales proceeds from carry value. Confirm that all are positive numbers in each row and in Total Losses.

For sample Gains and Losses schedules, see §§1.18 and 1.20.

§3.44 7. Assets on Hand—End of Period

The schedule Assets on Hand—End of Period will reflect all cash and asset values on the final date of the accounting period. For more details on this schedule, see chap 10. The schedule should be set up with the following headings:

Shares/ Par Value	Description	Carry Value	Market Value	Account #

To prepare the schedule, refer to the cash reconciliation spreadsheets and enter the account name, fund title (if necessary), and cash balance on hand at the end of the accounting period. For cash and cash equivalents, the carry values and market values will be identical, and thus the cash balance can be entered into both the Carry Value (CV) column and the Market Value column.

Add to the schedule Assets on Hand—End of Period each asset on hand at the end by referring to the asset reconciliation spreadsheets. For each asset account, copy and paste the entries listed under the CV End column. (This is a formula column, so the accountant will need to capture the resulting values, not the formulas.)

As the information is transferred from the asset reconciliation spreadsheets to the schedule, add the source account number for future reference. Sort the transactions by asset and categorize by type of asset. Up to this point, the accountant has not categorized assets by type. At this point, the accountant may refer to the final account statements and use asset headings that match the reporting by the brokerage firm. Categories might include equities, bonds, mutual funds, etc. This is also an opportunity to confirm that the final share balance reported on the schedule matches the statements. This step may have been done in the third pass, but should be reviewed again to ensure the transfer of information has not been lost during the fifth pass.

PRACTICE TIP➤ As with the cash accounts, it is a good idea to subtotal the assets by account, prior to categorizing them, to ensure that the totals match the asset reconciliation spreadsheets.

Once the assets are in the correct category, some additional formatting is needed. Confirm that shares, asset names, and carry values are listed in the correct columns. Subtotal each category and add a row for the Total Assets on Hand—End.

The Total Assets on Hand—End will match the Summary Reconciliation. If the total does not match, refer to the Summary Reconciliation to ensure that all assets that were on hand at the beginning of the accounting period have been accounted for. A common mistake is failing to list an asset that did not have any activity, such as a vehicle or real estate, that is on hand at the beginning and at the end of the accounting period.

Finally, referring to the brokerage statements, appraisals, etc., add the market values for each individual asset. This will provide a picture of the current market value for the trust. The market value may be significantly different from the carry value, particularly if the accounting spans a substantial period of time. See discussion of market values at §4.12.

For a sample Assets on Hand—End of Period schedule, see §1.22.

§3.45   8. Changes in Form of Assets

The Changes in Form of Assets schedule reports all activities, such as a purchase or a sale, in which there was a change from Cash to an Asset, or from an Asset to Cash, without a gain or loss. The Changes in Form of Assets schedule is also a convenient place to put other non-cash changes, such as a change in shares outside of a sale or a purchase. See discussion at §6.44. The schedule should be set up with the following headings:

§3.45

Date	Description	Cash	Carry Value	Account #

Referring to the asset reconciliation spreadsheet, copy all transactions for which a numeral appears in the Purchases column. Paste the transactions to the Changes in Form of Assets schedule. Once on the Changes in Form of Assets schedule, sort the transactions by the Purchases column and delete all transactions not reflected in this column.

Sort the transactions again, first by asset name and then by date. There will some additional formatting to move the shares into the correct column and the purchase amount into the Carry Value column.

For each purchase, carry value increases. This increase is reflected as a positive number in the Carry Value column. To reflect the corresponding cash transactions, simply multiply the numeral in the Carry Value column by −1 in the Cash column. This shows the change in form: cash out and carry value in.

Purchases that are part of a dividend reinvestment plan can be entered as Purchases, as outlined in §3.13. However, if there are multiple dividend reinvestment plans or a greater time period is included in the accounting, a separate category for Reinvestments may be used. In this case, the carry value on hand at the beginning can be reconciled to the carry value at the end of the accounting period.

For a sale without a gain or loss, the entry will be the opposite: cash in and carry value out. The accountant has already prepared the Gains and Losses schedules (see §3.43). A quick review of these two schedules will identify the transactions in which there was no gain or loss, and as such, these transactions will be moved to the Changes in Form of Assets schedule.

Non-cash transactions will be identified on the asset reconciliation spreadsheets and will be added as identified by date, asset name, and share increase/decrease. The Changes in Form of Assets schedule can also be used to list accounts opened or closed during the accounting.

For an example of a Changes in Form of Assets schedule, see §1.23.

§3.46   9. Summary of Account

The Summary of Account serves as the cover page for the accounting and reports the totals of each schedule within the accounting. For more on the Summary of Account, see chap 12. The Summary of Account is completed last, as the information for the summary is taken from the schedules within the accounting. For a sample Summary of Account, see §1.14.

The bottom of the schedule should contain a list of "additional schedules" that are included. This list always includes the Changes in Form of Assets schedule. It may also include a Liabilities schedule, or a schedule of Proposed Distributions. For more on these auxiliary schedules, see chap 11.

Copy the Total from each of the schedules within the accounting to the Summary of Account, under the heading Carry Value. Total the Charges and the Credits. The Charges and Credits must be equal on the Summary of Account. If all the cash and assets were reconciled (second pass and third pass) and the Summary Reconciliation was completed and balanced (fourth pass), the Summary of Account will balance.

If the accounting is not balanced at this point, you must go back to the fourth pass to confirm that the Summary Reconciliation is correct. If you identify an error, you must go back further to the second and third pass.

§3.47   F. Sixth Pass: Refining the Accounting

The goal of the sixth pass is to finalize the accounting. Already, the accounting is complete, balanced, and the accountant has a fairly good idea of what happened throughout the accounting period. However, to finalize the accounting, two additional reviews will need to be completed: a review for missing descriptions (§3.48) and a review to allocate income and principal (§3.49).

§3.48   1. Missing Descriptions

First review the accounting for missing descriptions. The accountant may have created a temporary category on the Receipts or Disbursements schedules called "Other" or "Unknown." This did not prevent the accountant from balancing the accounting.

Referring back to the fiduciary's statements, the accountant may quickly review for descriptions missed during the data entry. Using the check register, QuickBooks file, or box of receipts provided by the fiduciary, the accountant must add the source of funds for unknown deposits and payee, and determine the purpose of unknown payments. Once this information is complete, the schedules may need to be adjusted to put the previously unknown transactions into the correct category on the schedule.

§3.49   2. Allocating Income and Principal

Once each transaction has been described, the next review of the accounting allows the accountant to allocate additions, receipts, disbursements, and distributions between income and principal, if such an allocation is required. The accountant may have done this during the fifth pass, but any transactions that were previously unknown must be allocated during the sixth pass. (For information on how to allocate between income and principal, refer to the schedule-by-schedule chapters in this book.)

Once the allocations are complete, the subtotal of income and principal must be added to the Summary of Account. Using the information on the Summary of Account, calculate the income on hand at the end. This is the Income Additions subtotal plus Income Receipts subtotal minus Income Disbursements subtotal. The balance of the Assets on Hand—End of Period are allocated to principal.

§3.50   3. Missing Information

Ideally, the accountant will have every statement, a clear and concise description of each transaction, supporting documents for every appraised value, and zero questions. Because this rarely happens, the following recommendations may help handle any issues that arise.

The fiduciary has made consolidated deposits. Imagine that, when making a deposit at the bank, the fiduciary handed the teller a dividend check, a refund from the homeowners insurance, and some cash found in the residence. The teller added up and processed the three items as one deposit. Because the three items appear as a lump sum on the statements, the accountant lists this as an "unknown" deposit and completes the schedule. However, the fiduciary is responsible for identifying the transactions that make up the deposit. A good fiduciary will make a note of every separate transaction in his or her check register. In this case, the consolidated deposit requires an additional step: breaking down the deposit into the three separate transactions. Each transaction should be listed on the same date with the same source account number, but described and categorized separately.

Statements are missing. The accountant cannot finish the second pass through the fiduciary's data until the fiduciary has produced all of his or her account statements. However, while waiting for missing statements, the accountant can enter all of the data from the existing statements and create an adjustment to represent the missing statement. This adjustment will be the difference—net Receipts or net Disbursements—between the first statement provided and the subsequent statement provided. If the accountant is missing only cash statements (checking and savings accounts), the entire accounting may be completed, leaving an adjustment to deal with during the sixth pass. Once the missing statements are provided, the accountant will remove the adjustment and add the transactions to the schedule. The accountant should make a note of this on the Summary Reconciliation, as the numbers may have shifted a bit on the final schedules, making it harder to trace the transactions in the future.

New accounts are discovered. During the second pass, the accountant may discover the existence of accounts for which the fiduciary has provided no statements. These mystery accounts come to light, for example, when a trustee's checking account statement reveals a transfer out of a trust account to another, as yet unidentified account. Often—especially when the fiduciary is not a professional—the "new" account is revealed to be the fiduciary's personal account. The accountant must demand an explanation when he or she discovers transfers in or out of accounts for which the fiduciary has produced no statements. Occasionally, the mystery transaction reveals an account the fiduciary failed to mention and the accountant must get statements for that newly discovered account before finishing the fiduciary accounting. Just as frequently, the accountant's discovery reveals commingling that must be remedied as quickly as possible.

Transfers are discovered. The accountant will have to address transfers discovered as a result of breaking down lump deposits into their individual transactions, obtaining missing statements, or discovering an account that must be added to the accounting. As discussed earlier in this chapter, the accounting will not balance if a transfer in or transfer out is treated as a receipt or disbursement. The accountant must identify the offsetting transaction.

EXAMPLE▶ A disbursement is made to an unknown account. The disbursement is later identified as a transfer to an account to be included in the accounting. The accountant must go back and take out the deposit and reclassify it as a transfer. This will modify the transaction going all the way back to the first pass. For every transfer in, there must be a transfer out.

II. EXHIBITS

§3.51 A. Form: Spreadsheet for a Checking Account

A completed spreadsheet for a checking account will appear as follows.

WELLS FARGO BANK			
CHECKING A/C #XXXXXX9876			
APRIL CASH TRUST, SALLY CASH TTEE			
DATE	DESCRIPTION	DESCRIPTION	CHECK#
01/01/13	BALANCE		
01/02/13	ACME PLUMBING SUPPLY - WAGES 12/15/10 TO 12/31/10	OTHER RECEIPTS	
01/05/13	MARGARET'S RESTAURANT	MEMORIAL DINNER	204
01/05/13	FRED'S FUNERAL HOME	MEMORIAL SERVICE	205
01/15/13	INTEREST	METLIFE POLICY #XXXX4587 DTD 07/01/05	
03/01/13	BEST BUY	LAPTOP	206
03/15/13	ACME PLUMBING SUPPLY - UNION DEATH BENEFIT	OTHER RECEIPTS	
03/15/13	JAKE CASH	BIRTHDAY GIFT TO GRANDSON	207
03/15/13	SAVINGS ACCOUNT	TRANSFER IN	
03/15/13	RACHEL CASH	CASH DISTRIBUTION	WIRE
03/15/13	MIKE CASH	CASH DISTRIBUTION	WIRE
04/07/13	LAW OFFICES OF LUCY LAWYER	LEGAL FEES	208
06/28/13	WELLS FARGO BANK	WIRE TRANSFER FEE	AUTO
06/28/13	WELLS FARGO BANK	WIRE TRANSFER FEE	AUTO
06/30/13	WIDGET SUPPLIER LP	PARTNERSHIP INCOME	
06/30/13	SALLY CASH	TRUSTEE FEE	209
		TOTALS	

RECEIPTS	TRANSFERS IN	DISBURSEMENTS	TRANSFERS OUT	BALANCE
				$ 16,575.00
$ 3,200.00				$ 19,775.00
		$ 722.36		$ 19,052.64
		$ 1,750.00		$ 17,302.64
$ 21.92				$ 17,324.56
		$ 600.00		$ 16,724.56
$ 3,000.00				$ 19,724.56
		$ 1,000.00		$ 18,724.56
	$ 108,005.80			$ 126,730.36
		$ 50,000.00		$ 76,730.36
		$ 50,000.00		$ 26,730.36
		$ 500.00		$ 26,230.36
		$ 30.00		$ 26,200.36
		$ 30.00		$ 26,170.36
$ 5,200.00				$ 31,370.36
		$ 8,920.44		$ 22,449.92
$ 11,421.92	$ 108,005.80	$ 113,552.80	$ -	

Repeat this process for each checking and savings account to be included in the accounting, creating a separate spreadsheet for each account.

§3.52 B. Form: Spreadsheet for an Investment Account

A completed spreadsheet for an investment account will appear as follows.

\multicolumn{5}{l	}{CHARLES SCHWAB}
\multicolumn{5}{l	}{#XXXX-6549}
\multicolumn{5}{l	}{APRIL CASH TRUST, SALLY CASH TTEE}

DATE	DESCRIPTION	DESCRIPTION	SHARES	RECEIPTS
01/01/13	BALANCE ON HAND			
01/02/13	FRANKLIN CA TAX-FREE INCOME A	PURCHASE	57.063	
01/03/13	PEPSICO INC	DIVIDEND		$ 691.20
01/05/13	FRANKLIN CA TAX-FREE INCOME A	DIVIDEND		$ 383.46
01/07/13	MERCK & CO	DIVIDEND		$ 456.00
01/14/13	FRANKLIN UNIVERSAL TRUST	DIVIDEND		$ 38.00
01/28/13	SCHWAB PREMIER MONEY FUND	DIVIDEND		$ 0.69
02/01/13	NUVEEN CA INVT QUALITY MUN FD	DIVIDEND		$ 76.00
02/01/13	NUVEEN CA MUNICIPAL MKT OPP FD	DIVIDEND		$ 78.00
02/02/13	FRANKLIN CA TAX-FREE INCOME A	DIVIDEND		$ 385.00
02/02/13	FRANKLIN CA TAX-FREE INCOME A	PURCHASE	58.959	
02/09/13	ORACLE CORP	DIVIDEND		$ 120.00
02/15/13	FRANKLIN UNIVERSAL TRUST	DIVIDEND		$ 38.00
02/28/13	ML MONEY MARKET FUND	DIVIDEND		$ 0.85
03/01/13	WELLS FARGO & CO NEW	DIVIDEND		$ 864.00
03/01/13	NUVEEN CA INVT QUALITY MUN FD	DIVIDEND		$ 76.00
03/01/13	NUVEEN CA MUNICIPAL MKT OPP FD	DIVIDEND		$ 78.00
03/01/13	NUVEEN CA INVT QUALITY MUN FD	SHORT TERM CAPITAL GAIN		$ 12.00
03/01/13	NUVEEN CA MUNICIPAL MKT OPP FD	SHORT TERM CAPITAL GAIN		$ 14.00
03/01/13	NUVEEN CA INVT QUALITY MUN FD	LONG TERM CAPITAL GAIN		$ 82.00
03/01/13	NUVEEN CA MUNICIPAL MKT OPP FD	LONG TERM CAPITAL GAIN		$ 86.00
03/01/13	JP MORGAN CHASE & CO 7.900% APR/OCT 30 DUE 12/31/48	ACCRUED INTEREST ON PURCHASES		$ (608.12)
03/01/13	JP MORGAN CHASE & CO 7.900% APR/OCT 30 DUE 12/31/48 CALLABLE $100.00 ON 04/30/18	PURCHASE	24,000.000	
03/02/13	JP MORGAN CHASE & CO 7.900% APR/OCT 30 DUE 12/31/48 CALLABLE $100.00 ON 04/30/19	DIVIDEND		$ 405.20
03/02/13	FRANKLIN CA TAX-FREE INCOME A	PURCHASE	61.116	
03/10/13	CHEVRON CORP	DIVIDEND		$ 4,642.56
03/10/13	EXXON MOBIL CORP	DIVIDEND		$ 2,112.00
03/15/13	FRANKLIN UNIVERSAL TRUST	DIVIDEND		$ 38.00

§3.52

TRANSFERS IN	PROCEEDS OF SALE	DISBURSEMENTS	TRANSFERS OUT	PURCHASES	BALANCE
					$ 30,507.00
				$ 383.46	$ 30,123.54
					$ 30,814.74
					$ 31,196.20
					$ 31,654.20
					$ 31,692.20
					$ 31,692.89
					$ 31,768.89
					$ 31,846.89
					$ 32,231.89
				$ 385.00	$ 31,846.89
					$ 31,966.89
					$ 32,004.89
					$ 32,005.74
					$ 32,869.74
					$ 32,945.74
					$ 33,023.74
					$ 33,035.74
					$ 33,049.74
					$ 33,131.74
					$ 33,217.74
					$ 32,609.62
				$ 24,000.00	$ 8,609.62
					$ 9,014.82
				$ 405.20	$ 8,609.62
					$ 13,252.18
					$ 15,364.18
					$ 15,402.18

Date	Description	Type	Amount		Amount
06/28/13	BANK OF AMERICA CORP	DISTRIBUTION	1,100.000		
06/28/13	CHEVRON CORP	DISTRIBUTION	804.000		
06/28/13	BANK OF AMERICA CORP	DISTRIBUTION	1,100.000		
06/28/13	CHEVRON CORP	DISTRIBUTION	804.000		
03/25/13	BANK OF AMERICA CORP	DIVIDEND		$	22.00
03/31/13	PEPSICO INC	DIVIDEND		$	691.20
03/31/13	ML MONEY MARKET FUND	DIVIDEND		$	4.52
04/01/13	NUVEEN CA INVT QUALITY MUN FD	DIVIDEND		$	76.00
04/01/13	NUVEEN CA MUNICIPAL MKT OPP FD	DIVIDEND		$	78.00
04/04/13	FRANKLIN CA TAX-FREE INCOME A	DIVIDEND		$	406.93
04/04/13	FRANKLIN CA TAX-FREE INCOME A	PURCHASE	62.413		
04/07/13	MERCK & CO	DIVIDEND		$	456.00
04/15/13	FRANKLIN UNIVERSAL TRUST	DIVIDEND		$	38.00
04/15/13	FRANKLIN UNIVERSAL TRUST	SOLD	475.000		
04/20/13	CISCO SYS INC	DIVIDEND		$	116.40
04/30/13	ML MONEY MARKET FUND	DIVIDEND		$	7.59
04/30/13	JP MORGAN CHASE & CO 7.900% APR/OCT 30 DUE	INTEREST		$	948.00
05/02/13	NUVEEN CA INVT QUALITY MUN FD	DIVIDEND		$	76.00
05/02/13	NUVEEN CA MUNICIPAL MKT OPP FD	DIVIDEND		$	78.00
05/03/13	FRANKLIN CA TAX-FREE INCOME A	DIVIDEND		$	408.70
05/03/13	FRANKLIN CA TAX-FREE INCOME A	PURCHASE	61.551		
05/04/13	ORACLE CORP	DIVIDEND		$	144.00
05/05/13	NUVEEN CA MUNICIPAL MKT OPP FD	SOLD	700.000		
05/05/13	NUVEEN CA INVT QUALITY MUN FD	SOLD	1,000.000		
05/05/13	FRANKLIN UNIVERSAL TRUST	SOLD	475.000		
05/16/13	BANK OF AMERICA CORP 8.125% MAY/NOV 15 DUE	INTEREST		$	975.00
05/31/13	ML MONEY MARKET FUND	DIVIDEND		$	7.89
05/31/13	US TREASURY 3.5% DUE 05/31/11	SOLD			
06/01/13	WELLS FARGO & CO NEW	DIVIDEND		$	864.00
06/02/13	FRANKLIN CA TAX-FREE INCOME A	DIVIDEND		$	409.64
06/02/13	FRANKLIN CA TAX-FREE INCOME A	PURCHASE	62.022		
06/10/13	EXXON MOBIL CORP	DIVIDEND		$	2,256.00
06/30/13	PEPSICO INC	DIVIDEND		$	741.60
06/30/13	ML MONEY MARKET FUND	DIVIDEND		$	9.09
		TOTALS		$	**18,883.40**

						$	15,402.18
						$	15,402.18
						$	15,402.18
						$	15,402.18
						$	15,424.18
						$	16,115.38
						$	16,119.90
						$	16,195.90
						$	16,273.90
						$	16,680.83
					$ 406.93	$	16,273.90
						$	16,729.90
						$	16,767.90
		$ 2,932.02				$	19,699.92
						$	19,816.32
						$	19,823.91
						$	20,771.91
						$	20,847.91
						$	20,925.91
						$	21,334.61
					$ 408.70	$	20,925.91
						$	21,089.91
		$ 8,684.35				$	29,754.26
		$ 12,286.75				$	42,041.01
		$ 3,442.34				$	45,483.35
						$	46,458.35
						$	46,466.24
		$ 20,000.00				$	66,466.24
						$	67,330.24
						$	67,739.88
					$ 409.64	$	67,330.24
						$	69,586.24
						$	70,327.84
						$	70,336.93
$ -	$	47,345.46	$ -	$ -	$ 26,398.93		

Repeat this process for each investment account to be included in the accounting, creating a separate spreadsheet for each account.

§3.53 C. Form: Spreadsheet for Real Property

A completed spreadsheet for real property will appear as follows.

PROPERTY ADDRESS: 321 FRANCHISE ROW, ANYTOWN, CA		
TITLE: REAL ESTATE TRUST		
ESCROW STATEMENT TITLE: REAL ESTATE TRUST, THOMAS JONES, TRUSTEE		
DATE	DESCRIPTION	DESCRIPTION
05/15/12	CONTRACT PRICE	
05/15/12	STEWART TITLE COMPANY	REFUND OF PREPAID PROPERTY TAX
05/15/12	BETTER HOMES REAL ESTATE COMPANY	BROKER COMMISSION
05/15/12	PRUDENTIAL REAL ESTATE COMPANY	BROKER COMMISSION
05/15/12	SELLER CREDIT	CREDIT FOR CLOSING COSTS
05/15/12	SUPER CONSTRUCTION	LOADING DOCK REPAIRS REQUIRED FOR SALE
05/15/12	ERNEST EVIRONMENTAL	INSPECTION FEE
05/15/12	STEWART TITLE CO	PRO-RATED RENT COLLECTED FOR MAY 2012
05/15/12	STEWART TITLE CO	SECURITY DEPOSITS
05/15/12	STEWART TITLE CO	ESCROW AND TITLE FEES
05/15/12	STEWART TITLE CO	DOCUMENTATION FEE
05/15/12	STEWART TITLE CO	NOTARY FEE
05/15/12	STEWART TITLE CO	COURIER FEE
5/15/2012	TRANSFER OUT	
		TOTALS
		RECONCILIATION

RECEIPTS		TRANSFERS IN		DISBURSEMENTS		TRANSFERS OUT	
		$	1,675,000.00				
$	2,500.00						
				$	47,265.00		
				$	47,265.00		
				$	25,000.00		
				$	40,000.00		
				$	750.00		
				$	3,125.00		
				$	12,500.00		
				$	1,000.00		
				$	500.00		
				$	20.00		
				$	100.00		
						$	1,499,975.00
$	2,500.00	$	1,675,000.00	$	177,525.00	$	1,499,975.00
		$	**1,677,500.00**			$	**1,677,500.00**

Repeat this process for each parcel of real property to be included in the accounting, creating a separate spreadsheet for each property.

§3.54 D. Form: Spreadsheet for Personal Property

A completed spreadsheet for personal property will appear as follows.

PERSONAL PROPERTY		
FURNITURE AND FURNISHINGS		
DATE	DESCRIPTION	DESCRIPTION
06/01/13	SALES PRICE	
06/01/13	ALLY'S AUCTION HOUSE	CONSIGNMENT COMMISSION ON FURNITURE SALE
06/01/13	TRANSFER OUT	
		TOTALS
		RECONCILIATION

RECEIPTS	TRANSFERS IN	DISBURSEMENTS	TRANSFERS OUT
	$ 3,000.00		
		$ 1,500.00	
			$ 1,500.00
$ -	$ 3,000.00	$ 1,500.00	$ 1,500.00
	$ 3,000.00		$ 3,000.00

§3.55   E. Form: Third Pass Spreadsheet

A completed third pass spreadsheet will appear as follows.

CHARLES SCHWAB				
#XXXX-6549				
APRIL CASH TRUST, SALLY CASH TTEE				

DATE	DESCRIPTION	DESCRIPTION	SHARES	CARRY VALUE BEGINNING
01/01/13	FRANKLIN UNIVERSAL TRUST	ON HAND	1,000.000	$ 6,343.75
01/01/13	NUVEEN CA INVT QUALITY MUN FUND	ON HAND	1,000.000	$ 12,315.00
01/01/13	NUVEEN CA MUN MKT OPPORTUNITY	ON HAND	1,000.000	$ 12,490.00
01/01/13	US TREASURY 3.5% DUE 05/31/11	ON HAND	20,000.000	$ 20,000.00
01/01/13	BANK OF AMERICA CORP 8.125% MAY/NOV 15 DUE 12/31/48 CALLABLE $100.00 ON 05/15/18	ON HAND	24,000.000	$ 23,428.52
01/01/13	BANK OF AMERICA CORP	ON HAND	2,200.000	$ 26,466.00
01/01/13	CISCO SYS INC	ON HAND	1,940.000	$ 39,459.60
01/01/13	MERCK & CO INC	ON HAND	1,200.000	$ 49,608.00
01/01/13	ORACLE CORP	ON HAND	2,400.000	$ 83,256.00
01/01/13	FRANKLIN CA TAX-FREE INCOME FUND A	ON HAND	14,202.081	$ 95,722.03
01/01/13	PEPSICO INC	ON HAND	1,440.000	$ 99,835.20
01/01/13	CHEVRON CORP	ON HAND	1,608.000	$ 177,507.12
01/01/13	WELLS FARGO BANK & CO NEW	ON HAND	7,200.000	$ 252,360.00
01/01/13	EXXON MOBIL CORP	ON HAND	4,800.000	$ 425,808.00

CV CHANGES	CV END	PROCEEDS	GAIN/LOSS	PURCHASES

Date	Security	Transaction	Amount	
01/02/13	FRANKLIN CA TAX-FREE INCOME A	PURCHASE	57.063	
01/15/13	MERCK & CO INC	STOCK SPLIT	1,200.000	
02/02/13	FRANKLIN CA TAX-FREE INCOME A	PURCHASE	58.959	
03/01/13	JP MORGAN CHASE & CO 7.900% APR/OCT 30 DUE 12/31/48 CALLABLE $100.00 ON 04/30/18	PURCHASE	24,000.000	
03/02/13	FRANKLIN CA TAX-FREE INCOME A	PURCHASE	61.116	
03/15/13	BANK OF AMERICA CORP	TRANSFERRED OUT	1,100.000	
03/15/13	BANK OF AMERICA CORP	TRANSFERRED OUT	1,100.000	
03/15/13	CHEVRON CORP	TRANSFERRED OUT	804.000	
03/15/13	CHEVRON CORP	TRANSFERRED OUT	804.000	
04/04/13	FRANKLIN CA TAX-FREE INCOME A	PURCHASE	62.413	
04/15/13	FRANKLIN UNIVERSAL TRUST	SOLD	475.000	
05/03/13	FRANKLIN CA TAX-FREE INCOME A	PURCHASE	61.551	
05/05/13	FRANKLIN UNIVERSAL TRUST	SOLD	475.000	
05/05/13	NUVEEN CA MUN MKT OPPORTUNITY	SOLD	700.000	
05/05/13	NUVEEN CA INVT QUALITY MUN FUND	SOLD	1,000.000	
05/31/13	US TREASURY 3.5% DUE 05/31/11	SOLD		
06/02/13	FRANKLIN CA TAX-FREE INCOME A	PURCHASE	62.022	
		TOTALS		$ 1,324,599.22

			$	383.46
			$	385.00
			$	24,000.00
			$	405.20
			$	406.93
	$	2,932.02		
			$	408.70
	$	3,442.34		
	$	8,684.35		
	$	12,286.75		
	$	20,000.00		
			$	409.64
$ -	$ -	$ 47,345.46	$ -	$ 26,398.93

§3.56　　F. Form: Summary Reconciliation Spreadsheet

The following is an example of a completed Summary Reconciliation spreadsheet.

	TOTAL	WELLS FARGO CHECKING CASH	WELLS FARGO SAVINGS CASH	WELLS FARGO CD CASH
ON HAND - BEGINNING	$ 1,798,991.47	$ 16,575.00	$ 280,567.25	$ -
RECEIPTS	$ 138,729.76	$ 11,421.92	$ 6,424.44	$ 102,000.00
GAINS	$ 260.90	$ -	$ -	$ -
TRANSFERS IN	$ 240,493.19	$ 108,005.80	$ 58,743.00	$ -
TOTAL	$ 2,178,475.32	$ 136,002.72	$ 345,734.69	$ 102,000.00
DISBURSEMENTS	$ 115,052.80	$ 113,552.80	$ -	$ -
LOSSES	$ 2,000.00	$ -	$ -	$ -
DISTRIBUTIONS	$ 203,973.12	$ -	$ -	$ -
TRANSFERS OUT	$ 240,493.19	$ -	$ 108,005.80	$ -
ASSETS ON HAND	$ 1,616,956.21	$ 22,449.92	$ 237,728.89	$ 102,000.00
TOTAL	$ 2,178,475.32	$ 136,002.72	$ 345,734.69	$ 102,000.00

CHARLES SCHWAB/MERRILL LYNCH BROKERAGE		LP WIDGET	LIFE INSURANCE MET LIFE	PERSONAL PROPERTY
CASH	ASSET	ASSET	ASSET	ASSET
$ 30,507.00	$ 1,324,599.22	$ 82,000.00	$ 57,243.00	$ 7,500.00
$ 18,883.40	$ -	$ -	$ -	$ -
$ -	$ 260.90	$ -	$ -	$ -
$ 47,345.46	$ 26,398.93	$ -	$ -	$ -
$ 96,735.86	$ 1,351,259.05	$ 82,000.00	$ 57,243.00	$ 7,500.00
$ -	$ -	$ -	$ -	$ 1,500.00
$ -	$ -	$ -	$ -	$ 2,000.00
$ -	$ 203,973.12	$ -	$ -	$ -
$ 26,398.93	$ 47,345.46	$ -	$ 57,243.00	$ 1,500.00
$ 70,336.93	$ 1,099,940.47	$ 82,000.00	$ -	$ 2,500.00
$ 96,735.86	$ 1,351,259.05	$ 82,000.00	$ 57,243.00	$ 7,500.00

§3.57   G. Form: Summary of Account

The following is an example of a completed Summary of Account.

APRIL CASH TRUST			
SALLY CASH, TRUSTEE			
FIRST ACCOUNTING			
FOR THE PERIOD JANUARY 1, 2013 THRU JUNE 30, 2013			
SUMMARY OF ACCOUNT			
CHARGES			
			CARRY VALUE
ASSETS ON HAND - BEGINNING OF PERIOD			$ 1,798,991.47
ADDITIONS TO TRUST			$ 107,000.00
	INCOME	$ 2,000.00	
	PRINCIPAL	$ 105,000.00	
RECEIPTS - SCHEDULE A			$ 36,781.20
	INCOME	$ 30,413.20	
	PRINCIPAL	$ 6,368.00	
GAINS ON SALES - SCHEDULE B			$ 429.06
		TOTAL CHARGES	$ 1,943,201.73
CREDITS			
DISBURSEMENTS - SCHEDULE C			$ 14,052.80
	INCOME	$ 5,790.22	
	PRINCIPAL	$ 8,262.58	
LOSSES ON SALES - SCHEDULE D			$ 2,168.16
DISTRIBUTIONS - SCHEDULE E			$ 304,973.12
ASSETS ON HAND - SCHEDULE F			$ 1,622,007.65
	INCOME	$ 26,622.98	
	PRINCIPAL	$ 1,595,384.67	
		TOTAL CREDITS	$ 1,943,201.73
ADDITIONAL SCHEDULES			
CHANGES IN FORM OF ASSETS			
LIABILITIES			

4
Assets on Hand— Beginning of Period

I. A MEASURE OF THE FIDUCIARY'S RESPONSIBILITY ON DAY ONE §4.1
 A. Preparing the Schedule Is a Three-Step Process §4.2
 B. The Schedule's Appearance §4.3
 C. Minimum Requirements for Preparing the Schedule
  1. Step One: Identify the Beginning Date
   a. When the Accounts of Guardians and Conservators Begin §4.4
   b. When the Accounts of Personal Representatives of Decedents' Estates Begin §4.5
   c. When the Accounts of Trustees Begin
    (1) When an Income Interest Begins §4.6
    (2) When an Income Interest Ends §4.7
    (3) When the Trustee Starts After a Vacancy §4.8
  2. Step Two: Identify All Property for Which the Fiduciary Is Accountable
   a. First Account: Property for Which Guardians, Conservators, and Personal Representatives Are Responsible §4.9
   b. First Account: Property for Which Trustees Are Responsible §4.10
   c. Second and Subsequent Accounts: Property for Which All Fiduciaries Are Responsible §4.11
  3. Step Three: State the Carry Value of Each Item of Property
   a. Defining Carry Value §4.12
   b. Carry Value in First Accounts of Guardians, Conservators, and Personal Representatives §4.13
   c. Carry Value in Accounts of Trustees §4.14
 D. Differences Between First and Subsequent Accounts
  1. The First Account §4.15
  2. Assets on Hand at the Beginning of Subsequent Account Periods §4.16

E. Best Practices §4.17
F. Principal and Income §4.18
G. Insurance §4.19
H. Income Receipts and Disbursements at the Beginning §4.20
I. Income Received on Behalf of Terminated Mandatory Income Interest §4.21
J. Common Mistakes
   1. Using Negative Numbers §4.22
   2. Failing to Inventory an Asset for Which the Fiduciary Is Responsible §4.23
   3. Including Assets for Which the Fiduciary Has No Responsibility §4.24
   4. Excluding Assets for Which the Fiduciary *Is* Responsible §4.25
   5. Failing to Recognize That a Thing Is an Asset §4.26
   6. Failing or Refusing to Recognize Responsibility §4.27
   7. Failing to Recognize That Responsibility Begins *Now* §4.28
   8. Confusing the Notion of "Wealth" With the Notion of "Responsibility" §4.29
   9. Omitting Commingled Funds and Adjusting Carry Value to Make Account Balance §4.30
   10. Confusing Net Value or Market Value With Carry Value §4.31
   11. Treating Securities Accounts as a Single Property §4.32

II. EXHIBITS
   A. Form: Using Negative Numbers §4.33
   B. Form: Failing to Recognize That a Thing Is an Asset §4.34

§4.1 I. A MEASURE OF THE FIDUCIARY'S RESPONSIBILITY ON DAY ONE

The schedule Assets on Hand—Beginning may be thought of as the gross measure of the fiduciary's responsibility on the first day of an account period. In the fiduciary's first account, the weight of the fiduciary's responsibility is the aggregate gross fair market value of all the assets for which the fiduciary is responsible. In the fiduciary's second and later accountings, the burden of responsibility is no longer measured with gross fair market value. Instead, the fiduciary's responsibility for assets carried from one account period to another is measured with "carry value" (Prob C §1061(a)(10)), a term the Probate Code uses but does not define. For a discussion of carry value, see §§4.12–4.14.

§4.2 A. Preparing the Schedule Is a Three-Step Process

For the fiduciary preparing his or her first account, preparing the schedule Assets on Hand—Beginning of Period is a three-step process:

- The fiduciary must determine the beginning date of the account period;
- The fiduciary must list each asset for which the fiduciary was responsible on that date; and
- The fiduciary must identify the carry value of each such asset.

For fiduciaries preparing a second or subsequent accounting, the schedule Assets on Hand—Beginning of Period will be identical to the schedule Assets on Hand—End of Period from the previous account.

§4.3 B. The Schedule's Appearance

The following example, from the first accounting of the April Cash Trust (see chap 1), illustrates the appearance of the Assets on Hand—Beginning of Period schedule.

APRIL CASH TRUST		
SALLY CASH, TRUSTEE		
FIRST ACCOUNTING		
FOR THE PERIOD JANUARY 1, 2013 THRU JUNE 30, 2013		
ASSETS ON HAND—BEGINNING OF PERIOD		
SHARES/PAR VALUE	DESCRIPTION	CARRY VALUE

The next example, from the first accounting of the Real Estate Trust (see chap 1), further illustrates the appearance of the Assets on Hand—Beginning of Period schedule.

REAL ESTATE TRUST		
THOMAS JONES, TRUSTEE		
FIRST ACCOUNTING		
FOR THE PERIOD JANUARY 1, 2012 THRU JUNE 30, 2012		
ASSETS ON HAND—BEGINNING OF PERIOD		
SHARES/PAR VALUE	DESCRIPTION	CARRY VALUE

For complete sample schedules, see §§1.15, 1.41.

C. Minimum Requirements for Preparing the Schedule

1. Step One: Identify the Beginning Date

§4.4 **a. When the Accounts of Guardians and Conservators Begin**

The guardian's and the conservator's first account must begin on the date the fiduciary is appointed, *i.e.,* the date of the court's order, although there may be a gap between this date and the date the fiduciary's letters are issued and the court's order is otherwise effective.

NOTE▶ The date of appointment is the date used to inventory the guardianship and conservatorship estates. Prob C §2610(a).

There may be a gap between the date of appointment and the date that appointment becomes effective because conservators and guardians must take an oath, post a bond, and have letters issued before the appointment becomes effective. Prob C §§2300, 2310.

Second and subsequent accounts should begin on the date immediately after the ending date of the prior account. This rule is implied from Prob C §1061(a)(1), which mandates a beginning schedule identical to the prior account's ending schedule.

§4.5   b. When the Accounts of Personal Representatives of Decedents' Estates Begin

The first account of the personal representative of a decedent's estate will begin on the date of the decedent's death. Nowhere in the Probate Code is this explicitly stated, but the rule is derived from the following:

- The personal representative must account in the manner of Probate Code §§1060–1064 (Prob C §10900);

- The first account must begin with the "property initially received by the fiduciary" (Prob C §1061(a)(1)); and

- The personal representative's inventory must identify the property to be administered and state the value of each item as of the date of the decedent's death (Prob C §§8800–8802).

Second and subsequent accounts must begin on the day after the ending date of the personal representative's prior account. Again, this rule is implied by Prob C §1061(a)(1), which requires the fiduciary to state the assets on hand at the beginning and specifies that, in a second and subsequent account, this will be the property on hand at the end of the prior account.

NOTE▶ When a personal representative receives assets from the conservator of the estate of a deceased conservatee or from the guardian of a deceased ward, the personal representative may rely on the accountings of these fiduciaries and has no obligation to independently verify the transactions reported in them. Prob C §10902. In this situation, the court should allow the personal representative to begin his or her accounting on the ending date of the prior fiduciary's account, but because the Probate Code does not specifically authorize this, the personal representative may wish to include in the Petition for Probate (Judicial Council Form DE-111) a request for other orders allowing the alternative beginning date.

c. When the Accounts of Trustees Begin

§4.6   (1) When an Income Interest Begins

In practice, it usually is not difficult to determine the date a trustee's account should begin. It is impossible, however, to state a concise rule for making this determination. The problem is that trustees do not always take office promptly, and the trustee who comes late to his or her responsibility may be reluctant to account for the days or months the office of trustee was vacant. In a simple world, the office of trustee would never be vacant. Either the initial trustee would serve for the entire term of the trust, or trustees would succeed one another in lock step, with no intervening vacancies. In such a world, it would be easy to state the beginning date of the first account: it would begin on the date the first income interest began. Each successive account would begin the day after the ending date of the prior account.

The phrase, "when an income interest begins," and its corollary, "when an income interest ends," is used throughout the Uniform Principal and Income Act (UPAIA) (Prob C §§16320-16375) and is defined in Prob C §16345. An income interest begins on the date specified in the trust instrument or, if no date is specified, on the date an asset becomes subject to the trust or to the successive income interest. Prob C §16345. An asset becomes subject to a trust at the following times:

- **Date of transfer.** If a transferor transfers an asset to a trust during the transferor's lifetime, the asset becomes subject to the trust on the date of the transfer. Prob C §16345(b)(1).

    EXAMPLE▶ When a settlor establishes a qualified personal residence trust, the residence becomes subject to the trust on the date the trustee agrees in writing to administer the property, in the case of a third-party trustee, or on the date the settlor declares in writing that the settlor holds the property as trustee, if the settlor is the trustee. Prob C §15200 (methods of creating trusts), §15202 (trust created only if there is trust property), and §15206 (writing required for real property).

- **Testator's death.** If the transfer is by will, even if there is an intervening period of administration, the asset becomes subject to the trust on the date of the testator's death. The intervening administration may be as formal as a proceeding under Division 7 of the Probate Code (*i.e.,* a "probate") or as informal as one of the proceedings under Division 8 of the Probate Code. Often, trustees account for assets received at the end of a prior administration on a separate schedule—Additions to Trust, or

Late Acquired Assets—to emphasize the trustee's lack of control over the asset during the period of administration.

- **Settlor's death.** In the case of assets transferred to the trustee by a third party because of an individual's death, the asset becomes subject to the trust on the date of the individual's death. Prob C §16345(b)(3). For example, if a settlor owned life insurance on himself or herself and named the trustee as the beneficiary of the policy, the policy would become subject to the trust on the date of the settlor's death.

An asset becomes subject to a successive income interest on the day after the preceding income interest ends, even if there is an intervening period of administration to wind up the preceding income interest. Prob C §16345(c).

§4.7   (2) When an Income Interest Ends

An income interest ends on the day before an income beneficiary dies, or on the day before another "terminating event" occurs. Prob C §16345. A terminating event might be a beneficiary's birthday, if the beneficiary's interest in the trust ends as a result of reaching that age; or a terminating event might be the expiration of a term of years. For example, if a settlor created a grantor-retained annuity trust in which the settlor retained an income interest for 10 years, the terminating event would be the expiration of those 10 years.

PRACTICE TIP▶ With an example, the Uniform Principal and Income Act (UPAIA) makes a useful distinction between a trust ending and an income interest ending. If a trust has only one beneficiary and if the trust is to be distributed outright on the beneficiary's death, one might say that the beneficiary's death marks the end of the trust. Yet as long as the trustee holds trust property, he or she will owe duties to one or more persons, including the duty to account. For that reason, instead of speaking of a trust ending, the Act speaks of an income interest terminating. Comment to Prob C §16340.

Income interest ending at death. In many cases, the trustee will use the date of death as the beginning of the accounting period. As an example of an income interest ending at death, consider the qualified terminable interest property trust (QTIP trust) created for the benefit of a surviving spouse which, on the surviving spouse's death, is distributed to the settlor's children in trust. The first income interest in such a trust would be that of the surviving spouse, and the successive income interests would belong to the settlor's children. The first income interest would end the day before the surviving spouse's date of death and the successive income interests would begin on the date of the surviving spouse's death. One might speak of the QTIP trust ending on the day before the surviving spouse's death, but it would be misleading to speak of "the trust" ending on that day. As a result of the surviving spouse's death, the trustee owes duties to different beneficiaries, but the trust has not ended. As long as the trustee holds assets, the trustee will owe duties to someone and will be accountable for the performance of those duties.

In the example of a QTIP trust, if the surviving widow served as trustee during her entire lifetime, her trusteeship would end on her death and the person nominated as successor trustee would be expected to begin serving on that date. If this expectation was met, or even if the successor trustee delayed only briefly before accepting the office of trustee, the successor trustee likely would use the widow's date of death as the beginning date of the successor trustee's first accounting, *i.e.,* the first accounting for the children's trusts.

NOTE▶ If the trustee briefly administered the QTIP trust assets in an administrative trust, the same rules would apply. The beginning date of both the administrative trust and the trusts for the children would be the widow's date of death, but the children's trusts would receive their assets late, after the period of administration in the administrative trust.

§4.8 (3) When the Trustee Starts After a Vacancy

The rules in §§4.6–4.7 suggest the logical beginning point for a trustee's account, but the trustee who assumes office after a vacancy may wish to use as his or her beginning date the date he or she accepts the trust. The beginning date of a trustee's account signifies the date that a person becomes accountable to the beneficiaries. Trustees are accountable for their own actions (Prob C §§16060–16105), but with some exceptions, they are not liable for acts of their predecessors (Prob C §16403). A person nominated in a trust instrument does not become the trustee inadvertently; the person must affirmatively accept the trust and has no duty to do so. Prob C §15600.

All this suggests that a person might not be accountable for events that occurred while the office of trustee was vacant, *i.e.,* prior to the person's acceptance of the trust.

For an easy example of this idea, consider the QTIP trust illustrated in §4.7 and imagine that the successor trustee is a bank that learns of the widow's death a year or more after her passing. It might be a good idea for someone to account for the events of these months, but, depending on what has transpired, the bank might be unwilling or unable to do so. In this situation, the bank would be justified in choosing as the beginning date of its accounting the date the bank accepted the office of trustee.

This text is not the place to develop the arguments for or against holding a person accountable for the events that might have occurred before the person's acceptance of the trust, *i.e.,* before the person became trustee. Neither is it the place for arguments about whether a trustee appointed to fill a vacancy has a duty to account for the events that occurred during that vacancy. The authors only wish to acknowledge that, for some trustees, the beginning date of their first account might be the date the person accepts the office of trustee, which date might be different than the ending date of the trustee's predecessor's account and from the date an income interest began.

> **PRACTICE TIP▶** Successor trustees often wonder what to call their first account. If Tom Trustworthy is accounting for the first time, but his predecessor has twice accounted, is it the "First Account of Tom Trustworthy, trustee of the Wretched Mess Trust"? Is it the "Third Account of the Wretched Mess Trust, Tom Trustworthy, trustee"? In the authors' opinion, either title is defensible and the choice depends on how much the successor trustee wants to distance himself or herself from the predecessor trustee.

2. Step Two: Identify All Property for Which the Fiduciary Is Accountable

§4.9   a. First Account: Property for Which Guardians, Conservators, and Personal Representatives Are Responsible

Within 90 days of appointment, the guardian or conservator must file an Inventory and Appraisal of "all of the estate of the ward or conservatee of which the guardian or conservator has possession or knowledge." Prob C §2610. Using a form provided by the Judicial Council, the guardian or conservator must identify the fair market value of each asset, as of the date of appointment. Prob C §2610.

WARNING▶ Use of the form Inventory and Appraisal (Judicial Council Form CE-160/GC-040) is mandatory. Cal Rules of Ct 7.101(a).

Using the identical form, within 4 months of the date letters are issued, the personal representative of a decedent's estate must file with the court an Inventory and Appraisal of the "property to be administered in the decedent's estate." Prob C §8800. To prepare their schedules of Assets on Hand—Beginning of Period, these fiduciaries merely recapitulate the information reported on their inventories.

§4.10 b. First Account: Property for Which Trustees Are Responsible

The prudent trustee will identify and appraise each trust asset as quickly as reasonably possible. Trustees must provide beneficiaries with a "statement of the assets and liabilities of the trust as of the end of the last complete fiscal year of the trust or as of the end of the period covered by the account." Prob C §16063. The code prescribes no particular form the statement should take and sets no deadline for its preparation. Trustees have a duty to keep beneficiaries reasonably informed (Prob C §16060) and, on demand, trustees must inform beneficiaries about those trust assets relevant to each beneficiary's interest (Prob C §16061). However, trustees generally account only annually and, absent a demand from a beneficiary, no statute requires a trustee to provide a written inventory prior to serving the first annual account. For a full statement of the rules regarding frequency of accounting, see chap 2.

Nevertheless, it is good practice for trustees to prepare written inventories much more quickly than this. Trustees have a duty to:

- Take control of the trust's assets (Prob C §16006);

- Separate them from non-trust assets (Prob C §16009);

- Clearly designate them as trust assets (Prob C §16009); and

- Preserve them and make them productive (Prob C §16007).

Trustees also have a duty to make and keep a record of their administration of the trust. See, *e.g.,* Prob C §1062. It is hard to imagine that a trustee could perform all these duties without listing the assets subject to administration.

PRACTICE TIP➤ Trustee's counsel may wish to impose on their clients a deadline for inventorying and appraising trust assets. Counsel should not imply that the deadline is established by black letter law, but may say that the "authorities" recommend that the task be accomplished within the first 4 months of the trust administration.

§4.11 c. Second and Subsequent Accounts: Property for Which All Fiduciaries Are Responsible

Each fiduciary who prepares a second or subsequent account will prepare a schedule of assets on hand at the beginning of that second or subsequent account period. Guardians, conservators, and personal representatives are required to create a schedule identical to the schedule of assets on hand at the *end* of the prior account. Prob C §1061(a)(1). Trustees whose accounts are submitted for court approval also must do this. Prob C §1060. Trustees who will not petition for court approval also should prepare a beginning schedule identical to the prior account's ending schedule. Failing to do so invites questions about the trustee's administration of those assets that appear to have changed from one period to the next.

3. Step Three: State the Carry Value of Each Item of Property

§4.12 a. Defining Carry Value

Carry value is the value of an asset at the beginning of the fiduciary's relationship with that asset. The date on which carry value is assessed depends on the nature of the proceeding:

- **Conservatorship or guardianship.** In a conservatorship or guardianship, carry value is the asset's gross fair market value on the date of the fiduciary's appointment.

- **Decedent's trust or estate.** In a decedent's estate, or on the death of the settlor of a will-substitute trust, carry value will be the asset's fair market value on the date of the owner's or settlor's death.

- **Transfer of asset to a trust.** When a trust begins on a date unrelated to the settlor's death, carry value will be an asset's value on the date the settlor transferred it to the trust.

- **Acquisition by fiduciary.** When a fiduciary acquires an asset by purchase or trade, carry value is the purchase price or, in the case of an asset acquired by trade, the asset's fair market value on the date of acquisition.

Unlike market values, which will fluctuate during an account period, carry value, which represents the weight of the fiduciary's responsibility, generally does not change. Only if the asset itself changes will carry value change. For example, if a fiduciary carries 100 shares of Widget, Inc. through 7 years of administration, during which time the value of the stock triples, the fiduciary nevertheless will carry the stock at the value it had on the first day of administration. But if the fiduciary acquires more stock in Widget, Inc., the fiduciary will adjust the carry value of the whole position to reflect the additional responsibility.

EXAMPLE➤ If a trustee accepts a trust that owns 100 shares of Widget, Inc. and on the first day of the trust, the fair market value of the Widget, Inc. stock is $15 per share, the trustee will carry these 100 shares at $1500 regardless of what happens to the share price during the term of the trust. If the trustee later buys 12 additional shares of Widget, Inc. for $12 per share, the trustee will add the cost of the new shares to the carry value of the first 100 shares and will carry the whole position at $1644 (calculated: $1500 + (12 × $12) = $1644).

The few other exceptions to the rule that carry value remains unchanged throughout the period of trust or estate administration are discussed in Cantrell & Spoor, Fiduciary Accounting Answer Book, QQ 3:8–3:10 (CCH 2015).

PRACTICE TIP➤ Carry value should not be confused with basis. At times, an asset may have a tax basis that is identical to the asset's carry value, but an asset's basis is calculated according to the statutes and regulations of the Internal Revenue Code and carry value is a product of the state law rules that govern fiduciary accounting. The adjustments to basis required or allowed by federal tax law do not affect an asset's carry value. For example, the adjustment to basis required when a taxpayer depreciates an asset has no effect on the asset's carry value.

§4.13 **b. Carry Value in First Accounts of Guardians, Conservators, and Personal Representatives**

Responsibility for determining the value of the assets on hand at the beginning of a guardianship or conservatorship, or on hand in a decedent's estate as of the decedent's death, is divided between the fiduciary and a probate referee. The fiduciary is responsible for determining the value of all money and "cash items"—a phrase that refers to checks, drafts, money orders, and money market funds (Prob C §§2610(c), 8901), but logically also includes things like life insurance proceeds paid to a personal representative because of the decedent's death. These items are listed on Attachment Number One of the fiduciary's Inventory and Appraisal. The probate referee is responsible for determining the value of all other items of property, which are inventoried on Attachment Number Two. Prob C §§2610(c), 8902. In all cases, the value returned on the Inventory and Appraisal is the gross fair market value of the asset appraised.

NOTE▶ The Probate Code speaks only of a property's "value," without specifying gross or net value; however, the fiduciary's account would never balance if assets were carried at net values.

§4.14 **c. Carry Value in Accounts of Trustees**

Trustees must determine the beginning value of their assets using reasonable means and incurring no more than reasonable expenses. The Probate Code offers no specific guidance for discharging this obligation, but often the trust instrument empowers the trustee to determine the value of the trust estate. Certainly trustees may appraise money and cash assets themselves, and it is reasonable to assume that trustees themselves may appraise such things as securities traded on a public exchange, common vehicles, and other assets for which reliable information is readily available. For property that is more difficult to appraise, the trustee should hire qualified appraisers.

D. Differences Between First and Subsequent Accounts

§4.15 1. The First Account

The accounts of personal representatives, conservators, and guardians are always subject to court approval and therefore must be prepared in conformance with Prob C §§1061-1064. Prob C §1060. In court accountings, the schedule Assets on Hand—Beginning of Period is a recapitulation of the inventories these fiduciaries must file. Prob C §1060(a). The fiduciaries use as their beginning values the fair market values stated on their inventories. Prob C §8802 (personal representatives) and §2610 (conservators and guardians). Trustees who intend to seek court approval of their accounts must prepare their accounts in the same format required of these other fiduciaries. Prob C §1060. Trustees who will not submit their accounts for court approval are not subject to the rigid formatting rules of §§1061-1064, but may find that the format of a court account is nevertheless the best manner of presenting their information.

In a court accounting, the schedule Assets on Hand—Beginning of Period must list all the property on hand at the beginning of the account period. Prob C §1060(a)(1). If it is the fiduciary's first account, for each item the fiduciary must state the property's fair market value as of that date. Prob C §1060(a)(1). For second and subsequent accounts, the fiduciary must state the carry value for each item. Prob C §1061(a)(1), (a)(10). Again, the beginning date for guardians and conservators is the date of appointment. Prob C §2610(a). The beginning date for personal representatives of a decedent's estate is the date of the decedent's death. See Prob C §8802 (personal representative must inventory assets as of the date of death).

For trustees, the schedule Assets on Hand—Beginning of Period is a statement that the trustee has discharged his or her duty to take control of the trust property. Prob C §16006. Include on the schedule all assets for which the trustee was responsible and omit from the schedule assets for which the trustee had no responsibility. In the trustee's first account, the trustee will establish each asset's carry value. On carry value, see §4.12.

§4.16 2. Assets on Hand at the Beginning of Subsequent Account Periods

For court accountings, in the fiduciary's second and later accounts, the schedule Assets on Hand—Beginning of Period will be identical to the prior account's schedule, Assets on Hand—End of Period (Prob C §1061(a)(1)), and each asset must be stated at its carry value (Prob C §1061(a)(10)). Although the fiduciary must disclose market value (see below in §4.31 and the discussion of Auxiliary Schedules in §11.2), carry value will be used when determining whether the account balances. Prob C §1061(a)(1), (a)(10).

§4.17 E. Best Practices

The best way for a fiduciary to present his or her assets on hand at the beginning is to list the assets in a fashion that would allow the beneficiaries to easily compare the schedule to whatever other sources of information the beneficiaries might have about the estate or trust:

- **Guardians, conservators, and personal representatives.** These individuals should list assets in the same order as found in their Inventories and Appraisals.

- **Trustees.** Trustees have two options:

  - **As found on IRS Form 706.** If the trust relationship began on the date of the settlor's death and if an estate tax return is filed, the trustee may want to list assets in the same order as they are found on Form 706. Even if no estate tax return is filed, and if there is no schedule or assignment of assets, the trustee should consider listing assets as they would be found on Form 706.

  - **As found on the schedule or assignment.** Alternatively, if a schedule of assets is attached to the trust instrument, or if there is a separate and detailed assignment of assets, *and* if the schedule or assignment is fairly recent and representative of the assets on hand at the beginning, the trustee might list the assets in the same order as found on that schedule or the assignment.

Within categories such as stocks and bonds, individual holdings may be listed alphabetically. Real property should be listed by county and the counties should be listed alphabetically.

Fiduciaries who seek court approval of their accounts must provide an auxiliary schedule of the market value of the assets on hand at the beginning and end of an account. Prob C §1063. However, most beneficiaries would rather see this information displayed adjacent to the item's carry value on the beginning and ending schedules. The courts find this acceptable and it is therefore a good practice to add to the Assets on Hand—Beginning of Period schedule a column of figures representing market value. For sample accounting, see chap 1. Fiduciaries may not, however, carry the sum of the market-value figures forward to the Summary of Account, because doing so would throw the accounting out of balance.

For suggestions on the amount of detail to use when describing an asset, consider the probate referee's guide, *Using Probate Referees in Trusts, Probate, Conservatorships and Guardianships, Small Estates and Non-probate Matters* (California Probate Referee's Association 2005).

§4.18   F. Principal and Income

NOTE▶ Only personal representatives and trustees must account for principal and income. Prob C §16339.

Unless a more specific rule would allocate the item to income, all of the following are allocated to principal (Prob C §16355(a)):

- Assets received from a transferor during his or her lifetime;
- Assets received from the deceased transferor's estate;
- Assets received from a trust on the termination of an income interest; and
- Assets received from a payor under a contract that names the trust or the trustee as a beneficiary.

NOTE▶ Although life insurance appears to fall within these categories of assets, there is a specific statute that governs life insurance. See Prob C §16358.

Consider the following example of an uncashed check.

REAL ESTATE TRUST
THOMAS JONES, TRUSTEE

FIRST ACCOUNTING
FOR THE PERIOD JANUARY 1, 2012 THRU JUNE 30, 2012
ASSETS ON HAND—BEGINNING OF PERIOD

SHARES/PAR VALUE	DESCRIPTION	CARRY VALUE
	CASH AND CASH EQUIVALENTS	
	UNCASHED CHECK FROM OLD REPUBLIC TITLE PROCEEDS OF 555 RETIREMENT LANE, ANYTOWN SALE CLOSED PRIOR TO DATE OF DEATH	$22,530.00
	TOTAL CASH AND CASH EQUIVALENTS	*$22,530.00*

Note that at the end of the account period, this check will have been cashed and deposited into one of the trust's cash accounts. The check itself will no longer be on hand, but its carry value is accounted for in the sum on deposit at the bank.

One exception to the above rule is that the trustee must allocate to income any amount received as a distribution of income from a trust or a decedent's estate in which the trust has an interest other than a purchased interest. Prob C §16351. Concomitantly, the trustee must allocate to principal amounts received from such a trust or estate in the form of a distribution of principal. Prob C §16351.

Property received from a decedent's estate may be subject to an intervening administration and, although title passes to the trustee on the decedent's death (Prob C §7000), the trustee cannot administer the property until the personal representative distributes it to the trustee. In this situation, the trustee should account for the property as late-acquired assets on the schedule Assets Received During Period of Account. The following example contrasts the manner of accounting for assets received from a transferor during his lifetime with the manner of accounting for assets received from a deceased transferor's probate estate.

EXAMPLE➤ On Sam's death, his will-substitute trust became irrevocable and Tom Trustworthy succeeded to the office of trustee. During his lifetime, Sam had transferred his residence to the trust, but he had failed to transfer his commercial real property. In this situation, Tom Trustworthy would account for the residence as an asset on hand at the beginning and allocate the residence 100 percent to principal. (The carry value would be the property's fair market value on the date of Sam's death.) By contrast, the commercial real estate would be subject to administration in the probate of Sam's pour-over will. If the executor received rents from the tenants in excess of the expenses of administration, on order of final distribution, the executor would distribute to Tom Trustworthy both the real property and the net income from the rents. Tom Trustworthy then would report these two assets on the schedule Assets Received During Period of Account. In addition, he would allocate the commercial real property 100 percent to principal (Prob C §16355(a)) and he would allocate the cash attributable to the net rents 100 percent to income (Prob C §16356). On allocation between principal and income, see chap 13. Finally, if the probate concluded in a reasonable amount of time, the trustee would carry the commercial property at its date-of-death value, regardless of whether the personal representative had claimed a depreciation deduction for that property on an income tax return filed on behalf of the estate. If the probate was unusually protracted, however, the trustee might choose to carry the commercial property at its gross fair market value on the date of delivery to the trustee, to better represent the measure of the trustee's initial responsibility for the property.

§4.19   G. Insurance

The proceeds of a life insurance policy of which the trust is a beneficiary are allocated 100 percent to principal. Prob C §16358. Typically, the fiduciary would report these proceeds as an asset on hand at the beginning and, if the fiduciary is a personal representative, he or she would inventory these proceeds on his or her Inventory and Appraisal, as Attachment Number One items. If the insurance company does not pay the insurance proceeds promptly on the death of the insured and as a result, the company distributes interest on the policy proceeds, this interest would be allocated to income. Prob

C §16357(a). Customarily, the interest also is reported on the schedule Assets on Hand—Beginning of Period, although the interest is in the nature of a receipt.

§4.20 H. Income Receipts and Disbursements at the Beginning

The Uniform Principal and Income Act (UPAIA) (Prob C §§16320-16375) provides extensive guidance for distinguishing between principal and income during the course of the estate or trust administration. These rules are discussed in detail in chap 6. The rules for allocating between income and principal at the beginning of the administration, *i.e.*, on the decedent's death or when an income interest begins, are the topic of the present section. Distinct rules apply to receipts and disbursements with respect to a specific gift. See chap 9. Otherwise, the fiduciary should be mindful of the following rules when preparing his or her schedule of Assets on Hand—Beginning of Period.

At the beginning, a receipt or disbursement that otherwise might be allocated to income may instead be allocated to principal, depending on the item's due date. The pivotal date is the date the income interest ends, discussed above and charted below.

End of Prior Interest	Beginning of Successive Interest
An income interest ends on the day before an income beneficiary dies, or another terminating event occurs, or on the last day of a period during which there is no beneficiary to whom a trustee may distribute income. Prob C §16345(d).	An asset becomes subject to a successive income interest on the day after the preceding income interest ends—even if there is an intervening period of administration to wind up the precedent income interest. Prob C §16345(c).

Allocation to principal. The fiduciary must allocate an income receipt or disbursement 100 percent to principal if it is due before the end of the prior interest, *i.e.*, if its due date is before the date of the decedent's death or before the successive income interest begins. Prob C §16346(a). In other words, such a "receipt" will be treated as an asset on hand at the beginning of the account period, whereas such a "disbursement" will have the effect of reducing the property carried on that schedule.

Allocation to income. By contrast, the fiduciary must allocate an income receipt or disbursement 100 percent to income if (Prob C §16345(b)):

- It is due on or after the date the successive income interest begins, *i.e.,* if it is due on or after the date of death or the date of a terminating event; and

- The item is due periodically.

NOTE▶ A due date is periodic if the item must be paid at regular intervals under a lease, or an obligation to pay interest, or if an entity customarily makes distributions at regular intervals. Prob C §16345(c).

The receipts and disbursements allocated to income are indeed receipts and disbursements and would be accounted for on the schedules bearing those titles.

Apportionment between income and principal. The fiduciary must apportion an income receipt or disbursement between income and principal if the item's due date is not periodic or if it has no due date. The trustee must treat these items as accruing from day to day and must allocate to principal the portion that accrues prior to the date of the decedent's death or the date the income interest begins, and must allocate to income the portion that accrues on or after those dates. Prob C §16345(b).

Income is due or payable on the date the payer is required to make the payment, but if the payment date is not stated, there is no due date for the purpose of the UPAIA. Prob C §16345(c). Distributions from entities described in §16350 are deemed to be due on the date fixed by the entity for determining who is entitled to receive the distribution or, if no date is fixed, on the declaration date for the distribution. Prob C §16345(c). This applies to distributions to shareholders; partners; members of limited liability companies; owners of shares in a regulated investment company, a real estate investment trust (REIT), or a common trust fund; as well as to distributions from entities for which the trustee is accounting separately and from asset-backed securities. Prob C §§16345, 16350.

§4.21   I. Income Received on Behalf of Terminated Mandatory Income Interest

A "mandatory income interest" refers to the right given an income beneficiary to receive net income distributions from an estate or trust. The most common example of a mandatory income interest is the interest of the surviving spouse in a qualified terminable interest property trust (a "QTIP" trust). If a beneficiary has a mandatory income interest in the trust and that beneficiary's interest ends, special rules govern distribution of any "undistributed income" received before the date on which the income interest ended. These rules are found in Prob C §16347.

J. Common Mistakes

§4.22   1. Using Negative Numbers

With few exceptions, negative numbers have no place on the schedules of assets on hand. Liabilities such as margin debt, mortgages, and tax liabilities do not decrease the trustee's responsibility, yet including them on a schedule of assets would reduce the trustee's charges. Fiduciaries must account for liabilities (Prob C §§1063(g), 16063(a)(1)), but should do so on a separate auxiliary schedule, not on the Assets on Hand—Beginning of Period schedule.

NOTE▶ A separate Liabilities schedule is *required* in a court accounting. Prob C §1063(g). See chap 11.

There are only two occasions when negative numbers are stated on the Assets on Hand—Beginning of Period schedule. One is when the account beginning date bisects the purchase of a security. See the example in §4.33, which illustrates the reinvestment of a $383.46 dividend.

In that example, the Schwab Premier Money Fund paid a dividend before April Cash's death. That dividend was being reinvested in more money fund shares, but the purchase had not settled by the date of death. Typically, there is a 2-day delay between the date of a purchase and the date the security is reregistered in the purchaser's name. If the purchaser dies during this delay, the statement for her securities account may show the cash on hand on the date of death, when in fact it has been spent; the statement may also omit the recently purchased securities, though in fact the decedent owns them. In this situation, the accountant would subtract the cash on the Asset on Hand—Beginning of Period schedule.

The second example of when a negative number might appear on the schedule Assets on Hand—Beginning of Period is when there is an overdrawn account. On the schedule Assets on Hand—Beginning of Period, the fiduciary is representing how much cash is in each account *and* the sum of the cash on hand. Listing the overdrawn account only as a liability would overstate the cash on hand.

§4.23 2. Failing to Inventory an Asset for Which the Fiduciary Is Responsible

Guardians, conservators, and personal representatives sometimes account for assets that they have failed to inventory. When the court discovers this problem, it will not accept the accounting until the asset has been inventoried and appraised. The best practice, therefore, is for the fiduciary to reconsider the inventories before petitioning for court approval of his or her accounting. If the fiduciary has collected receipts from an asset not inventoried, unless the asset was purchased during the period of the account, the fiduciary must inventory the asset. Similarly, the fiduciary also should double check that the values of Attachment Number One items were correctly stated.

§4.24 3. Including Assets for Which the Fiduciary Has No Responsibility

The fiduciary who creates a schedule Assets on Hand—Beginning of Period is saying, "This is the extent of my responsibility." Trustees must account for *trust* assets, but nothing else. For example, typically trustees will *not* account for:

- Joint tenancy property;
- Pay-on-death accounts;
- Probate assets;
- IRA proceeds;
- Life insurance proceeds;
- Annuity payments; and
- Social security payments.

Concomitantly, the other fiduciaries—guardians, conservators, and personal representatives—do not account for trust assets. A conservator might account for a joint tenancy account, but a personal representative would not. Before listing an asset on the schedule, Assets on Hand—Beginning of Period, the fiduciary should be sure that he or she is responsible for the asset. Fiduciaries should not include on this schedule assets for which they bear no responsibility.

§4.25 4. Excluding Assets for Which the Fiduciary *Is* Responsible

Just as it is a mistake to account for assets for which the fiduciary has no responsibility, it is a mistake to omit from the schedule, Assets on Hand—Beginning of Period, assets for which the fiduciary *is* responsible. Household goods are among the most commonly forgotten assets, for example:

- Appliances, such as a washer or a dryer;
- Televisions;
- Computers, including tablets and other mobile devices; and
- Furnishings.

§4.26 5. Failing to Recognize That a Thing Is an Asset

Inexperienced fiduciaries may not recognize that something is an asset. For example, the right to sue to redress a wrong, sometimes called a "chose in action," is an asset, and the fiduciary has a duty to take reasonable steps to collect it. Prob C §2401 (guardians and conservators), §9650 (personal representatives), §16010 (trustees). If the estate on hand at the beginning includes a chose in action, this asset belongs on the schedule Assets on Hand—Beginning of Period, even though the asset's carry value may be exceedingly difficult to determine. See §4.34, in which the settlor's home burned during his lifetime and at his death he had yet to resolve a dispute with his insurance company over the amount the company should pay.

§4.27 6. Failing or Refusing to Recognize Responsibility

Trustees also may not recognize, or may wish to ignore, responsibility for an asset. For example, the daughter who becomes the trustee on her mother's death may not want to collect the debt her brother owes the trust. Or even more likely, she may not want to collect the debt she herself owes the trust. In the first instance, the trustee's failure to collect her brother's debt would be a breach of the trustee's duty to enforce the claims that are a part of the trust property. Prob C §16010. In the second, the trustee's failure to collect from herself would be a breach of the trustee's duty not to deal with trust property for her own benefit. Prob C §16004(a). In either instance, failing to list the receivable as an asset on hand would misstate the measure and nature of the fiduciary's responsibility.

§4.28 7. Failing to Recognize That Responsibility Begins *Now*

Regarding hard-to-collect assets, a trustee may recognize his or her responsibility to collect an asset, but fail to realize that the responsibility alights the day the fiduciary takes office. Accounts receivable are a good example of this phenomenon. If a receipt is due when the fiduciary takes office, it is an asset on hand at the beginning (Prob C §16346) and should be identified as such on the schedule Assets on Hand—Beginning of Period. Omitting a receivable from this schedule and accounting for it only when it is received, *i.e.,* on the Receipts schedule, suggests that the fiduciary's responsibility for the asset only began on collection. In fact, if the receivable existed at the beginning of the account period, the trustee's duty to administer the receivable existed then, too.

The proper way to account for such a receivable would be to state it on the Assets on Hand—Beginning of Period schedule and when the fiduciary finally collects the receivable, show the collection as a change in form of asset. Prob C §1063(b). See chap 11. If the trustee accepts less than full payment as payment in full, he or she must account for the transaction as a loss. See chap 7. If the trustee receives payment in full plus interest, the principal amount due would be accounted for as a change in form of principal asset and the interest would be accounted for as a receipt. See chap 6.

Refunds are another example of this phenomenon. Some refunds are in fact receipts—for example, the refund paid when the personal representative cancels the decedent's magazine subscriptions. But if the right to collect the refund existed on the beginning date, the trustee should account for the refund as an asset on hand at the beginning. Prob C §16346. For example, if the decedent was awaiting the receipt of an income tax refund claimed on a return filed during his or her lifetime, the personal representative should report this refund as an asset on hand at the beginning. The right to collect is also the duty to collect (Prob C §16006), and one purpose of the accounting is to show the trustee's discharge of his or her duties.

§4.29   8. Confusing the Notion of "Wealth" With the Notion of "Responsibility"

Trustees may recognize that a fund contributes nothing to the value of the trust and, unclear on the purpose of a fiduciary account, omit the fund from the schedule of assets on hand. Tenant security deposits are an example of this problem. Although these funds add nothing to the value of the trust estate, they are yet another thing for which the trustee is responsible. When the trustee takes office, if he or she assumes responsibility for tenant security deposits, they should be scheduled as an "asset" on hand. See Prob C §16356 (amounts received as refundable deposits, including security deposits or for future rent, "shall be added to principal and held subject to the terms of the lease ... until the trustee's contractual obligations have been satisfied"). Because the funds are also a liability, they should be identified as such on an auxiliary schedule. See chap 11.

§4.30   9. Omitting Commingled Funds and Adjusting Carry Value to Make Account Balance

Fiduciaries often omit from their schedules of assets the funds the fiduciary has commingled, but commingled funds are trust and estate assets, even though they are in the "wrong" account. *Kobida v Hinkelmann* (1942) 53 CA2d 186. The best practice for a fiduciary who administers a commingled fund is to disclose the commingling in an accounting that also reveals that the fiduciary has remedied the breach by segregating the trust or estate assets and designating them as such.

Another mistake that implicates the trustee's fiduciary duty involves adjusting carry values. If the trustee's account does not balance, the trustee should not hide the imbalance by adjusting carry values. Indeed, it would be dishonest to do so.

§4.31   10. Confusing Net Value or Market Value With Carry Value

Assets on hand are always stated at their gross *carry* value. Prob

C §1061(a)(1), (a)(10). At the beginning of the trustee's administration, carry value and market value may be identical, but it is a mistake to confuse the two.

§4.32 11. Treating Securities Accounts as a Single Property

An account at a securities brokerage is not an asset. Such accounts are more like containers full of assets. The fiduciary must report each stock position as a separate asset. Similarly, each bond is a separate asset, as is each mutual fund. Additionally, the cash held in a securities account must be accounted for separately, as cash.

II. EXHIBITS

§4.33 A. Form: Using Negative Numbers

In the example below, the Schwab Premier Money Fund paid a dividend before April Cash's death. For a discussion of this schedule, see §4.22.

CASH TRUST
SALLY CASH, TRUSTEE
FIRST ACCOUNTING
FOR THE PERIOD JANUARY 1, 2013 THRU JUNE 30, 2013
ASSETS ON HAND - BEGINNING OF PERIOD

SHARES / PAR VALUE	DESCRIPTION	CARRY VALUE	
CASH AND CASH EQUIVALENTS			
	CHARLES SCHWAB CASH INVESTMENT A/C #XXXX-6549	$ (383.46)	
	CHARLES SCHWAB SCHWAB PREMIER MONEY FUND INVESTMENT A/C #XXXX-6549	$ 30,890.46	
	TOTAL CASH AND CASH EQUIVALENTS	$ 30,507.00	
	TOTAL ASSETS	$ **30,507.00**	

CASH TRUST
SALLY CASH, TRUSTEE
FIRST ACCOUNTING
FOR THE PERIOD JANUARY 1, 2013 THRU JUNE 30, 2013
CHANGES IN FORM OF ASSETS

DATE	SHARES	DESCRIPTION	CASH	CARRY VALUE
REINVESTMENTS				
01/01/13	14,202.081	BALANCE		$ 95,722.03
01/02/13	57.063	FRANKLIN CA TAX-FREE INCOME A	$ (383.46)	$ 383.46

§4.34 B. Form: Failing to Recognize That a Thing Is an Asset

In the following example, the settlor's home burned during his lifetime and at his death he had yet to resolve a dispute with his insurance company over the amount the company should pay. For a discussion of this scenario, see §4.26.

DAVID JONES TRUST
THOMAS JONES, TRUSTEE

FIRST ACCOUNTING
FOR THE PERIOD JANUARY 1, 2012 THRU JUNE 30, 2012
ASSETS ON HAND - BEGINNING OF PERIOD

SHARES / PAR VALUE	DESCRIPTION	CARRY VALUE
CASH AND CASH EQUIVALENTS		
	BANK OF AMERICA CHECKING A/C #XXXXXX6789	$ 5,279.53
	BANK OF AMERICA SAVINGS A/C #XXXXXX6789	$ 75,002.15
	PROPERTY MANAGEMENT COMPANY	$ 1,000.00
	UNCASHED CHECK FROM OLD REPUBLIC TITLE PROCEEDS OF 555 RETIREMENT LANE, ANYTOWN SALE CLOSED PRIOR TO DATE OF DEATH	$ 22,530.00
	TOTAL CASH AND CASH EQUIVALENTS	$ 103,811.68
REAL ESTATE		
	RESIDENCE 987 SUNNYSIDE STREET, ANYTOWN, CALIFORNIA	$ 750,000.00
	RESIDENCE 654 FORECLOSURE WAY, ANYTOWN, CALIFORNIA	$ 275,000.00
	COMMERICAL PROPERTY 321 FRANCHISE ROW, ANYTOWN, CALIFORNIA	$ 1,500,000.00
	APARTMENT BUILDING 111 MANAGEMENT AVE, ANYTOWN, CALIFORNIA	$ 1,200,000.00
	LAND (UNIMPROVED) ANYTOWN, CALIFORNIA	$ 200,000.00
	TOTAL REAL ESTATE	$ 3,925,000.00

SHARES / PAR VALUE	DESCRIPTION		CARRY VALUE
RECEIVABLES			
	DUE FROM REBECCA JONES (12 MOS RENT ON FORECLOSURE WAY)	$	24,000.00
	TOTAL RECEIVABLES	*$*	*24,000.00*
OTHER ASSETS			
	STATE FARM INSURANCE CO CLAIM PENDING RE: FIRE AT 555 RETIREMENT LANE, ANYTOWN, CA	$	125,000.00
	2010 MERCEDES C230 VIN K47834N923498M	$	7,000.00
	2007 MALIBU SPEEDBOAT VIN B987345H0934	$	15,000.00
	OTHER ASSETS	*$*	*147,000.00*
	TOTAL ASSETS	**$**	**4,199,811.68**

5
Additional Property Received During Period of Account

I. DEFINING THE "ADDITIONAL PROPERTY RECEIVED DURING PERIOD OF ACCOUNT" SCHEDULE §5.1
   A. Defining Carry Value §5.2
   B. The Additional Property Schedule's Appearance §5.3

II. MINIMUM REQUIREMENTS FOR PREPARING THE SCHEDULE
   A. Preparing the Schedule for the Fiduciary's First Account §5.4
   B. Preparing the Schedule for the Fiduciary's Second and Subsequent Accounts §5.5p
   C. Supplemental Inventory §5.6

III. PRINCIPAL AND INCOME: RECEIPTS FROM DECEDENT'S ESTATE AND OTHER TRUSTS §5.7

IV. FORM: ADDITIONS TO TRUST SCHEDULE §5.8

§5.1 I. DEFINING THE "ADDITIONAL PROPERTY RECEIVED DURING PERIOD OF ACCOUNT" SCHEDULE

The schedule Additional Property Received During Period of Account is where the fiduciary reports assets that are received during an account period in which assets are neither receipts nor assets on hand at the beginning of the period. Prob C §1061. This schedule is sometimes referred to as the "Late Acquired Assets" schedule and in many trust and probate administrations the fiduciary collects no assets that would belong on this schedule.

§5.2 A. Defining Carry Value

Carry value is the "unifying element" that links the beginning of a fiduciary's account to the end of the account period. English & Whitman, Fiduciary Accounting and Trust Administration Guide, chap 3 (ALI ABA, 2d ed 2009). Carry value allows beneficiaries to track the fiduciary's handling of an asset from the date the fiduciary shoulders responsibility for the property until the date the fiduciary has discharged his or her responsibility. On carry value, see §§4.12-4.14. On the schedule Additional Property Received During Period of Account, carry value is almost always the value of the asset when the fiduciary receives it.

§5.3 B. The Additional Property Schedule's Appearance

The schedule Additional Property Received During Period of Account is similar in appearance to the schedule Assets on Hand—Beginning of Period, except that the Additional Property schedule also has a column in which the fiduciary reports the date the property was received.

The example in §5.8 accounts for the trustee's late discovery of cash found in the settlor's residence and for the receipt of a certificate of deposit after the order of final distribution in the deceased settlor's estate.

II. MINIMUM REQUIREMENTS FOR PREPARING THE SCHEDULE

§5.4 A. Preparing the Schedule for the Fiduciary's First Account

In the fiduciary's first account, the schedule Additional Property Received During Period of Account is used to report assets received by the fiduciary after the beginning date of the accounting.

EXAMPLE 1▸ A father established a trust for his son and named Tom Trustworthy as trustee. Trustworthy began serving as trustee after the father transferred $100,000 to the trust and Trustworthy's schedule Assets on Hand—Beginning of Period shows this amount. Three months into the period of the first account, if the father transfers real property to the trust, the real property would be reported on the schedule Additional Property Received During Period of Account.

This schedule is also used to report assets received on distribution from a decedent's estate.

EXAMPLE 2▶ When Julia created her revocable trust, she transferred her real property to herself as trustee, but never re-titled her financial assets to reflect trust ownership. On Julia's death, her financial assets were subject to administration in the probate of her pour-over will and the trustee received the assets 9 months after Julia's death, on order of final distribution from the probate court. The financial assets had been "subject" to the trust from the date of Julia's death (Prob C §16345(b)(2)), *i.e.*, from the beginning date of the trustee's account, but they were not received by the trustee until late in the first year of the trust administration. The trustee would account for the receipt of these financial assets on the schedule Additional Property Received During Period of Account.

In Example 1 above, the carry value of the real property would be the fair market value of the real property on the date the father transferred it to the trust. In Example 2, the carry value of Julia's financial assets would be the value of those assets on the date the trustee received the assets, even though the assets had been subject to the trust since the date of Julia's death. Prob C §16345(b)(2). Such an adjustment, from the date-of-death value (*i.e.*, the value at which the personal representative carried the assets) to the value on receipt by the trustee, allows beneficiaries to measure the trustee's performance in isolation. If the late-received asset was instead carried at its date-of-death value, either the trustee would receive credit for the asset's appreciation in the decedent's estate or the trustee would appear responsible for the asset's loss of value during the prior administration.

On carry value generally, see Cantrell & Spoor, Fiduciary Accounting Answer Book, QQ 3:8–3:10 (CCH 2015) or English & Whitman, Fiduciary Accounting and Trust Administration Guide, chap 3 (ALI ABA, 2d ed 2009).

§5.5 B. Preparing the Schedule for the Fiduciary's Second and Subsequent Accounts

In a fiduciary's second or a subsequent account, the schedule Assets on Hand—Beginning of Period should be identical to the ending schedule of the prior account. (This is required of accounts filed with the court. Prob C §1061(a)(1).) Thus, the fiduciary who would report additional property must do so on the schedule Additional Property Received During Period of Account. On this schedule the fiduciary would report, for example, an item once thought worthless and later found to be valuable. The Additional Property schedule is also where the fiduciary would report assets transferred between two trusts.

EXAMPLE▶ Tom Trustworthy assumed the office of trustee after a car accident in which married settlors perished. The trust required Trustworthy to allocate the wife's trust estate to one sub-trust and the husband's to another. Sometime after serving his first account on the trust's respective beneficiaries, Trustworthy learned that he had made a mistake. He had carried the painting by Picasso as an asset belonging to the husband's trust when in fact, the painting had belonged to the wife. In his second account for the husband's trust, Trustworthy will report the solution to this problem by reporting the transfer of the painting from to the wife's trust on the schedule Losses on Sales or Other Dispositions. In his second account for the wife's trust, Trustworthy will report receiving the painting on the schedule Additional Property Received During Period of Account.

§5.6 C. Supplemental Inventory

Early in their administrations, guardians, conservators, and trustees are required to inventory the assets they administer. Often, when preparing their first accounts, these fiduciaries realize they are accounting for an asset that was not inventoried. It is imperative the fiduciary promptly inventory that asset on a Supplemental Inventory. The court will not approve the account of a guardian, conservator, or personal representative if the account contains assets that were not properly inventoried. *Conservatorship of Hume* (2006) 139 CA4th 393.

§5.7 III. PRINCIPAL AND INCOME: RECEIPTS FROM DECEDENT'S ESTATE AND OTHER TRUSTS

When the trustee receives a distribution from a decedent's estate or from another trust, the trustee must allocate to income any amounts identified as income by the distributing fiduciary and must allocate to principal amounts identified as principal. Prob C §16351.

NOTE▶ The fiduciary responsible for the distributing entity, *i.e.*, the trustee or personal representative, is also required to account for principal and income, and so should identify the property distributed as one or the other, or some proportion of each. Indeed, every trustee and every personal representative must account for principal and income as required by the Uniform Principal and Income Act (UPAIA) (Prob C §§16320-16375), unless the trust or will provides otherwise. Prob C §§16320, 16335, and 16339.

Typically, such distributions would not be "receipts" to the receiving trustee because, all along, the property had been "subject" to the receiving trust, even though there was an "intervening period of administration" in a decedent's estate or another trust. Prob C §16345(b). The trustee should report such late-received property on the schedule Additional Property Received During Period of Account. Fiduciaries accounting to the court must report collection of the property on this schedule and may not report the transaction on the Receipts schedule. Prob C §1061(a)(2).

§5.8   IV. FORM: ADDITIONS TO TRUST SCHEDULE

The following sample schedule from the April Cash Trust accounts for the trustee's late discovery of cash found in the settlor's residence, and for the receipt of a certificate of deposit after the order of final distribution in the deceased settlor's estate.

APRIL CASH TRUST

SALLY CASH, TRUSTEE

FIRST ACCOUNTING

FOR THE PERIOD JANUARY 1, 2013 THRU JUNE 30, 2013

ADDITIONS TO TRUST

DATE	DESCRIPTION	INCOME	PRINCIPAL
02/20/13	CASH FOUND IN SETTLORS RESIDENCE APARTMENT 2A		$ 5,000.00
06/25/13	CERTIFICATE OF DEPOSIT RECEIVED FROM ESTATE OF CARSON CASH, FATHER OF DECEDENT (INCLUDES INCOME FROM 12/31/12)	$ 2,000.00	$ 100,000.00
	TOTAL INCOME AND PRINCIPAL	$ 2,000.00	$ 105,000.00
	TOTAL ADDITIONS TO TRUST	$ **107,000.00**	

6
Receipts

I. ACCOUNTING FOR RECEIPTS §6.1

II. THE RECEIPTS SCHEDULE'S APPEARANCE §6.2

III. PREPARING THE SCHEDULE, AT A MINIMUM §6.3
   A. Categorize §6.4
   B. Receipts in Escrow §6.5
   C. Disclose Mistakes §6.6
   D. Borrowed Funds §6.7

IV. RECEIPTS OF PRINCIPAL AND INCOME
   A. Income Is a Defined Term §6.8
   B. Receipts From Entities Are Generally Income §6.9
   C. Receipts From Entities, Allocation to Principal §6.10
   D. Receipts From Entities, Mutual Funds §6.11
   E. Receipts From a Decedent's Estate and Other Trusts; Trust-Owned Businesses Accounting Separately; Derivatives, Options, and Asset-Backed Securities §6.12
      1. Receipts From a Decedent's Estate and Other Trusts §6.13
      2. Receipts From Trust-Owned Businesses for Which Trustee Accounts Separately §6.14
      3. Receipts From Derivatives, Options, and Asset-Backed Securities §6.15
   F. Receipts Normally Allocated 100 Percent to Principal §6.16
   G. Receipts From Rental Properties §6.17
   H. Bank Account Interest Owed to Trustee §6.18
   I. Interest on Bonds Owed to Trustee §6.19
   J. Special Rules for Assets Listed in Prob C §16357(c) §6.20
   K. Insurance Against Loss of Occupancy, Income, or Profits; Property Insurance; Life Insurance

1. Allocation of Insurance Proceeds Between Income and Principal §6.21
2. Which Schedule? §6.22
    a. Accounting for Property Insurance Proceeds §6.23
    b. Accounting for Title Insurance Proceeds §6.24
    c. Accounting for Life Insurance Proceeds §6.25
3. Dividends §6.26

L. Insubstantial Receipts §6.27
M. Deferred Compensation, Qualified and Non-Qualified Plans, IRAs, Annuities §6.28
    1. Trusts Not Described in IRC §2056(b)(5) or §2056(b)(7) §6.29
    2. Trusts Described in IRC §2056(b)(5) or §2056(b)(7) §6.30
        a. If Payor Provides Documentation §6.31
        b. If Separate Fund Payor Provides No Documentation §6.32
N. Liquidating Assets: Leasehold Interests, Patents, Copyrights, Royalty Rights, Notes With No Stated Interest §6.33
O. Mineral, Water, and Natural Resources §6.34
    1. Receipts Allocated 100 Percent to Income §6.35
    2. Production Payments Under an Agreement That Provides for Interest or Its Equivalent §6.36
    3. Other Receipts; the 90:10 Rule §6.37
    4. Trust-Owned Interests Acquired On or Before January 1, 2000 §6.38
P. Timber and Related Products §6.39
    1. Timberland Acquired After January 1, 2000 §6.40
    2. Timberland Acquired On or Before January 1, 2000 §6.41
Q. Derivatives and Options §6.42
R. Collateral-Backed Securities §6.43
S. Dividend Reinvestment Programs §6.44
T. Specifically Gifted Property §6.45

V. COMMON MISTAKES
    A. Late-Received Assets Are Not Receipts §6.46
    B. In General, Sales Proceeds Are Not Receipts §6.47
    C. Receipts Collected During a Sale Are Not Gross Sales Proceeds §6.48
    D. Omitting From Assets on Hand the Source of a Receipt §6.49

E. Failing to Account for Receipts From Commingled Assets §6.50
F. Form 1099 Phantom Income Is Not a Receipt §6.51
G. Transfers Between Accounts Are Not Receipts §6.52

VI. EXHIBITS
   A. Form: Receipts Schedule §6.53
   B. Form: Receipts From Entities §6.54
   C. Form: Dividends and Capital Gains §6.55
   D. Form: Receipts From Rental Properties §6.56
   E. Form: Bank Account Interest §6.57
   F. Form: Interest on Bonds Owed to Trustee §6.58
   G. Form: Assets Listed in Prob C §16357(c) §6.59
   H. Form: Dividend Reinvestment Programs §6.60

§6.1   I. ACCOUNTING FOR RECEIPTS

Personal representatives, conservators, and guardians must report the amount of any receipts of income or principal, "showing the nature or purpose of each item, the source of the receipt and the date thereof." Prob C §§1061, 1062(a). Receipts do *not* include (Prob C §1061(a)(3)):

- Property on hand at the beginning of the account period;
- The value of any assets received during the period of the account that are not assets on hand at the beginning, *i.e.*, late received assets (see chap 5); or
- Amounts received from a trade or business if the fiduciary is accounting for these receipts separately.

By contrast, all the law requires of trustees is "a statement of receipts and disbursement of principal and income that have occurred in the last complete fiscal year." Prob C §16063(a)(1). Nevertheless, the best practice is for trustees to account for receipts in the same manner as would a personal representative. That method of accounting is the subject of this chapter.

§6.2   II. THE RECEIPTS SCHEDULE'S APPEARANCE

Fiduciaries who account to a California court must report "receipts" on a schedule separate from their schedule of Gains on Sales or Other Dispositions. Prob C §1062(a), (d). For an example of the appearance of this schedule, see §6.53.

§6.3 III. PREPARING THE SCHEDULE, AT A MINIMUM

In court accountings, for each receipt the fiduciary must state (Prob C §§1061–1062):

- The date;
- The source;
- The purpose; and
- The amount.

The fiduciary may not lump together common items and disclose only their sum.

EXAMPLE▶ The following would not be allowed (Prob C §1062(a)):

| Annual rent on 100 Main Street, Unit A | $120,000 |

The presentation in the example above is impermissible because of the information that might be obscured by such a summary presentation. Consider the below illustration of all the information that might be revealed if the fiduciary accounted as the Probate Code required. (Imagine the fiduciary's name is Frederic Basso.) Accounting only for the sum of the rents collected obscures the fact that the fiduciary failed to collect rent from The Hat Shop in February and June, appears to have rented the property to himself for 3 months (at a reduced rate), and is now renting to a high-risk tenant.

Date	Payor	Income
January 1, 2010	The Hat Shop	$10,000
March 1, 2010	The Hat Shop	$10,000
April 1, 2010	The Hat Shop	$10,000
May 30, 2010	The Hat Shop	$10,000
July 1, 2010	Frederic Basso	$5,000
August 1, 2010	Frederic Basso	$5,000
September 1, 2010	Frederic Basso	$5,000
November 1, 2010	Ye Local Marijuana Shoppe	$20,000

Date	Payor	Income
December 1, 2010	Ye Local Marijuana Shoppe	$45,000
TOTAL		**$120,000**

§6.4   A. Categorize

Rather than reporting receipts in a purely chronological fashion, the fiduciary should group them by payor—for example, "Tenant, 100 Main Street." Beneath each payor's name, the receipts should be organized chronologically. This allows the beneficiaries to see, for example, that the fiduciary has collected the rent on the same day each month. It is also a good practice to list the payors in exactly the same order as they appear in the schedule Assets on Hand—Beginning of Period. This makes it easy for beneficiaries, the court, and other interested parties to determine whether the fiduciary has collected the return due from each asset and to identify those assets that were not productive.

§6.5   B. Receipts in Escrow

Typically, the transactions conducted through an escrow are disbursements, including loan repayments, realtor's commissions, notary fees, payments of property taxes, and processing fees. Occasionally, however, the fiduciary will also collect a receipt in escrow. These receipts are often accounted for under the general heading "Refunds" on the Receipts schedule. See the example in the Real Estate Trust Receipts schedule in §1.42, which accounts for the refund of prepaid property tax.

§6.6   C. Disclose Mistakes

When accounting for a mistake, plainly reveal it and identify the entry that shows the fiduciary has fixed the problem. For example, consider the problem of the trustee who has commingled trust money in a personal bank account by depositing a trust receipt into this account. The best practice would be for this trustee to:

- Disclose the commingling when accounting for the receipt;
- Show the problem has been remedied by transferring an appropriate amount from the trustee's personal account to the appropriate trust account;

- Disclose the transfer from the personal account on the Changes in Form of Assets schedule;
- Calculate any interest earned while commingling and deposit this amount (a receipt of income under Prob C §16357) into the trust account;
- Have the trustee's attorney examine the trust for exculpatory language, since many trusts exculpate trustees for all but bad faith and gross negligence; and
- If exculpatory language exists, point out the language in a footnote explaining the transaction.

§6.7   D. Borrowed Funds

Borrowed money is accounted for as a receipt and the concomitant obligation to repay the money is accounted for on the Liabilities schedule. Accountants accustomed to preparing financial accounts will recognize that the borrowed funds do not increase the value of the estate accounted for, but because these funds increase the variety and amount of property for which the fiduciary is responsible, the funds must be reported amongst the fiduciary's other charges. The Receipts schedule is the place to do this.

IV. RECEIPTS OF PRINCIPAL AND INCOME

§6.8   A. Income Is a Defined Term

The Uniform Principal and Income Act (UPAIA) (Prob C §§16320–16375) broadly defines "income" as (Prob C §16324)

> money or property that a fiduciary receives as a current return from a principal asset. The term includes a portion of receipts from a sale, exchange, or liquidation of a principal asset, to the extent provided in Article 5.1 (commencing with Section 16350), 5.2 (commencing with Section 16335), or 5.3 (commencing with Section 16360).

The Act does not, however, define principal. Principal is identified by reference to when and how the property was obtained. Principal receipts are discussed in this chapter. For a discussion of initial principal, see §4.18.

Under the Act, receipts fall into three categories:

- Receipts from entities;
- Receipts not normally apportioned (*i.e.,* receipts that are usually 100 percent income or 100 percent principal); and
- Receipts normally apportioned.

Within these categories, the Act addresses nearly every receipt imaginable. The three categories of receipts presented in the Act are discussed in §§6.10–6.12.

§6.9   B. Receipts From Entities Are Generally Income

In general, money received from an "entity" is income. Prob C §16350(b). There are, however, two broad exceptions to the general rule. The first exception arises from the definition of "entity." Under Prob C §16350(a)(1):

"Entity" includes:	"Entity" does not include:
• Corporations;	• Trusts;
• Partnerships;	• Decedent's estates;
• Limited liability companies;	• A business for which the trustee is accounting separately; and
• Regulated investment companies;	• Asset-backed securities.
• Real estate investment trusts;	
• Common trust funds; and	
• Any other organization in which a trustee has an interest.	

Trusts, decedent's estates, businesses for which the trustee accounts separately, and asset-backed securities are discussed at §§6.12–6.15. The second exception is found in Prob C §16350(c), and is discussed in §§6.10–6.11.

For a sample receipts schedule showing money received from an entity, see §6.54.

§6.10 C. Receipts From Entities, Allocation to Principal

When the fiduciary receives any of the following from an entity, the fiduciary must allocate the receipt 100 percent to principal:

NOTE► These transactions often are not receipts but are instead sales or other dispositions, accounted for on the schedule of Gains on Sales or Other Dispositions, the schedule of Losses on Sales or Other Dispositions, or the schedule of Changes in Form of Assets.

- Property other than money (Prob C §16350(c)(1));
- Money received in one distribution or a series of related distributions in exchange for a part or all of a trust's interest in the entity (Prob C §16350(c)(2));
- Money received in total or partial liquidation of the entity, as defined in Prob C §16350(d) (Prob C §16350(c)(3)); and
- Money received from an entity that is a regulated investment company or a real estate investment trust if the money distributed is a capital gain dividend for federal income tax purposes (Prob C §16350(c)(4)).

Although few reported cases analyze the Uniform Principal and Income Act (UPAIA) (Prob C §§16320–16375), two address the meaning of "money received in total or partial liquidation of an entity": *Hasso v Hasso* (2007) 148 CA4th 329 and *Manson v Shepherd* (2010) 188 CA4th 1244. These cases predate the 2014 amendment to Prob C §16350(d), which now defines partial liquidations as follows:

> (d) For purposes of [determining whether money is received as part of a partial liquidation], money shall be treated as received in partial liquidation to the extent the amount received from the distributing entity is attributable to the proceeds from a sale by the distributing entity, or by the distributing entity's subsidiary or affiliate, of a capital asset. The following shall apply to determine whether money is received in partial liquidation:
>
> (1) A trustee may rely without investigation on a written statement made by the distributing entity regarding the receipt.
>
> (2) A trustee may rely without investigation on other information actually known by the trustee regarding whether the receipt is attributable to the proceeds from a sale by the distributing entity, or by the distributing entity's subsidiary or affiliate, of a capital asset.

(3) With regard to each receipt from a distributing entity, if within 30 days from the date of the receipt the distributing entity provides no written statement to the trustee that the receipt is a distribution attributable to the proceeds from a sale of a capital asset by the distributing entity or by the distributing entity's subsidiary or affiliate and the trustee has no actual knowledge that the receipt is a distribution attributable to the proceeds from a sale of a capital asset by the distributing entity or by the distributing entity's subsidiary or affiliate, then the following shall apply:

(A) The trustee shall have no duty to investigate whether the receipt from the distributing entity is in partial liquidation of the entity.

(B) If, on the date of receipt, the receipt from the distributing entity is in excess of 10 percent of the value of the trust's interest in the distributing entity, then the receipt shall be deemed to be received in partial liquidation of the distributing entity, and the trustee shall allocate all of the receipt to principal. For purposes of this subparagraph, the value of the trust's interest in the distributing entity shall be determined as follows:

(i) In the case of an interest that is a security regularly traded on a public exchange or market, the closing price of the security on the public exchange or market occurring on the last business day before the date of the receipt.

(ii) In the case of an interest that is not a security regularly traded on a public exchange or market, the trust's proportionate share of the value of the distributing entity as set forth in the most recent appraisal, if any, actually received by the trustee and prepared by a professional appraiser with a valuation date within three years of the date of the receipt. The trustee shall have no duty to investigate the existence of the appraisal or to obtain an appraisal nor shall the trustee have any liability for relying upon an appraisal prepared by a professional appraiser. The term "professional appraiser" shall refer to an appraiser who has earned an appraisal designation for valuing the type of property subject to the appraisal from a recognized professional appraiser organization.

(iii) If the trust's interest in the distributing entity cannot be valued under clause (i) or clause (ii), the trust's proportionate share of the distributing entity's net assets, to be calculated as gross assets minus liabilities, as shown in the distributing entity's yearend financial statements immediately preceding the receipt.

(iv) If the trust's interest in the distributing entity cannot be valued under clause (i), (ii), or (iii), the federal cost basis of the trust's interest in the distributing entity on the date immediately before the date of the receipt.

§6.11 D. Receipts From Entities, Mutual Funds

In general, the Uniform Principal and Income Act (UPAIA) (Prob C §§16320–16375) characterizes receipts as either income or principal without respect to how the Internal Revenue Code would characterize the transaction. Receipts from mutual funds are an exception to this rule. Short-term capital gain, which is taxed as ordinary income and reported on Form 1099-DIV as an ordinary dividend, is allocated to income. Comment to Prob C §16350. By comparison, money distributed from a mutual fund or real estate investment trust, which money is a capital gain dividend for federal income tax purposes, is allocated to principal. Prob C §16350(c)(4).

In the example in §6.55, Sally Cash regularly received dividends from mutual funds—for example, Nuveen CA Municipal Market Opportunity Fund—which she accounted for as receipts of income. She also received short-term capital gains and long-term capital gains from the same funds. She accounted for these as income and principal, respectively.

§6.12 E. Receipts From a Decedent's Estate and Other Trusts; Trust-Owned Businesses Accounting Separately; Derivatives, Options, and Asset-Backed Securities

Also excluded from the general rule that receipts from entities are allocated to income, are receipts from decedent's estates and other trusts; receipts from trust-owned businesses for which the trustee is accounting separately; and receipts from derivatives, options, and asset-backed securities. These exceptions are discussed in §§6.13–6.15.

§6.13 1. Receipts From a Decedent's Estate and Other Trusts

When the trustee receives a distribution from a decedent's estate or from another trust, the trustee must allocate to income any amounts identified as income by the distributing fiduciary. Likewise, the trustee must allocate to principal amounts identified as principal. Prob C §16351. See chap 5.

§6.14 2. Receipts From Trust-Owned Businesses for Which Trustee Accounts Separately

The trustee's authority to account separately for a trust-owned business is discussed in §§13.2-13.4. When this election is properly made, the trustee may characterize the receipts from the business as principal or income, at the trustee's discretion. Prob C §16352(b). Trustees who make this election, and who intend to present their accounts to the court for approval, must account for the receipts on a separate schedule: Receipts From Trade or Business.

§6.15 3. Receipts From Derivatives, Options, and Asset-Backed Securities

Historically, derivatives, options, and asset-backed securities have been considered high-risk investments and as a result, one seldom finds such investments in a fiduciary's portfolio. Therefore, this text does not cover the procedure for accounting for the receipts from these investments. Receipts from derivatives, options, and asset-backed securities are the subject of Prob C §§16366-16367 and the practitioner who must account for receipts from these assets should consult those statutes. On sales of options, see §6.42. On sales of asset-backed securities, see §6.43.

§6.16 F. Receipts Normally Allocated 100 Percent to Principal

Under the heading "Receipts Not Normally Apportioned" (see Prob C §§16353-16358) the Uniform Principal and Income Act (UPAIA) (Prob C §§16320-16375) identifies six categories of "receipts" that usually are allocated to principal. However, in a fiduciary accounting prepared in the manner of Prob C §§1060-1064, not all of these receipts are reported on the schedule of Receipts. For example, sales and condemnation proceeds would be reported on either the Losses on Sales or Other Dispositions schedule, the Gains on Sales or Other Dispositions schedule, or the Changes in Form of Assets schedule. Other such "receipts" are noted below.

The trustee must allocate to principal all of the following:

- To the extent the UPAIA does not allocate the receipt to income, assets received from a transferor during the transferor's lifetime, assets received from a decedent's estate or from a trust with a terminating income interest, and assets received from a payor under a contract naming the trust or its trustee as beneficiary. Prob C §16355(a), referring to Ch 3, Pt 4, Div 9, of the Probate Code. See also Assets on Hand—Beginning of Period, discussed in chap 4, and Additional Property Received During Period of Account, discussed in chap 5.

- Subject to any contrary rules in Probate Code §§16350–16367, money or other property received from the sale, exchange, liquidation, or change in form of a principal asset, including realized profit. Prob C §16355(b), referring to Art 5.2, Ch 2, Pt 4, Div 9, of the Probate Code.

NOTE▶ When the money or property received exceeds the asset's carry value, report the transaction on the schedule Gains on Sales or Other Dispositions, discussed in chap 7. When the asset's carry value exceeds the money or property received, report the transaction on the schedule Losses on Sales or Other Dispositions, also discussed in chap 7. When the asset's carry value and the value of the money or other property received are the same, report the transaction on the schedule Changes in Form of Assets.

- Amounts recovered from third parties to reimburse the trust for disbursements related to environmental matters, including the cost of inspections, the cost of environmental remediation, the expense of preventing the future release of toxic substances, penalties for violating environmental laws, and the cost of collecting from those liable for the environmental contamination, to the extent the recovery is not based on the loss of income. Prob C §16355(c).

- Proceeds of property taken by eminent domain (but allocate to income any separate award made for the loss of income during an accounting period during which a current income beneficiary had a mandatory income interest). Prob C §16355(d).

NOTE▶ When the money received exceeds the condemned asset's carry value, report the transaction on the schedule Gains on Sales or Other Dispositions, discussed in chap 7. When the condemned asset's carry value exceeds the money received, report the transaction on the schedule Losses on Sales or Other Dispositions, also discussed in chap 7. When the condemned asset's carry value and the condemnation proceeds are equal, the transaction is reported on the schedule Changes in Form of Assets.

- Net income received in an accounting period during which there is no beneficiary to whom a trustee may or must distribute income. Prob C §16355(e). On receipts generally, see chap 6.

PRACTICE TIP▶ In an accounting period during which there is no income beneficiary, the fiduciary would account for principal and income as one normally would. Then, on the schedule Assets on Hand—End of Period, the fiduciary would make an adjusting entry, allocating the net income to principal.

- Other receipts allocated to principal as provided in Prob C §§16360-16367. Prob C §16355(f). See chap 13.

§6.17   G. Receipts From Rental Properties

Rents from real or personal property are allocated 100 percent to income, as is any payment received when a lease is canceled or renewed. Prob C §16356. By contrast, amounts received as a refundable deposit (including security deposits and deposits toward future rent, *e.g.*, "last month's rent") are allocated 100 percent to principal and held subject to the terms of the lease. Prob C §16356. Until the trustee's contractual obligations are fulfilled, the trustee may not distribute such principal to a beneficiary. Prob C §16356. The trustee may alert beneficiaries to this impediment by identifying the refundable deposit on the Liabilities schedule.

In the example in §6.56, the trustee reports rents from Betty's Bargain Boutique, Cheryl's Cheesesteaks, and Ernie's Electronics—all tenants in 321 Franchise Row—and reports rental income from an apartment building at 111 Management Avenue unit by unit.

§6.18   H. Bank Account Interest Owed to Trustee

Interest on obligations payable to the trustee is allocated 100 percent to income. Prob C §16357(a). This rule applies to interest paid on bank deposits such as savings accounts, certificates of deposit, and checking accounts, as well as to interest paid on notes held by the trustee, and to interest paid on promises not evidenced by a promissory note. For an example of the trustee accounting for income from Bank of America, see §6.57.

§6.19 I. Interest on Bonds Owed to Trustee

Interest on bonds, like interest on bank deposits, is also allocated 100 percent to income. This rule applies to bonds acquired at a discount, short-term obligations such as United States Treasury Bills, long-term obligations such as United States Savings bonds, zero-coupon bonds, and discount bonds that pay interest during part, but not all, of the period before maturity. Comment to Prob C §16357. On the purchase of a bond, if interest has accrued since the last date the bond paid interest, that accrued interest is the property the seller; and the buyer purchases not only the bond, but the accrued interest as well. Thus, when the fiduciary purchases the bond, the amount expended exceeds the carry value of the bond. To accurately reflect the carry value of the bond, the fiduciary will account for the purchase by deducting the accrued interest on the Receipts schedule. This is the only occasion when a fiduciary would use a negative number on the Receipts schedule.

For an example of a trustee accounting for income from a J.P. Morgan Chase bond, see the example in §6.58. This example has a Changes in Form of Assets schedule, a Receipts schedule, and an Assets on Hand—End of Period schedule. In this example, the fiduciary expended $24,608.12 to purchase the $24,000 J.P. Morgan bond. The bond is carried at $24,000 and on the Receipts schedule, the trustee subtracts the $608.12 of interest that belongs to the selling party. By so doing, when the bond pays interest, in this example $948.00, the net accurately reflects what the trustee has earned.

Special rules apply to the sale of such obligations to pay money to the trustee. (Note that sales are reported on schedules of gains, losses, or changes in the form of principal assets, not on schedules of receipts.) See chap 7.

§6.20 J. Special Rules for Assets Listed in Prob C §16357(c)

Before characterizing an asset as "an obligation to pay money to the trustee," the practitioner must determine whether the asset is one of those listed in Prob C §16357(c), for which the Uniform Principal and Income Act (UPAIA) has special rules. For example, there are special rules for receipts from deferred compensation plans, individual retirement accounts, annuities, and other contractual arrangements requiring payments for services rendered to, or property transferred to, the payor. Prob C §§16357(c), 16361. There are special rules for "liquidating assets," such as patents, copyrights, leaseholds, and royalties. Prob C §§16357(c), 16362. There are also special rules for mineral and water interests (Prob C §§16357(c), 16363), for timber (Prob C §§16357(c), 16364), for derivatives (Prob C §§16357(c), 16366), and for collateral financial assets and asset-backed securities (Prob C §§16357(c), 16367).

The example in §6.59 shows the trustee collecting principal and interest payments from the obligor on a promissory note payable to the trustee. That payor, Land Investors LLC, paid monthly interest of $666.67 and made one payment of principal in the amount of $5000. These transactions are reported on the Receipts schedule and the Changes in Form of Assets schedule, respectively.

K. Insurance Against Loss of Occupancy, Income, or Profits; Property Insurance; Life Insurance

§6.21   1. Allocation of Insurance Proceeds Between Income and Principal

The rules governing allocation of insurance proceeds between income and principal are summarized below.

Allocate the following to principal:	Allocate the following to income:
• Proceeds of life insurance (Prob C §16358);	• Proceeds of a contract insuring the trustee against the loss of occupancy or other use by an income beneficiary; loss of income; or, subject to Prob C §16352, loss of profits from a buiness; and
• Proceeds on a contract insuring the trust or the trustee against the loss of, damage to, or destruction of a trust asset (Prob C §16358);	
• Proceeds of title insurance (Prob C §16357); and	• Dividends, if paid on a policy, the premiums of which are paid from income.
• Dividends, if paid on a policy, the premiums of which are paid from principal (Prob C §16358).	

The above does not apply to annuities or other contracts described in Prob C §16361. Prob C §16358(c).

§6.22   2. Which Schedule?

Which schedule a fiduciary will use to report the collection of insurance proceeds depends on the nature of the contract and the nature of the claim. If the contract remains in force after the fiduciary makes and collects on a claim, the money received as payment of the claim would be a receipt. On the procedure for handling property insurance proceeds, see §6.23. On handling title insurance proceeds, see §6.24. On life insurance proceeds, see §6.25.

§6.23   a. Accounting for Property Insurance Proceeds

The procedure for handling property insurance proceeds depends on the nature of the claim.

EXAMPLE 1▶ Trust property is damaged by a small fire isolated in the property's kitchen. The trustee would account for the insurance proceeds as a receipt. Because this property insurance normally would not be carried as an asset on hand, and because the policy's value would not be diminished by the claim, the trustee is simply charged with responsibility for the proceeds.

EXAMPLE 2▶ A trust-owned vehicle is totaled. The trustee would report the receipt of insurance proceeds on either the Gains on Sales or Other Dispositions or the Losses on Sales or Other Dispositions schedule, where the trustee could show that the proceeds have replaced the vehicle as an asset of the trust estate. See §1.45.

§6.24   b. Accounting for Title Insurance Proceeds

The reasoning behind the treatment of property insurance proceeds also dictates the treatment of title insurance proceeds. If a title dispute resulted in a trust or estate losing all or a significant portion of some real property, the fiduciary would report collecting the title insurance proceeds on either the Gains on Sales or Other Dispositions or the Losses on Sales or Other Dispositions schedule. Reporting in this fashion would allow the fiduciary to show both that he or she had collected the insurance proceeds and that the insured property had either diminished in value or had been lost. On the other hand, if the title dispute were minor and at its conclusion the subject property was little changed, the trustee might report the collection of insurance proceeds on the Receipts schedule. In all cases, the proceeds would be trust accounting principal. Prob C §16358.

§6.25   c. Accounting for Life Insurance Proceeds

Life insurance proceeds are almost always accounted for as assets on hand at the beginning of an account period because the death of the insured so often marks the end of an income interest. Only rarely do fiduciaries collect on a policy insuring someone who is not either the decedent, in the case of a decedent's estate, or the settlor or beneficiary of a trust. In this rare situation, which schedule the fiduciary would use to report the "receipt" depends on whether the policy was owned by the estate or trust the fiduciary administered.

EXAMPLE 1► If a trust becomes irrevocable on the death of the settlor and the trustee receives the proceeds of a life insurance policy that insured the settlor's life, the trustee would report the policy as a principal asset (Prob C §16358) on hand at the beginning of the account period. Traditionally, the trustee also would report on this schedule any interest paid on the policy proceeds, although the interest is trust accounting income (Prob C §16357(a)) and could be reported on the Receipts schedule.

EXAMPLE 2► **Policy owned by the trust.** If the policy was a trust-owned policy on the life of the settlor's business partner, the trustee would report collecting the policy proceeds on either the Gains on Sales or Other Dispositions or the Losses on Sales or Other Dispositions schedule, or the Changes in Form of Assets schedule, depending on whether the trustee collected more than, less than, or the equivalent of the carry value of the policy.

EXAMPLE 3► **Policy not owned by the trust.** By contrast, if the trustee received policy proceeds from a policy not owned by the trust, the trustee should report the money on the schedule Assets Received During Period of Account.

§6.26 3. Dividends

Dividends paid by insurance companies are routinely reported as receipts. The trustee should allocate such dividends to principal or income depending on the source of the premium payments. The trustee should report dividends as receipts of income when the policy premiums are paid from income; when premiums are paid from principal, any dividends would be receipts of principal. Prob C §16358.

§6.27 L. Insubstantial Receipts

Instead of allocating an "insubstantial" receipt partially to income and partially to principal, the trustee may allocate the receipt entirely to principal when all of the below conditions are met (Prob C §16360):

- An allocation otherwise would be required under Prob C §16361, §16362, §16363, §16364, or §16367 (sections addressing payments from individual retirement accounts, annuities, pension plans, profit-sharing plans, stock bonus plans, stock ownership plans, receipts from liquidating assets, receipts from mineral and water interests or other natural resources, receipts from timber harvests and timber products, and payments from asset-backed securities);

- The trust is not one of the trusts described in Prob C §16336(b);

- The trust is one that requires all income to be paid to a surviving spouse in order to qualify the trust assets for the marital deduction from the gift or estate tax; and

- The settlor intended that transfers to the trust would qualify for a gift tax exclusion and the adjustment would affect the actuarial value of an income interest in the trust.

Probate Code §16360 was enacted to relieve trustees of the duty to make relatively small allocations between income and principal, while preserving the trustee's ability to do so when the absolute dollars are significant. Comment to Prob C §16360.

§6.28 M. Deferred Compensation, Qualified and Non-Qualified Plans, IRAs, Annuities

Fiduciaries who collect receipts from a "separate fund" that will pay for a fixed number of years or during an individual's lifetime, must allocate those receipts as provided in Prob C §16361. This section governs receipts from (Prob C §16361):

- Deferred compensation plans;
- Qualified and non-qualified retirement plans;
- Individual retirement accounts;
- Annuities; and
- Other contracts that pay to the trustee because of services rendered or property transferred to the payor in exchange for future payments.

Prob C §16361 provides two sets of rules for receipts from such separate funds. One set applies to all trusts except those for which an election was made to qualify for the marital deduction from the estate tax under IRC §2056(b)(7) or which qualifies for the marital deduction under IRC §2056(b)(5). Another set applies to all other trusts, *i.e.*, trusts that are qualified terminal interest property trusts (QTIP trusts) or power of appointment marital trusts.

§6.29   1. Trusts Not Described in IRC §2056(b)(5) or §2056(b)(7)

If the trust is not a trust described in either IRC §2056(b)(5) or §2056(b)(7), *i.e.*, the trust is not a QTIP trust nor a marital-deduction power of appointment trust, and the trustee receives a payment from a separate fund described in Prob C §16361, the trustee must allocate the payment between principal and income in keeping with the payor's characterization of the payment. The rules are as follows:

- If the payor characterizes any portion of the payment as interest, as a dividend, or as a payment made instead of interest or a dividend, the trustee must allocate that portion of the payment to income (Prob C §16361(b));

- If the payor characterizes no portion of the payment as interest, as a dividend, or as a payment instead of interest or a dividend, and all or part of the payment is required to be made, the trustee must allocate the payment 10 percent to income and 90 percent to principal (Prob C §16361(c)); or

- If no part of a payment is required to be made or the payment received is the entire amount to which the trustee is entitled, the trustee must allocate the entire payment to principal. (A payment is not "required to be made" if it is made because the trustee exercises a right of withdrawal.) Prob C §16361(c).

§6.30 2. Trusts Described in IRC §2056(b)(5) or §2056(b)(7)

The so-called 90:10 rule of Prob C §16361(c) could pose a problem in trusts where the trustee has elected that the trust qualify for the marital deduction under either IRC §2056(b)(5) or §2056(b)(7). To guard against this, in 2009, the Legislature enacted subsections (d)–(f) of Prob C §16361.

NOTE▶ Subsections (d)–(f) apply to the affected trusts on the following dates: (1) if the trust is not funded by January 1, 2010, on the date of the decedent's death; (2) if the trust is initially funded in 2010, on the date of the decedent's death; (3) if the trust is not described in (1) or (2), on January 1, 2010.

These subsections allow the trustee to allocate more to income and less to principal and also allow the trustee to demand greater distributions from the payor. Prob C §16361(f). These rules for allocating between principal and income apply only if their application is necessary to qualify a series of payments for the marital deduction. Prob C §16361(e). If necessary, which of the rules the trustee must use depends on whether the separate fund payor provides documentation reflecting the internal income of the separate fund.

§6.31 a. If Payor Provides Documentation

If the separate fund payor provides documentation reflecting the internal income of the separate fund, such as a Form 1099, the trustee must allocate payments from the separate fund between principal and income, as follows (Prob C §16361(f)):

- The trustee must allocate to income a payment from the separate fund, to the extent of the internal income of the separate fund, and must distribute that amount to the surviving spouse;
- Even if the separate fund does not pay the trust the full share of the separate fund's internal income allocable to the trust, if the separate fund provides documentation reflecting the internal income of the separate fund, the trustee must allocate the internal income of the separate fund as if that fund were a

separate trust subject to the Uniform Principal and Income Act (UPAIA) (Prob C §§16320-16375). And note:

- The surviving spouse may compel the trustee to require the person administering the separate fund to distribute this internal income to the trustee;
- If the payments to the trust from the separate fund are less than the trust's share of the separate fund's internal income, the surviving spouse may compel the trustee to allocate principal to income in an amount equal to the difference between the separate fund's internal income and the amount paid to the trust;
- The trustee must allocate to principal that portion of the payment from the separate fund not allocated to income.

§6.32   b. If Separate Fund Payor Provides No Documentation

If the separate fund payor does not provide the trustee with documentation regarding the separate fund's internal income, the trustee must allocate the receipt from the separate fund with one of the methods described below (Prob C §16361(g)):

- **Value of separate fund can be determined.** If the trustee can determine the value of the separate fund, the internal income of the separate fund is deemed to equal 4 percent of the fund's value, according to the most recent statement of value preceding the beginning of the accounting period.

- **Value of separate fund cannot be determined.** If the trustee cannot determine the value of the separate fund,

    the internal income of the fund is deemed to equal the product of the interest rate and the present value of the expected future payments, as determined under Section 7520 of the Internal Revenue Code for the month preceding the accounting period for which the computation is made.

§6.33   N. Liquidating Assets: Leasehold Interests, Patents, Copyrights, Royalty Rights, Notes With No Stated Interest

In general, the trustee will allocate receipts from liquidating assets

10 percent to interest and 90 percent to principal. Prob C §16362(b). Liquidating assets include leasehold interests, patents, copyrights, royalties, and notes with no stated interest. Prob C §16362(a). Different rules apply to assets described in §16361, to resources described in §16363, to timber, to derivatives and options, to collateral-backed securities, and to assets for which the trustee has established a reserve for depreciation. Prob C §16362.

§6.34   O. Mineral, Water, and Natural Resources

If a trustee administers real property from which minerals or other natural resources are extracted, or if the trustee receives receipts from an interest in minerals, water, or other natural resources, the trustee may elect to account for these activities as a separate business. Prob C §16352(c). See §§13.2-13.4. The trustee who does not so elect, must contend with the lengthy rules for allocating receipts from mineral interests, water, and natural resources. See Prob C §16363. The open mine doctrine has been abolished (Comment to Prob C §16363) and receipts from these activities must be allocated between principal and income on the basis of the nature of the receipt.

§6.35   1. Receipts Allocated 100 Percent to Income

The trustee must allocate 100 percent to income the receipts described below (Prob C §16363(a)(1)):

- Nominal bonus;
- Nominal delay rental; and
- Nominal annual rent on a lease.

Additionally, an amount received on account of an interest in renewable water is allocated 100 percent to income. Prob C §16363(b).

§6.36   2. Production Payments Under an Agreement That Provides for Interest or Its Equivalent

If the trustee receives a production payment and the agreement creating the production payment provides a factor for interest or its equivalent, the trustee must allocate the payment to income to the extent it represents interest, or the equivalent, under the agreement. The trustee must allocate the balance of the payment to principal. Prob C §16363(a)(2).

§6.37   3. Other Receipts; the 90:10 Rule

Receipts are allocated 90 percent to principal and 10 percent to income, unless the receipt is nominal.

NOTE▶ As mentioned in §6.35, nominal bonuses, delay rentals, and annual rent are allocated 100 percent to income. Prob C §16363(a)(1).

If the receipt is a royalty, shut-in-well payment, take-or-pay payment, bonus, or delay rental payment, the 90:10 rule applies. Prob C §16363(a)(3). The 90:10 rule also applies to all receipts not described in Prob C §16363(a)(1), §16363(a)(2), or §16363(a)(3). Prob C §16363(a)(4). Additionally, an amount received on account of an interest in water that is not renewable is allocated 90 percent to principal and 10 percent to income. Prob C §16363(b).

§6.38   4. Trust-Owned Interests Acquired On or Before January 1, 2000

The rules described in §§6.34–6.37 apply to interests acquired by a trustee after January 1, 2000. For trust-owned interests acquired on or before that date, the trustee may account according to the Uniform Principal and Income Act (UPAIA) (Prob C §§16320–16375) or in the manner reasonably used by the trustee prior to January 1, 2000. Prob C §16363(d).

§6.39   P. Timber and Related Products

A trustee who accounts for receipts from timber and related products must allocate those receipts between principal and income in the manner of Prob C §16364, regardless of the nature of the timber or source of receipts. Prob C §16364(a). Lumber operations, ornamental-tree nurseries, Christmas-tree farms, and trees sold for pulp are all subject to this section. See Cantrell & Spoor, Fiduciary Accounting Answer Book, chap 13 (CCH 2015). The section applies whether or not the decedent or settlor was harvesting timber when the timberland became subject to the trust. Prob C §16364(c).

Before calculating net receipts from the sale of timber or related products, the trustee must deduct from income and allocate to principal a reasonable amount for depletion. Prob C §16364(b). At least one author suggests that a reasonable depletion reserve is that amount permitted as a depletion deduction under the Internal Revenue Code and Treasury Regulations. See Cantrell & Spoor, Fiduciary Accounting, Q 13:24.

§6.40   1. Timberland Acquired After January 1, 2000

For timberland acquired by a trustee after January 1, 2000, the trustee must allocate receipts 100 percent to income during all periods in which a beneficiary has a mandatory income interest if the amount of timber removed from the land does not exceed the rate of growth during the account period.

The trustee must allocate receipts 100 percent to principal to the extent the receipts are attributable to timber removed in excess of the timber's rate of growth. The trustee also must allocate the receipts 100 percent to principal if the net receipts are from the sale of standing timber.

The trustee also must allocate to principal advance payments, bonuses, and other payments not allocated to principal and income, or between them, under Prob C §16364(a)(1), (2), or (3).

If the trustee leases timberland, and that trust-owned timberland is subject to a contract that allows a third party to cut timber, the trustee must allocate receipts from the lease or contract between income and principal by applying the rules of Prob C §16364(a)(1) and (a)(2), discussed above.

§6.41   2. Timberland Acquired On or Before January 1, 2000

For receipts from trust-owned timberland acquired on or before January 1, 2000, the trustee may account according to the Uniform Principal and Income Act (UPAIA) (Prob C §§16320-16375), or in the manner reasonably used by the trustee prior to January 1, 2000. Prob C §16363(d).

§6.42   Q. Derivatives and Options

Trustees who invest in derivative financial instruments, asset-backed securities, and options to buy or sell, often own these investments indirectly—for example, when the trust is a partner in a partnership that makes such investments. Such trustees must account for receipts from these investments as receipts from entities and apply the rules of Prob C §16350. Otherwise, trustees who invest directly in derivatives, asset-backed securities, and options must allocate receipts from these transactions to principal (Prob C §16366), unless the trustee elects to account for the investments as a separate trade or business (Prob C §16352(c)(7)).

§6.43   R. Collateral-Backed Securities

Collateral-backed securities are assets, such as collections of mortgages, which give the security owner a right to distributions defined in the security contract. For example, the contract might entitle the owner to a share of mortgage-interest payments, or to distributions of principal when the underlying mortgages are paid.

If a trustee receives payments from interest or other current return and from other proceeds of the collateral-backed security, the trustee must allocate to income the portion of the payment identified by the payor as interest or other current return and must allocate the balance of the payment to principal. Prob C §16367(b).

If the trust receives one or more distributions during a single account period and the distributions are in exchange for the trust's entire interest in the security, the trustee must allocate all the receipts to principal. Prob C §16367(c). On the other hand, if the trustee receives a series of distributions that will result in the liquidation of the trust's interest in the security and the distributions are received over more than one account period, the trustee must allocate the receipts 10 percent to income and 90 percent to principal. Prob C §16367(c).

§6.44   S. Dividend Reinvestment Programs

Many companies that pay dividends offer shareholders the opportunity to reinvest their dividends in additional shares of the company, through a "dividend reinvestment program," or DRIP. As an enticement, these companies usually do not charge shareholders a commission on the shares purchased through reinvestment and a small number of companies even sell shares purchased through reinvestment at a discount.

Broken into its constituent parts, a DRIP transaction is always (1) a receipt, followed by (2) a purchase, that (3) increases the number of shares the shareholder owns. The trustee who participates in a DRIP must account for each step of the transaction, as follows:

- Report the dividend as a receipt on the schedule of Receipts;
- Report the purchase of additional shares on the schedule Changes in Form of Assets; and
- Adjust the quantity and carry value of the aggregate shares.

PRACTICE TIP▶ The trustee should add the number of pre-existing shares to the number purchased through reinvestment and should add the carry value of the pre-existing shares to the purchase price of the new shares.

Are the new shares received through dividend reinvestment allocated to income or to principal? The answer to this question is found in the commentary to Prob C §16350, which on first reading suggests that the dividends are principal. The commentary says:

> If a trustee elects (or continues an election made by its predecessor) to reinvest dividends in shares of stock of a distributing corporation or fund, . . . , the new shares would be principal. Making or continuing such an election would be equivalent to deciding under Section 10 [Prob C §16336] to transfer income to principal in order to comply with Section 103(b) [Prob C §16335(b), duty of impartiality]. However if the trustee makes or continues the election for a reason other than to comply with Section 103(b) [Prob C §16335(b)], *e.g.*, to make an investment without incurring brokerage commissions, the trustee should transfer cash from principal to income in an amount equal to the reinvested dividends. [Footnote 87: Law Revision Commission Comments (Background from Uniform Act) to Prob C §16350.]

On close reading, however, it becomes apparent that the new shares increase trust principal only in narrow circumstances. The trustee may characterize the reinvested dividends as principal only in circumstances that would justify transferring income to principal under Prob C §16335(b), a transfer necessary to the trustee's discharge of the duty of impartiality. If the trustee makes or continues an election to participate in a dividend reinvestment program for the same reason most investors initially make the election—to purchase shares without paying a commission—the dividends must be characterized as income.

PRACTICE TIP➤ In the authors' experience, most lay fiduciaries who participate in dividend reinvestment programs are following the practice of their predecessor or the advice of their investment advisor. Usually, these fiduciaries make or continue the election to participate in the DRIP without giving any thought to the competing interests of the income and principal beneficiaries. The election cannot, therefore, be characterized as an exercise of the trustee's power to make adjustments between principal and income. This power exists only when three conditions are met, and one condition is that the trustee "determines" that he or she is unable to treat the classes of beneficiaries impartially. Prob C §16336(a)(3). (The other two conditions being that the trustee invests and manages trust assets under the prudent investor rule, and that the trust describes the amount that shall or may be distributed to a beneficiary by referring to the trust's income. Prob C §16336(a)(1)-(2).) The trustee who participates in a dividend reinvestment program without first considering the program's effect on the beneficiaries' competing interests, must characterize the dividends received as income.

The example in §6.60 shows dividends paid by Franklin California Tax-Free Income Fund A and reinvested in the same fund.

§6.45 T. Specifically Gifted Property

When a fiduciary distributes a specific gift, the fiduciary also must distribute any net income attributable to that gift. Prob C §16340(a). In his or her accounting, the fiduciary should report receipts attributable to the gift as the fiduciary would report any other receipts: on the Receipts schedule. In a decedent's estate, the fiduciary should repeat this information on the Proposed Distribution schedule, to show the court and beneficiaries the calculation of net income. See §1.50. Similarly, a trustee who distributes a specific gift and its net income may wish to show the calculation of net income on an auxiliary schedule. See §§11.7-11.8.

V. COMMON MISTAKES

§6.46 A. Late-Received Assets Are Not Receipts

The trustee who receives assets subject to the trust after the beginning of the trust administration, should account for them on the schedule Additional Property Received During Period of Account. In the beginning of a trust administration, assets subject to the trust may yet be administered by a different fiduciary, such as when the assets are subject to the personal representative's administration during the probate of a pour-over will. When these assets are finally collected by the trustee, such as on an order of final distribution in the probate, the trustee should not account for the assets as receipts. Though subject to administration in the decedent's estate, these assets become subject to the trust on the date of the decedent's death. Prob C §§7000-7001. These assets should appear on the schedule Additional Property Received During Period of Account.

§6.47 B. In General, Sales Proceeds Are Not Receipts

With few exceptions, sales proceeds are not receipts and should not be reported on the Receipts schedule. Instead, sales should be reported on one of the following schedules:

- Gains on Sales or Other Dispositions;
- Losses on Sales or Other Dispositions; or
- Changes in Form of Assets.

A sale mistakenly reported as a receipt overstates the fiduciary's charges, inflates the basis of the personal representative's statutory fee, and obscures the details of the sale that would be revealed if the sale were accounted for properly.

§6.48 C. Receipts Collected During a Sale Are Not Gross Sales Proceeds

In some sales transactions, particularly sales of real property, the seller may receive amounts from the buyer instead of refunds from third parties. In a real estate sale, for example, the buyer might reimburse the seller some portion of the pre-paid property tax. Though received in an escrow, these amounts are not "gains" on sale, they are receipts and should be accounted for as such.

§6.49 D. Omitting From Assets on Hand the Source of a Receipt

Fiduciaries in general. As a general rule, if the fiduciary collects receipts from an asset or an entity, that asset or entity should appear on either the schedule Assets on Hand—Beginning of Period, the schedule Additional Property Received During Period of Account, or the schedule Changes in Form of Assets. Most likely, the asset or entity will also appear on the schedule Assets on Hand—End of Period. An exception would lie if the fiduciary acquired the asset in the middle of the account period and sold or disposed of it *during* the account period. Such an asset would appear on hand neither at the beginning nor at the end, but nevertheless should appear on the Changes in Form of Assets schedule.

Conservators and guardians. For conservators and guardians, the rule is somewhat different. These fiduciaries administer only the ward's or conservatee's real property located in California. Although these fiduciaries may collect receipts from out-of-state real properties, and although they must report the receipts in their accountings, conservators and guardians do not carry the out-of-state real properties as assets on hand. In other words, these fiduciaries do not list their out-of-state real properties on the schedules Assets on Hand— Beginning of Period or Assets on Hand—End of Period. Instead, guardians and conservators must list the out-of-state real property on an auxiliary schedule. Prob C §1063(h). See chap 11.

§6.50 E. Failing to Account for Receipts From Commingled Assets

Misplacing a receipt does not eliminate the fiduciary's duty to account for it. A fiduciary who commingles must account for the trust's or estate's portion of all payments received from the commingled property. And the fiduciary who puts trust or estate receipts in his or her personal account must account for administering that receipt (and may owe the trust interest). Putting a receipt into the wrong container does not change the nature of the receipt, nor the duty to account for it. *Gunter v Janes* (1858) 9 C 643; Prob C §16062.

§6.51 F. Form 1099 Phantom Income Is Not a Receipt

Partnerships, S corporations, and limited liability companies may report to their owners taxable income that the entity did not distribute during the tax year. It is a mistake to account for this retained income as if it were a receipt. If the entity distributed no money or property, the fiduciary has no receipt to account for.

For a discussion of the payment of tax attributable to phantom income, see Business Succession Planning: Strategies for California Estate Planners and Business Attorneys §20.54 (Cal CEB).

§6.52 G. Transfers Between Accounts Are Not Receipts

If a fiduciary transfers assets from one account to another, the transfer is not a receipt. Moreover, the fiduciary need not report the transfer on his or her accounting. Prob C §1063(b). See discussion regarding disbursements in §8.28.

VI. EXHIBITS

§6.53   A. Form: Receipts Schedule

The following example illustrates the appearance of the Receipts schedule. See §6.2.

DAVID JONES TRUST

THOMAS JONES, TRUSTEE

FIRST ACCOUNTING

FOR THE PERIOD JANUARY 1, 2012 THRU JUNE 30, 2012

RECEIPTS

SCHEDULE A

DATE	DESCRIPTION	INCOME	PRINCIPAL
INTEREST			
01/31/12	BANK OF AMERICA SAVINGS A/C #XXXXXX6789	$ 64.59	
02/29/12	BANK OF AMERICA SAVINGS A/C #XXXXXX6789	$ 60.42	
03/31/12	BANK OF AMERICA SAVINGS A/C #XXXXXX6789	$ 64.59	
04/30/12	BANK OF AMERICA SAVINGS A/C #XXXXXX6789	$ 62.50	
05/31/12	BANK OF AMERICA SAVINGS A/C #XXXXXX6789	$ 64.59	
06/30/12	BANK OF AMERICA SAVINGS A/C #XXXXXX6789	$ 62.50	
05/31/12	NOTE RECEIVABLE FROM LAND INVESTORS LLC	$ 666.67	
06/30/12	NOTE RECEIVABLE FROM LAND INVESTORS LLC	$ 666.67	
	TOTAL INTEREST	$ 1,712.53	$

§6.53

RENTAL INCOME - 321 FRANCHISE ROW

01/02/12	BETTY'S BARGAIN BOUTIQUE, FRANCHISE ROW	$	2,000.00
02/01/12	BETTY'S BARGAIN BOUTIQUE, FRANCHISE ROW	$	2,000.00
03/01/12	BETTY'S BARGAIN BOUTIQUE, FRANCHISE ROW	$	2,000.00
04/01/12	BETTY'S BARGAIN BOUTIQUE, FRANCHISE ROW	$	2,000.00
05/01/12	BETTY'S BARGAIN BOUTIQUE, FRANCHISE ROW	$	2,000.00
01/02/12	CHERYL'S CHEESESTEAKS, FRANCHISE ROW	$	750.00
02/01/12	CHERYL'S CHEESESTEAKS, FRANCHISE ROW	$	750.00
03/01/12	CHERYL'S CHEESESTEAKS, FRANCHISE ROW	$	750.00
04/01/12	CHERYL'S CHEESESTEAKS, FRANCHISE ROW	$	750.00
05/01/12	CHERYL'S CHEESESTEAKS, FRANCHISE ROW	$	750.00
01/02/12	ERNIE'S ELECTRONICS, FRANCHISE ROW	$	3,500.00
02/01/12	ERNIE'S ELECTRONICS, FRANCHISE ROW	$	3,500.00
03/01/12	ERNIE'S ELECTRONICS, FRANCHISE ROW	$	3,500.00
04/01/12	ERNIE'S ELECTRONICS, FRANCHISE ROW	$	3,500.00
05/01/12	ERNIE'S ELECTRONICS, FRANCHISE ROW	$	3,500.00
	TOTAL RENTAL INCOME - 321 FRANCHISE ROW $		31,250.00 $

RENTAL INCOME - 111 MANAGEMENT AVE

Date	Description	Amount	Amount
01/05/12	111 MANAGEMENT AVE, APT A	$ 700.00	
02/05/12	111 MANAGEMENT AVE, APT A	$ 700.00	
03/05/12	111 MANAGEMENT AVE, APT A	$ 700.00	
01/05/12	111 MANAGEMENT AVE, APT B	$ 800.00	
02/05/12	111 MANAGEMENT AVE, APT B	$ 800.00	
03/05/12	111 MANAGEMENT AVE, APT B	$ 800.00	
01/05/12	111 MANAGEMENT AVE, APT C	$ 900.00	
02/05/12	111 MANAGEMENT AVE, APT C	$ 900.00	
03/05/12	111 MANAGEMENT AVE, APT C	$ 900.00	
02/01/12	111 MANAGEMENT AVE, APT D - SECURITY DEPOSIT		$ 2,000.00
02/05/12	111 MANAGEMENT AVE, APT D	$ 1,000.00	
03/05/12	111 MANAGEMENT AVE, APT D	$ 1,000.00	
	TOTAL RENTAL INCOME - 111 MANAGEMENT AVE	$ 9,200.00	$ 2,000.00

OTHER INCOME

Date	Description	Amount	Amount
03/31/12	EXPLORERS OIL LEASE INCOME ON LAND (UNIMPROVED) ANYTOWN, CA	$ 1,000.00	
	TOTAL OTHER INCOME	$ 1,000.00	$ -

REFUNDS

Date	Description	Amount	Amount
04/30/12	SAFE INSURANCE - REFUND OF AUTO INSURANCE UPON CANCELLATION OF POLICY	$ 200.00	
05/15/12	STEWART TITLE COMPANY - REFUND OF PREPAID PROPERTY TAX ON 321 FRANCHISE ROW, RECEIVED IN ESCROW		$ 2,500.00
	TOTAL REFUNDS	$ 200.00	$ 2,500.00
	TOTAL INCOME AND PRINCIPAL	$ 43,362.53	$ 4,500.00
	TOTAL RECEIPTS	$ 47,862.53	

§6.54   B. Form: Receipts From Entities

The following example illustrates an accounting of money received from an entity. See §6.9.

APRIL CASH TRUST
SALLY CASH, TRUSTEE

FIRST ACCOUNTING
FOR THE PERIOD JANUARY 1, 2013 THRU JUNE 30, 2013
RECEIPTS
SCHEDULE A

DATE	DESCRIPTION	INCOME	PRINCIPAL
PARTNERSHIP INCOME			
06/30/13	WIDGET SUPPLIER LP	$ 5,200.00	
	TOTAL PARTNERSHIP INCOME	$ 5,200.00	$ -
	TOTAL INCOME AND PRINCIPAL	$ 5,200.00	$ -
	TOTAL RECEIPTS	$ **5,200.00**	

APRIL CASH TRUST
SALLY CASH, TRUSTEE

FIRST ACCOUNTING
FOR THE PERIOD JANUARY 1, 2013 THRU JUNE 30, 2013
ASSETS ON HAND - END OF PERIOD
SCHEDULE F

SHARES / PAR VALUE	DESCRIPTION		CARRY VALUE	MARKET VALUE
CASH AND CASH EQUIVALENTS				
	MERRILL LYNCH INVESTMENT A/C #XXXX-2222	CASH	$ 5,200.00	$ 5,200.00
	TOTAL CASH AND CASH EQUIVALENTS		$ 5,200.00	$ 5,200.00
	TOTAL ASSETS		$ **5,200.00**	$ 5,200.00

§6.55   C. Form: Dividends and Capital Gains

The following example illustrates the receipt of dividends from mutual funds (accounted for as receipts of income), and short-term capital gains and long-term capital gains (accounted for as income and principal, respectively). See §6.11.

APRIL CASH TRUST
SALLY CASH, TRUSTEE

FIRST ACCOUNTING
FOR THE PERIOD JANUARY 1, 2013 THRU JUNE 30, 2013
RECEIPTS
SCHEDULE A

DATE	DESCRIPTION	INCOME	PRINCIPAL
DIVIDENDS			
01/14/13	FRANKLIN UNIVERSAL TRUST	$ 38.00	
02/15/13	FRANKLIN UNIVERSAL TRUST	$ 38.00	
03/15/13	FRANKLIN UNIVERSAL TRUST	$ 36.00	
04/15/13	FRANKLIN UNIVERSAL TRUST	$ 38.00	
02/01/13	NUVEEN CA INVT QUALITY MUN FD	$ 76.00	
03/01/13	NUVEEN CA INVT QUALITY MUN FD	$ 76.00	
04/01/13	NUVEEN CA INVT QUALITY MUN FD	$ 76.00	
05/02/13	NUVEEN CA INVT QUALITY MUN FD	$ 76.00	
02/01/13	NUVEEN CA MUNICIPAL MKT OPP FD	$ 78.00	
03/01/13	NUVEEN CA MUNICIPAL MKT OPP FD	$ 78.00	
04/01/13	NUVEEN CA MUNICIPAL MKT OPP FD	$ 78.00	
05/02/13	NUVEEN CA MUNICIPAL MKT OPP FD	$ 78.00	
01/28/13	SCHWAB PREMIER MONEY FUND	$ 0.69	
02/28/13	ML MONEY MARKET FUND	$ 0.85	
03/31/13	ML MONEY MARKET FUND	$ 4.52	
04/30/13	ML MONEY MARKET FUND	$ 7.59	
05/31/13	ML MONEY MARKET FUND	$ 7.89	
06/30/13	ML MONEY MARKET FUND	$ 9.09	
	TOTAL DIVIDENDS	$ 798.63	$ -

§6.55

SHORT TERM CAPITAL GAINS				
03/01/13	NUVEEN CA INVT QUALITY MUN FD	$	12.00	
03/01/13	NUVEEN CA MUNICIPAL MKT OPP FD	$	14.00	
	TOTAL SHORT TERM CAPITAL GAINS	$	26.00	$ -
LONG TERM CAPITAL GAINS				
03/01/13	NUVEEN CA INVT QUALITY MUN FD			$ 82.00
03/01/13	NUVEEN CA MUNICIPAL MKT OPP FD			$ 86.00
	TOTAL LONG TERM CAPITAL GAINS	$	-	$ 168.00
	TOTAL INCOME AND PRINCIPAL	$	824.63	$ 168.00
	TOTAL RECEIPTS	$	992.63	

APRIL CASH TRUST

SALLY CASH, TRUSTEE

FIRST ACCOUNTING

FOR THE PERIOD JANUARY 1, 2013 THRU JUNE 30, 2013

ASSETS ON HAND - END OF PERIOD

SCHEDULE F

SHARES / PAR VALUE	DESCRIPTION		CARRY VALUE	MARKET VALUE
CASH AND CASH EQUIVALENTS				
	MERRILL LYNCH INVESTMENT A/C #XXXX-2222	CASH	$ 992.63	$ 992.63
	TOTAL CASH AND CASH EQUIVALENTS		$ 992.63	$ 992.63
	TOTAL ASSETS		$ 992.63	$ 992.63

§6.56   D. Form: Receipts From Rental Properties

The following example illustrates the receipt of rents from commercial and residential tenants. See §6.17.

REAL ESTATE TRUST
THOMAS JONES, TRUSTEE

FIRST ACCOUNTING
FOR THE PERIOD JANUARY 1, 2012 THRU JUNE 30, 2012

RECEIPTS
SCHEDULE A

DATE	DESCRIPTION	INCOME	PRINCIPAL
RENTAL INCOME - 321 FRANCHISE ROW			
01/02/12	BETTY'S BARGAIN BOUTIQUE, FRANCHISE ROW	$ 2,000.00	
02/01/12	BETTY'S BARGAIN BOUTIQUE, FRANCHISE ROW	$ 2,000.00	
03/01/12	BETTY'S BARGAIN BOUTIQUE, FRANCHISE ROW	$ 2,000.00	
04/01/12	BETTY'S BARGAIN BOUTIQUE, FRANCHISE ROW	$ 2,000.00	
05/01/12	BETTY'S BARGAIN BOUTIQUE, FRANCHISE ROW	$ 2,000.00	
01/02/12	CHERYL'S CHEESESTEAKS, FRANCHISE ROW	$ 750.00	
02/01/12	CHERYL'S CHEESESTEAKS, FRANCHISE ROW	$ 750.00	
03/01/12	CHERYL'S CHEESESTEAKS, FRANCHISE ROW	$ 750.00	
04/01/12	CHERYL'S CHEESESTEAKS, FRANCHISE ROW	$ 750.00	
05/01/12	CHERYL'S CHEESESTEAKS, FRANCHISE ROW	$ 750.00	
01/02/12	ERNIE'S ELECTRONICS, FRANCHISE ROW	$ 3,500.00	
02/01/12	ERNIE'S ELECTRONICS, FRANCHISE ROW	$ 3,500.00	
03/01/12	ERNIE'S ELECTRONICS, FRANCHISE ROW	$ 3,500.00	
04/01/12	ERNIE'S ELECTRONICS, FRANCHISE ROW	$ 3,500.00	
05/01/12	ERNIE'S ELECTRONICS, FRANCHISE ROW	$ 3,500.00	
	TOTAL RENTAL INCOME - 321 FRANCHISE ROW	$ 31,250.00	$ -

RENTAL INCOME - 111 MANAGEMENT AVE				
01/05/12	111 MANAGEMENT AVE, APT A	$ 700.00		
02/05/12	111 MANAGEMENT AVE, APT A	$ 700.00		
03/05/12	111 MANAGEMENT AVE, APT A	$ 700.00		
01/05/12	111 MANAGEMENT AVE, APT B	$ 800.00		
02/05/12	111 MANAGEMENT AVE, APT B	$ 800.00		
03/05/12	111 MANAGEMENT AVE, APT B	$ 800.00		
01/05/12	111 MANAGEMENT AVE, APT C	$ 900.00		
02/05/12	111 MANAGEMENT AVE, APT C	$ 900.00		
03/05/12	111 MANAGEMENT AVE, APT C	$ 900.00		
02/01/12	111 MANAGEMENT AVE, APT D - SECURITY DEPOSIT		$ 2,000.00	
02/05/12	111 MANAGEMENT AVE, APT D	$ 1,000.00		
03/05/12	111 MANAGEMENT AVE, APT D	$ 1,000.00		
	TOTAL RENTAL INCOME - 111 MANAGEMENT AVE	$ 9,200.00	$ 2,000.00	
	TOTAL INCOME AND PRINCIPAL	$ 40,450.00	$ 2,000.00	
	TOTAL RECEIPTS	$ **42,450.00**		

REAL ESTATE TRUST

THOMAS JONES, TRUSTEE

FIRST ACCOUNTING

FOR THE PERIOD JANUARY 1, 2012 THRU JUNE 30, 2012

ASSETS ON HAND - END OF PERIOD

SCHEDULE F

SHARES / PAR VALUE	DESCRIPTION	CARRY VALUE	MARKET VALUE
CASH AND CASH EQUIVALENTS			
	BANK OF AMERICA CHECKING A/C #XXXXXX6789	$ 42,450.00	$ 42,450.00
	TOTAL CASH AND CASH EQUIVALENTS	$ 42,450.00	$ 42,450.00
	TOTAL ASSETS	$ **42,450.00**	$ 42,450.00

§6.57   E. Form: Bank Account Interest

The following example illustrates the receipt of bank account interest. See §6.18.

REAL ESTATE TRUST
THOMAS JONES, TRUSTEE
FIRST ACCOUNTING
FOR THE PERIOD JANUARY 1, 2012 THRU JUNE 30, 2012
RECEIPTS
SCHEDULE A

DATE	DESCRIPTION	INCOME	PRINCIPAL
INTEREST			
01/31/12	BANK OF AMERICA SAVINGS A/C #XXXXXX6789	$ 64.59	
02/29/12	BANK OF AMERICA SAVINGS A/C #XXXXXX6789	$ 60.42	
03/31/12	BANK OF AMERICA SAVINGS A/C #XXXXXX6789	$ 64.59	
04/30/12	BANK OF AMERICA SAVINGS A/C #XXXXXX6789	$ 62.50	
05/31/12	BANK OF AMERICA SAVINGS A/C #XXXXXX6789	$ 64.59	
06/30/12	BANK OF AMERICA SAVINGS A/C #XXXXXX6789	$ 62.50	
	TOTAL INTEREST	$ 379.19	$ —
	TOTAL INCOME AND PRINCIPAL	$ 379.19	$ —
	TOTAL RECEIPTS	$ 379.19	

REAL ESTATE TRUST
THOMAS JONES, TRUSTEE
FIRST ACCOUNTING
FOR THE PERIOD JANUARY 1, 2012 THRU JUNE 30, 2012
ASSETS ON HAND - END OF PERIOD
SCHEDULE F

SHARES / PAR VALUE	DESCRIPTION	CARRY VALUE	MARKET VALUE
CASH AND CASH EQUIVALENTS			
	BANK OF AMERICA SAVINGS A/C #XXXXXX6789	$ 379.19	$ 379.19
	TOTAL CASH AND CASH EQUIVALENTS	$ 379.19	$ 379.19
	TOTAL ASSETS	$ 379.19	$ 379.19

§6.58 F. Form: Interest on Bonds Owed to Trustee

The following example illustrates the receipt of income from a J.P. Morgan Chase bond. See §6.19.

APRIL CASH TRUST
SALLY CASH, TRUSTEE
FIRST ACCOUNTING
FOR THE PERIOD JANUARY 1, 2013 THRU JUNE 30, 2013
RECEIPTS
SCHEDULE A

DATE	DESCRIPTION	INCOME	PRINCIPAL
INTEREST			
04/30/13	JP MORGAN CHASE & CO 7.900% APR/OCT 30 DUE 12/31/48	$ 948.00	
	TOTAL INTEREST	$ 948.00	$ --
ACCRUED INTEREST ON PURCHASES			
03/01/13	JP MORGAN CHASE & CO 7.900% APR/OCT 30 DUE 12/31/48	$ (608.12)	
	TOTAL ACCRUED INTEREST ON PURCHASES	$ (608.12)	$ --

APRIL CASH TRUST
SALLY CASH, TRUSTEE
FIRST ACCOUNTING
FOR THE PERIOD JANUARY 1, 2013 THRU JUNE 30, 2013
CHANGES IN FORM OF ASSETS

DATE		DESCRIPTION	CASH	CARRY VALUE
PURCHASES				
03/01/13	24,000.000	JP MORGAN CHASE & CO 7.900% APR/OCT 30 DUE 12/31/48 CALLABLE $100.00 ON 04/30/18	$ (24,000.00)	$ 24,000.00

APRIL CASH TRUST
SALLY CASH, TRUSTEE

FIRST ACCOUNTING
FOR THE PERIOD JANUARY 1, 2013 THRU JUNE 30, 2013
ASSETS ON HAND - END OF PERIOD
SCHEDULE F

SHARES / PAR VALUE	DESCRIPTION	CARRY VALUE	MARKET VALUE
CORPORATE BONDS			
24,000.000	JP MORGAN CHASE & CO 7.900% APR/OCT 30 DUE 12/31/48	$ 24,000.00	$ 24,125.00
	TOTAL CORPORATE BONDS	$ 24,000.00	$ 24,125.00

§6.59   G. Form: Assets Listed in Prob C §16357(c)

The following example illustrates the receipt of principal and interest payments from the obligor on a promissory note payable to the trustee. These transactions are reported on the Receipts schedule and the Changes in Form of Assets schedule, respectively. See §6.20.

		REAL ESTATE TRUST		
		THOMAS JONES, TRUSTEE		
		FIRST ACCOUNTING		
	FOR THE PERIOD JANUARY 1, 2012 THRU JUNE 30, 2012		
		RECEIPTS		
		SCHEDULE A		
DATE	DESCRIPTION		INCOME	PRINCIPAL
INTEREST				
05/31/12	NOTE RECEIVABLE FROM LAND INVESTORS LLC	$	666.67	
06/30/12	NOTE RECEIVABLE FROM LAND INVESTORS LLC	$	666.67	
	TOTAL INTEREST	$	1,333.34	$ -
	TOTAL INCOME AND PRINCIPAL	$	1,333.34	$ -
	TOTAL RECEIPTS	$	**1,333.34**	

		REAL ESTATE TRUST		
		THOMAS JONES, TRUSTEE		
		FIRST ACCOUNTING		
	FOR THE PERIOD JANUARY 1, 2012 THRU JUNE 30, 2012		
		CHANGES IN FORM OF ASSETS		
DATE	DESCRIPTION		CASH	CARRY VALUE
COLLECTION OF RECEIVABLES				
06/30/12	LAND INVESTORS INC PRINCIPAL PAYMENT NOTE RECEIVABLE 10 YEARS, DUE 4/01/22 INT MONTHLY, 4% P.A. PRIN $5,000 QTR	$	5,000.00	$ (5,000.00)

§6.60 H. Form: Dividend Reinvestment Programs

The following example illustrates the receipt and reinvestment of dividends paid by Franklin CA Tax-Free Income Fund A. See §6.44.

APRIL CASH TRUST
SALLY CASH, TRUSTEE

FIRST ACCOUNTING
FOR THE PERIOD JANUARY 1, 2013 THRU JUNE 30, 2013
ASSETS ON HAND - BEGINNING OF PERIOD

SHARES / PAR VALUE	DESCRIPTION	CARRY VALUE
MUTUAL FUNDS		
14,202.081	FRANKLIN CA TAX FREE INCOME FUND CL A	$ 95,722.03
	TOTAL MUTUAL FUNDS	$ 95,722.03
	TOTAL ASSETS	$ 95,722.03

APRIL CASH TRUST
SALLY CASH, TRUSTEE

FIRST ACCOUNTING
FOR THE PERIOD JANUARY 1, 2013 THRU JUNE 30, 2013
RECEIPTS
SCHEDULE A

DATE	DESCRIPTION	INCOME	PRINCIPAL
DIVIDENDS			
01/01/13	FRANKLIN CA TAX-FREE INCOME A	$ 383.46	
02/02/13	FRANKLIN CA TAX-FREE INCOME A	$ 385.00	
03/02/13	FRANKLIN CA TAX-FREE INCOME A	$ 405.20	
04/04/13	FRANKLIN CA TAX-FREE INCOME A	$ 406.93	
05/03/13	FRANKLIN CA TAX-FREE INCOME A	$ 408.70	
06/02/13	FRANKLIN CA TAX-FREE INCOME A	$ 409.64	
	TOTAL DIVIDENDS	$ 2,398.93	$ --
	TOTAL INCOME AND PRINCIPAL	$ 2,398.93	$ --
	TOTAL RECEIPTS	$ 2,398.93	

APRIL CASH TRUST

SALLY CASH, TRUSTEE

FIRST ACCOUNTING

FOR THE PERIOD JANUARY 1, 2013 THRU JUNE 30, 2013

ASSETS ON HAND - END OF PERIOD

SCHEDULE F

SHARES / PAR VALUE	DESCRIPTION	CARRY VALUE	MARKET VALUE
MUTUAL FUNDS			
14,565.205	FRANKLIN CA TAX FREE INCOME FUND CL A	$ 98,120.96	
	TOTAL MUTUAL FUNDS	$ 98,120.96	$ -
	TOTAL ASSETS	**$ 98,120.96**	$ -

APRIL CASH TRUST

SALLY CASH, TRUSTEE

FIRST ACCOUNTING

FOR THE PERIOD JANUARY 1, 2013 THRU JUNE 30, 2013

CHANGES IN FORM OF ASSETS

DATE	SHARES / PAR VALUE	DESCRIPTION	CASH	CARRY VALUE
REINVESTMENTS				
01/01/13	14,202.081	BALANCE		$ 95,722.03
01/01/13	57.063	FRANKLIN CA TAX-FREE INCOME A	$ (383.46)	$ 383.46
02/02/13	58.959	FRANKLIN CA TAX-FREE INCOME A	$ (385.00)	$ 385.00
03/02/13	61.116	FRANKLIN CA TAX-FREE INCOME A	$ (405.20)	$ 405.20
04/04/13	62.413	FRANKLIN CA TAX-FREE INCOME A	$ (406.93)	$ 406.93
05/03/13	61.551	FRANKLIN CA TAX-FREE INCOME A	$ (408.70)	$ 408.70
06/02/13	62.022	FRANKLIN CA TAX-FREE INCOME A	$ (409.64)	$ 409.64
	14,565.205			$ 98,120.96

7
Gains and Losses

I. IN GENERAL
   A. Distinguishing Gains from Losses §7.1
   B. Separate Schedules Are Required §7.2
   C. Appearance of the Schedules
      1. Gains §7.3
      2. Losses §7.4

II. PREPARING THE SCHEDULES, AT A MINIMUM
   A. Gains on Sales or Other Dispositions §7.5
   B. Losses on Sales or Other Dispositions §7.6

III. BEST PRACTICES §7.7

IV. PRINCIPAL AND INCOME
   A. In General §7.8
   B. Mineral and Water Interests, Other Natural Resources, Timber §7.9
   C. Sale, Redemption, or Other Disposition of Obligation to Pay Money §7.10
      1. Obligations That Mature More Than 1 Year After Acquisition §7.11
      2. Obligations That Mature in Less Than 1 Year §7.12
   D. Options §7.13
   E. Asset-Backed Securities §7.14
   F. Insurance Proceeds §7.15
   G. Marital Deduction Trusts §7.16

V. COMMON MISTAKES
   A. It Is a Mistake to Calculate Gain Using *Net* Sales Price §7.17
   B. It Is a Mistake to Calculate Loss Using *Net* Sales Price §7.18

VI. EXHIBITS
   A. Form: Gains on Sales or Other Dispositions §7.19
   B. Form: Insurance Proceeds §7.20
   C. Form: Sales in Which Expenses Were Paid in the Course of the Sale §7.21

I. IN GENERAL

§7.1 A. Distinguishing Gains from Losses

When a fiduciary disposes of an asset in an exchange for cash or other property, the fiduciary must characterize the transaction as a gain if the gross fair market value of the property received exceeds the *carry* value of the property exchanged. This rule is true of sales, condemnations, redemptions, casualty "losses," and exchanges. This rule applies even when the cost of the transaction results in an economic loss.

EXAMPLE▶ At her death, the decedent's residence had a fair market value of $100,000. Shortly after the decedent's death, her personal representative sold the residence for $105,000. The realtors' commissions were 6 percent and the realtors were paid $6000 from the escrow. As a result, the most the personal representative might receive from this transaction is $99,000. Yet when he accounts for the sale, the personal representative must report the sale on the schedule of Gains on Sales or Other Dispositions. On that schedule, he will seek credit for a $5000 gain, which is the difference between the property's carry value and the gross sales proceeds.

A transaction is reported as a loss if the gross fair market value received is less than the asset's carry value.

§7.2 B. Separate Schedules Are Required

In general, in a court accounting, the fiduciary is charged with additional responsibility when he or she sells an asset at a gain and is credited with discharging a measure of responsibility when he or she sells an asset at a loss. Stated differently, any sale or other disposition that increases the trustee's burden of responsibility should be reported on the schedule Gains on Sales or Other Dispositions, and any sale or other disposition that decreases the trustee's burden should be reported on the schedule Losses on Sales or Other Dispositions. In a fiduciary accounting that will be submitted for court approval in a California court, the fiduciary would never combine these transactions in one schedule. Prob C §1061(b).

NOTE▶ California law is contrary to Fiduciary Accounting Principal V, 1983 Report of Fiduciary Accounting Standards Committee, but otherwise the committee's report provides good guidance for California fiduciaries.

Despite that prohibition, gains and losses are discussed together in this chapter because their presentation in a fiduciary accounting is so similar.

C. Appearance of the Schedules

§7.3   1. Gains

The schedule Gains on Sales or Other Dispositions should include the date sold, a description of the property, the sales price, the carry value, and the gain on sale. For example:

Date Sold	Property Description	Sales Price	Carry Value	Gain on Sale
8/1/2015	10,000 U.S. Treas. Nt 6.5% due 12/31/2016	$9,025.00	$8,000.00	$1,025.00

§7.4   2. Losses

The schedule Losses on Sales or Other Dispositions should include the date sold, a description of the property, the carry value, the sales price, and the loss on sale. For example:

Date Sold	Property Description	Carry Value	Sales Price	Loss on Sale
10/1/2015	200 shares of XYZ Telephone Co. 6% first preferred stock, par value of $100	$20,000.00	$17,750.00	$2,250.00

II. PREPARING THE SCHEDULES, AT A MINIMUM

§7.5 A. Gains on Sales or Other Dispositions

Personal representatives, conservators, and guardians must report their gains on sales and must calculate the amount of the gain. Prob C §16061(a)(5). The Probate Code says nothing more than this, but because it requires the account to balance (Prob C §16061(c)), when one considers the rules for reporting receipts and disbursements, the formula for calculating gain emerges. That formula could be stated:

> Gross Sales Price − Carry Value = Gain on Sale

NOTE▶ If the above formula produces a negative number, the transaction must be reported as a loss. Do not report losses by using negative numbers on the schedule of gains. Doing so would understate the fiduciary's charges.

For an example of an accounting of a gain on the sale, see §7.19. This transaction appears on the Gains on Sales or Other Dispositions schedule.

Personal representatives, conservators, and guardians must report the disposition of each asset carried in an account period and may not aggregate sales and report them as a sum. This rule is not clearly stated in the Probate Code, but is an artifact of the code's requirement of an "itemized list of property on hand [at the end], describing each item at its carry value." Prob C §1062(f). In many counties, the court employees who examine fiduciary accountings will trace each asset from beginning (or acquisition) to end and will recommend against approving an account that does not report the disposition of an asset disposed of during the account period.

The law of trusts does not require trustees to report gains on one schedule and losses on another. Neither does trust law require trustees to report each sale or each transaction in which one asset is exchanged for another. All that is *required* of trustees is a "statement of the assets and liabilities of the trust as of the end of the last complete fiscal year of the trust or as of the end of the period covered by the account." Prob C §16063. But the trustee who seeks court approval of his or her account must account in the manner of Prob C §§1061–1064. Prob C §1060.

§7.6   B. Losses on Sales or Other Dispositions

Personal representatives, conservators, and guardians must report their losses on sales and must calculate the amount of the loss. Prob C §16061(a)(5). The Probate Code says nothing more than this, but because it requires the account to balance (Prob C §16061(c)), when one considers the rules for reporting receipts and disbursements, the formula for calculating loss emerges. That formula could be stated:

Carry Value − Gross Sales Price = Loss on Sale

NOTE▶ If the above formula produces a negative number, the transaction must be reported as a gain.

As with gains, the law of trusts contains no requirement that the trustee report each transaction individually. All that is *required* of trustees is a "statement of the assets and liabilities of the trust as of the end of the last complete fiscal year of the trust or as of the end of the period covered by the account." Prob C §16063.

§7.7   III. BEST PRACTICES

If there have been only a few sales during the period of the report, report the sales chronologically, even if the various properties are accounted for elsewhere in some other order—for example, alphabetically. By contrast, if there was a mass sell off (for example, if an entire stock portfolio was liquidated), account for each property sold by listing the sale in the same order as the property appeared on the schedule of assets on hand. Remember, the person examining the schedules of losses and gains is trying to answer the question, "What happened to a particular asset?" These schedules should make it easy for those interested in the administration to figure out why an asset on hand at the beginning (or a late-acquired asset) cannot be found on the schedule Assets on Hand—End of Period.

IV. PRINCIPAL AND INCOME

§7.8   A. In General

In general, money or other property received from the sale, exchange, liquidation, or other disposition of a principal asset, including realized profit, is itself principal. Prob C §16355(b). The exceptions to this rule are those exceptions found in Articles 5.1, 5.2, and 5.3

of the Uniform Principal and Income Act (UPAIA) (Prob C §§16320–16375) and discussed below. Concomitantly, the proceeds of the sale of an income asset are trust accounting income.

§7.9 B. Mineral and Water Interests, Other Natural Resources, Timber

The Uniform Principal and Income Act (UPAIA) speaks of the "sale of timber and related products" and alludes to the sale of minerals, water, and other natural resources. Prob C §§16363–16364. However, the fiduciary who administers timberland, minerals, water, and other natural resources would *not* account for the periodic sale of these renewable resources on the schedules of gains and losses. Receipts from such sales are accounted for on the Receipts schedule unless the fiduciary sells all, or a substantial portion of, the timberland or the interest in minerals, water, or other natural resources. A sale of this nature would be reported on either the gains or losses schedule and falls within the general rule of Prob C §16355, *i.e.,* the money received would be allocated 100 percent to principal. Prob C §16355(b).

On the Receipts schedule, see chap 6.

§7.10 C. Sale, Redemption, or Other Disposition of Obligation to Pay Money

In general, if a fiduciary sells, redeems, or otherwise disposes of an obligation to pay money, the fiduciary must allocate the receipt between principal and income as provided below. This rule applies to bonds, including those acquired at a discount; short-term obligations such as United States Treasury Bills; long-term obligations such as United States Savings bonds; zero-coupon bonds; and discount bonds that pay interest during part, but not all, of the period before maturity. Comment to Prob C §16357. Although §16357(c) suggests that there are a host of exceptions to the rule of §16357, when it comes to sales of obligations to pay money, the exceptions apply only to sales of options (see §7.13) and asset-backed securities (see §7.14).

NOTE➤ Probate Code §16357(c) says that "this section does not apply to an obligation to which Section 16361, 16362, 16363, 16364, 16366 or 16367 applies." However, the listed sections deal primarily with receipts from assets. Only §§16366 and 16367 address sales.

§7.11 1. Obligations That Mature More Than 1 Year After Acquisition

If the trust owns an obligation that matures more than 1 year after its acquisition, and if the trustee sells that obligation, the trustee must allocate the entire receipt to principal, whether the obligation is sold for a gain or a loss. Prob C §16357(b). This is true even if the obligation's purchase price, or value at acquisition, was less when acquired than at maturity.

§7.12 2. Obligations That Mature in Less Than 1 Year

If the trust owns an obligation to pay money and the obligation matures within 1 year of its acquisition, if the trustee sells the obligation for more than its purchase price, or value, when otherwise acquired, the trustee must allocate the excess to income and the rest to principal. If the trustee disposes of the obligation for less than the purchase price, or for less than the acquisition value, the fiduciary must allocate the entire receipt to principal. Prob C §16355(b). Because Prob C §16357 states no rule for the sale of a short-term obligation at a loss, the more general rule of Prob C §16355(b) applies.

§7.13 D. Options

Subject to the prudent investor rule and the terms of the trust, trustees may buy, exercise, and sell options. The sale (sometimes called a "grant") of an option and the exercise of an option are accounted for as follows. The amount received for granting an option to purchase trust property, whether or not the trust owns the property at the time the option is granted, is allocated 100 percent to principal. Prob C §16366(c). Any gain or loss realized by the trustee on the exercise of an option, even an option granted to the trust's settlor for services rendered, also is allocated 100 percent to principal. Prob C §16366(c).

§7.14 E. Asset-Backed Securities

If, during one account period, the trustee receives one or more payments in exchange for the trust's entire interest in an asset-backed security, the trustee must allocate the payments received 100 percent to principal. Prob C §16367(c). If a series of payments would liquidate the trust's interest in the security over a period that extends beyond that of one accounting period, *i.e.,* 1 year (see Prob C §16322), the trustee must allocate each payment 10 percent to income and 90 percent to principal. In either case, the trustee would report the transaction either on the schedule of Gains on Sales or Other Dispositions, the schedule of Losses on Sales or Other Dispositions, or the schedule of Changes in Form of Assets.

NOTE▶ The Uniform Principal and Income Act (UPAIA) defines "accounting period" as a period no longer than 12 months. Prob C §16322.

§7.15   F. Insurance Proceeds

Fiduciaries should report the receipt of insurance proceeds on the Gains schedule, or on the Losses schedule if the event that justified the insurance claim resulted in the loss of a trust or estate asset. For example, the trustee who collects on an insurance claim after a trust-owned vehicle has been totaled should treat the insurance proceeds as a replacement for the vehicle. The trustee should report the transaction as a gain if the insurance company pays more than the vehicle's carry value, but as a loss if the proceeds are less than the carry value. In either case, the proceeds are trust principal. Prob C §16358. For an example showing the receipt of insurance proceeds following an accident that totaled a Mercedes, see §7.20.

If the car in the example in §7.20 had been totaled in one account period, but the insurance company had not paid on the claim by the close of the period, an alternate method of accounting would be acceptable. In the account period during which the accident occurred, the fiduciary would show the vehicle as a total loss on the date of the accident and, using a footnote, alert the beneficiaries to the existence of a claim. In the following account period, when the fiduciary collects the insurance proceeds, he or she would report that receipt as a receipt of principal on the Receipts schedule.

§7.16   G. Marital Deduction Trusts

If a transfer to a trust for the benefit of the settlor's spouse qualifies for the marital deduction from the estate tax, the trust must give the surviving spouse the right to all income. IRC §2056. For that right to be meaningful, the surviving spouse must have the power to compel the trustee to make the trust property productive of income.

Early versions of the prudent investor rule looked at productivity on an asset-by-asset basis and earlier versions of the Uniform Principal and Income Act were in accord: when an unproductive asset was sold, the surviving spouse would receive a "delayed payment." See Cantrell & Spoor, Fiduciary Accounting Answer Book, chap 14 (CCH 2015), discussing Section 12 of the 1962 Act and Section 11 of the 1931 Act. This is no longer the case. California's Uniform Prudent Investor Act (UPIA) (Prob C §§16045-16054) requires trustees to evaluate investments in the context of the trust portfolio as a whole (Prob C §16047(b)), and California's Uniform Principal and Income Act (UPAIA) (Prob C §§16320-16375) gives trustees a variety of ways to cope with underproductive assets. The trustee may adjust between principal and income (see Prob C §16336), convert the trust to a unitrust (Prob C §§16336.4-16336.6), or "convert" the asset to more productive property (Prob C §16226). And the Treasury regulations make clear that giving the surviving spouse the power to demand that the trustee choose between these options is sufficient to preserve the marital deduction. Treas Reg §20.2056(b)-5(f)(4); IRC §2056. The exception to this rule is the "estate trust," for which income may be accumulated provided the principal and income are paid to the surviving spouse's estate on his or her death. Treas Reg §20.2056(c)-2(b)(1)(iii); Cantrell & Spoor, Fiduciary Accounting, Q 14:5. Probate Code §16365 gives the surviving spouse the power to demand that the trustee make property productive in one of these ways, but gives the trustee the power to choose which action to take.

V. COMMON MISTAKES

§7.17 A. It Is a Mistake to Calculate Gain Using *Net* Sales Price

Accustomed to accounting for *value* instead of *responsibility*, accountants are often tempted to report the gain on sale by subtracting basis from *net* sales price, as in the following erroneous formula:

Gross Sales Price − (sales expenses + basis) = Gain

Fiduciaries should not account in this fashion, because doing so would obscure the disbursement of the expenses of the sale. Consider the sale of a house. It is customary to pay from escrow all mortgages encumbering the property, realtor commissions, fees to title companies, and transfer taxes. These disbursements should be listed on the schedule of Disbursements, so that beneficiaries can assure themselves that the trustee is not paying excessive commissions, commissions to family members, commissions to unlicensed "realtors," and so forth. Beneficiaries also are entitled to see whether the trustee agreed to pay through the escrow costs usually borne by the buyer (for example, a portion of any city transfer tax), or more egregiously, expenses personal to the trustee.

§7.18   B. It Is a Mistake to Calculate Loss Using *Net* Sales Price

Fiduciaries also should not calculate their losses using net sales price. In other words, the following formula is wrong:

Carry Value − (sales expenses + sales price) = Loss

The above formula obscures the disbursements made during the sales process, but also overstates the fiduciary's loss.

When accounting for sales in which expenses were paid in the course of the sale, use the model provided in the example in §7.21.

VI. EXHIBITS

§7.19   **A. Form: Gains on Sales or Other Dispositions**

The following example illustrates a gain on the sale of 1000 shares of the Franklin Universal Trust. See §7.5.

APRIL CASH TRUST
SALLY CASH, TRUSTEE

FIRST ACCOUNTING
FOR THE PERIOD JANUARY 1, 2013 THRU JUNE 30, 2013

ASSETS ON HAND - BEGINNING OF PERIOD

SHARES / PAR VALUE	DESCRIPTION	CARRY VALUE
	MUTUAL FUNDS	
1,000.000	FRANKLIN UNIVERSAL TRUST FD	$ 6,343.75
	TOTAL MUTUAL FUNDS	$ 6,343.75
	TOTAL ASSETS	$ **6,343.75**

APRIL CASH TRUST
SALLY CASH, TRUSTEE

FIRST ACCOUNTING
FOR THE PERIOD JANUARY 1, 2013 THRU JUNE 30, 2013

GAINS ON SALES
SCHEDULE B

DATE	SHARES	DESCRIPTION	CARRY VALUE	PROCEEDS	GAINS
05/05/13	1,000.000	FRANKLIN UNIVERSAL TRUST FD	$ 6,343.75	$ 6,374.35	$ 30.60
		TOTALS	$ 6,343.75	$ 6,374.35	$ **30.60**

§7.20 B. Form: Insurance Proceeds

In the following example, a Mercedes carried at $7000 was totaled in an accident. The insurance company, Safe Insurance, paid only $2350 on the claim. The transaction is accounted for as a loss of $4650. See §7.15.

REAL ESTATE TRUST
THOMAS JONES, TRUSTEE

FIRST ACCOUNTING
FOR THE PERIOD JANUARY 1, 2012 THRU JUNE 30, 2012
ASSETS ON HAND - BEGINNING OF PERIOD

SHARES / PAR VALUE	DESCRIPTION	CARRY VALUE	
OTHER ASSETS			
	2010 MERCEDES C230 VIN K47834N923498M	$	7,000.00
	OTHER ASSETS	$	7,000.00
	TOTAL ASSETS	**$**	**7,000.00**

REAL ESTATE TRUST
THOMAS JONES, TRUSTEE

FIRST ACCOUNTING
FOR THE PERIOD JANUARY 1, 2012 THRU JUNE 30, 2012
LOSSES ON SALES
SCHEDULE D

DATE	DESCRIPTION	CARRY VALUE	PROCEEDS	LOSSES
04/03/12	2010 MERCEDES C230 VIN K47834N923498M (TOTALED IN ACCIDENT ON 02/15/12, PROCEEDS FROM SAFE INSURANCE CO)	$ 7,000.00	$ 2,350.00	$ 4,650.00
	TOTALS	$ 7,000.00	$ 2,350.00	**$ 4,650.00**

§7.21 C. Form: Sales in Which Expenses Were Paid in the Course of the Sale

In the following example, furniture was sold for a gross price of $3000, resulting in a $2000 loss. This loss was reported on the Losses schedule. The sales expense of $1500 was reported on the Disbursements schedule. See §7.18.

APRIL CASH TRUST
SALLY CASH, TRUSTEE

FIRST ACCOUNTING
FOR THE PERIOD JANUARY 1, 2013 THRU JUNE 30, 2013
ASSETS ON HAND - BEGINNING OF PERIOD

SHARES / PAR VALUE		DESCRIPTION	CARRY VALUE
PERSONAL PROPERTY			
	FURNITURE AND FURNISHINGS		$ 5,000.00
		TOTAL PERSONAL PROPERTY	$ 5,000.00
		TOTAL ASSETS	$ 5,000.00

APRIL CASH TRUST
SALLY CASH, TRUSTEE

FIRST ACCOUNTING
FOR THE PERIOD JANUARY 1, 2013 THRU JUNE 30, 2013
DISBURSEMENTS
SCHEDULE C

DATE	PAID TO	FOR	INCOME	PRINCIPAL
ADMINISTRATIVE EXPENSES				
06/01/13	ALLY'S AUCTION HOUSE	CONSIGNMENT COMMISSION ON FURNITURE SALE	$ 750.00	$ 750.00
		TOTAL ADMINISTRATIVE EXPENSES	$ 750.00	$ 750.00
		TOTAL INCOME AND PRINCIPAL	$ 750.00	$ 750.00
		TOTAL DISBURSEMENTS	$ 1,500.00	

APRIL CASH TRUST
SALLY CASH, TRUSTEE

FIRST ACCOUNTING
FOR THE PERIOD JANUARY 1, 2013 THRU JUNE 30, 2013
LOSSES ON SALES
SCHEDULE D

DATE	SHARES	DESCRIPTION	CARRY VALUE	PROCEEDS	LOSSES
06/01/13		FURNITURE AND FURNISHINGS	$ 5,000.00	$ 3,000.00	$ 2,000.00
		TOTALS	$ 5,000.00	$ 3,000.00	$ 2,000.00

8
Disbursements

I. WHAT A DISBURSEMENTS SCHEDULE MUST INCLUDE §8.1
   A. Disbursements: Payments to Third Parties §8.2
   B. The Disbursements Schedule's Appearance
      1. Requirements for Different Types of Fiduciaries §8.3
      2. Sample Complete Disbursements Schedules
         a. Form: Disbursements From the Cash Trust §8.4
         b. Form: Disbursements From the Real Estate Trust §8.5

II. PREPARING THE SCHEDULE, AT A MINIMUM §8.6

III. BEST PRACTICES
   A. Disclose, Explain, and Atone for Mistakes §8.7
   B. List Categorically, Then Chronologically §8.8
   C. Each Real Property and Business Is Its Own Category §8.9
   D. Amounts Disbursed in Escrow §8.10
   E. Use Subtotals §8.11

IV. DISBURSEMENTS OF PRINCIPAL AND INCOME
   A. Debts of a Decedent, Expenses of Final Illness, and Expenses of Prior Administrations §8.12
      1. Payments From Principal §8.13
      2. Discretion to Pay From Either Income or Principal §8.14
      3. Paid Equally From Income and Principal §8.15
   B. Disbursements During Administration §8.16
      1. Expenses Paid Half From Income, Half From Principal §8.17
      2. Expenses Paid 100 Percent From Principal §8.18
      3. Expenses Paid 100 Percent From Income §8.19
   C. Payment of Taxes
      1. Gift, Estate, Inheritance, and Other Similar Taxes §8.20

     2. Property Taxes §8.21
     3. Income and Capital Gains Tax §8.22
  D. Expenses of Administering Real Property §8.23
  E. Loan Payments, Payments on Trust Debts §8.24
  F. Specifically Gifted Property §8.25

V. COMMON MISTAKES
  A. Payments From Sources Other Than the Res §8.26
  B. Asset Purchases Are Not Disbursements §8.27
  C. Transfers Are Not Disbursements §8.28

VI. EXHIBITS
  A. Form: Receipts Related to Real Property §8.29
  B. Form: Amounts Disbursed in Escrow §8.30
  C. Form: Debts Associated With a Decedent's Death Paid From Principal §8.31
  D. Form: Expenses Associated With Real Property §8.32
  E. Form: Loan Payments, Payments on Trust Debts §8.33

§8.1 I. WHAT A DISBURSEMENTS SCHEDULE MUST INCLUDE

In the Disbursements schedule of a court accounting, the fiduciary must state, with respect to each receipt (Prob C §§1061-1062):

- The date;
- The payee;
- The purpose; and
- The amount.

Trustees who are not concerned about whether a judge will review the account can meet their statutory duty to account for disbursements by furnishing the trust beneficiaries "a statement of . . . disbursements of principal and income that have occurred during the last complete fiscal year of the trust or since the last account." Prob C §16063(a).

§8.2 A. Disbursements: Payments to Third Parties

In general, disbursements are payments to third parties and distributions are payments to or for the benefit of beneficiaries. However, disbursements and distributions are distinguished from one another more by the nature of the payment than by the identity of the payee. Distributions are payments in satisfaction of a beneficial interest. See chap 9. Disbursements are all the other payments a fiduciary makes in the course of the administration. Disbursements include the debts of the decedent or of the deceased settlor, funeral expenses, taxes, and the expenses of administration. Disbursements also may include payments for rent, interest on a debt or obligation, or the cost of goods or services. Confusingly, a fiduciary might disburse money to a person who is also receiving distributions.

EXAMPLE 1▶ The personal representative who pays a creditor's claim for funeral expenses is making a disbursement, regardless of whether the creditor is also a beneficiary.

EXAMPLE 2▶ If a trustee rents a climate-controlled storage locker for 3 months, awaiting the day the trust's residual beneficiaries can gather to divide the settlor's valuable art collection, the trustee's rent payments are expenses of administration, accounted for as disbursements.

EXAMPLE 3▶ The sole beneficiary of the settlor's valuable art collection is traveling abroad at the time the trustee proposes distributing the art. At the beneficiary's request, the trustee places the art in a climate-controlled storage locker. In a decedent's estate, the rent on this storage locker is an expense of administration, *i.e.*, a disbursement. Prob C §11754. However, for the trustee who stores the art at the beneficiary's request, it would be a distribution.

EXAMPLE 4▶ A trustee pays herself a trustee fee. This is a disbursement, even if the trustee is also a beneficiary.

Unlike in trusts, in guardianships and conservatorships the fiduciary reports as disbursements expenses paid for the benefit of the ward or conservatee. Such expenses include living expenses such as clothing, food, and shelter. The expenses of medical and personal care are also treated as disbursements, as are a ward's education expenses. The only distribution a conservator or guardian would report on a Distribution schedule would be one that had been ordered by the court.

B. The Disbursements Schedule's Appearance

§8.3   1. Requirements for Different Types of Fiduciaries

Guardians and conservators who are not using the Judicial Council forms must account for disbursements on a schedule organized into five columns, as follows:

Date	Check No.	Payee	Purpose	Amount
5/13/2013	123	Superior Court	Letters of Conservatorship	$13.00

Although the Probate Code does not require fiduciaries to disclose how payment was made (*e.g.*, by check or electronic funds transfer), including this data in the account makes it easier to correlate individual disbursements with the fiduciary's financial records and facilitates proving the account.

Personal representatives and trustees should account for disbursements in a similar fashion as guardians and conservators. However, for each disbursement, the personal representative or trustee must also identify whether the payment is made from income, from principal, or partly from each. Personal representatives and trustees may represent the payment in either of two ways. Some fiduciaries use one schedule to account for payments from principal and another for payments from income. Thus, a personal representative might account for the expense of letters testamentary as follows:

Disbursements of Income

Date	Check No.	Payee	Purpose	Amount
5/13/2013	123	Superior Court	Letters Testamentary	$6.50

Disbursements of Principal

Date	Check No.	Payee	Purpose	Amount
5/13/2013	123	Superior Court	Letters Testamentary	$6.50

More commonly, and perhaps less confusingly, personal representatives and trustees may aggregate on one schedule their distributions of principal and income.

Disbursements

Date	Check No.	Payee	Purpose	Income	Principal
5/13/2013	123	Superior Court	Letters Testamentary	$6.50	$6.50

2. Sample Complete Disbursements Schedules

§8.4   a. Form: Disbursements From the Cash Trust

The example below is the complete Disbursements schedule of the Cash Trust described in chap 1.

SALLY CASH, TRUSTEE

FIRST ACCOUNTING

FOR THE PERIOD JANUARY 1, 2013 THRU JUNE 30, 2013

DISBURSEMENTS

SCHEDULE C

DATE	PAID TO	CHK #	FOR	INCOME	PRINCIPAL
ADMINISTRATIVE EXPENSES					
01/05/13	MARGARET'S RESTAURANT	204	MEMORIAL DINNER		$ 722.36
01/05/13	FRED'S FUNERAL HOME	205	MEMORIAL SERVICE		$ 1,750.00
03/01/13	BEST BUY	206	LAPTOP	$ 300.00	$ 300.00
04/07/13	LAW OFFICES OF LUCY LAWYER	208	LEGAL FEES	$ 250.00	$ 250.00
06/01/13	ALLY'S AUCTION HOUSE		CONSIGNMENT COMMISSION ON FURNITURE SALE	$ 750.00	$ 750.00
06/28/13	WELLS FARGO BANK	AUTO	WIRE TRANSFER FEE	$ 15.00	$ 15.00
06/28/13	WELLS FARGO BANK	AUTO	WIRE TRANSFER FEE	$ 15.00	$ 15.00
06/30/13	SALLY CASH	209	TRUSTEE FEE	$ 4,460.22	$ 4,460.22
			TOTAL ADMINISTRATIVE EXPENSES	$ 5,790.22	$ 8,262.58
			TOTAL INCOME AND PRINCIPAL	$ 5,790.22	$ 8,262.58
			TOTAL DISBURSEMENTS	$ 14,052.80	

§8.5 b. Form: Disbursements From the Real Estate Trust

The example below is the complete Disbursements schedule of the David Jones Real Estate Trust described in chap 1.

DAVID JONES TRUST
THOMAS JONES, TRUSTEE

FIRST ACCOUNTING
FOR THE PERIOD JANUARY 1, 2012 THRU JUNE 30, 2012
DISBURSEMENTS
SCHEDULE C

DATE	PAID TO	CHK #	FOR	INCOME		PRINCIPAL
ADMINISTRATIVE EXPENSES						
01/03/12	FANCY FUNERAL HOME		MEMORIAL SERVICE		$	1,200.00
01/04/12	FANCY FUNERAL HOME		BURIAL FEES		$	6,000.00
01/29/12	LAW OFFICE OF DUDLEY SMITH		REIMBURSMENT FOR COSTS ADVANCED	$ 52.00	$	52.00
01/31/12	BANK OF AMERICA		MONTHLY SERVICE FEE	$ 5.00	$	5.00
01/31/12	DISCOVER CARD		CREDIT CARD - DEBT OF DECEDENT		$	521.34
02/15/12	ANYTOWN HOSPITAL		DEBT OF DECEDENT		$	600.00
02/15/12	ANYTOWN MEDICAL GROUP		DEBT OF DECEDENT		$	230.00
02/28/12	BANK OF AMERICA		MONTHLY SERVICE FEE	$ 5.00	$	5.00
03/31/12	BANK OF AMERICA		MONTHLY SERVICE FEE	$ 5.00	$	5.00
04/16/12	LAW OFFICE OF DUDLEY SMITH		LEGAL FEES	$ 500.00	$	500.00
04/20/12	INTERNAL REVENUE SERVICE		2011 FEDERAL TAX DUE		$	5,230.00
04/20/12	FRANCHISE TAX BOARD		2011 STATE TAX DUE		$	2,140.00
04/30/12	BANK OF AMERICA		MONTHLY SERVICE FEE	$ 5.00	$	5.00
05/05/12	LOUIE & LOUIE, CPA		TAX PREPARATION	$ 250.00	$	250.00
05/31/12	BANK OF AMERICA		MONTHLY SERVICE FEE	$ 5.00	$	5.00
06/30/12	BANK OF AMERICA		MONTHLY SERVICE FEE	$ 5.00	$	5.00
			TOTAL ADMINISTRATIVE EXPENSES	$ 832.00	$	16,753.34

REAL ESTATE EXPENSES - 987 SUNNYSIDE STREET

Date	Payee	Description	Amount		
01/05/12	QUALITY MORTGAGE COMPANY	MORTGAGE PAYMENT	$	787.50	$ 712.50
01/17/12	PACIFIC GAS & ELECTRIC	UTILITIES	$	52.75	
01/28/12	EBMUD	WATER SERVICE	$	62.45	
01/28/12	KILLER PEST CONTROL	EXTERMINATOR	$	150.00	
01/30/12	WASTE MANAGEMENT COMPANY	GARBAGE SERVICE	$	142.00	
01/30/12	COMCAST	CABLE AND TELEPHONE SERVICE	$	160.80	
02/05/12	QUALITY MORTGAGE COMPANY	MORTGAGE PAYMENT	$	784.53	$ 715.47
02/15/12	PACIFIC GAS & ELECTRIC	UTILITIES	$	53.21	
02/29/12	COMCAST	CABLE AND TELEPHONE SERVICE	$	162.90	
03/05/12	QUALITY MORTGAGE COMPANY	MORTGAGE PAYMENT	$	781.55	$ 718.45
03/12/12	ROOTER ROOTER	PLUMBING REPAIR	$	475.00	
03/15/12	GORGEOUS GARDENS	GARDENING SERVICE (3 MONTHS)	$	300.00	
03/17/12	PACIFIC GAS & ELECTRIC	UTILITIES	$	50.98	
03/27/12	EBMUD	WATER SERVICE	$	65.01	
03/28/12	WASTE MANAGEMENT COMPANY	GARBAGE SERVICE	$	142.00	
03/31/12	COMCAST	CABLE AND TELEPHONE SERVICE	$	161.75	
04/05/12	QUALITY MORTGAGE COMPANY	MORTGAGE PAYMENT	$	778.56	$ 721.44
04/07/12	A-1 ROOFING	ROOF REPAIR	$	3,600.00	
04/18/12	PACIFIC GAS & ELECTRIC	UTILITIES	$	51.37	
04/30/12	COMCAST	CABLE AND TELEPHONE SERVICE	$	160.90	
05/05/12	QUALITY MORTGAGE COMPANY	MORTGAGE PAYMENT	$	775.55	$ 724.45
05/17/12	PACIFIC GAS & ELECTRIC	UTILITIES	$	51.22	

Date	Payee	Description	Amount	
05/31/12	EBMUD	WATER SERVICE	$ 61.98	
05/31/12	COMCAST	CABLE AND TELEPHONE SERVICE	$ 161.85	
06/01/12	WASTE MANAGEMENT COMPANY	GARBAGE SERVICE	$ 142.00	
06/05/12	QUALITY MORTGAGE COMPANY	MORTGAGE PAYMENT	$ 772.53	$ 727.47
06/15/12	PACIFIC GAS & ELECTRIC	UTILITIES	$ 53.01	
06/30/12	COMCAST	CABLE AND TELEPHONE SERVICE	$ 162.25	
		TOTAL REAL ESTATE EXPENSES - 987 SUNNYSIDE STREET	$ 11,103.65	$ 4,319.78

REAL ESTATE EXPENSES - 321 FRANCHISE ROW

Date	Payee	Description	Amount	
01/15/12	COUNTY TAX COLLECTOR	SECOND INSTALLMENT OF 2011-2012 PROPERTY TAX	$ 7,550.00	
01/18/12	JOE'S ELECTRICAL	INSTALLATION OF OUTDOOR LIGHTING	$ 1,200.00	
01/26/12	WASTE MANAGEMENT	GARBAGE SERVICE	$ 450.00	
02/08/12	PAT'S PAVING	PARKING LOT REPAVING	$ 4,500.00	
02/15/12	PAUL'S PAINTING	PARKING LOT PAINTING	$ 2,300.00	
02/25/12	WASTE MANAGEMENT	GARBAGE SERVICE	$ 450.00	
02/27/12	SAL'S PLUMBING	PLUMBING REPAIR	$ 752.00	
03/25/12	WASTE MANAGEMENT	GARBAGE SERVICE	$ 450.00	
04/25/12	WASTE MANAGEMENT	GARBAGE SERVICE	$ 450.00	
		TOTAL REAL ESTATE EXPENSES - 321 FRANCHISE ROW	$ 18,102.00	$ -

REAL ESTATE EXPENSES PAID IN ESCROW UPON SALE OF 321 FRANCHISE ROW

Date	Payee	Description	Amount
05/15/12	BETTER HOMES REAL ESTATE COMPANY	BROKER COMMISSION	$ 47,265.00
05/15/12	PRUDENTIAL REAL ESTATE COMPANY	BROKER COMMISSION	$ 47,265.00
05/15/12	SELLER CREDIT	CREDIT FOR CLOSING COSTS	$ 25,000.00
05/15/12	SUPER CONSTRUCTION	LOADING DOCK REPAIRS REQUIRED FOR SALE	$ 40,000.00
05/15/12	ERNEST EVIRONMENTAL	INSPECTION FEE	$ 750.00
05/15/12	STEWART TITLE CO	PRO-RATED RENT COLLECTED FOR MAY 2012	$ 3,125.00
05/15/12	STEWART TITLE CO	SECURITY DEPOSITS	$ 12,500.00
05/15/12	STEWART TITLE CO	ESCROW AND TITLE FEES	$ 1,000.00
05/15/12	STEWART TITLE CO	DOCUMENTATION FEE	$ 500.00
05/15/12	STEWART TITLE CO	NOTARY FEE	$ 20.00
05/15/12	STEWART TITLE CO	COURIER FEE	$ 100.00
		TOTAL REAL ESTATE EXPENSES PAID IN ESCROW $ -	$ 177,525.00

§8.5

REAL ESTATE EXPENSES - 111 MANAGEMENT AVE

Date	Payee	Description	Amount	Total
01/02/12	MAGNIFICENT MANAGEMENT	PROPERTY MANAGEMENT FEE	$ 225.00	
01/15/12	FINE FENCES	FENCE REPAIR - UNIT B	$ 1,500.00	
01/22/12	GUPPY GLASS	WINDOW REPAIR - UNIT B	$ 250.00	
01/31/12	AMY'S APPLIANCES	WASHER / DRYER - UNIT D	$ 600.00	
01/31/12	CAPPY'S CARPET	CARPET REPLACEMENT - UNIT D	$ 550.00	
01/31/12	DOLLY'S DECORATING	INTERIOR PAINTING - UNIT D	$ 750.00	
02/02/12	MAGNIFICENT MANAGEMENT	PROPERTY MANAGEMENT FEE	$ 225.00	
02/17/12	JOE'S ELECTRICAL	INTERCOM REPAIR	$ 325.00	
03/02/12	MAGNIFICENT MANAGEMENT	PROPERTY MANAGEMENT FEE	$ 225.00	
03/15/12	PAUL'S PAINTING	EXTERIOR PAINTING OF BUILDING IN PREPARATION FOR SALE		$ 7,000.00
03/15/12	FANNIE'S FURNACE	FURNACE REPAIR IN PREPARATION FOR SALE		$ 2,500.00
		TOTAL REAL ESTATE EXPENSES - 111 MANAGEMENT AVE	$ 4,650.00	$ 9,500.00

REAL ESTATE EXPENSES PAID IN ESCROW UPON SALE OF 111 MANAGEMENT AVE

Date	Payee	Description	Amount	Total
04/01/12	COLDWELL BANKER	BROKER COMMISSION		$ 31,500.00
04/01/12	ZEPHYER REAL ESTATE	BROKER COMMISSION		$ 31,500.00
04/01/12	DAN'S DISCLOSURES	HAZARD DISCLOSURES		$ 200.00
04/01/12	COUNTY TAX COLLECTOR	PRO-RATED PROPERTY TAX DUE		$ 3,650.00
04/01/12	OLD REPUBLIC TITLE	TITLE AND ESCROW FEES		$ 750.00
04/01/12	OLD REPUBLIC TITLE	DOCUMENTATION FEE		$ 250.00
04/01/12	OLD REPUBLIC TITLE	SECURITY DEPOSITS		$ 6,800.00
		TOTAL REAL ESTATE EXPENSES PAID IN ESCROW	$ -	$ 74,650.00

OTHER DISBURSEMENTS

Date	Payee	Description	Amount	Total
01/17/12	MIKE MECHANIC	SMOG CHECK	$ 75.00	
01/31/12	DEPARTMENT OF MOTOR VEHICLES	AUTO REGISTRATION	$ 129.00	
01/31/12	SAFE INSURANCE	AUTO INSURANCE	$ 400.00	
02/16/12	TOWING SERVICE OF AMERICA	TOWING FEE TO REMOVE MERCEDES AT ACCIDENT SITE	$ 200.00	
		TOTAL OTHER DISBURSEMENTS	$ 804.00	$ -
		TOTAL INCOME AND PRINCIPAL	$ 35,491.65	$ 282,748.12
		TOTAL DISBURSEMENTS	$ 318,239.77	

§8.6 II. PREPARING THE SCHEDULE, AT A MINIMUM

A fiduciary accounting should alert the beneficiaries to all significant transactions occurring during the account period. National Fiduciary Accounting Standards Project, Principle III. Consistent with this principal, the fiduciary who accounts to the court may not lump together common items and disclose only their sum. Prob C §1062(b). For example, the fiduciary who rents a storage unit for which rent is paid periodically must *not* account as follows:

Annual storage fee: $60,000

The above example would be impermissible in a court accounting, both because it omits the name of the payee and because it does not show the payment of "each item." Prob C §1062(b). Even in a non-court trust accounting, where such aggregation might be permissible (Prob C §16063(a)), the above might be insufficient because it does not show to whom payments were made.

Consider the below example, taken from the Disbursements schedule of the trustee Prudence Lightly.

Date	Payee	Purpose	Amount
1/1/2010	P. Lightly	Storage	$5,000
3/1/2010	P. Lightly	Storage	$5,000
4/1/2010	P. Lightly	Storage	$5,000
5/30/2010	P. Lightly	Storage	$5,000
7/1/2010	Mary Lightly	Storage	$2,500
8/1/2010	Chris Lightly	Storage	$2,500
9/1/2010	Harry Lightly	Storage	$2,500
12/25/2010	P. Lightly	Storage	$10,000
12/25/2010	Mary Lightly	Storage	$22,500
			$60,000

In her accounting, Prudence needs to disclose any potential breaches of trust in order to trigger the running of the statute of limitations. See §§15.12, 15.25. By accounting in the manner required by the Probate Code, Prudence Lightly has disclosed three potential breaches of trust. First, she has disclosed a likely breach of her duty not to use trust property for her own benefit. The payments to herself appear to be a breach of the duty codified in Prob C

§16004(a), sometimes called the duty to avoid conflicts of interest. Second, she has disclosed a potential breach of her duty to administer the trust solely in the interests of the beneficiaries. Payments to family members appear to breach the duty codified in Prob C §16002(a). Lastly, if these storage fees are otherwise legitimate, failing to pay the fee in February, June, October, and November might risk losing trust property in a lien sale. The disclosure of these missed payments reveals a possible breach of Prudence's duty to control and preserve the trust property. Prob C §16006. The impermissible accounting shown in the first example would not be sufficient to trigger the running of the statute of limitations; only the detailed accounting shown in the second example achieves this goal.

III. BEST PRACTICES

§8.7   A. Disclose, Explain, and Atone for Mistakes

Many beneficiaries find fiduciary accountings confusing, but everyone understands spending money. As a result, when beneficiaries examine a fiduciary accounting, they often turn first to the Disbursements schedule and give it their greatest scrutiny. This is the schedule that most quickly reveals the mistakes of inexperienced trustees and the breaches of the more culpable. But practitioners should not obfuscate! Fiduciaries who act in bad faith and unreasonably when opposing an objection to an account may be ordered to pay the objector's attorney fees. Prob C §2622.5 (conservators and guardians), §11003(b) (personal representatives), §17211 (trustees). See California Trust and Probate Litigation §§13.48–13.49 (Cal CEB). It is unreasonable to hide improper disbursements by mischaracterizing them. The best practice is to honestly disclose any improper disbursements, while simultaneously calling attention to any actions the fiduciary has taken to remedy the breach.

§8.8   B. List Categorically, Then Chronologically

As with receipts, disbursements should be listed categorically, then chronologically within each category. Traditionally, the categories and the order of presentation are as follows:

- Debts of the decedent;

- Expenses of administration;
- Taxes;
- Expenses of each individual real property;
- Amounts disbursed in escrow; and
- Note payments.

The above categories are not the only acceptable presentation of disbursements, however. For example, the trustee who administers several properties within the same utility district might write one check each month, or each quarter, to pay the various properties' water bills. This trustee might categorize these payments under the heading, "East Bay Municipal Utilities District." As another example, consider the trustee who hires an attorney to review the trust's leases with tenants in various properties. Unless the attorney bills separately for each lease reviewed, the trustee may be unable to allocate the attorney's fees to any particular property. This trustee might account for each payment to the attorney under the heading, "Attorney Fees, Real Property Management."

The trustee should approach the question of how to best categorize expenses by asking, "To what use will this information be put?" In a terminating trust that distributes only to residual beneficiaries, if the trustee is selling real properties as quickly as reasonably possible, the beneficiaries may be uninterested in assessing the carrying costs of any particular property. This trustee may wish to categorize expenses by payor, or by type, and not bother with allocating each expense to a particular property. By contrast, the trustee who administers an ongoing trust has a duty to assess whether his or her investments are prudent. Prob C §§16045–16054. To do this, the trustee must be able to assess each individual property's carrying cost. This trustee should categorize disbursements by property. Similarly, the trustee who administers a property that will be distributed as a specific gift must categorize disbursements (and receipts) by property because, typically, a specific gift carries with it the benefits and burdens of the property. Prob C §16340.

§8.9   C. Each Real Property and Business Is Its Own Category

If the fiduciary administers income-producing real property, or a business for which the trustee is not accounting separately, the fiduciary may wish to treat each enterprise as a separate category of expense. Within these categories, the fiduciary might create sub-categories of the enterprise-specific expenses. This practice is best explained with an example. Imagine the trust estate consists of two apartment buildings in two different counties. For each, the trustee pays some expenses semi-annually, such as insurance and property tax, and some expenses monthly, including utilities and gardening. This fiduciary would account for disbursements related to the two properties by creating a separate category for each property and sub-categorizing the disbursements made on behalf of the particular property, as follows:

Date	Payee (Purpose)	Amount
	Clearlake Property	
1/15/2010	Calfarm Ins. Co. (liability insurance)	$1,250
1/30/2010	Mighty Midge (mosquito abatement)	$400
4/1/2010	Lake County Tax Assessor (property tax)	$1,000
	Subtotal, Clearlake Property	$2,650
	Truckee Property	
1/15/2010	State Farm Ins. Co. (liability insurance)	$2,250
1/30/2010	Jose Aguillar (weed abatement)	$600
4/1/2010	Nevada County Tax Assessor (property tax)	$3,000
	Subtotal, Truckee Property	$5,850

Also see the example in §8.29, which accounts for receipts from two different properties.

§8.10 D. Amounts Disbursed in Escrow

Use a separate category for amounts disbursed in escrow, even though some of the disbursements might also fit nicely in one of the Disbursements schedule's other categories. For an example illustrating such disbursements, see §8.30.

§8.11 E. Use Subtotals

Anticipate the beneficiaries' concerns and, using subtotals, answer the questions they can be expected to ask. Such questions may include, "How much was spent on attorneys?" At a minimum, subtotal

IV. DISBURSEMENTS OF PRINCIPAL AND INCOME

§8.12 A. Debts of a Decedent, Expenses of Final Illness, and Expenses of Prior Administrations

Often, the fiduciary's first account begins as the result of a testator's or settlor's death, or as the result of an income interest ending, such as when the surviving-spouse beneficiary of a QTIP trust dies or when a trust for a term of years terminates. These events do not necessarily terminate a trust. Often, one income interest is followed by another, such as when the settlor of a grantor trust dies and the settlor's interest is followed by trusts established for the benefit of the settlor's children. Even when the end of an income interest is followed by outright distribution of the entire trust estate, the trustee's powers will continue during the period of winding up the trust. Whether the trust continues for new income beneficiaries or terminates in an outright distribution, the termination of the prior interest often gives rise to expenses that the fiduciary will pay after the termination. The Uniform Principal and Income Act (UPAIA) (Prob C §§16320–16375) distinguishes these disbursements from those associated with the terminated income interest, sometimes called "disbursements during administration."

§8.13 1. Payments From Principal

The rules for paying the debts and expenses associated with a decedent's death or the termination of an income interest are the subject of Prob C §16340(c)(2)–(3). Most practitioners are familiar with the rule that the following payments are payments from principal:

- Debts of the decedent;
- Funeral expenses;
- Disposition of remains;
- Family allowances;
- Death taxes and related penalties that are apportioned to the

estate or terminating income interest by the will, the trust, or Division 10 of the Probate Code (see also Prob C §16371(a)(6) (characterizing as payments of principal all "[e]state, inheritance, and other transfer taxes, including penalties, apportioned to the trust")); and

- The disbursements made or incurred in connection with the settlement of a decedent's estate, or the winding up of a terminating income interest, which disbursements are not taken as an income tax deduction and accordingly paid from income under Prob C §16340(c)(2).

For an example accounting of debts and expenses associated with a decedent's death, see §8.31.

§8.14   2. Discretion to Pay From Either Income or Principal

Practitioners are less familiar with the rule that gives fiduciaries the discretion to pay certain disbursements from income or principal, provided the disbursements are made after a decedent's death (in the case of a decedent's estate) or after an income interest in a trust ends. In those circumstances, the items below may be paid from income or principal, at the fiduciary's discretion (Prob C §16340(c)(2)):

- Fees of attorneys, accountants, and other fiduciaries;
- Court costs and other expenses of administration;
- Interest on death taxes.

NOTE▶ Such expenses may not be paid from income of property passing to a trust that qualifies for the marital or charitable deduction from the estate tax if that payment would cause the loss of the deduction. Prob C §16340(c)(2).

§8.15   3. Paid Equally From Income and Principal

In certain situations, fiduciaries do not have the discretion to choose between principal and income when paying such expenses. During the administration, as opposed to at the beginning, the above disbursements are governed by the rules of Prob C §§16370–16371. These sections contain the familiar rule that trustee fees, attorney fees, and accounting fees are paid equally from income and principal; that the costs of court proceedings are similarly shared; and that interest is paid 100 percent from income. Prob C §16370(c). The rule of Prob C §16340(c) applies at the beginning of an income interest to make it easier for the fiduciary to treat the income and principal beneficiaries fairly. As the Comment to Prob C §16340 explains:

> An advantage of permitting the fiduciary to choose the source of the payment is that, if the fiduciary's decision is consistent with the decision to deduct these expenses for income tax purposes or estate tax purposes, it eliminates the need to adjust between principal and income that may arise when, for example, an expense that is paid from principal is deducted for income tax purposes or an expense that is paid from income is deducted for estate tax purposes.

§8.16 B. Disbursements During Administration

The expenses of administration not subject to Prob C §16340 are paid from income and principal as explained in the following sections.

§8.17 1. Expenses Paid Half From Income, Half From Principal

Many of the disbursements made during the course of administration are governed by Prob C §§16370–16371, which most publishers misleadingly label Disbursements From Income and Disbursements From Principal.

NOTE▶ Section headings do not impart meaning to the provisions of the Probate Code (Prob C §4). Because they are often the publishers' creation, consider the statutes as the legislature enacts them.

In fact, these statutes allocate the disbursements listed below equally between principal and income, except as ordered by the court:

- The trustee's regular compensation (Prob C §§16370(a), 16371(a)(1));

- The compensation of any person providing investment advisory or custodial services to the trustee (Prob C §§16370(a), 16371(a)(1));

- The expenses for accountings (Prob C §§16370(b), 16371(a)(1)); and

- The expense, including attorney fees, of judicial proceedings or other matters that involve both the income and remainder interests (Prob C §§16370(b), 16371(a)(1)).

§8.18 2. Expenses Paid 100 Percent From Principal

The following expenses of administration are paid 100 percent from principal:

- Except as the court may order, all of the trustee's compensation calculated on principal as a fee for acceptance, distribution, or termination of the trust (Prob C §16371(a)(2));

- Expenses of a proceeding that concerns primarily principal, including a proceeding to construe the trust or to protect the trust or its property (Prob C §16371(a)(4)); and

- Premiums on insurance not described in Prob C §16370(d), provided the trust is the owner and beneficiary of the policy (Prob C §16371(a)(5)).

NOTE▶ The insurance described in Prob C §16370(d) is insurance covering the loss of a principal asset or the loss of income from the use of a principal asset.

§8.19 3. Expenses Paid 100 Percent From Income

The following disbursements are paid 100 percent from income (Prob C §16370(c)):

- Except those expenses paid equally from income and principal (see §8.17), the ordinary expenses incurred in connection with the administration, management, or preservation of trust property and the distribution of income, including interest, ordinary repairs, and regularly recurring taxes assessed against principal; and

- Expenses of a proceeding or other matter that concerns primarily the income interest.

EXAMPLE▶ The legal fees incurred to evict a tenant from a rental property are paid from income.

C. Payment of Taxes

§8.20   1. Gift, Estate, Inheritance, and Other Similar Taxes

Estate, inheritance, and other taxes on gratuitous transfers, including penalties, apportioned to the trust are paid 100 percent from principal. Prob C §16371(a)(6). Interest on these taxes, however, may be paid from income at the trustee's discretion. Prob C §16340(c)(2).

§8.21   2. Property Taxes

Property taxes are "regularly recurring taxes assessed against principal," and accordingly are paid 100 percent from income. Prob C §16370(c). Property taxes include the taxes assessed on real property and also those assessed against tangible and intangible personal property.

§8.22   3. Income and Capital Gains Tax

Regardless of whether a taxing authority calls its tax an "income" tax, the source of the tax payment depends on whether the receipts that generate the tax are income receipts or principal receipts. The "income" tax on receipts allocable to principal is paid from principal. Prob C §16374.

When the trustee is required to pay a tax on the trust's share of an entity's taxable income, the trustee must pay the tax from income or principal in the same proportion as the trustee allocates receipts from the entity to income or principal. Prob C §16374(c). An exception lies when the tax allocable to the trust's share in the entity exceeds the receipts from that entity. Then, the trustee will pay from principal that portion of the tax that exceeds the trust's receipts from the entity. Prob C §16374(c)(4). To offset the shifting of economic interests such a payment might create, the Uniform Principal and Income Act (UPAIA) gives the trustee the power to make adjustments between principal and income. Prob C §16375(a).

§8.23   D. Expenses of Administering Real Property

There is no single statute that governs payment of the expenses of administering real property, and many of the rules cited below would apply equally to the administration of personal property.

The following are paid 100 percent from income:

- All recurring premiums on insurance covering the loss of a principal asset or the loss of income from, or use of, the asset (Prob C §16370(d));

- Ordinary repairs (Prob C §16370(c));

- Regularly recurring taxes assessed against principal (Prob C §16370(c)); and

- Expenses of a proceeding or other matter that primarily concerns the income interest (Prob C §16370(c)), such as the expense of evicting a tenant.

The following are paid 100 percent from principal:

- Disbursements made to prepare a property for sale (Prob C §16371(a)(2));

- Expenses of environmental remediation, amounts spent to prevent future releases of contamination, expenses of pursuing other potentially liable parties, and the like (Prob C §16371(a)(7));

- The expense of a proceeding that concerns primarily principal (Prob C §16371(a)(4)), such as a boundary-line dispute;

- The return of a tenant's security deposit; and

- Payment of principal amounts due on a mortgage (Prob C §16371(a)(3)).

For an example of a Disbursements schedule showing payments made to prepare a property for sale, see §8.32.

§8.24   E. Loan Payments, Payments on Trust Debts

Interest payments on a loan, whether consumer credit, mortgage, or other type of loan, are paid from income (Prob C §16370(c)), and principal payments are paid from principal (Prob C §16371(a)(3)).

Payments on the principal of the trust's debt are paid 100 percent from principal. Prob C §16371(a)(3). For an illustration of mortgage payments that reduce a trust's outstanding liabilities, see §8.33.

§8.25   F. Specifically Gifted Property

Until a specific gift is distributed, a fiduciary must account for the receipts and payments related to that gift just as the fiduciary would account for any receipts or payments. Just prior to distributing the specific gift, the fiduciary must calculate the net income attributable to the gift. See §§9.27-9.30. In a decedent's estate, the personal representative would show this calculation on the auxiliary schedule, Proposed Distributions. See §§11.5-11.8. Only after the court has authorized the distribution could the personal representative distribute the specific gift and its net income. If the personal representative then had to file a further account, he or she would report the distribution on the Distributions schedule, including the distribution of net income. See chap 9.

In a trust administration, the trustee also would report receipts and payments on behalf of a specific gift on the Receipts and Disbursements schedules. And like personal representatives, before distributing a specific gift, the trustee must calculate any net income attributable to the gift. Trustees would not, however, report their calculation on the schedule, Proposed Distributions. Instead, the trustee probably would distribute the property and its net income, then report these distributions on the Distributions schedule. The trustee may show the calculation of net income either in a note on the Distributions schedule, or as an auxiliary schedule. See chap 11.

V. COMMON MISTAKES

§8.26   A. Payments From Sources Other Than the Res

The schedule of disbursements is a statement by the fiduciary that he or she has disbursed a particular amount from the res (guardianship or conservatorship estate, probate estate, or income or principal of the trust) on a specific date, to an identified payee, for the stated purpose. Prob C §§1061-1062. It is a mistake to use the Disbursements schedule to account for expenditures made from any fund other than the res. The following examples illustrate this common mistake.

EXAMPLE 1▶ Daughter serves as conservatee for Mother. As a favor to his sister, and because he is a dutiful son, Son purchased supplies for Mother. Son made the purchase with his own money, with the expectation of being reimbursed. Son's expenditures were not disbursements of conservatorship funds and should not be stated on the conservator's schedule of Disbursements. If the conservator reimbursed Son during the account period, that payment is a disbursement of conservatorship funds, in which case the payment *to Son* should be accounted for as a disbursement. By contrast, if at the end of the account, the conservator still owes Son for his purchase, the amount Son spent is carried as a liability and should be reported on the schedule of Liabilities, with all the particularity that would be required if Son's purchases had been a disbursement of conservatorship funds.

EXAMPLE 2▶ Joe is the personal representative of his mother's estate, which has only one asset: the decedent's vacant single-family home. To ready the home for sale, Joe spent his own money on repairs. As personal representative, Joe may not account for this expense as a disbursement of estate funds. The estate had no funds to disburse and in any case, the purchases were made by Joe, individually. Perhaps Joe lent money to himself as personal representative, a transaction which raises its own issues. On accounting for borrowed money, see §6.7. Just as likely, Joe was acting as a volunteer when he rehabilitated his mother's property. Joe may expect and hope to be reimbursed, but he should not characterize the transaction as something it was not. It was not a disbursement of estate funds.

EXAMPLE 3▶ Theresa is a trustee of her mother's trust, which became irrevocable on the death of her mother. Theresa also is the surviving joint tenant of a bank account established by her mother, with the mother's funds. After her mother died, Theresa used the joint account to pay for the funeral. If Theresa takes the position that the joint account is not a trust asset, she will not carry it on the schedule of Assets on Hand—Beginning of Period, and she may not treat the payment of funeral expenses as a disbursement of trust assets. Like Joe in the prior example, Theresa may be a creditor or she may be a mere volunteer, but she is not entitled to account for the payment of funeral expenses as if they were disbursements from the trust.

§8.27 B. Asset Purchases Are Not Disbursements

Many purchases are disbursements. For example, when a fiduciary purchases postage stamps, the purchase is an administrative expense and is properly accounted for on the schedule of Disbursements. One of the most common mistakes fiduciaries make, however, is accounting for the purchase of an *asset* as if the purchase were a disbursement of cash. For example, the purchase of an annuity is not a disbursement. Neither is the purchase of corporate shares, partnership interests, or the like. When the fiduciary exchanges cash for some other type of asset, presumably the fiduciary receives something of like value. Such transactions therefore should be accounted for on the schedule, Changes in Form of Assets. See §11.11.

§8.28 C. Transfers Are Not Disbursements

Moving money from one cash account to another, or from one money market mutual fund to another, is not a disbursement and fiduciaries are not required to account for those transfers. Prob C §1063(b). If the transfer has some other significance, such as marking the beginning of a relationship with an attorney, the transaction may merit mention. For example, if the trustee makes a deposit toward the attorney's future services and the attorney puts the deposit into a client-trust account, the trustee may wish to account for the transfer on the schedule, Changes in Form of Assets. While the money is on deposit in the attorney's client-trust account, the money is still a trust asset, *i.e.*, giving the deposit to the attorney is not a disbursement. The money is not *disbursed* until the attorney is paid some portion of it, and any portion of the money remaining in the attorney's client-trust account at the end of the account period should be reported on the schedule of Assets on Hand—End of Period.

Treating a transfer as a disbursement is not an error without consequence. Consider the personal representative who closes one bank account and deposits the money in another. If this fiduciary mistakenly treats the closure as a disbursement, the credits will exceed the charges by the amount of the transfer. To rebalance the account, the fiduciary would have to treat opening the account as a receipt (disbursements are credits; receipts are charges), but doing this would increase the fiduciary's statutory fee because one of the bases of the statutory fee is the fiduciary's receipts. Prob C §10800(b). Therefore, if a fiduciary must report a transfer of money from one account to another, the transfer should be accounted for on the Changes in Form of Assets schedule.

VI. EXHIBITS

§8.29   A. Form: Receipts Related to Real Property

The example below shows Thomas Jones, Trustee, accounting for receipts from 321 Franchise Row and 111 Management Avenue. For a further discussion of this schedule, see §8.9.

REAL ESTATE TRUST
THOMAS JONES, TRUSTEE

FIRST ACCOUNTING
FOR THE PERIOD JANUARY 1, 2012 THRU JUNE 30, 2012
DISBURSEMENTS
SCHEDULE C

DATE	PAID TO	CHK #	FOR	INCOME	PRINCIPAL
REAL ESTATE EXPENSES - 321 FRANCHISE ROW					
01/15/12	COUNTY TAX COLLECTOR		SECOND INSTALLMENT OF 2011-2012 PROPERTY TAX	$ 7,550.00	
01/18/12	JOE'S ELECTRICAL		INSTALLATION OF OUTDOOR LIGHTING	$ 1,200.00	
01/26/12	WASTE MANAGEMENT		GARBAGE SERVICE	$ 450.00	
02/08/12	PAT'S PAVING		PARKING LOT REPAVING	$ 4,500.00	
02/15/12	PAUL'S PAINTING		PARKING LOT PAINTING	$ 2,300.00	
02/25/12	WASTE MANAGEMENT		GARBAGE SERVICE	$ 450.00	
02/27/12	SAL'S PLUMBING		PLUMBING REPAIR	$ 752.00	
03/25/12	WASTE MANAGEMENT		GARBAGE SERVICE	$ 450.00	
04/25/12	WASTE MANAGEMENT		GARBAGE SERVICE	$ 450.00	
			TOTAL REAL ESTATE EXPENSES - 321 FRANCHISE ROW	$ 18,102.00	$ -
REAL ESTATE EXPENSES - 111 MANAGEMENT AVE					
01/02/12	MAGNIFICENT MANAGEMENT		PROPERTY MANAGEMENT FEE	$ 225.00	
01/15/12	FINE FENCES		FENCE REPAIR - UNIT B	$ 1,500.00	
01/22/12	GUPPY GLASS		WINDOW REPAIR - UNIT B	$ 250.00	
01/31/12	AMY'S APPLIANCES		WASHER / DRYER - UNIT D	$ 600.00	
01/31/12	CAPPY'S CARPET		CARPET REPLACEMENT - UNIT D	$ 550.00	
01/31/12	DOLLY'S DECORATING		INTERIOR PAINTING - UNIT D	$ 750.00	
02/02/12	MAGNIFICENT MANAGEMENT		PROPERTY MANAGEMENT FEE	$ 225.00	

02/17/12	JOE'S ELECTRICAL		INTERCOM REPAIR	$	325.00		
03/02/12	MAGNIFICENT MANAGEMENT		PROPERTY MANAGEMENT FEE	$	225.00		
03/15/12	PAUL'S PAINTING		EXTERIOR PAINTING OF BUILDING IN PREPARATION FOR SALE			$	7,000.00
03/15/12	FANNIE'S FURNACE		FURNACE REPAIR IN PREPARATION FOR SALE			$	2,500.00
		TOTAL REAL ESTATE EXPENSES - 111 MANAGEMENT AVE		$	4,650.00	$	9,500.00

§8.30 B. Form: Amounts Disbursed in Escrow

The example below shows disbursements made when Thomas Jones, Trustee, sold 321 Franchise Row and 111 Management Avenue. For further discussion of this schedule, see §8.10.

REAL ESTATE TRUST
THOMAS JONES, TRUSTEE

FIRST ACCOUNTING
FOR THE PERIOD JANUARY 1, 2012 THRU JUNE 30, 2012
DISBURSEMENTS
SCHEDULE C

DATE	PAID TO	CHK #	FOR	INCOME	PRINCIPAL
REAL ESTATE EXPENSES PAID IN ESCROW UPON SALE OF 321 FRANCHISE ROW					
05/15/12	BETTER HOMES REAL ESTATE COMPANY		BROKER COMMISSION		$ 47,265.00
05/15/12	PRUDENTIAL REAL ESTATE COMPANY		BROKER COMMISSION		$ 47,265.00
05/15/12	SELLER CREDIT		CREDIT FOR CLOSING COSTS		$ 25,000.00
05/15/12	SUPER CONSTRUCTION		LOADING DOCK REPAIRS REQUIRED FOR SALE		$ 40,000.00
05/15/12	ERNEST EVIRONMENTAL		INSPECTION FEE		$ 750.00
05/15/12	STEWART TITLE CO		PRO-RATED RENT COLLECTED FOR MAY 2012		$ 3,125.00
05/15/12	STEWART TITLE CO		SECURITY DEPOSITS		$ 12,500.00
05/15/12	STEWART TITLE CO		ESCROW AND TITLE FEES		$ 1,000.00
05/15/12	STEWART TITLE CO		DOCUMENTATION FEE		$ 500.00
05/15/12	STEWART TITLE CO		NOTARY FEE		$ 20.00
05/15/12	STEWART TITLE CO		COURIER FEE		$ 100.00
			TOTAL REAL ESTATE EXPENSES PAID IN ESCROW $	-	$ 177,525.00

REAL ESTATE EXPENSES PAID IN ESCROW UPON SALE OF 111 MANAGEMENT AVE

DATE	PAID TO	FOR		
04/01/12	COLDWELL BANKER	BROKER COMMISSION	$	31,500.00
04/01/12	ZEPHYER REAL ESTATE	BROKER COMMISSION	$	31,500.00
04/01/12	DAN'S DISCLOSURES	HAZARD DISCLOSURES	$	200.00
04/01/12	COUNTY TAX COLLECTOR	PRO-RATED PROPERTY TAX DUE	$	3,650.00
04/01/12	OLD REPUBLIC TITLE	TITLE AND ESCROW FEES	$	750.00
04/01/12	OLD REPUBLIC TITLE	DOCUMENTATION FEE	$	250.00
04/01/12	OLD REPUBLIC TITLE	TRANSFER OF SECURITY DEPOSITS	$	6,800.00
		TOTAL REAL ESTATE EXPENSES PAID IN ESCROW $ -	$	74,650.00

§8.31 C. Form: Debts Associated With a Decedent's Death Paid From Principal

The example below shows disbursements made to pay various debts of the decedent. See §8.13.

REAL ESTATE TRUST
THOMAS JONES, TRUSTEE

FIRST ACCOUNTING
FOR THE PERIOD JANUARY 1, 2012 THRU JUNE 30, 2012
DISBURSEMENTS
SCHEDULE C

DATE	PAID TO	CHK #	FOR	INCOME		PRINCIPAL
ADMINISTRATIVE EXPENSES						
01/31/12	DISCOVER CARD		CREDIT CARD - DEBT OF DECEDENT		$	521.34
02/15/12	ANYTOWN HOSPITAL		DEBT OF DECEDENT		$	600.00
02/15/12	ANYTOWN MEDICAL GROUP		DEBT OF DECEDENT		$	230.00
			TOTAL ADMINISTRATIVE EXPENSES $	-	$	1,351.34
			TOTAL INCOME AND PRINCIPAL $	-	$	1,351.34
			TOTAL DISBURSEMENTS $	1,351.34		

§8.32 D. Form: Expenses Associated With Real Property

The example below shows disbursements made to prepare real property for sale. See §8.23.

REAL ESTATE TRUST
THOMAS JONES, TRUSTEE

FIRST ACCOUNTING
FOR THE PERIOD JANUARY 1, 2012 THRU JUNE 30, 2012
DISBURSEMENTS
SCHEDULE C

DATE	PAID TO	CHK #	FOR	INCOME		PRINCIPAL
REAL ESTATE EXPENSES - 111 MANAGEMENT AVE						
03/15/12	PAUL'S PAINTING		EXTERIOR PAINTING OF BUILDING IN **PREPARATION FOR SALE**		$	7,000.00
03/15/12	FANNIE'S FURNACE		FURNACE REPAIR IN **PREPARATION FOR SALE**		$	2,500.00
	TOTAL REAL ESTATE EXPENSES - 111 MANAGEMENT AVE			$ -	$	9,500.00

§8.33 E. Form: Loan Payments, Payments on Trust Debts

The example below shows the mortgage payments made to Quality Mortgage Company, on the Disbursements schedule, and shows how these disbursements reduce the trust's outstanding liabilities. See §8.24.

REAL ESTATE TRUST
THOMAS JONES, TRUSTEE

FIRST ACCOUNTING
FOR THE PERIOD JANUARY 1, 2012 THRU JUNE 30, 2012
DISBURSEMENTS
SCHEDULE C

DATE	PAID TO	CHK #	FOR	INCOME	PRINCIPAL
REAL ESTATE EXPENSES - 987 SUNNYSIDE STREET					
01/05/12	QUALITY MORTGAGE COMPANY		MORTGAGE PAYMENT	$ 787.50	$ 712.50
02/05/12	QUALITY MORTGAGE COMPANY		MORTGAGE PAYMENT	$ 784.53	$ 715.47
03/05/12	QUALITY MORTGAGE COMPANY		MORTGAGE PAYMENT	$ 781.55	$ 718.45
04/05/12	QUALITY MORTGAGE COMPANY		MORTGAGE PAYMENT	$ 778.56	$ 721.44
05/05/12	QUALITY MORTGAGE COMPANY		MORTGAGE PAYMENT	$ 775.55	$ 724.45
06/05/12	QUALITY MORTGAGE COMPANY		MORTGAGE PAYMENT	$ 772.53	$ 727.47
	TOTAL REAL ESTATE EXPENSES - 987 SUNNYSIDE STREET			$ 4,680.22	$ 4,319.78

REAL ESTATE TRUST
THOMAS JONES, TRUSTEE

FIRST ACCOUNTING
FOR THE PERIOD JANUARY 1, 2012 THRU JUNE 30, 2012
LIABILITIES

DATE	DESCRIPTION	INCREASE	DECREASE	BALANCE
DUE TO QUALITY MORTGAGE COMPANY				
SECURED BY PROPERTY LOCATED AT				
987 SUNNYSIDE STREET, ANYTOWN, CALIFORNIA				
01/01/12	BALANCE DUE			$ 189,000.00
01/05/12	PRINCIPAL PAYMENT		$ 712.50	$ 188,287.50
02/05/12	PRINCIPAL PAYMENT		$ 715.47	$ 187,572.03
03/05/12	PRINCIPAL PAYMENT		$ 718.45	$ 186,853.58
04/05/12	PRINCIPAL PAYMENT		$ 721.44	$ 186,132.14
05/05/12	PRINCIPAL PAYMENT		$ 724.45	$ 185,407.69
06/05/12	PRINCIPAL PAYMENT		$ 727.47	$ **184,680.22**

9
Distributions

I. WHEN DISTRIBUTIONS CAN BE MADE §9.1
   A. Distributions Versus Disbursements §9.2
   B. The Appearance of the Distributions Schedule §9.3

II. PREPARING THE SCHEDULE, AT A MINIMUM
   A. Account for Distributions Using Carry Value §9.4
      1. Example One: Distribution of Depreciated Asset §9.5
      2. Example Two: Distribution of Appreciated Asset §9.6
   B. The Appearance of the Schedule: Favored Gifts First §9.7

III. ABATEMENT; PRORATION OF TAXES; SATISFACTION OF OMITTED SPOUSE, REGISTERED DOMESTIC PARTNER, OR CHILD §9.8
   A. Abatement: Which Gifts Shrink to Pay Debts and Expenses? §9.9
      1. Specific Gifts §9.10
      2. General Gifts §9.11
      3. Demonstrative Gifts §9.12
      4. General Pecuniary Gifts §9.13
      5. Annuity §9.14
      6. Residuary Gifts and Property Not Distributed by the Instrument §9.15
      7. Categorization of People §9.16
      8. Rules of Abatement §9.17
         a. Property Not Disposed of by the Instrument §9.18
         b. Remaining Gifts §9.19
      9. Gift Exonerated From Mortgage, Deed of Trust, or Other Lien §9.20
      10. Abatement in Action §9.21
   B. Proration of Taxes §9.22
   C. Transfers to Omitted Spouse, Registered Domestic Partner, or Child

1. Omitted Spouse or Registered Domestic Partner §9.23
2. Omitted Child §9.24
3. Manner of Satisfying Share of Omitted Spouse, Registered Domestic Partner, or Child §9.25

IV. PRINCIPAL AND INCOME
   A. In General §9.26
   B. Allocation of Income After the Decedent's Death or After an Income Interest in a Trust Ends
      1. Specific Gifts
         a. Expenses and Receipts Attributable to Specific Gifts §9.27
            (1) Receipts and Disbursements, At the Beginning §9.28
            (2) Receipts and Disbursements, During the Administration §9.29
            (3) Receipts and Disbursements, At the End §9.30
         b. Debts and General Expenses of Administration §9.31
      2. General Pecuniary Gifts, Annuities, and Gifts of Maintenance §9.32
      3. Net Income Distributable to Residuary Beneficiaries §9.33

V. TAX ATTRIBUTES OF DISTRIBUTIONS §9.34

VI. AVOIDING COMMON MISTAKES
   A. Do Not Report Distributions Using Market Value §9.35
   B. Give Interest Where Due §9.36

VII. ABATEMENT EXAMPLES AND SELF-TESTS
   A. Abatement: Example One and Self-Test §9.37
   B. Abatement: Example Two and Self-Test §9.38
   C. Abatement: Example Three and Self-Test §9.39
   D. Abatement: Example Four and Self-Test §9.40
   E. Abatement: Example Five and Self-Test §9.41
   F. Abatement: Example Six and Self-Test §9.42

VIII. EXHIBITS
   A. Form: Expenses and Receipts Applicable to a Specific Gift §9.43
   B. Form: Accounting for the Accrual of Interest on a General Pecuniary Gift §9.44

§9.1 I. WHEN DISTRIBUTIONS CAN BE MADE

NOTE▶ Conservators and Guardians. Although conservators and guardians will find this chapter helpful in formatting their Distributions schedules, the focus of the chapter is on the challenges that personal representatives and trustees face when accounting for distributions. A conservator or guardian might make distributions to the conservatee or ward, but because these fiduciaries owe duties only to one person and usually distribute only a minuscule portion of the assets of the estate, these fiduciaries avoid the challenges that the others often face. For example, when making distributions, personal representatives and trustees must account for principal and income. They also must determine which gifts abate to pay debts and expenses. Additionally, personal representatives and trustees must worry about the receipts and expenses attributable to specific gifts and the interest owed on late-distributed general pecuniary gifts. Conservators and guardians have none of these concerns. Additionally, conservatorships and guardianships are disregarded for income tax purposes.

Whenever a fiduciary gives money or property to a beneficiary in full or partial satisfaction of the beneficiary's beneficial interest, the fiduciary is said to have made a distribution. With the exception noted below, personal representatives may distribute property only after the court orders a preliminary or the final distribution of the estate.

NOTE▶ Probate Code §9650(c) provides:

> Real property or tangible personal property may be left with or surrendered to the person presumptively entitled to it unless or until, in the judgment of the personal representative, possession of the property by the personal representative will be necessary for purposes of administration.

When property is distributed after an order of distribution, the date of distribution is the date the personal representative delivers the property. (Often, delivery is memorialized with a receipt that bears the date.) This is also true of property left with, or surrendered to, the person presumptively entitled to its possession. If the property will not be necessary for the purposes of the administration, the personal representative may leave real or tangible personal property with the person presumptively entitled to it, provided this person agrees to return the property to the personal representative on request. Prob C §9650(c). For example, the personal representative may allow a beneficiary to continue living in real property if the personal representative expects to distribute that property to the occupant-beneficiary. Or the personal representative may distribute the contents of the decedent's residence to the beneficiaries who have inherited that tangible personal property. The personal representative who exercises this power should account for the delivery or surrender as if the property were distributed on the date the personal representative leaves or surrenders it to its presumptive owner, even though that person's duty to return the property is not extinguished until later, when the court orders distribution.

Trustees may distribute income or principal at regular intervals throughout the term of a trust, as would for example, the trustee of a QTIP trust. Trustees also may distribute income or principal episodically, as would the trustee of a trust that terminates in stages, such as a trust for a young person who is entitled to outright distributions on reaching certain milestone birthdays. Or, trustees may distribute a trust all at once, as trustees of will-substitute revocable trusts often do.

§9.2   A. Distributions Versus Disbursements

A person entitled to distributions also may receive *disbursements*. For example, a trustee may also be a trust beneficiary, in which case the trustee's fee is a disbursement, whereas satisfaction of the trustee's beneficial interests is a distribution. Similarly, the beneficiary of a decedent's estate may also be a creditor of the estate, in which case payment of the creditor's claim would be a disbursement, but satisfaction of the beneficiary's interest in the estate would be a distribution. Whether the transaction is a distribution or a disbursement, unless the trust or will otherwise provides, trustees and personal representatives must refer to the Uniform Principal and Income Act (UPAIA) (Prob C §§16320-16375) to determine whether the transaction affects principal, income, or both. Prob C §§16335, 16374.5.

§9.3   B. The Appearance of the Distributions Schedule

Below is an example of a Distributions schedule that shows the trustee distributing cash and securities. (See chap 1 about the Cash Trust.)

APRIL CASH TRUST
SALLY CASH, TRUSTEE

FIRST ACCOUNTING
FOR THE PERIOD JANUARY 1, 2013 THRU JUNE 30, 2013
DISTRIBUTIONS
SCHEDULE E

DATE	SHARES	DESCRIPTION		AMOUNT/CARRY VALUE
RACHEL CASH				
06/28/13		CASH DISTRIBUTION	$	50,000.00
06/28/13	1,100.000	BANK OF AMERICA CORP	$	13,233.00
06/28/13	804.000	CHEVRON CORP	$	88,753.56
		TOTAL DISTRIBUTION TO RACHEL CASH	$	*151,986.56*
MIKE CASH				
06/28/13		CASH DISTRIBUTION	$	50,000.00
06/28/13	1,100.000	BANK OF AMERICA CORP	$	13,233.00
06/28/13	804.000	CHEVRON CORP	$	88,753.56
		TOTAL DISTRIBUTION TO MIKE CASH	$	*151,986.56*
		TOTAL DISTRIBUTIONS	$	**303,973.12**

The example below shows the trustee distributing a speed boat.

REAL ESTATE TRUST
THOMAS JONES, TRUSTEE

FIRST ACCOUNTING
FOR THE PERIOD JANUARY 1, 2012 THRU JUNE 30, 2012
DISTRIBUTIONS
SCHEDULE E

DATE	DESCRIPTION		AMOUNT/CARRY VALUE
REBECCA JONES			
01/05/12	2007 MALIBU SPEEDBOAT B987345H0934	VIN $	15,000.00
	TOTAL DISTRIBUTIONS	$	**15,000.00**

II. PREPARING THE SCHEDULE, AT A MINIMUM

§9.4 A. Account for Distributions Using Carry Value

When accounting for a distribution, the amount accounted for is the property's *carry value*. Prob C §1062(e). Somewhat confusingly, this is true even though market value is used to determine whether a distribution in kind is sufficient to satisfy a pecuniary bequest.

§9.5 1. Example One: Distribution of Depreciated Asset

Imagine the settlor has left his nephew a general pecuniary gift of $50,000. Eleven months after the settlor's death, the trustee distributes the settlor's Facebook stock to the nephew, who accepts the stock in full satisfaction of the pecuniary gift. At the settlor's death, the Facebook stock had been valued at $90,000, but by the date of distribution its fair market value had dropped to $50,000.

The trustee would account for this transaction on the schedule of Distributions as follows:

Date	Distribution	Carry Value	Market Value
1/15/10	Facebook stock, distributed to John White in full satisfaction of the $50,000 general pecuniary gift (see Trust, p. 10, §3.4)	$90,000	$50,000

PRACTICE TIP▶ Remember, it is the carry value that is carried forward to the Summary schedule. If the trustee mistakenly uses market value as the measure of the distribution, after making the above distribution, it would appear that the fiduciary had on hand $40,000 more than he or she actually has. In the parlance of fiduciary accounting, if this trustee accounted for the distribution at market value, the fiduciary would not claim sufficient credit for the transaction.

§9.6 2. Example Two: Distribution of Appreciated Asset

Imagine the settlor has left his niece a general pecuniary gift of $1 million. Eleven months after the settlor's death, with the niece's consent, the trustee distributes to her the trust-owned real property, Green Springs. At the settlor's death, Green Springs had been valued at $850,000, but its fair market value on the date of distribution is $1 million.

The trustee would account for this transaction on the schedule of Distributions as follows:

Date	Distribution	Carry Value	Market Value
2/14/12	Green Springs, distributed to Sara Jones in full satisfaction of the $1 million general pecuniary gift (see Trust, p. 12, §3.7)	$850,000	$1,000,000

For income tax purposes, the trustee would recognize capital gain on this transaction (Treas Reg §1.661(a)-2(f); see *Kenan v Commissioner* (2d Cir 1940) 114 F2d 217), but that does not affect the manner in which the transaction is accounted for in the trustee's account. As with a distribution of depreciated property, the value carried forward to the summary of account, *i.e.,* the value for which credit is given, is the asset's carry value. In the above example, the trustee would get $850,000 credit for distributing Green Springs to the settlor's niece.

§9.7   B. The Appearance of the Schedule: Favored Gifts First

The statutory abatement scheme, discussed below, suggests a method for organizing the schedule of Disbursements. Favored gifts, such as specific gifts to the transferor's relatives, should be listed first, followed by specific gifts to persons who are not the transferor's relatives. The third category of distributions would be general pecuniary gifts to the transferor's relatives. The fourth category would be such gifts to non-relatives, followed by residuary gifts. See categorization of gifts at §§9.10-9.15.

§9.8   III. ABATEMENT; PRORATION OF TAXES; SATISFACTION OF OMITTED SPOUSE, REGISTERED DOMESTIC PARTNER, OR CHILD

It is the public policy of the State of California to protect against the inadvertent disinheritance of spouses, registered domestic partners (RDPs), and children, and that policy is codified in the omitted spouse/partner and omitted child statutes found in Prob C §§21610-21623 and Fam C §297.5(c). Protecting the intention of settlors and testators is also a matter of public policy, and the tension between these policies has resulted in a statutory scheme not easily summarized. Basically, the omitted spouse/partner statutes give rights to a surviving spouse or partner if the decedent:

- Had a will or trust at the time of the marriage or registration;
- Died without updating the testamentary instrument; and
- Did not otherwise provide for the surviving spouse or RDP.

Similarly, the omitted child statute gives rights to a surviving child if:

- The child was born after a parent created a will or trust;
- The parent died without updating the testamentary instrument; and
- The deceased parent did not otherwise provide for the child.

On transfers to an omitted child or omitted spouse/partner, see §§9.23-9.24. For further discussion of the rights of an omitted spouse, RDP, or child, see California Decedent Estate Practice §28.34 (Cal CEB).

With each disbursement, and when satisfying the shares of an omitted spouse or child, the fiduciary necessarily diminishes the expectations of one or more beneficiaries. More colloquially, whenever the fiduciary spends a penny, he or she is spending a penny that would otherwise be distributed to a beneficiary. The Distributions schedule is where this shrinkage is made apparent. The testator or settlor may specify which gifts should be applied to satisfy which obligations, but if the instrument is silent, the fiduciary must follow the rules of the Probate Code.

Disbursements implicate three sets of rules. Disbursements for debts of a decedent and expenses of administration are governed by the rules of Part 4, Division 11 of the Probate Code (Prob C §§21400-21406). Prob C §21400.

PRACTICE TIP➤ If the instrument is silent on the manner of abatement, yet the fiduciary believes the testator's plan, or the purpose of the transfer, would be frustrated by application of Part 4, Division 9 of the Probate Code (Prob C §§16000–16015), the fiduciary would be wise to seek instructions under Prob C §11700 or §17200(a)(4).

Disbursements for estate or generation-skipping transfer taxes are subject to the rules of Division 10 of the Probate Code (Prob C §§20100–20225). Transfers to satisfy the beneficial interests of an omitted spouse or child are subject to the rules of Part 6, Division 11 of the Probate Code (Prob C §§21600–21700).

§9.9   A. Abatement: Which Gifts Shrink to Pay Debts and Expenses?

To determine which gifts abate to pay the debts of the decedent and the expenses of administration, the fiduciary looks first to the instrument, and if it is silent, to the codified rules of abatement. Prob C §§21400–21401. Before applying the codified rules of abatement, the fiduciary first must categorize each gift and each relationship between the beneficiary and donor. Every gift belongs in one of the categories discussed in §§9.10–9.15.

§9.10   1. Specific Gifts

A specific gift is a transfer of specifically identifiable property. Prob C §21117(a). Each of the following would be a specific gift:

- I leave my double wedding ring quilt to Emily.
- The trustee shall distribute the settlor's Gran Torino to the boy next door.
- The trustee shall distribute White Acre in equal shares to the settlor's children who survive the settlor.

§9.11   2. General Gifts

A general gift is a transfer from the general assets of the transferor that does not give specific property. Prob C §21117(b). Each of the following would be a general gift:

- I leave any automobile I may own at my death to the boy next door.
- I leave one-third of my cash to my nephew.

- I leave my tangible personal property of a personal nature to my sister.

§9.12   3. Demonstrative Gifts

A demonstrative gift is a general gift from a specified fund or property. Prob C §21117(c). Each of the following would be a demonstrative gift:

- I leave my nephew those securities held in my Dodge & Cox account.
- I leave my jewelry to my nieces, who shall choose items in round-robin fashion until all of my jewelry has been disposed of or until no niece wants any of the remaining jewelry, which my executor shall sell.

§9.13   4. General Pecuniary Gifts

A general pecuniary gift is either a transfer described in the instrument as a fixed dollar amount or a dollar amount determinable by the provisions of the instrument. Prob C §§21117(d), 21118. Each of the following is a gift of a general pecuniary amount:

- I leave $10,000 to each of my grandchildren.
- I leave my son an amount sufficient to pay the principal balance due on his home mortgage, determined on the date of my death.
- The trustee shall distribute to the QTIP Trust the smallest pecuniary amount that, if allowed as a federal estate tax marital deduction, would result in the least possible federal estate tax being payable on the deceased settlor's death, after taking into account allowable credits.

§9.14   5. Annuity

An annuity is a general pecuniary gift that is payable periodically. Prob C §21117(e). Each of the following is a gift of an annuity:

- My executor shall distribute One Thousand Dollars ($1000) each month to my daughter, for the duration of the administration of my estate.
- During the trust term, the trustee shall distribute to the settlor

an annuity at the times and in the amounts set forth in this Article Five. If the settlor is not then living, the trustee shall distribute the required annuity amount to the settlor's estate.

§9.15 6. Residuary Gifts and Property Not Distributed by the Instrument

Residuary gifts. A residuary gift is the transfer of the property that remains after all specific and general gifts have been satisfied. Prob C §21117(f). In a well-drafted instrument, the residuary gift will be plainly described. For example, a testator might say in the will, "I leave the residue of my estate to my descendants, by right of representation." The law presumes that a person who bothers to make a will or trust intended to avoid intestacy, and wills and trusts are interpreted according to this presumption. Prob C §21120. Courts will give the provision of a will a "broad and liberal interpretation to the end that intestacy may be prevented." *Estate of Plumer* (1958) 159 CA2d 389. If there is a total or partial failure of the residuary gift, the affected portion of the residue will pass under the laws of intestate succession. *Estate of Russell* (1968) 69 C2d 200. See also *Estate of Barnes* (1965) 63 C2d 580 (will did not establish "dominant dispositive plan" with respect to residuary gift contingent on simultaneous death of testator and spouse). On residuary gifts, see California Will Drafting §§12.79–12.80 (3d ed Cal CEB).

Property Not Distributed by the Instrument. In attorney-drafted wills and trusts, one rarely finds the type of flaws that might result in a partial intestacy, but in holographic wills they are not uncommon. A lay person might, for example, leave a will that consists of a list of specific gifts and which contains no residual clause. If such a testator died owning property in addition to that which was specifically given away in the will, such property would be "property not disposed of by the instrument" and would pass by intestacy.

§9.16 7. Categorization of People

To determine which gifts abate, the fiduciary must classify not only the gifts but also the donees. Each beneficiary is either a relative of the transferor or a person other than a relative. A person is a relative of the transferor if the person is one to whom property would pass from the transferor if the transferor died intestate and there were no other persons having priority. Prob C §21402(b), referring to Prob C §§6401–6402. For the purpose of determining abatement, all of the following people are relatives of the transferor:

- Spouses or registered domestic partners of the transferor (§6401(a));
- Children of the transferor (§6402(a)), including those born to unmarried parents (§6450(a));
- Grandchildren of the transferor and more remote issue (§6402(a));
- Parents of the transferor (§6402(b));
- Issue of the transferor's parents, including siblings, nieces, nephews, and their issue (§6402(c));
- Grandparents of the transferor (§6402(d));
- Issue of the grandparents of the transferor, including uncles, aunts, first cousins, etc. (§6042(c));
- The transferor's "next of kin" (great-grandparents and more remote ancestors, and the issue of these ancestors (§6402(f))); and
- Issue of a predeceased spouse (§6402(e)).

Half-blood relatives are relatives to the same extent as are full-blood relatives, provided adoption has not severed the parent-child relationship. Prob C §6406.

A person who on the transferor's death has not yet been born, will be a relative of the transferor if the person was conceived before the transferor's death and born after. Prob C §6407.

A child of a deceased transferor who is conceived and born after the transferor's death (called a "posthumously-conceived child") is deemed to have been born during the transferor's lifetime, but after the execution of all of the transferor's testamentary instruments, provided all of the requirements of Prob C §249.5 are met. One of these requirements is that the child be in utero within 2 years of the date of the transferor's death. Prob C §249.5(c).

NOTE➤ Probate Code §249.5 is lengthy and not easily summarized. Practitioners should read the statute before assuming that a posthumously-conceived person is a relative of a transferor within the meaning of Prob C §21402(b).

Adopted children are the children of the parents who adopt them. Prob C §6450(a). Adoption severs the parent-child relationship between the natural parent and the child, unless the adoption is by a step-parent and the conditions of Prob C §6451 are met. Prob C §6451. Before assuming an exception to the rule that adoption severs the parent-child relationship, practitioners should read the statute and the Law Revision Commission Comments thereto.

Persons not defined as relatives by the statutes that determine intestate succession are "persons other than the transferor's relatives" for the purpose of the abatement statute.

§9.17   8. Rules of Abatement

If the will or trust is silent and Part 4, Division 11 of the Probate Code (Prob C §§21400-21406) can be applied without frustrating the transferor's plan or the purpose of the transfer, the shares of beneficiaries abate as described in §§9.18-9.19. Prob C §§21400-21406.

§9.18   a. Property Not Disposed of by the Instrument

The fiduciary spends first the property not disposed of by the instrument. The cases that illustrate this phenomenon predate Prob C §21111(b), which abolished the "no residue of a residue" rule. Comment to Prob C §21111. For example, in *Estate of Stauffer* (1959) 53 C2d 124, the testator left the residue of her estate to three named individuals not identified as a class. One of these people was found guilty of unduly influencing the testator. The court denied probate as to that gift, which passed by intestacy. So passing, this share was property not disposed of by the instrument and therefore was liable for the expenses of administration. Now, under Prob C §21111(b), the failed residuary gift would enlarge the valid residuary gifts, meaning the two "good" residual beneficiaries would split the share of the "bad" beneficiary. After enactment of Prob C §21111(b), "property not disposed of by the instrument" usually is found only in the following situation: if a testator has left a will that has no residual clause—for example, because she has made only specific gifts—and the testator dies owning more property than she has identified in her will, that additional property is "property not disposed of by the instrument." Similarly, if a settlor's trust has no residual clause and the dispositive provisions are a collection of specific gifts (general pecuniary devises and the like), any property included in the trust estate in addition to that identified in the dispositive provisions, is "property not disposed of by the instrument."

§9.19   b. Remaining Gifts

The remaining gifts abate as follows:

- Second: Residuary gifts. Prob C §21402(a)(2).
- Third: General gifts to persons other than the transferor's relatives. Prob C §21402(a)(3).
- Fourth: General gifts to the transferor's relatives. Prob C §21402(a)(4).
- Fifth: Specific gifts to persons other than the transferor's relatives. Prob C §21402(a)(5).
- Last: Specific gifts to the transferor's relatives. Prob C §21402(a)(6).

An annuity that is satisfied out of a fund or property specifically identified in the gift abates as would a specific gift. Prob C §21403(b). An annuity that cannot be wholly satisfied out of a specifically identified fund or property is treated as a specific gift to the extent it is satisfied out of the specifically identified fund or property, and as a general gift to the extent it is satisfied out of property other than the fund or property specified in the gift. Prob C §21403(b).

The rules of abatement for demonstrative gifts are the same as those for annuities, above. Prob C §21403(b).

Within a class of gifts—for example, the class of general gifts to persons other than the transferor's relatives—gifts abate ratably. Prob C §21403.

EXAMPLE 1▶ In her will, Wendy left the residue of her estate one half to Sonny and gave each of her three grandchildren one sixth of the residue. Each disbursement to pay debts and expenses would be paid one half from Sonny's expectancy and one sixth from each of the expectancies of the grandchildren. In this situation, it is common to say that the debts and expenses are paid "off the top."

EXAMPLE 2▶ In his holographic will, Walter inventoried everything he owned and gave each item to a specifically identified person. Most of these specific gifts were to relatives, but Walter gave his gun collection, appraised at $50,000, to his hunting buddy and his coin collection, appraised at $25,000, to the son of his housekeeper. Walter was not related to either of these beneficiaries. Walter's personal representative would be expected to sell enough of the guns and the coins to pay Walter's debts and expenses and the burden of these payments would fall two-thirds on the hunting buddy and one-third on the housekeeper's son. In the alternative, the fiduciary may collect cash from these beneficiaries sufficient to pay these obligations. Prob C §21405. The code speaks of the court fixing the amount each distributee must contribute to abatement (Prob C §21405(a)), but in a situation such as this, the personal representative or trustee should seek instructions before selling the property. That way, the affected beneficiaries can be given the opportunity to argue that the fiduciary's plan for abatement thwarts the donor's intent and must be modified. See Prob C §21400 ("If the transferor's plan or if the purpose of the transfer would be defeated by abatement as provided in [Prob C §§21400-21406], the shares of the beneficiaries abate as is necessary to effectuate the instrument, plan, or purpose").

§9.20   9. Gift Exonerated From Mortgage, Deed of Trust, or Other Lien

Generally, a specific gift passes property subject to mortgages, deeds of trust, and other liens without exoneration. Prob C §21131. This is true even if the instrument contains a general directive to pay all debts and expenses. Prob C §21131. An exception lies when the property is encumbered during a period when the transferor is incapacitated and the encumbrance is the consequence of an action taken by the incapacitated transferor's conservator, agent, or trustee. Prob C §21134. Other than this narrow exception, however, the beneficiary of a specific gift that is encumbered may demand that the fiduciary pay the encumbrance from another source only if the instrument so provides. Prob C §21131.

An instrument may provide that property subject to a mortgage, deed of trust, or other lien passes free of that obligation. For example, a will may require the personal representative to pay the mortgage on a specific gift of real property before distributing the property to the beneficiary. If the instrument specifies the source of the payment, the fiduciary must pay the debt from that source. Prob C §21400. With one exception, if the instrument does not specify the source of payment, the fiduciary must pay the debt as provided in the abatement statute. Prob C §21400. The exception applies when the only source of payment would be another specific gift. One specific gift does not abate to exonerate another specific gift (Prob C §21404), and if no other property were available for the payment, presumably the transferor's intention would be frustrated and the encumbered gift would remain encumbered.

§9.21   10. Abatement in Action

When there is an abatement in a decedent's estate, the court fixes the amount each beneficiary must contribute. Prob C §21405(a). If a specific gift must abate, the beneficiary who does not want his or her gift sold to pay debts and expenses may contribute for abatement from other property. Prob C §21405(b). In a trust administration, the trustee must fix the amount each gift abates. Trustees in this situation should propose a scheme of abatement, perhaps by accounting to the beneficiaries and including in the accounting an auxiliary schedule showing the proposed distribution. The trustee should seek the beneficiaries' consents to the proposed distribution and if the beneficiaries do not consent, the trustee should consider seeking the court's approval before distributing the trust property.

See §§9.37–9.43 for examples of abatement in action.

§9.22   B. Proration of Taxes

The abatement statutes discussed above do not allocate responsibility for the estate and generation-skipping transfer taxes. These taxes are the subject of Division 10 of the Probate Code (Prob C §§20100–20225). A thorough discussion of these statutes is beyond the scope of this text, but in general, unless the settlor or testator provides otherwise, the estate tax and the generation-skipping transfer tax are equitably prorated among the persons interested in the estate, on the one hand, or persons receiving property on which a generation-skipping tax is imposed, on the other. Prob C §§20110, 20210.

On proration of estate taxes generally, see California Decedent Estate Practice §§31.89–31.90 (2d ed Cal CEB).

C. Transfers to Omitted Spouse, Registered Domestic Partner, or Child

§9.23 1. Omitted Spouse or Registered Domestic Partner

The so-called "omitted spouse" statutes protect widows and widowers, as well as registered domestic partners (RDPs) (see Fam C §297.5(c)), from inadvertent disinheritance. If all of the conditions of Chapter 2, Part 6, Division 11 of the Probate Code (Prob C §§21610-21623) are met, the omitted spouse or RDP is entitled to a share of the decedent's probate estate and all property held in any revocable trust that becomes irrevocable on the death of the decedent. Prob C §§21600-21623; Fam C §297.5. Specifically, the surviving spouse or RDP is entitled to (Prob C §21610; Fam C §297.5(c)):

- The decedent's one half of any community property;
- The decedent's one half of any quasi-community property; and
- A share of the decedent's separate property equal in value to what the survivor would have received, had the decedent died intestate.

§9.24 2. Omitted Child

The so-called "omitted child" statutes are meant to protect children from inadvertent disinheritance and function much like the omitted spouse statues. A child born after the execution of all of the decedent's testamentary instruments, who is not provided for in those instruments, is entitled to a share of the decedent's estate equal in value to the share the child would have received if the decedent had died without executing any testamentary instruments. Prob C §§21620-21623.

§9.25 3. Manner of Satisfying Share of Omitted Spouse, Registered Domestic Partner, or Child

Obviously, giving an omitted spouse, RDP, or child such a large share of the decedent's property will diminish the expectancy of those persons provided for in the decedent's testamentary instruments.

The share of an omitted spouse, RDP, or child is satisfied from the following property, in the following order:

- The decedent's estate not disposed of by will or trust, if any; and

- The property otherwise passing to the beneficiaries of the decedent's testamentary instruments, in proportion to these beneficiaries' expectancies, which proportions are to be determined using date-of-death values. Prob C §21612(a) and Fam C §297.5(c) (omitted spouse/RDP); Prob C §21623(a) (omitted child).

If the above scheme for satisfying the share of the omitted spouse, RDP, or child would frustrate the decedent's "obvious intention" regarding a specific gift or a specific devise, the specific gift or specific devise may be exempted from apportionment and a different apportionment may be adopted. Prob C §21612(b) and Fam C §297.5(c) (omitted spouse/RDP); Prob C §21623(b) (omitted child). Fiduciaries facing this challenge should seek court approval of any deviation from the strict statutory scheme.

IV. PRINCIPAL AND INCOME

§9.26   A. In General

The rules governing distributions under the Uniform Principal and Income Act (UPAIA) (Prob C §§16320-16375) work in concert with the abatement statutes (Prob C §§21400-21406) and with Prob C §§12000-12007 to protect the transferor's presumed intent to favor the specific over the general and family over non-relatives.

NOTE▶ Probate Code §16340 cross references Prob C §12000 and allocates debts and expenses in the same manner.

These rules are built on the assumption that the transferor of a specific gift intends the gift to be distributed intact, undiminished by debts and the general expenses of administration, and augmented by any net income the gift property might earn during the period of administration. Similarly, the rules protect general devises from debts and expenses, provided the residuary gifts are sufficient to cover these disbursements. Additionally, if distribution of a general devise is delayed beyond the anniversary of the decedent's death, for gifts made in a will, or the anniversary of the date an income interest in a trust ends, the beneficiary of the general devise is entitled to interest. Prob C §16340(b).

B. Allocation of Income After the Decedent's Death or After an Income Interest in a Trust Ends

1. Specific Gifts

§9.27   a. Expenses and Receipts Attributable to Specific Gifts

If a will or trust makes a specific gift and the instrument does not specify a contrary rule, the fiduciary must distribute to the beneficiary the net income and principal receipts attributable to the gift, subject to the rules of Prob C §§16340 and 12002. Prob C §16340(a), which cross-references Prob C §12002.

NOTE▶ If a trustee has distributed a specific gift or a general pecuniary gift before January 1, 2007, the trustee may allocate income and principal as set forth in California's Uniform Principal and Income Act (UPAIA) (Prob C §§16320–16375), or in the manner allowed by the law in effect at the time of distribution. Prob C §16340(f).

The fiduciary must determine the net income and principal receipts by netting against the receipts all amounts paid with respect to the property. Prob C §16340(a)(1). "Expenses attributable to the property" are expenses arising directly from use or ownership and include property tax and income tax, but exclude the estate tax and generation-skipping transfer tax. Prob C §12002(b).

The example in §9.43 models what would have happened had Thomas Jones distributed 111 Management Avenue to the beneficiary Rebecca Jones, instead of selling the property. (In the master accounting for this trust, the property is sold. See chap 1.)

When determining the net income and principal receipts attributable to a property, the fiduciary will be concerned with at least two, and possibly three, time periods, discussed below.

§9.28   (1) Receipts and Disbursements, At the Beginning

At the beginning, *i.e.*, after a decedent's death or after an income interest in a trust ends, when calculating the net income and principal receipts from a specifically given property, it is immaterial whether an amount collected accrued before, on, or after the death or the end of the income interest. Prob C §16340(a)(1). Similarly, it does not matter whether a post-death (or post-end-of-income-interest) payment became due before, on, or after the death or the end of the income interest. Prob C §16340(a)(1). All that matters is the timing of the receipt or payment. Amounts received and payments made after the death or the end of the income interest are included in, or deducted from, the net income due to the beneficiary of the specific devise. Prob C §16340(a)(1). At the beginning, one might say that the calculation of net income and principal receipts is a cash basis calculation.

EXAMPLE▶ The testator's will makes a specific gift of a three-unit apartment building to the testator's son. Just before the testator's death in January, the testator collected and deposited in his own bank account the following: January's rent ($800) from the tenant in apartment A and both January's and February's rent ($1600) from the tenant in apartment B. The tenant in apartment C did not pay January's rent until after the personal representative had been appointed. When the personal representative calculates the net rent attributable to the specific gift, only the rent from unit C will be included in the calculation.

§9.29 (2) Receipts and Disbursements, During the Administration

If the income from a specifically devised property is insufficient to carry the property, the fiduciary must pay the carrying cost from other property. Up to a point, defined below, the expenses that exceed the property's income are paid out of the "estate," causing gifts to abate in the manner provided by Prob C §21400, unless the instrument provides otherwise.

NOTE▶ Part 4, Division 11 of the Probate Code (Prob C §§21400–21406) applies to "payment of expenses on specifically devised property pursuant to Section 12002." Prob C §21401.

Past that point, these excess expenses become a burden on the specific property. The point in time referred to here is the earlier of:

- The date the property is distributed to the devisee or the devisee takes possession of the property, whichever occurs first; or

- The anniversary of either the testator's death or the date the prior income interest ended. Prob C §12002.

In the first instance, when property is distributed to, or possessed by, the distributee, the fiduciary should stop paying expenses.

NOTE▶ The Probate Code does not prescribe consequences for the fiduciary who continues paying expenses on a specifically devised property after distribution to, or possession by, a beneficiary. Presumably, these expenses should be a lien against the property or the distributee's other interests in the estate. This result is suggested by the method of allocating expenses when distribution is delayed past the anniversary of the decedent's death or date the prior income interest terminated.

In the second instance, when distribution is delayed, the fiduciary must continue paying the expenses, but they become a charge against the share of the distributee, and the fiduciary has a lien against the specifically devised property in the amount paid. Prob C §12002.

At this turning point, when excess expenses no longer burden the estate and instead become a lien on the specific gift, timing is again an issue. No matter when the deficiency is paid, if it accrued after the turning point, it is a charge against the beneficiary's share of the specific gift. Prob C §12002(c). In other words, prepaying an expense that would have accrued after the turning point does not make the expenses a charge against the estate.

EXAMPLE▶ The testator's will makes a specific gift of real property to the testator's son. Eleven months after the testator's death, the personal representative pays the premium on the property's insurance, even though that premium is not due until after the anniversary of the testator's death. If the property produces insufficient income to cover this expense, the payment will be a lien on the son's share of the estate, even though the payment was made before the anniversary of death.

At the turning point, one might characterize the calculation of net income and principal receipts as an accrual basis accounting.

§9.30   (3) Receipts and Disbursements, At the End

Before distributing a specific gift, the fiduciary may deduct from income amounts the fiduciary believes the estate or terminating income interest may become obligated to pay after the property is distributed. Prob C §12002(c). Examples of common post-distribution disbursements related to real property include property taxes, utility bills, and the expenses of gardening and maintenance.

§9.31 b. Debts and General Expenses of Administration

California's Uniform Principal and Income Act (UPAIA) (Prob C §§16320-16375) makes it clear that fiduciaries may not reduce the income and principal receipts of a specific gift on account of a payment described in Prob C §16370 or §16371 (generally, expenses of administration and certain debts) if the will, the trust, or Prob C §12002 dictates that payment must be made from other property. Prob C §16340(a)(2). Nor may the fiduciary reduce income or principal receipts if the fiduciary makes disbursements on behalf of the property and later recovers the disbursed amounts from a third party. Prob C §16340(a)(2). It is not the case, however, that the UPAIA generally protects specific gifts from responsibility for the debts of the decedent and the general expenses of administration. This protection, to the extent it exists, is provided by California's abatement statutes (Prob C §§21400-21406), discussed in §§9.10-9.23, not the UPAIA.

NOTE► Comparing Prob C §16430 with §201 of the Uniform Principal and Income Act of 1997, one finds many differences. Probate Code §16340 is based on §201, but was modified in a number of ways to conform with the California rule on specific gifts and "to improve readability." Comment to Prob C §16340.

Therefore, when accounting for distributions, fiduciaries must integrate these two statutory schemes; they cannot rely on the commentary to the model UPAIA for guidance on abatement.

§9.32 2. General Pecuniary Gifts, Annuities, and Gifts of Maintenance

When made in trust, a general pecuniary gift, an annuity, or a gift of maintenance carries with it income and bears interest in the same manner as would such a gift under a will. Prob C §16340(b). As is always the case, the intention of the settlor or testator, as expressed in the instrument, applies; Chapter 8, Part 10, Division 7 of the Probate Code (Prob C §§12000–12007) applies only when the instrument is silent. Prob C §12000, applied to trusts by Prob C §16340(b). Under the Probate Code, a general pecuniary devise bears no interest for the first year and thereafter bears interest of "three percentage points less than the legal rate on judgments in effect one year after the date of the testator's death." Prob C §12003, applied to trusts by Prob C §16340(b). Currently, the rate of interest on judgments is 10 percent annually (CCP §685.010); thus, the rate of interest on gifts is 7 percent. For trustees, the point at which interest begins accruing is the anniversary of the date the prior income interest ended. Prob C §12003, applied to trusts by Prob C §16340(b).

The fiduciary must pay the income or interest to the beneficiary who receives the pecuniary amount, whether outright or in trust, from the net income attributable to the reserve, and if that income is insufficient, from the principal of the reserve. Prob C §16340(b). If the reserve is insufficient, the source of payment is found by reference to the abatement statutes.

NOTE▶ Probate Code §21401 provides that the shares of beneficiaries abate "for all purposes, including. . . ." Although interest on general pecuniary devises is not one of the enumerated purposes, it should be included under the catch-all term, "all purposes."

Under the abatement statutes, one finds that interest on a general pecuniary devise may be paid from property not disposed of by the instrument or the residue, and in the case of a general pecuniary devise to a relative of the transferor, from a general pecuniary devise to a person who is not a relative of the transferor. Prob C §21402(a)(3). If none of these sources is sufficient, presumably no interest can be paid.

For an example of accounting for interest that accrued on a general pecuniary gift, see §9.44.

§9.33 3. Net Income Distributable to Residuary Beneficiaries

To determine whether there is any net income distributable to residuary beneficiaries, the fiduciary should take the following steps:

- Distribute any specific gifts and all the net income attributable to those gifts (Prob C §16340(a));
- Distribute any general pecuniary gifts, annuities, and gifts of maintenance, and any interest due on those gifts (Prob C §16340(b));
- Include in net income any income from property disbursed to discharge liabilities (Prob C §16340(c)(1));
- Pay all of the following, from income or principal at the fiduciary's discretion, provided that paying these expenses from property passing to a marital or charitable trust would not cause a reduction or loss of the marital or charitable deduction (Prob C §16340(c)(2)):
  - Fees of attorneys, accountants, and fiduciaries;
  - Court costs and other expenses of administration; and
  - Interest on estate taxes;
- Pay from principal all other disbursements made or incurred in connection with the settlement of a decedent's estate or the winding up of a terminating income interest, including (Prob C §16340(c)(3)):
  - Debts;
  - Funeral expenses;
  - Disposition of remains;
  - Family allowances; and
  - Estate taxes and related penalties that are apportioned to the estate or terminating income interest by the will, the trust, or Division 10 of the Probate Code (beginning with Prob C §20100).

Residuary beneficiaries are entitled to distributions of the net income so calculated in proportion to their interests in the undistributed principal assets, using asset values as of the date of distribution and without reducing those values by any unpaid principal obligations. Prob C §16341(a). The "date of distribution" must be reasonably near the date used in the fiduciary's calculation, but the date of distribution and the date of the calculation need not be identical. Prob C §16341(c). The fiduciary who does not distribute the income to which the residual beneficiaries are entitled must keep appropriate records of each beneficiary's entitlement. Prob C §16341(b).

§9.34 V. TAX ATTRIBUTES OF DISTRIBUTIONS

Except as otherwise provided in the trust instrument, distributions to beneficiaries must be considered paid in the following order from the following sources (Prob C §16374.5):

- From net taxable income other than capital gains;
- From net realized short-term capital gains;
- From net realized long-term capital gains;
- From tax-exempt and other income; and
- From principal of the trust.

After distributing property to the beneficiaries, the trustee must adjust income or principal receipts to the extent the trust's taxes were reduced by a distribution deduction taken on the trust's income tax return. Prob C §16374.9(d).

Probate Code §16374.5 is not a tracing rule; it imposes responsibility for the tax on income and capital gains without regard to the nature of the asset distributed.

EXAMPLE▶ A will-substitute trust has become irrevocable due to the settlor's death. The trustee should administer the trust with all due speed, but during the first year of administration, the trustee manages to distribute only one asset, a grand piano. Assume the grand piano's carry and market values are the same: $80,000. Also assume that the trust had $80,000 of net ordinary income during the first year of administration. Probate Code §16374.5 would characterize the distribution of the piano as entirely ordinary income.

As the above example illustrates, applied in isolation, Prob C §16374.5 might unfairly burden one beneficiary with a disproportionate share of the trust's taxable income and capital gain. The Uniform Principal and Income Act (UPAIA) (Prob C §§16320-16375) guards against this by giving trustees the power to adjust between income and principal to offset the shifting of economic interests or tax benefits. Prob C §16375. See discussion in §§13.18-13.20.

VI. AVOIDING COMMON MISTAKES

§9.35 A. Do Not Report Distributions Using Market Value

Distributions must be shown at carry value. Prob C §16062(e). Reporting distributions at market value, or at any value other than carry value, makes the fiduciary look as if he or she is trying to hide something. It is acceptable to include on the Distributions schedule both carry and market value, but on the Summary of Account, one reports only carry value.

§9.36 B. Give Interest Where Due

Pecuniary bequests bear interest if not distributed within 1 year. Prob C §12003. Probate Code §16340(b) imports this rule into the law of trusts. This rule, and the others found in Prob C §§16340, 12000-12007, often catch trustees unaware. To avoid paying interest unnecessarily, practitioners should review these sections of the Probate Code early in the trust administration.

VII. ABATEMENT EXAMPLES AND SELF-TESTS

§9.37 A. Abatement: Example One and Self-Test

The testator's will is only one sentence. It says, "I leave my Gran Torino to the boy next door and my house to the girl next door." The testator is not related to his next-door neighbors. The testator has two children who survive him and no deceased children. The testator's estate consists of the following:

- The Gran Torino;
- The testator's home; and
- $25,000 on deposit at the Bank of America.

The sum of the decedent's debts and the expenses of administration is $25,000.

Classify the gift of the Gran Torino.

- Property not disposed of by the instrument;
- A residuary gift;

- A general gift to persons other than the testator's relatives;
- A general gift to the testator's relatives;
- A specific gift to persons other than the testator's relatives; or
- A specific gift to the testator's relatives.

Classify the gift of the house.

- Property not disposed of by the instrument;
- A residuary gift;
- A general gift to persons other than the testator's relatives;
- A general gift to the testator's relatives;
- A specific gift to persons other than the testator's relatives; or
- A specific gift to the testator's relatives.

Classify the $25,000 in the testator's bank account.

- Property not disposed of by the instrument;
- A residuary gift;
- A general gift to persons other than the testator's relatives;
- A general gift to the testator's relatives;
- A specific gift to persons other than the testator's relatives; or
- A specific gift to the testator's relatives.

What abates to pay the debts and expenses?

- The Gran Torino;
- The home; or
- The cash.

Do the testator's children get anything?

- Yes
- No

Answer: Both the Gran Torino and the house are specific gifts to persons other than the testator's relatives. The cash is property not disposed of by the instrument and would pass to the testator's children by intestacy. However, because this gift abates first, the children get nothing.

§9.38 B. Abatement: Example Two and Self-Test

The testator's will says, "I leave my Gran Torino to the boy next door and I leave my house and its contents to the girl next door. I leave one half of my cash to my daughter and I leave one half of my cash to my son." The testator is not related to the boy and girl who live next door. He has two children who survive him and no deceased children.

The testator's estate consists of the following:

- The Gran Torino, with a date-of-death value of $5000;
- The testator's home, with a date-of-death value of $95,000; and
- $25,000 on deposit at the Bank of America.

The sum of the testator's debts and the expenses of administration is $25,000.

Classify the gifts of the cash.

- Property not disposed of by the instrument;
- Residuary gifts;
- General gifts to persons other than the testator's relatives;
- General gifts to the testator's relatives;
- Specific gifts to persons other than the testator's relatives; or
- Specific gifts to the testator's relatives.

Which gifts abate?

- The Gran Torino;
- The home; or
- The gifts of cash.

Answer: The gifts of cash are general gifts to the testator's relatives; these gifts abate first to pay the debts and expenses of administration. The children get nothing.

§9.39   C. Abatement: Example Three and Self-Test

This example is identical to Example Two (§9.38), except that the debts and expenses of administration are $35,000, rather than $25,000.

Which gift(s) abate first?

- The Gran Torino;
- The home; or
- The gifts of cash.

Which gift abates second?

- The Gran Torino;
- The home;
- The residue; or
- None of the above.

Answer: Again, the general gifts to the testator's relatives (cash to kids) abate first, but the cash is insufficient to pay expenses. Thus, the specific gifts must abate by $10,000 to pay the excess of the debts and expenses not covered by the $25,000 cash. The specific gifts are of the same class and abate pro rata. Prob C §21043. In other words, the boy must pay 5 percent of the excess debts and expenses and the girl must pay 95 percent. Either these beneficiaries will contribute cash to the administration, or the personal representative must sell the gift of the beneficiary who does not make a contribution.

§9.40   D. Abatement: Example Four and Self-Test

The testator's will says, "I leave my Gran Torino to the boy next door and I leave my house and its contents to the girl next door. I leave my Wells Fargo bank account to my daughter and I leave my Bank of America account to my son." The testator is not related to the boy and girl next door. The testator has two children who survive him and no deceased children.

The testator's estate consists of the following:

- The Gran Torino, worth $5000;
- The testator's home, worth $95,000;
- $15,000 on deposit at Wells Fargo Bank; and
- $10,000 on deposit at the Bank of America.

The sum of the testator's debts and the expenses of administration is $25,000.

Classify the gift of the Wells Fargo account.

- Property not disposed of by the instrument;
- A residuary gift;
- A general gift to persons other than the testator's relatives;
- A general gift to the testator's relatives;
- A specific gift to persons other than the testator's relatives; or
- A specific gift to the testator's relatives.

Classify the gift of the Bank of America account.

- Property not disposed of by the instrument;
- A residuary gift;
- A general gift to persons other than the testator's relatives;
- A general gift to the testator's relatives;
- A specific gift to persons other than the testator's relatives; or
- A specific gift to the testator's relatives.

Which gifts abate?

- The Gran Torino;
- The home;
- The Wells Fargo account;
- The Bank of America account; or

- None of the above.

Answer: In contrast to the will in Examples Two (§9.38) and Three (§9.39), the will in Example Four refers to specifically identifiable properties, *i.e.,* two bank accounts. In Example Four, the testator is making specific gifts to his relatives and they abate after specific gifts to non-relatives. The gifts to the boy and girl next door abate ratably to pay the $25,000 in debts and expenses.

§9.41   E. Abatement: Example Five and Self-Test

The testator's will says, "I leave my Gran Torino to the boy next door and I leave my cash to my children, to share equally. I leave the residue of my estate equally to the boy and girl next door." The testator is not related to the boy and girl who live next door. The testator is survived by his two children.

The testator's estate consists of the following:

- The Gran Torino;
- The testator's home; and
- $25,000 on deposit at the Bank of America.

The sum of the testator's debts and the expenses of administration is $25,000.

From what property will the personal representative pay the debts and expenses?

- The Gran Torino;
- The home; or
- The cash.

Answer: The debts and expenses must be paid from the residue, even though this may mean selling the house.

§9.42   F. Abatement: Example Six and Self-Test

The testator's will says, "I leave my Gran Torino to the boy next door. I leave my house and its contents to the mother of the boy next door. I leave my Wells Fargo bank account to my daughter.

I leave my Bank of America account to my son." Again, the testator is not related to the boy next door. He is survived by two children. His estate consists of the following:

- The Gran Torino, worth $5000;
- The testator's home, worth $95,000;
- $15,000 on deposit at Wells Fargo Bank; and
- $10,000 on deposit at the Bank of America.

The sum of the testator's debts and the expenses of administration is $35,000.

The decedent held his Wells Fargo bank account in joint tenancy with his daughter and his Bank of America account in joint tenancy with his son.

From what property will the personal representative pay the debts and expenses?

- The Gran Torino;
- The home; or
- The cash.

Answer: The joint tenancy accounts are not liable for the expenses of administration, because these accounts are not subject to administration. Generally, joint tenancy property also is not subject to the debts of the decedent. In a joint tenancy, each tenant owns an equal undivided life estate in the property and both have a contingent remainder in the fee, "the contingency being dependent upon which joint tenant survives." *Ziegler v Bonnell* (1942) 52 CA2d 217, 220. When one tenant dies, nothing passes to the other, "rather, the survivor takes from the instrument by which the joint tenancy was created." *Grothe v Cortlandt* (1992) 11 CA4th 1313, 1371. In other words, on the deceased joint tenant's death, the property belongs automatically to the other tenant. If the joint tenancy is not severed during the joint tenant's lifetime, the death of a debtor joint-tenant defeats his or her creditors' ability to reach the property. The death of a debtor joint-tenant defeats even the interests of a creditor who has secured a judgment lien against the debtor joint-tenant's interest during the debtor's lifetime. *Ziegler v Bonnell* (1942) 52 CA2d 217. The death of a debtor joint-tenant after the creditor records a levy but before the execution sale also defeats the creditor's interests in the property. *Grothe v Cortlandt* (1992) 11 CA4th 1313. To protect the right to collect from joint tenancy property, the creditor must complete the execution sale while the debtor joint-tenant is still alive. *Grothe v Cortlandt, supra.*

VIII. EXHIBITS

§9.43   **A. Form: Expenses and Receipts Applicable to a Specific Gift**

The following example models what would have happened had Thomas Jones distributed 111 Management Avenue to the beneficiary Rebecca Jones, instead of selling the property. The example shows a cash distribution of rental income, less expenses, in addition to the distribution of the property. See §9.27.

THIS EXAMPLE IS NOT IN THE MASTER ACCOUNTING. THIS REFLECTS IF THE APARTMENT BUILDING HAD BEEN DISTRIBUTED WITH INCOME AND EXPENSES, RATHER THAN SOLD.

REAL ESTATE TRUST
THOMAS JONES, TRUSTEE

FIRST ACCOUNTING
FOR THE PERIOD JANUARY 1, 2012 THRU JUNE 30, 2012
ASSETS ON HAND - BEGINNING OF PERIOD

SHARES / PAR VALUE	DESCRIPTION	CARRY VALUE
REAL ESTATE		
	APARTMENT BUILDING 111 MANAGEMENT AVE, ANYTOWN, CALIFORNIA	$ 1,200,000.00
	TOTAL REAL ESTATE	$ 1,200,000.00
	TOTAL ASSETS	$ 1,200,000.00

REAL ESTATE TRUST
THOMAS JONES, TRUSTEE

FIRST ACCOUNTING
FOR THE PERIOD JANUARY 1, 2012 THRU JUNE 30, 2012
RECEIPTS
SCHEDULE A

DATE	DESCRIPTION	INCOME	PRINCIPAL
RENTAL INCOME - 111 MANAGEMENT AVE			
01/05/12	111 MANAGEMENT AVE, APT A	$ 700.00	
02/05/12	111 MANAGEMENT AVE, APT A	$ 700.00	
03/05/12	111 MANAGEMENT AVE, APT A	$ 700.00	
01/05/12	111 MANAGEMENT AVE, APT B	$ 800.00	
02/05/12	111 MANAGEMENT AVE, APT B	$ 800.00	
03/05/12	111 MANAGEMENT AVE, APT B	$ 800.00	
01/05/12	111 MANAGEMENT AVE, APT C	$ 900.00	
02/05/12	111 MANAGEMENT AVE, APT C	$ 900.00	
03/05/12	111 MANAGEMENT AVE, APT C	$ 900.00	
02/01/12	111 MANAGEMENT AVE, APT D - SECURITY DEPOSIT		$ 2,000.00
02/05/12	111 MANAGEMENT AVE, APT D	$ 1,000.00	
03/05/12	111 MANAGEMENT AVE, APT D	$ 1,000.00	
	TOTAL RENTAL INCOME - 111 MANAGEMENT AVE $	9,200.00	$ 2,000.00
	TOTAL INCOME AND PRINCIPAL $	9,200.00	$ 2,000.00
	TOTAL RECEIPTS $	11,200.00	

REAL ESTATE TRUST
THOMAS JONES, TRUSTEE

FIRST ACCOUNTING
FOR THE PERIOD JANUARY 1, 2012 THRU JUNE 30, 2012
DISBURSEMENTS
SCHEDULE C

DATE	PAID TO	FOR	INCOME
REAL ESTATE EXPENSES - 111 MANAGEMENT AVE			
01/02/12	MAGNIFICENT MANAGEMENT	PROPERTY MANAGEMENT FEE	$ 225.00
01/15/12	FINE FENCES	FENCE REPAIR - UNIT B	$ 1,500.00
01/22/12	GUPPY GLASS	WINDOW REPAIR - UNIT B	$ 250.00
01/31/12	AMY'S APPLIANCES	WASHER / DRYER - UNIT D	$ 600.00
01/31/12	CAPPY'S CARPET	CARPET REPLACEMENT - UNIT D	$ 550.00
01/31/12	DOLLY'S DECORATING	INTERIOR PAINTING - UNIT D	$ 750.00
02/02/12	MAGNIFICENT MANAGEMENT	PROPERTY MANAGEMENT FEE	$ 225.00
02/17/12	JOE'S ELECTRICAL	INTERCOM REPAIR	$ 325.00
03/02/12	MAGNIFICENT MANAGEMENT	PROPERTY MANAGEMENT FEE	$ 225.00
		TOTAL REAL ESTATE EXPENSES - 111 MANAGEMENT AVE	$ 4,650.00
		TOTAL INCOME AND PRINCIPAL	$ 4,650.00
		TOTAL DISBURSEMENTS	$ **4,650.00**

REAL ESTATE TRUST

THOMAS JONES, TRUSTEE

FIRST ACCOUNTING

FOR THE PERIOD JANUARY 1, 2012 THRU JUNE 30, 2012

DISTRIBUTIONS

SCHEDULE E

DATE	DESCRIPTION	AMOUNT/CARRY VALUE
REBECCA JONES		
04/01/12	APARTMENT BUILDING 111 MANAGEMENT AVE, ANYTOWN, CALIFORNIA	$ 1,200,000.00
04/01/12	CASH DISTRIBUTION (EQUAL TO NET INCOME ON RENTAL PROPERTY, RENTS OF $11,200 LESS EXPENSES OF $4,650)	$ 6,550.00
	TOTAL DISTRIBUTIONS	**$ 1,206,550.00**

§9.44 B. Form: Accounting for the Accrual of Interest on a General Pecuniary Gift

The following example shows the distribution of $75,000 to the Animal Rescue Foundation, plus interest of $3937.50.

THIS IS NOT IN THE MASTER ACCOUNTING AS THIS ASSUMES A DISTRIBUTION AFTER THE END OF OUR MASTER ACCOUNTING OF $75,000 SPECIFIC GIFT AT SEPTEMBER 30, 2013

REAL ESTATE TRUST
THOMAS JONES, TRUSTEE

FIRST ACCOUNTING
FOR THE PERIOD JANUARY 1, 2012 THRU SEPTEMBER 30, 2013
ASSETS ON HAND - BEGINNING OF PERIOD

SHARES / PAR VALUE	DESCRIPTION	CARRY VALUE
CASH AND CASH EQUIVALENTS		
	BANK OF AMERICA CHECKING A/C #XXXXXX6789	$ 5,279.53
	BANK OF AMERICA SAVINGS A/C #XXXXXX6789	$ 75,002.15
	PROPERTY MANAGEMENT COMPANY	$ 1,000.00
	UNCASHED CHECK FROM OLD REPUBLIC TITLE PROCEEDS OF 555 RETIREMENT LANE, ANYTOWN SALE CLOSED PRIOR TO DATE OF DEATH	$ 22,530.00
	TOTAL CASH AND CASH EQUIVALENTS	$ 103,811.68

REAL ESTATE TRUST
THOMAS JONES, TRUSTEE

FIRST ACCOUNTING
FOR THE PERIOD JANUARY 1, 2012 THRU **SEPTEMBER 30, 2013**
DISTRIBUTIONS
SCHEDULE E

DATE	DESCRIPTION	AMOUNT/CARRY VALUE
ANIMAL RESCUE FOUNDATION		
09/30/13	CASH DISTRIBUTION GENERAL PECUNIARY DEVISE	$ 75,000.00
09/30/13	CASH DISTRIBUTION - ACCRUED INTEREST ON SPECIFIC GIFT OF 7% FROM ANNIVERSARY DATE TO DISTRIBUTION DATE	$ 3,937.50
	TOTAL DISTRIBUTIONS	**$ 78,937.50**

10
Assets on Hand—End of Period

I. SUMMARY OF THE ASSETS ON HAND—END OF PERIOD SCHEDULE §10.1

II. PREPARING THE SCHEDULE, AT A MINIMUM
   A. Ending Date
      1. Guardians and Conservators §10.2
      2. Personal Representatives §10.3
      3. Trustees §10.4
   B. Assets on Hand §10.5

III. BEST PRACTICES
   A. Check Beginning Schedules §10.6
   B. Personal Representatives: Check Inventories and Appraisals §10.7

IV. PRINCIPAL AND INCOME §10.8

V. COMMON MISTAKES
   A. Assets Not Inventoried §10.9
   B. Substituting Market Value for Carry Value §10.10

VI. EXHIBITS
   A. Form: Sample Assets on Hand—End of Period Schedule (Cash, Real Estate, and Receivables) §10.11
   B. Form: Sample Assets on Hand—End of Period Schedule (Cash, Equities, Corporate Bonds, Mutual Funds, a Limited Partnership, and Personal Property) §10.12

§10.1 I. SUMMARY OF THE ASSETS ON HAND—END OF PERIOD SCHEDULE

Just as the schedule Assets on Hand—Beginning of Period might be described as a snapshot of the gross estate on the first day of the account period, the schedule Assets on Hand—End of Period presents a picture of the gross estate as of the last day of the account period. In the first account period, unlike the schedule Assets on Hand—Beginning, the schedule Assets on Hand—End of Period usually states two values for each asset: carry value and market value. In the second and subsequent account periods, the schedule Assets on Hand—End of Period has the same appearance as the schedule Assets on Hand—Beginning of Period. For the beginning schedule of a first account, carry and market values are often the same. See chap 4.

II. PREPARING THE SCHEDULE, AT A MINIMUM

A. Ending Date

§10.2 1. Guardians and Conservators

The guardian's or conservator's account will be either an annual account or a final account, depending on the fiduciary's circumstances. As illustrated below, after filing the first annual account, guardians and conservators must account biennially. Thus, annual accounts should end on the following dates (Prob C §2620(a)):

- For the first account, on the first anniversary of the fiduciary's appointment;
- For the second account, on the third anniversary of the fiduciary's appointment;
- For the third account, on the fifth anniversary; and
- For the fourth account, on the seventh anniversary; and so on.

As a logical alternative to the above dates, the fiduciary may choose to end the account at the end of a month or the end of the year, provided the fiduciary does not unreasonably delay filing the accounting.

NOTE▶ The Probate Code does not explicitly allow this, but the courts generally allow some deviation from the requirements of Prob C §2620(a) if the fiduciary explains why the deviation benefits the ward or conservatee.

Guardianships of the estate terminate when the ward reaches age 18 or dies (Prob C §1600(a)), or when a court determines that it is in the ward's best interest to terminate the guardianship (Prob C §1601). Generally, after a guardianship is terminated, the court retains jurisdiction until the guardian's accounts have been settled. Prob C §2630. If the guardianship ends because the ward has attained majority, the ward may settle the guardian's accounts and give the guardian a release (Prob C §2627), but most courts require the ward to appear in court for this purpose. See, *e.g.,* Contra Costa Ct R 806(b).

Conservatorships terminate on the death of the conservatee or by order of the court. Prob C §1860. When a guardianship or conservatorship is terminated by death, the fiduciary must file what the Probate Code calls the "final" account and this account must end on the date of the ward's or conservatee's death. Prob C §2620(b). This "final" account is in fact only the penultimate account because the fiduciary also must file an account for the period that begins the day after the date of death and ends on or about the date that the guardian or conservator no longer administers any assets, *i.e.,* the date the fiduciary distributes the last asset to the ward's or conservatee's successor in interest. Prob C §2620(b). The successor in interest may be the personal representative of the deceased ward's or conservatee's estate, or that person who collects the estate using one of the procedures in Prob C §§13000–13660.

§10.3   2. Personal Representatives

When the estate is in a condition to be closed, the personal representative must file a final account and petition for an order of final distribution. The ending date of these accounts should be a date as close in time to the date of the hearing on the petition as reasonably possible.

Typically, personal representatives need not file a stub account like that required of conservators and sometimes of guardians. See §2.15. Instead, after getting an order of final distribution, the personal representative must file receipts from the beneficiaries.

If the personal representative has been removed, or if his or her powers have been suspended, he or she is required to file an account within 60 days of the termination of authority. Prob C §10952. This requirement is understandable given the court's likely concerns, but the court also should require an account for the period that ends on the date the removed or suspended fiduciary finally possesses no estate property. The code does not require this, but the fiduciary may offer it for his or her own protection.

§10.4   3. Trustees

With certain exceptions, trustees must account at least annually, on termination of the trust, and on a change of trustee. Prob C §16062(a). For exceptions, see §5.5. In the definition of "accounting period," the Uniform Principal and Income Act (UPAIA) (Prob C §§16320–16375) explains that the accounting should end on the date an income interest ends (Prob C §16322), which is either "the day before an income beneficiary dies, or another terminating event occurs, or the last day of a period during which there is no beneficiary to whom a trustee may distribute income." Prob C §16345(c).

The trustee who is accounting for a trust termination should prepare a final account that ends on the date the trust terminates. If the trustee still administers assets on that date, the trustee may wish to prepare a final-final account. This stub account would end on the date the trustee finally administers only the fund reserved for the final expenses of administration.

§10.5   B. Assets on Hand

The schedule Assets on Hand—End of Period must report every asset carried by the fiduciary at the end of the account period, whether the asset was on hand at the beginning or acquired during the period of the account.

III. BEST PRACTICES

§10.6   A. Check Beginning Schedules

The fiduciary should check that every asset listed on the schedule Assets on Hand—End of Period also appears on one of the following three schedules:

- Assets on Hand—Beginning of Period;

- Assets Received During Period of Account; or
- Changes in Form of Assets.

In other words, the assets listed on the schedule Assets on Hand—End of Period are credits, and these credits should be traceable to a charge found elsewhere in the accounting. More colloquially, if it is on hand at the end, it came from somewhere and the accounting had better show where it came from.

§10.7 B. Personal Representatives: Check Inventories and Appraisals

Personal representatives must make sure that every asset on hand at the end of the account period may be found on one of the personal representative's Inventories and Appraisals. If the personal representative determines that he or she has been administering an asset that should have been inventoried but was not, the personal representative should remedy this problem before seeking court approval of the accounting. The court will not approve an accounting for assets that should have been inventoried but were not.

§10.8 IV. PRINCIPAL AND INCOME

Every asset on hand at the end is either a principal asset, undistributed income, or partly both. For example, a cash account may be partly principal and partly undistributed income. The character of the asset is a consequence of the transactions reported on the other schedules of the account. On the schedule Assets on Hand—End of Period, the fiduciary reports only the net effect of these transactions. For each asset listed on the schedule Assets on Hand—End of Period, the fiduciary must say whether the asset is principal or income, or if the asset is a mix of the two, the fiduciary must state how much is principal and how much is income.

V. COMMON MISTAKES

§10.9 A. Assets Not Inventoried

Personal representatives, guardians, and conservators must inventory all assets on hand at the beginning of the administration and any late-discovered assets. Only assets purchased with estate money need not be inventoried. The court will not approve the account of a fiduciary who fails to inventory an asset that must be inventoried.

§10.10 B. Substituting Market Value for Carry Value

Assets on hand at the end must be reported at their carry value (Prob C §1061(a)(10)), and it is a mistake to substitute market value for carry value on the schedule Assets on Hand—End of Period. Nevertheless, unscrupulous fiduciaries often do so, in an attempt to disguise the paucity of their credits. Market value belongs on an auxiliary schedule (Prob C §1063(a)) and those fiduciaries who choose to combine the Estimated Market Value of Assets on Hand at End of Account Period auxiliary schedule with the schedule Assets on Hand—End of Period must be careful not to confuse the two values.

VI. EXHIBITS

§10.11 A. Form: Sample Assets on Hand— End of Period Schedule (Cash, Real Estate, and Receivables)

The sample schedule below accounts for cash, real estate, and receivables.

DAVID JONES TRUST

THOMAS JONES, TRUSTEE

FIRST ACCOUNTING

FOR THE PERIOD JANUARY 1, 2012 THRU JUNE 30, 2012

ASSETS ON HAND - END OF PERIOD

SCHEDULE F

SHARES / PAR VALUE	DESCRIPTION	CARRY VALUE	MARKET VALUE
CASH AND CASH EQUIVALENTS			
	BANK OF AMERICA CHECKING A/C #XXXXXX6789	$ 99,754.44	$ 99,754.44
	BANK OF AMERICA SAVINGS A/C #XXXXXX6789	$ 2,768,030.00	$ 2,768,030.00
	TOTAL CASH AND CASH EQUIVALENTS	$ 2,867,784.44	$ 2,867,784.44
REAL ESTATE			
	RESIDENCE 987 SUNNYSIDE STREET ANYTOWN, CALIFORNIA	$ 773,000.00	$ 755,000.00
	TOTAL REAL ESTATE	$ 773,000.00	$ 755,000.00
RECEIVABLES			
	DUE FROM REBECCA JONES (12 MOS RENT ON FORECLOSURE WAY)	$ 24,000.00	$ 24,000.00
	NOTE RECEIVABLE DUE FROM LAND INVESTORS LLC SECURED BY LAND (UNIMPROVED) ANYTOWN, CA	$ 195,000.00	$ 195,000.00
	TOTAL RECEIVABLES	$ 219,000.00	$ 219,000.00
	TOTAL ASSETS	$ **3,859,784.44**	$ 3,622,784.44

§10.12 B. Form: Sample Assets on Hand—End of Period Schedule (Cash, Equities, Corporate Bonds, Mutual Funds, a Limited Partnership, and Personal Property)

The sample schedule below accounts for cash, equities, corporate bonds, mutual funds, a limited partnership, and personal property.

APRIL CASH TRUST

SALLY CASH, TRUSTEE

FIRST ACCOUNTING

FOR THE PERIOD JANUARY 1, 2013 THRU JUNE 30, 2013

ASSETS ON HAND - END OF PERIOD

SCHEDULE F

SHARES / PAR VALUE	DESCRIPTION	CARRY VALUE	MARKET VALUE
CASH AND CASH EQUIVALENTS			
	WELLS FARGO BANK CHECKING A/C #XXXXXX9876	$ 22,449.92	$ 22,449.92
	WELLS FARGO BANK SAVINGS A/C #XXXXXX4321	$ 237,728.89	$ 237,728.89
	WELLS FARGO BANK CERTIFICATE OF DEPOSIT	$ 102,000.00	$ 102,000.00
	MERRILL LYNCH CASH INVESTMENT A/C #XXXX-2222	$ 4,477.11	$ 4,477.11
	MERRILL LYNCH ML MONEY MARKET FUND INVESTMENT A/C #XXXX-2222	$ 65,859.82	$ 65,859.82
	TOTAL CASH AND CASH EQUIVALENTS	$ 432,515.74	$ 432,515.74
EQUITIES			
1,940.000	CISCO SYS INC	$ 39,459.60	$ 47,219.60
4,800.000	EXXON MOBIL CORP	$ 425,808.00	$ 433,680.00
2,400.000	MERCK & CO INC	$ 49,608.00	$ 111,480.00
2,400.000	ORACLE CORP	$ 83,256.00	$ 73,704.00
1,440.000	PEPSICO INC	$ 99,835.20	$ 117,777.60
7,200.000	WELLS FARGO & CO NEW	$ 252,360.00	$ 297,144.00
	TOTAL EQUITIES	$ 950,326.80	$ 1,081,005.20

CORPORATE BONDS					
24,000.000	BANK OF AMERICA CORP 8.125% MAY/NOV 15 DUE 12/31/48	$	23,428.52	$	23,150.00
24,000.000	JP MORGAN CHASE & CO 7.900% APR/OCT 30 DUE 12/31/48	$	24,000.00	$	24,125.00
	TOTAL CORPORATE BONDS	$	47,428.52	$	47,275.00
MUTUAL FUNDS					
14,565.205	FRANKLIN CA TAX FREE INCOME FUND CL A	$	98,120.96	$	104,578.17
50.000	FRANKLIN UNIVERSAL TRUST	$	317.19	$	341.50
300.000	NUVEEN CA MUN MKT OPPORTUNITY	$	3,747.00	$	3,909.00
	TOTAL MUTUAL FUNDS	$	102,185.15	$	108,828.67
LIMITED PARTNERSHIPS					
5.000	WIDGET SUPPLIER LP	$	82,000.00	$	82,000.00
	TOTAL LIMITED PARTNERSHIPS	$	82,000.00	$	82,000.00
PERSONAL PROPERTY					
	JEWELRY	$	2,500.00	$	2,500.00
	TOTAL PERSONAL PROPERTY	$	2,500.00	$	2,500.00
	TOTAL ASSETS	$	**1,616,956.21**	$	1,754,124.61

11
Auxiliary Schedules

I. IN GENERAL §11.1

II. THE AUXILIARY SCHEDULES, BRIEFLY
   A. Schedule of Estimated Market Value §11.2
   B. Purchases, Sales, or Other Changes in Form §11.3
   C. Allocation of Receipts and Disbursements Between Principal and Income §11.4
   D. Proposed Distributions §11.5
      1. Distribution to Income Beneficiary §11.6
      2. Specifically Devised Property §11.7
      3. Interest on Bequests, Gifts of Annuities, and Gifts for Maintenance §11.8
   E. Schedule of Liabilities §11.9
   F. Guardians and Conservators §11.10

III. CHANGES IN FORM OF ASSETS §11.11
   A. Disbursements and Exchanges §11.12
   B. Sale Price Equal to Asset's Carry Value §11.13
   C. Payments of Principal From a Debtor Obligated to the Trust §11.14
   D. Transactions That Affect an Asset's Carry Value §11.15
   E. Transfers Between Accounts §11.16

IV. EXHIBITS
   A. Form: Spreadsheet Illustrating Sale Price Equal to Asset's Carry Value §11.17
   B. Form: Spreadsheet Showing Payments of Principal From a Debtor to the Trust §11.18
   C. Spreadsheets Showing Transactions Affecting an Asset's Carry Value
      1. Form: Purchase of Bond and Reinvestment of Dividends §11.19
      2. Form: Disbursement of Funds to Improve Real Property §11.20

D. Spreadsheets Showing Liabilities
  1. Form: Spreadsheet Accounting for Tenant Security Deposit §11.21
  2. Form: Spreadsheet Showing Increase in Liabilities §11.22

§11.1   I. IN GENERAL

In court accountings, the fiduciary must report certain information on the auxiliary schedules listed below (Prob C §1063):

- Estimated Market Value of Assets on Hand at End of Account Period;
- Estimated Market Value of Assets on Hand at Beginning of Account Period (for all accounts subsequent to the initial account);
- Changes in Form of Assets;
- Allocation of Receipts and Disbursements Between Principal and Income;
- Specifically Devised Property;
- Interest to Be Paid on Gifts;
- Proposed Distributions;
- Liabilities; and
- Conservators, Guardians: Real Property Located in Foreign Jurisdiction.

This chapter addresses in detail only two of the above schedules: Changes in Form of Assets and Liabilities. The six other auxiliary schedules are covered elsewhere in this book, and are discussed here only briefly.

II. THE AUXILIARY SCHEDULES, BRIEFLY

§11.2   A. Schedule of Estimated Market Value

Guardians, conservators, and personal representatives, as well as trustees who seek court approval of their accounts, must show the estimated market value of the assets on hand as of the end of the account period. Prob C §1063(a).

PRACTICE TIP▶ Although the Probate Code requires fiduciaries to state the market value on an "additional schedule," many fiduciaries omit the additional schedule and list market value adjacent to the carry value on the schedules of assets on hand. This method of representing market values is preferable because it helps beneficiaries avoid the confusion that carry value sometimes creates, and facilitates a comparison between carry and market values. Fiduciaries who choose to report estimated market values on a separate schedule should clone the schedule Assets on Hand—End of Period and then substitute market value for carry value.

Trustees who will not submit their accounts for court approval must provide a "statement of the assets and liabilities of the trust as of the end of the last complete fiscal year of the trust or as of the end of the period covered by the account." Prob C §1063(a). Presumably, this statement must provide the market values of the assets of the trust.

§11.3   B. Purchases, Sales, or Other Changes in Form

If a fiduciary has purchased assets during the account period, has sold assets for carry value, or otherwise has engaged in transactions that affect the form of the assets, those transactions must be reported on the schedule Changes in Form of Assets. Prob C §1063(b). This schedule is also the place to report transfers of funds or property from one account to another—for example, closing and opening bank accounts (if the fiduciary feels these transactions should be reported). This schedule is the subject of §11.11.

§11.4   C. Allocation of Receipts and Disbursements Between Principal and Income

The Probate Code requires fiduciaries to provide an auxiliary schedule allocating receipts and disbursements between principal and income. However, it is preferable to account for principal and income on the Receipts and Disbursements schedules, instead.

§11.5 D. Proposed Distributions

Except as provided in Prob C §9650(c), personal representatives may not distribute property to beneficiaries without prior court authorization.

NOTE▶ Probate Code §9650(c) provides:

> Real property or tangible personal property may be left with or surrendered to the person presumptively entitled to it unless or until, in the judgment of the personal representative, possession of the property by the personal representative will be necessary for purposes of administration.

If the personal representative seeks an order for distribution in conjunction with the petition for approval of his or her accounting, the accounting must contain a schedule setting forth the proposed distribution. Prob C §1063(f). In three situations, briefly discussed in §§11.6–11.8, the code mandates certain disclosures. The schedule Proposed Distributions is identical to the schedule a fiduciary would use to report distributions already made, and that schedule is discussed at length in chap 9.

§11.6 1. Distribution to Income Beneficiary

If a personal representative or a trustee will distribute the estate or trust to an income beneficiary, the fiduciary must show the allocation of receipts and disbursements between principal and income. Prob C §1063(c).

NOTE▶ Income beneficiary means "a person to whom the income of a trust is or may be payable." Prob C §16325.

The code requires fiduciaries to report this information on an auxiliary schedule, but fiduciaries customarily distinguish between income and principal on their schedules of Receipts and Disbursements, eliminating the need for an auxiliary schedule. See §§6.8–6.45, 8.12–8.25.

§11.7 2. Specifically Devised Property

Under Prob C §12002, if property is specifically devised, the personal representative must provide an additional schedule accounting for the income and disbursements with respect to the property, and if the specifically gifted property is sold, the schedule must show an accounting of the sales proceeds. Prob C §1063(d). The format of this schedule is that described in chap 9. See §§9.27-9.30.

§11.8   3. Interest on Bequests, Gifts of Annuities, and Gifts for Maintenance

Certain testamentary gifts must be distributed within 1 year of the testator's death or the gift bears interest thereafter. Prob C §§12003-12005. These gifts are those described in Prob C §12003 (general pecuniary devise), §12004 (annuity), or §12005 (devise for maintenance). If the personal representative will pay interest on such a gift, he or she must include in the accounting a schedule showing the calculation of interest he or she proposes paying. Prob C §1063(e). Trustees also must pay interest on such gifts, under the same conditions that apply to gifts from decedent's estates. Prob C §16340(d). To account for these proposed or actual distributions of income, see §9.32.

§11.9   E. Schedule of Liabilities

For court accountings, the fiduciary's schedule of Liabilities should list *all* liabilities that exist at the end of the account period, excluding recurring expenses such as rent, salaries, insurance premiums, and the like, but including the following (Prob C §1063(g)):

- Liabilities that are a lien on estate property;
- Taxes due but unpaid;
- All notes payable;
- Any judgments for which the estate or trust is liable; and
- Any other material liability.

A common example of a liability is a tenant's security deposit. For a spreadsheet illustrating this situation, see §11.21.

For an example of regular principal payments on a mortgage, see §8.33. For a spreadsheet showing liabilities that increased due to missed payments on a mortgage, see §11.22.

When liabilities increase during the period of an account, reflect these increases as shown in §11.22.

When a fiduciary pays a liability, the payments are reported on the Disbursements schedule, and if the fiduciary pays the debt in full before the end of the account period, the Liabilities schedule should reflect this fact. Prob C §1063(g).

Finally, if the debt was incurred during the account period, this should be disclosed on the Liabilities schedule, even if the debt is paid in full before the close of the account period. Nevertheless, the fiduciary may wish to repeat the payment information on the Liabilities schedule, where it will be more apparent that the liability was paid in full.

§11.10 F. Guardians and Conservators

If a guardian or conservator has knowledge of real property outside of California, the fiduciary must file with his or her account a separate schedule that (Prob C §1063(h)):

- Identifies the real property;
- Provides a good-faith estimate of the property's fair market value; and
- States what action, if any, will be or has been taken to preserve and protect the real property, including a recommendation whether an ancillary proceeding is necessary.

§11.11 III. CHANGES IN FORM OF ASSETS

Any transaction that changes the form of an asset without triggering a gain or a loss should be reported on the schedule Changes in Form of Assets. For example, when cash is exchanged for other property (a purchase), that transaction is reported on the schedule. Similarly, when property is sold for carry value, the transaction is reported on the schedule. The fiduciary who fails to account for these transactions will not be able to reconcile his or her cash.

§11.12 A. Disbursements and Exchanges

Fiduciaries must distinguish between those purchases that are treated as disbursements and those that are better described as an exchange of one type of property for another. Disbursements may be thought of as purchases that decrease the estate accounted for. Disbursements may include the purchase of sundries such as office supplies, stamps, packing material, paint, and light bulbs. By contrast, the purchase of stocks, bonds, annuities, certificates of deposit, real property, or durable goods such as vehicles, represent the exchange of one type of asset—money—for another. Exchanges do not alter the measure of the trustee's responsibility; they merely change the form of the asset for which the trustee is responsible. Such purchases are reported on the Changes in Form of Assets schedule.

NOTE▶ The Uniform Principal and Income Act (UPAIA) (Prob C §§16320-16375) is generally silent on the topic of purchases, but it specifies that an amount paid to acquire an option "shall be paid from principal." Prob C §16366(c).

§11.13   B. Sale Price Equal to Asset's Carry Value

On the schedule Changes in Form of Assets, the trustee also should report any sale in which the sale price was equal to the asset's carry value. In such a transaction, the fiduciary again exchanges one property—tangible, intangible, or real property—for another type of property: money. In general, the proceeds of such a sale would be principal. Prob C §16355(b). However, see chap 6 for a discussion of the exceptions to this rule.

The example in §11.17 illustrates this situation by showing the trustee collecting the proceeds of a life insurance policy and the sale of a U.S. Treasury Bond.

§11.14   C. Payments of Principal From a Debtor Obligated to the Trust

The Changes in Form of Assets schedule is also the place to report payments of principal from a debtor who is obligated to the trust. These principal payments change one type of asset, a receivable, to another, money.

NOTE▶ Interest payments are reported on the Receipts schedule, usually as receipts of income. See §6.18.

The sample spreadsheet in §11.18 shows the collection of a State Farm Insurance claim that was pending on the settlor's date of death.

§11.15   D. Transactions That Affect an Asset's Carry Value

The Changes in Form of Assets schedule is also the place to

recapitulate transactions that have affected an asset's carry value. For example, if the trustee is participating in a dividend reinvestment program, he or she probably accounts for each dividend as a receipt of income (see §6.44), but at the end of the account, the trustee must explain why he or she carries more of the security and not more cash. The Changes in Form of Assets schedule is the place to report the many small purchases that result from participation in a dividend reinvestment program.

The sample spreadsheet in §11.19 shows the purchase of a J.P. Morgan bond and reinvestment of dividends in a mutual fund.

Another example of a transaction that affects an asset's carry value is the disbursement of funds for improvement of real property. The example in §11.20 illustrates such disbursements.

§11.16   E. Transfers Between Accounts

In a court accounting, fiduciaries need not account for transfers of cash or securities between accounts (Prob C §1063(b)), but they may wish to do so if disclosing the transactions would serve a purpose. For example, if the settlor had established multiple trust-owned bank accounts, scattered across town, and if the trustee closed them all and consolidated the deposits at one institution, accounting for these transactions might alleviate a beneficiary's suspicions about the closed accounts while simultaneously illustrating the trustee's efforts to efficiently administer the trust. The trustee would report these transactions on the Changes in Form of Assets schedule.

Fiduciaries who disclose transfers from one account to another should not treat such transfers as if the transaction were a disbursement and an offsetting receipt. Accounting for the transaction this way would inflate the fiduciary's charges, making the administration appear more burdensome than it is. For personal representatives, such erroneous reporting also would inflate the "estate accounted for," and concomitantly, the personal representative's statutory fee. Prob C §10800(b). Fiduciaries who account for the transfer of assets between one account and another should do so on the auxiliary schedule Changes in Form of Assets.

IV. EXHIBITS

§11.17 A. Form: Spreadsheet Illustrating Sale Price Equal to Asset's Carry Value

The example below illustrates the collection of the proceeds of a life insurance policy and the sale of a U.S. Treasury Bond. See §11.13. For discussion of the Cash Trust, see chap 1.

APRIL CASH TRUST

SALLY CASH, TRUSTEE

FIRST ACCOUNTING

FOR THE PERIOD JANUARY 1, 2013 THRU JUNE 30, 2013

CHANGE IN FORM OF ASSETS

DATE	DESCRIPTION	CASH	CARRY VALUE
SALES W/O GAIN OR LOSS			
01/15/13	METLIFE POLICY #XXXX4587 DTD 07/01/05	$ 57,243.00	$ (57,243.00)
05/31/13	US TREASURY 3.5% DUE 05/31/11	$ 20,000.00	$ (20,000.00)

§11.18 B. Form: Spreadsheet Showing Payments of Principal From a Debtor to the Trust

The spreadsheet below that will become part of the Changes in Form of Assets schedule illustrates the collection of a State Farm Insurance claim that was pending on the date of the settlor's death. See §11.14.

REAL ESTATE TRUST

THOMAS JONES, TRUSTEE

FIRST ACCOUNTING

FOR THE PERIOD JANUARY 1, 2012 THRU JUNE 30, 2012

CHANGE IN FORM SCHEDULE

SCHEDULE A

DATE	DESCRIPTION	CASH	CARRY VALUE
COLLECTION OF RECEIVABLES			
01/05/12	STATE FARM INSURANCE CO CLAIM PENDING RE: FIRE AT 555 RETIREMENT LANE, ANYTOWN, CA	$ 125,000.00	$ (125,000.00)

C. Spreadsheets Showing Transactions Affecting an Asset's Carry Value

§11.19 1. Form: Purchase of Bond and Reinvestment of Dividends

The example below illustrates the purchase of a bond and the trustee's participation in a dividend reinvestment program. See §11.15.

APRIL CASH TRUST

SALLY CASH, TRUSTEE

FIRST ACCOUNTING

FOR THE PERIOD JANUARY 1, 2013 THRU JUNE 30, 2013

CHANGES IN FORM OF ASSETS

DATE		DESCRIPTION	CASH	CARRY VALUE
PURCHASES				
03/01/13	24,000.000	JP MORGAN CHASE & CO 7.900% APR/OCT 30 DUE 12/31/48 CALLABLE $100.00 ON 04/30/18	$ (24,000.00)	$ 24,000.00
REINVESTMENTS				
01/01/13	14,202.081	BALANCE		$ 95,722.03
01/01/13	57.063	FRANKLIN CA TAX-FREE INCOME A	$ (383.46)	$ 383.46
02/02/13	58.959	FRANKLIN CA TAX-FREE INCOME A	$ (385.00)	$ 385.00
03/02/13	61.116	FRANKLIN CA TAX-FREE INCOME A	$ (405.20)	$ 405.20
04/04/13	62.413	FRANKLIN CA TAX-FREE INCOME A	$ (406.93)	$ 406.93
05/03/13	61.551	FRANKLIN CA TAX-FREE INCOME A	$ (408.70)	$ 408.70
06/02/13	62.022	FRANKLIN CA TAX-FREE INCOME A	$ (409.64)	$ 409.64
	14,565.205			$ 98,120.96

§11.20 2. Form: Disbursement of Funds to Improve Real Property

The spreadsheet below illustrates the disbursement of funds to improve real property. See §11.15.

DAVID JONES TRUST

THOMAS JONES, TRUSTEE

FIRST ACCOUNTING

FOR THE PERIOD JANUARY 1, 2012 THRU JUNE 30, 2012

CHANGES IN FORM OF ASSETS

DATE	DESCRIPTION		CASH	CARRY VALUE
CAPITAL IMPROVEMENTS - 987 SUNNYSIDE STREET				
01/01/12	CARRY VALUE ON HAND - BEGINNING OF PERIOD			$ 750,000.00
04/15/12	CREATIVE CONSTRUCTION	DEPOSIT FOR BATHROOM ADDITION	$ (5,000.00)	$ 5,000.00
04/30/12	CREATIVE CONSTRUCTION	BATHROOM ADDITION	$ (10,000.00)	$ 10,000.00
05/15/12	CREATIVE CONSTRUCTION	BATHROOM ADDITION FINAL PAYMENT	$ (8,000.00)	$ 8,000.00
06/30/12	CARRY VALUE ON HAND - END OF PERIOD			$ 773,000.00

DAVID JONES TRUST

THOMAS JONES, TRUSTEE

FIRST ACCOUNTING

FOR THE PERIOD JANUARY 1, 2012 THRU JUNE 30, 2012

ASSETS ON HAND - BEGINNING OF PERIOD

SHARES / PAR VALUE	DESCRIPTION	CARRY VALUE
REAL ESTATE		
	RESIDENCE 987 SUNNYSIDE STREET ANYTOWN, CALIFORNIA	$ 750,000.00
	TOTAL REAL ESTATE	$ 750,000.00
	TOTAL ASSETS	$ **750,000.00**

DAVID JONES TRUST

THOMAS JONES, TRUSTEE

FIRST ACCOUNTING

FOR THE PERIOD JANUARY 1, 2012 THRU JUNE 30, 2012

ASSETS ON HAND - END OF PERIOD

SCHEDULE F

SHARES / PAR VALUE REAL ESTATE	DESCRIPTION		CARRY VALUE	MARKET VALUE
	RESIDENCE 987 SUNNYSIDE STREET ANYTOWN, CALIFORNIA		$ 773,000.00	$ 755,000.00
		TOTAL REAL ESTATE $	773,000.00	$ 755,000.00
		TOTAL ASSETS $	**773,000.00**	$ 755,000.00

D. Spreadsheets Showing Liabilities

§11.21   1. Form: Spreadsheet Accounting for Tenant Security Deposit

The spreadsheet below illustrates accounting for a tenant security deposit. See §11.9.

REAL ESTATE TRUST

THOMAS JONES, TRUSTEE

FIRST ACCOUNTING

FOR THE PERIOD JANUARY 1, 2012 THRU JUNE 30, 2012

LIABILITIES

DATE	DESCRIPTION	INCREASE	DECREASE	BALANCE
DUE TO TENANTS /SECURITY DEPOSITS				
01/01/12	BETTY'S BARGAIN BOUTIQUE, FRANCHISE ROW			$ 4,000.00
05/15/12	SECURITY DEPOSIT TRANSFERRED IN ESCROW		$ 4,000.00	$ -

§11.22 2. Form: Spreadsheet Showing Increase in Liabilities

In the example below, liabilities increased due to missed payments on a mortgage. See §11.9.

REAL ESTATE TRUST
THOMAS JONES, TRUSTEE

FIRST ACCOUNTING
FOR THE PERIOD JANUARY 1, 2012 THRU JUNE 30, 2012
LIABILITIES

DATE	DESCRIPTION	INCREASE	DECREASE	BALANCE
DUE TO SECRET MORTGAGE COMPANY				
SECURED BY PROPERTY LOCATED AT				
654 FORECLOSURE WAY, ANYTOWN, CALIFORNIA				
01/01/12	BALANCE DUE			$ 289,500.00
01/15/12	LATE FEE	$ 250.00		$ 289,750.00
01/30/12	INTEREST DUE	$ 1,206.25		$ 290,956.25
02/15/12	LATE FEE	$ 250.00		$ 291,206.25
02/15/12	FORECLOSURE NOTICE FEE	$ 500.00		$ 291,706.25
02/15/12	MORTAGE BANK FEES	$ 300.00		$ 292,006.25
02/29/12	INTEREST DUE	$ 1,225.25		$ 293,231.50
03/15/12	LATE FEE	$ 250.00		$ 293,481.50
03/30/12	INTEREST DUE	$ 1,250.50		$ 294,732.00
03/30/12	LOAN PAYOFF		$ 275,000.00	$ 19,732.00
03/30/12	BANK WRITE-OFF		$ 19,732.00	$ -

12
Summary of Account, Reconciliation

I. SUMMARY OF ACCOUNT §12.1

II. APPEARANCE OF THE SUMMARY OF ACCOUNT
   A. Statutory Form and Requirements for Summary of Account §12.2
   B. Improved Summary of Account §12.3

III. BEST PRACTICES
   A. Use the "Equals" Function §12.4
   B. Charges Equal Credits, From Time to Time §12.5
   C. What to Do When Account Will Not Balance §12.6

IV. AVOIDING COMMON MISTAKES §12.7

§12.1   I. SUMMARY OF ACCOUNT

In a court accounting, "total charges shall equal total credits." Prob C §1061(c). The Summary of Account is where the fiduciary demonstrates that he or she has met this requirement. When allowed credits equal allowed charges, the fiduciary is said to have discharged his or her responsibility; hence fiduciary accountings are sometimes called "discharge accountings." The Summary of Account is the first page of the accounting, but we discuss it here, in chap 12, because it cannot be finalized until every other schedule has been completed.

II. APPEARANCE OF THE SUMMARY OF ACCOUNT

§12.2 A. Statutory Form and Requirements for Summary of Account

Probate Code §1061(b) requires a summary "in a format substantially the same as the following" for court accountings.

NOTE▶ For an improved format that shows the allocation of income and principal by schedule, see §12.3.

CHARGES	
Property on Hand, Beginning (or Inventories)	$
Additional Property Received (or Supplemental Inventories)	$
Receipts (Schedule ___)	$
Gains on Sales or Other Dispositions (Schedule ___)	$
Net Income From Trade or Business (Schedule ___)	$
Total Charges	$
CREDITS	
Disbursements (Schedule ___)	$
Losses on Sales or Other Dispositions (Schedule ___)	$
Net Loss From Trade or Business (Schedule ___)	$
Property on Hand at Close of Account (Schedule ___)	$
Total Credits	$

The practitioner must support the summary with detailed schedules showing (Prob C §1062):

- Receipts that reveal the nature or purpose of each item, the source of the receipt, and the date;
- Disbursements, including the nature or purpose of each item, the name of the payee, and the date;
- Net income or loss from a trade or business;
- Calculation of gains or losses on sale or other distribution;
- Distributions of cash or property to beneficiaries, ward, or conservatee, showing the date and amount of each, with the distribution of property shown as its carry value; and
- An itemized list of property on hand, describing each item at its carry value.

In addition, Prob C §1063 requires the following schedules:

ADDITIONAL SCHEDULES

Estimated Market Value of Assets on Hand at End of Account Period

Estimated Market Value of Assets on Hand at Beginning of Account Period (for all accounts subsequent to the initial account)

Changes in Form of Assets

Specifically Devised Property

Calculation of Interest (general pecuniary devise, etc.)

Proposed Distributions

Liabilities

§12.3   B. Improved Summary of Account

The summary of account below improves on the requirements of the statute by showing the sum of the:

- Income disbursements;
- Principal disbursements;
- Income receipts; and
- Principal receipts.

The format suggested by the Probate Code hides this vital information in auxiliary schedules.

APRIL CASH TRUST
SALLY CASH, TRUSTEE

FIRST ACCOUNTING
FOR THE PERIOD JANUARY 1, 2013 THRU JUNE 30, 2013
SUMMARY OF ACCOUNT

CHARGES

				CARRY VALUE
ASSETS ON HAND - BEGINNING OF PERIOD			$	1,798,991.47
ADDITIONS TO TRUST			$	107,000.00
INCOME	$	2,000.00		
PRINCIPAL	$	105,000.00		
RECEIPTS - SCHEDULE A			$	31,729.76
INCOME	$	25,361.76		
PRINCIPAL	$	6,368.00		
GAINS ON SALES - SCHEDULE B			$	429.06
TOTAL CHARGES			$	1,938,150.29

CREDITS

DISBURSEMENTS - SCHEDULE C			$	14,052.80
INCOME	$	5,790.22		
PRINCIPAL	$	8,262.58		
LOSSES ON SALES - SCHEDULE D			$	2,168.16
DISTRIBUTIONS - SCHEDULE E			$	304,973.12
ASSETS ON HAND - SCHEDULE F			$	1,616,956.21
INCOME	$	21,571.54		
PRINCIPAL	$	1,595,384.67		
TOTAL CREDITS			$	1,938,150.29

ADDITIONAL SCHEDULES
    CHANGES IN FORM OF ASSETS
    LIABILITIES

III. BEST PRACTICES

§12.4   A. Use the "Equals" Function

Most practitioners skilled in the preparation of fiduciary accountings use spreadsheets for their work. Such spreadsheets permit the user to fill one cell with a value copied from another cell. For example, on the Summary of Account, the value adjacent to the title "Assets on Hand—Beginning of Period" would be copied from a cell on the spreadsheet used to prepare the schedule, Assets on Hand—Beginning of Period. Specifically, the summary page would capture the sum at the bottom of each of the various schedules.

Though the beginning and ending schedules of assets on hand may provide two values for each asset (carry value and market value), only the carry value is listed on the Summary of Account. Prob C §1061(a)(10).

§12.5   B. Charges Equal Credits, From Time to Time

Once the Summary of Account worksheet has been laid out, and after the cells have been encoded to capture the sum total of the various supporting worksheets, it is a good idea to keep track of whether the charges equal credits. To do this, set up an equation in a corner of the summary worksheet:

$$X \text{ (Total Charges)} - Y \text{ (Total Credits)} = Z$$

When the difference between charges and credits (Z, in the above example) is a negative number, the accounting is out of balance because either the charges are understated or the credits are excessive.

When the difference between charges and credits is a positive number, the accounting is out of balance because either the charges are excessive or the credits are understated.

§12.6   C. What to Do When Account Will Not Balance

Practitioners who adhere to the instructions in chap 3 will reduce, or completely eliminate, the risk that their accounts will not balance. But on the rare occasion that an account does not balance at the end of the project, take a deep breath and try some, or all, of the following (not necessarily in this order):

- Find a quiet place where interruptions can be minimized;
- Verify the beginning and ending cash balances with the inventory(ies) (if applicable) and bank statements;
- Check the formulas in each spreadsheet to make sure each transaction is properly included in the sum total at the bottom of the spreadsheet;
- Verify that the summary of account is picking up the sum total from the bottom of each spreadsheet;
- Make sure that property accounted for as on hand at the beginning (or received late) is not also included on the Receipts schedule;
- Take the amount by which the account is out of balance (total Charges less total Credits, or vice versa) and divide that number by nine. If the product is a whole number (no decimals), then the problem is most likely a transposition in a cash transaction entry—for example, $29.75 has been recorded as $29.57; and
- Determine whether the problem is in the principal assets or the cash by doing the following:
  - Total all beginning principal (non-cash) assets;
  - Add any additions to principal;
  - Subtract the carry value (or tax costs) of any sales items;
  - Add the total purchases (from your Changes in Form of Assets schedule); and
  - Compare the resulting total with the total of non-cash assets on the Property on Hand at Close of Account schedule.

NOTE➤ If the numbers do not match, the initial values of non-cash assets is likely incorrect (although the initial value of the cash might also be incorrect). If the numbers match, then the problem lies solely with a cash transaction such as a missing dividend, missing disbursement(s), mis-entered gross sales proceeds of an asset, or a failure to verify ending balances.

Pay attention to whether charges outweigh credits, or vice versa, and think about what the discrepancy means. If charges outweigh credits, it is unlikely the assets on hand at the beginning are overstated, but the assets on hand at the end might be. Alternatively, a sale may have been mischaracterized as a gain when it was in fact a loss. Receipts might have been double-counted, or an asset might have been counted as both on hand and as a receipt. By contrast, if credits outweigh charges, the fiduciary might have failed to inventory a property on hand at the end. Alternatively, the fiduciary might have characterized a gain as a loss, or double-counted a disbursement. The point is, to balance the account that is out of balance, the accountant must think about the way each transaction tips the balance between charges and credits and look for a transaction erroneously recorded in a manner that tips the scales too far in one direction or the other.

NOTE► The authors wish to thank Paige Eldredge, the principal of Estate Minders, Inc., for compiling these useful tips.

§12.7 IV. AVOIDING COMMON MISTAKES

The mistakes one finds in the Summary of Account usually have their origins in the supporting schedules, with the following two exceptions:

- **Use carry value.** First, practitioners often carry forward the market value of property on hand when the proper measure of the fiduciary's charge or credit is carry value. The Probate Code specifically says, "property on hand at the end of the accounting period [shall be] stated at its carry value." Prob C §1061(a)(10).

- **Liabilities only on auxiliary schedule.** Second, practitioners often incorporate liabilities into the schedules of charges and credits. Liabilities are not irrelevant, but they do not belong on either side of the "charges = credits" equation. Liabilities must be reported on the auxiliary schedule, Liabilities.

13
Adjustments Between Principal and Income

I. THE FOUR COMPONENTS OF CALIFORNIA'S UNIFORM PRINCIPAL AND INCOME ACT §13.1

II. ACCOUNTING SEPARATELY FOR A TRUST-OWNED BUSINESS §13.2
   A. Activities for Which Trustees May Account Separately §13.3
   B. Guidelines for Accounting Separately for an Activity §13.4

III. ADJUSTMENTS BETWEEN PRINCIPAL AND INCOME, GENERALLY §13.5
   A. Threshold Criteria §13.6
   B. When Prohibited §13.7
   C. Factors for Trustee to Consider §13.8
   D. Notice of Proposed Action §13.9

IV. INCREASING INCOME IN ORDER TO OBTAIN MARITAL DEDUCTION §13.10
   A. When Income Beneficiary May Compel Trustee to Make Trust Property Productive §13.11
   B. How Trustee May Respond to a Demand to Make Trust Property Productive §13.12

V. DEPRECIATION RESERVE §13.13
   A. When to Create a Depreciation Reserve §13.14
   B. How to Create a Depreciation Reserve §13.15
   C. Cash in Depreciation Reserve Cannot Be Recharacterized §13.16

VI. TRANSFERS FROM INCOME TO PRINCIPAL IN ANTICIPATION OF PRINCIPAL DISBURSEMENT §13.17

VII. ADJUSTMENTS TO OFFSET SHIFTING ECONOMIC
INTERESTS OR TAX BENEFITS
A. Mandatory Allocation of Prob C §16374 **§13.18**
B. Discretionary Adjustment of Prob C §16375(a) **§13.19**
C. Mandatory Adjustment of Prob C §16375(b) **§13.20**

§13.1   I. THE FOUR COMPONENTS OF CALIFORNIA'S UNIFORM PRINCIPAL AND INCOME ACT

Roughly speaking, California's Uniform Principal and Income Act (UPAIA) (Prob C §§16320–16375) consists of four components. First, it is the set of rules that trustees and personal representatives must use when allocating receipts and disbursements between income and principal. (One of the UPAIA's rules is that the fiduciary must comply with the terms of the trust or of the decedent's will when that instrument contains a provision contrary to the Act. Prob C §16335.) This component of the UPAIA is discussed throughout those chapters of this book devoted to the preparation of the fiduciary's schedules of account.

The UPAIA's second component is a set of powers that trustees, but not personal representatives, may use to adjust these allocations if strict adherence to the rules of the Act would favor one beneficiary or class of beneficiaries over another in a manner unintended by the settlor or testator.

The UPAIA's third component lets the sole-proprietor trustee account for a trust-owned business entity separately, using generally accepted accounting principles, provided certain conditions are met. These latter two component—adjustments between principal and income and accounting separately for a trade or business—are the subjects of this chapter.

The fourth component of the UPAIA allows a trustee to convert the trust to a "unitrust," and by so doing, redefine the trust instrument's use of the word "income." After conversion to a unitrust, "income" means the annual payout settled on in the conversion process. (Income is 4 percent, or a greater amount as agreed on by the beneficiaries or ordered by the court. Prob C §16336.4(e)(2).) Defining income in this way raises the question of whether a unitrust conversion renders meaningless the distinction between fiduciary accounting income and principal. The Act simply says that, after a trust is converted to a unitrust (Prob C §16336.4(e)(2)),

> [t]he term "income" in the governing instrument shall mean an annual distribution, the unitrust amount, equal to 4 percent, which is the payout percentage, of the net fair market value of the trust's assets, whether those assets would be considered income or principal under other provisions of this chapter, averaged over the lesser of the following [periods].

In light of this, might the trustee of a unitrust account for his or her administration as would a guardian or conservator, *i.e.*, without allocating receipts and disbursements between income and principal? Perhaps; and if the trustee is administering a trust that has been a unitrust since its creation, certainly. Such a trustee will not face the question of whether to reconvert the trust to a traditional income trust.

By contrast, the trustee who administers a trust that has been converted to a unitrust may reconvert to a traditional income trust if the conversion has not achieved its purpose and other conditions are met. Prob C §16336.6. The purpose of the unitrust conversion is to allow the trustee to administer the trust "impartially, except to the extent that the trust or the will expresses an intention that the fiduciary shall or may favor one or more of the beneficiaries." Prob C §§16335(b), 16336(a), 16336.4(b)(1). Only by accounting for principal and income in the traditional manner can a trustee assess whether the conversion has achieved this purpose. Thus, the author recommends that trustees who convert to unitrusts continue accounting for principal and income as they were required to do prior to the conversion.

A thorough discussion of unitrust conversions is beyond the scope of this book. Readers interested in this topic should see California Trust Administration §§8.3F, 14A.2–14A.5 (Cal CEB).

§13.2   II. ACCOUNTING SEPARATELY FOR A TRUST-OWNED BUSINESS

A trustee who conducts a business or other activity as a sole proprietor may find himself or herself allocating to income more of his or her receipts than is in the beneficiaries' best interests. For example, consider the trustee who holds only rental properties, and the rents received from the properties' tenants. Absent other provisions in the trust instrument, this trustee must allocate to income 100 percent of the rents (Prob C §16356), but must pay from principal one-half of the trustee's fee, all principal payments on trust debt, and the cost of environmental remediation. It would not be in the beneficiaries' best interests for the trustee to forgo those principal disbursements, but absent a power to reallocate income to principal, this trustee would be unable to pay the trust's debts, fix environmental problems, and pay himself or herself in full. By contrast, if the properties were held in a corporation wholly owned by the trust, the trustee's receipts would be limited to those dividends issued by the corporate board. Prob C §16350(b). The board would consider the business's need for operating capital before issuing dividends and would withhold enough cash to meet those needs. Section 16352 is intended to give trustees who operate businesses and other activities as sole proprietors some of the flexibility and control they would have if they operated their businesses as a corporation or limited liability company.

§13.3   A. Activities for Which Trustees May Account Separately

The activities for which trustees may account separately include the following (Prob C §16352(c)):

(1) Retail, manufacturing, service, and other traditional business activities;
(2) Farming;
(3) Raising and selling livestock and other animals;
(4) Managing rental properties;
(5) Extracting minerals and other natural resources;
(6) Timber operations; and
(7) Transactions in derivatives and options.

This list includes a broad range of activities, and Prob C §16352(c) uses the liberal "includes" in the preface to the list. The authors believe a trustee may account separately for any activity for which there are generally accepted accounting principles. The trustee may not, however, account separately for a traditional securities portfolio. 29 Cal L Rev'n Comm'n Reports 301 (1999), *Proposed Prob C §16352 Background from Uniform Act,* adapted from Uniform Principal and Income Act §403 comment (1997).

§13.4   B. Guidelines for Accounting Separately for an Activity

The trustee who operates a business or other activity and who determines that it is in the interests of *all* the beneficiaries may account separately for the activity, instead of accounting for it as part of the trust's general accounting records. Prob C §16352. Such a trustee may retain cash receipts for working capital, for acquisition or replacement of fixed assets, and for other reasonably foreseeable needs. Prob C §16352. Additionally, such a trustee has some discretion to allocate the remaining receipts between income and principal. Prob C §16352.

The trustee who elects to account separately for an activity should account for that activity using the business and record-keeping methods of the decedent or transferor, if those methods are generally acceptable. 29 Cal L Rev'n Comm'n Reports 300 (1999), *Proposed Prob C §16352 Background from Uniform Act*. In an accounting submitted to the court for its approval, the trustee must report the net income or net losses on a schedule separate from the other schedules of receipts or losses. Prob C §1061(a)(4), (a)(8).

Finally, electing to account separately for a trade or business is not a license for the trustee to alter the interests of the income and remainder beneficiaries. The trustee may elect this form of accounting only if it is in the interests of all the beneficiaries. And the election gives the trustee no authority with regard to certain sales of business assets. If the trustee sells assets other than in the ordinary course of the business, and if the trustee determines that the amount received is no longer needed to conduct the business, the trustee must allocate the receipt to principal. Prob C §16352(b).

§13.5   III. ADJUSTMENTS BETWEEN PRINCIPAL AND INCOME, GENERALLY

The trustee of a trust with multiple beneficiaries must treat the beneficiaries impartially. Prob C §16003. The Uniform Principal and Income Act (UPAIA) (Prob C §§16320-16375) generally requires trustees to reduce investment risk by diversifying their investments while investing for total return, following modern portfolio theory. Prob C §§16045-16054; Cal L Rev'n Comm'n Comments. Due to the UPAIA's rigid rules, investing may skew the trust's receipts toward income or toward principal, making it difficult for the trustee to both invest prudently and treat beneficiaries fairly and reasonably. For example, in periods of high inflation, investing for total return might lead the trustee to invest heavily in bonds, the return from which is allocated 100 percent to interest. Prob C §16357. This strategy might produce the best total return, but also might unfairly favor the interests of the income beneficiaries over those of the remainder beneficiaries. By contrast, in a different investment environment, investing for total return might lead the trustee to prefer capital appreciation over assets that return rents, interest, and dividends. In a low-interest investment environment, such a strategy might produce the highest total return, but would favor the remainder beneficiaries' interests over those of the income beneficiaries.

The UPAIA gives trustees the power to make adjustments between principal and income so that the trustee will not be forced to choose between the duty to invest prudently and the duty to allocate between principal and income as the Act dictates. Trustees may not use this power to increase or decrease the beneficial enjoyment to which the beneficiaries are entitled; the power exists only to allow the trustee to perform his or her duties. 29 Cal L Rev'n Comm'n Reports 300 (1999), *Background from Uniform Act.*

§13.6   A. Threshold Criteria

A trustee may make an adjustment between principal and income only if three criteria are met and many prohibitions avoided. The three criteria are as follows (Prob C §16336(a)(1)-(3)):

- First, the trustee must invest and manage trust assets under the prudent investor rule.

- Second, the trust must be what is sometimes called an "income rule" trust, meaning that at least one beneficiary is entitled to mandatory or discretionary distributions described in the trust instrument as distributions of income.

- Third, after considering his or her other powers, the trustee determines either that he or she is unable to administer the trust impartially, if impartiality is called for, or that he or she is unable to favor the beneficiaries whose interests are to be favored.

To meet this third criteria, the trustee must determine that the power granted by the trust instrument, for example the power to invade principal or accumulate income, does not enable the trustee to strike the right balance between the interests of the income and principal beneficiaries. Prob C §16336(a)(3).

§13.7   B. When Prohibited

If the three criteria described in §13.6 are met, the trustee may yet be prohibited from making an adjustment under Prob C §16336—for example, if the adjustment would have adverse tax consequences or if the trustee is also a beneficiary. Adjustments under Prob C §16336 are *prohibited* in all of the following circumstances:

- The trustee is a beneficiary of the trust. Prob C §16336(b)(7).

  NOTE▶ If there is more than one trustee, a trustee who is not a beneficiary may make the adjustment, unless prohibited from doing so by the trust (Prob C §16336(c)) or by trust law.

- During any period in which the trust is administered as a unitrust, whether under the trust instrument or because the trustee has converted the trust to a unitrust under Prob C §16336.4 or §16336.5. Prob C §16336(b)(8).

- The adjustment would disqualify the trust from the marital deduction from the gift or estate tax. Specifically, the adjustment is prohibited if it would *diminish* the income interest in a trust that:

  - Requires all of the trust's income to be paid to a spouse at least annually; and

  - Would qualify for the marital deduction from the gift or estate tax, if the trustee did not have the power to adjust between principal and income. Prob C §16336(b)(1).

  NOTE▶ The trustee is not prohibited from making an adjustment that would *increase* income distributions to a spouse. Additionally, the prohibition does not apply to the so-called "estate trust," which qualifies for the marital deduction because the trust terms require that all undistributed income and principal be paid to the spouse's estate at his or her death. Finally, the prohibition applies to a qualified terminable interest trust (QTIP trust) only to the extent the fiduciary has elected to qualify as marital deduction property that property which passes from the deceased spouse to the trust.

- The adjustment would change the actuarial value of an income interest in a trust to which the settlor had transferred property, with the expectation of qualifying all or a portion of the transfer for a gift tax exclusion. Prob C §16336(b)(2).
- The adjustment would change the amount payable to a beneficiary as a fixed annuity or a fixed fraction of the value of the trust assets. Prob C §16336(b)(3).
- The adjustment would be made from an amount permanently set aside for charitable purposes. Prob C §16336(b)(4).

NOTE▶ This prohibition does not apply to a trust in which both the income and principal is set aside for charitable purposes. The prohibition applies only to trusts with charitable lead or remainder interests.

- Possessing or exercising the power would cause an individual to be treated as the owner of all or part of the trust for income tax purposes and the individual would not be treated as such, absent the power. Prob C §16336(b)(5).
- Possessing or exercising the power would cause all or part of the trust assets to be included in an individual's estate for estate tax purposes, and such would not be the case if the trustee did not have the power to make the adjustment. Prob C §16336(b)(6).

NOTE▶ A co-trustee who might exercise the power without being treated as an owner would be allowed to do so, if not otherwise prohibited. Prob C §16336(c).

§13.8   C. Factors for Trustee to Consider

When the legislature enacted Prob C §16336, it did not intend to create a duty for trustees to make adjustments between principal and income. Prob C §16336(h). Trustees who never consider making such adjustments, as well as trustees who consider and reject the idea, are not liable for forgoing the opportunity Prob C §16336 presents.

On the other hand, the trustee who considers making an adjustment between principal and income must proceed with caution. At a minimum, the trustee should consider, and document his or her consideration of, all of the following factors (Prob C §16336(g)):

(1) The nature, purpose, and expected duration of the trust;
(2) The intent of the settlor;
(3) The identity and circumstances of the beneficiaries;
(4) The needs for liquidity, regularity of income, and preservation and appreciation of capital;
(5) Regarding the trust's assets, the trustee should consider all of the following:

- The extent to which they consist of financial assets, interests in closely held enterprises, tangible and intangible personal property, or real property;
- Whether, and the extent to which, an asset is used by a beneficiary; and
- Whether an asset was purchased by the trustee or received from the settlor;

(6) The net amount allocated to income under other statutes and the increase or decrease in the value of the principal assets, which the trustee may estimate as to assets for which market values are not readily available;
(7) Whether, and to what extent, the trust instrument prohibits, or authorizes, the trustee to invade principal or accumulate income, and whether the trustee has exercised such a power from time to time;
(8) The actual and anticipated effect of economic conditions on principal and income and the effects of inflation and deflation; and
(9) The anticipated tax consequences of an adjustment.

§13.9   D. Notice of Proposed Action

Before making an adjustment between principal and income under Prob C §16336, the trustee should consider giving notice of the proposed action. See Prob C §16337. If the trustee gives a proper notice (see Prob C §§16500–16504) and no beneficiary objects, the trustee is not liable to any current or future beneficiary for taking the proposed action. Prob C §16503(b). If the trustee believes he or she cannot discharge his or her duty of impartiality without making an adjustment, but a beneficiary objects to the proposed adjustment, the trustee may petition for court approval of the adjustment. Prob C §§16338, 17200.

Trustees also may give notice of a proposal to forgo an adjustment between principal and income (Prob C §16337) and are advised to do so if their passivity might cause or perpetuate a seeming breach of the duty of impartiality. Likewise, trustees may petition for approval of a decision to take no action. Prob C §16338.

§13.10 IV. INCREASING INCOME IN ORDER TO OBTAIN MARITAL DEDUCTION

A transfer to a trust may qualify for the marital deduction from the gift and estate tax only if the trust is one of the types described in IRC §2056(b). Two such trusts require that the surviving spouse receive sufficient income to meet the "beneficial interest" requirement of Treas Reg §20.2056(b)-5(f)(4). IRC §2056(b). This regulation says that transfers to a trust may qualify for the marital deduction from the estate tax only if the surviving-spouse beneficiary has the power, under the trust instrument or state law, to demand that the trustee make trust property productive. Probate Code §16365 is California's answer to the challenge of giving surviving-spouse beneficiaries of marital deduction trusts the power to compel trustees to make trust property productive.

§13.11 A. When Income Beneficiary May Compel Trustee to Make Trust Property Productive

If the two conditions below are met, the income beneficiary of a marital deduction trust may, but is not required to, compel the trustee to make trust property productive of income (Prob C §16365):

- The marital deduction was allowed for all or part of a trust, the assets of which consist substantially of assets that do not provide the spouse with sufficient income; and

- The amounts of principal distributed by the trustee to the surviving spouse, either under a power granted by the trust instrument or by the trustee's exercise of the adjustment power of Prob C §16336 (see §§13.5-13.9), are not sufficient to provide the spouse with the beneficial enjoyment required to obtain the marital deduction.

§13.12 B. How Trustee May Respond to a Demand to Make Trust Property Productive

The trustee of a marital-deduction trust who receives a demand to make the trust property productive has the discretion to respond in any of three ways. The trustee may (Prob C §16365):

- Make the property productive of income;
- Convert the property to productive property; or
- Make an adjustment between principal and income under Prob C §16336(a).

The trustee has discretion to decide which action or combination of actions to take.

NOTE▶ Probate Code §16365 does not apply to so-called "estate" trusts, which qualify for the marital deduction from the estate tax because the trust's undistributed income and principal will be paid to the surviving spouse's estate on his or her death. 29 Cal L Rev'n Comm'n Reports 317 (1999), *Proposed Prob C §16365 Background from Uniform Act.*

§13.13 V. DEPRECIATION RESERVE

Except when prohibited by statute, the trustee has the discretion to create a depreciation reserve if a trustee administers a principal asset that (Prob C §16372):

- Has a useful life of more than 1 year; and
- Is subject to reduction in value due to wear, tear, decay, corrosion, or gradual obsolescence.

§13.14 A. When to Create a Depreciation Reserve

Trustees are prohibited from creating depreciation reserves in the following circumstances (Prob C §16372(b)):

- Regarding real property, if the property is available for use by a beneficiary as a residence;
- Regarding personal property, if the property is available for a beneficiary's use or enjoyment;

- During the administration of a decedent's estate; and
- When the trustee is accounting for the property as a separate business under Prob C §16352.

Additionally, a trustee may set aside a depreciation reserve only if the property is in fact declining in value. ("Depreciation" means a reduction in value. Prob C §16372(a).) If the property *is* declining in value, the trustee may set aside a depreciation reserve regardless of whether the trustee claims a depreciation deduction on the trust's income tax return.

There are reasons a trustee might not set aside a depreciation reserve—for example, the trustee may believe that a real property's gradual appreciation is sufficient to offset any depreciation due to wear and tear. Some trustees are reluctant to establish depreciation reserves for any property not depreciated under generally accepted accounting principals, *i.e.*, for any property that is not part of a business.

§13.15   B. How to Create a Depreciation Reserve

To create a depreciation reserve, the trustee transfers net cash receipts (trust accounting income) from the depreciating property to principal. Prob C §16372(b). The amount transferred must be reasonable under generally accepted accounting principles. Prob C §16372(b).

If the trustee exercises the discretion to set aside a depreciation reserve, the reserve need not be segregated in a separate account, but must be properly accounted for. Prob C §16372(b)-(c). The transfer from income to principal should be reported on the schedule Changes in Form of Assets, and in subsequent years the reserve is carried as an asset on hand, stated separately from the trust's other cash. The depreciation reserve may be used for any principal disbursements related to the property—for example, principal payments on debt secured by the property, replacement of fixtures, or capital improvements. Such disbursements should be identified on the schedule of Disbursements and perhaps given additional visibility by repeating the information on an auxiliary schedule.

A depreciation reserve may be created only from the income of the property being depreciated, and the reserve should be set aside for that property. See Prob C §16372(b): "A trustee may transfer from income to principal a reasonable amount of the *net cash receipts from a principal asset that is subject to depreciation.*" (Emphasis added.) Thus, depreciation reserves do not solve the problem a trustee faces when the trustee must disburse principal with regard to a property that generates too little income or none at all. Additionally, a depreciation reserve is an amount of cash set aside for future *principal* disbursements and does not solve the problem of the trustee who anticipates making, or who has made, a large disbursement chargeable to income. Facing problems like these, the trustee may find help in Prob C §16373, which allows transferring income to principal in certain limited situations.

§13.16   C. Cash in Depreciation Reserve Cannot Be Recharacterized

Once the trustee has allocated cash to a depreciation reserve, the trustee cannot later recharacterize the reserve account as income, even if the property has appreciated rather than depreciated. *Stahl v Wells Fargo Bank* (1998) 63 CA4th 396. In *Stahl,* the trustee set aside $300,000 in two reserve accounts, one for depreciation and one for maintenance. The properties increased in value and when the trustee later sold them, the trustee sought to characterize the reserve accounts as income, rather than principal. The principal beneficiaries objected. The trial court found for the trustee, but the court of appeal reversed. The court of appeal construed former Prob C §16312(b)(2), (b)(11) (see now Prob C §§6335, 16324, respectively), and acknowledged that the trustee possessed the discretion to determine whether funds should be allocated to a reserve account for depreciation. The court also concluded that the trustee could not be held liable for failing to establish a reserve account. Nevertheless, the court held that once a reserve had been established, the amounts set aside must be allocated to principal and may not be recharacterized as income.

§13.17   VI. TRANSFERS FROM INCOME TO PRINCIPAL IN ANTICIPATION OF PRINCIPAL DISBURSEMENT

The trustee who has made or who expects to make a principal disbursement described in Prob C §16373 may transfer an "appropriate" amount from income to principal either to reimburse principal or to create a reserve for future principal disbursements. Prob C §16373(a). The trustee may make the transfer from income to principal over successive accounting periods (Prob C §16373(a)), and if the asset that gives rise to the disbursements becomes subject to a successive income interest, the trustee may continue to transfer amounts from income to principal, if circumstances allow. Prob C §16373(b).

Trustees may transfer income to principal only in the circumstances described below, and only if the trustee has not been, and does not expect to be, reimbursed by a third party:

- If the trustee must disburse an amount chargeable to income, and because the payment is so large that the trustee needs to make the payment from principal, the trustee may shift income to principal in anticipation of the payment, or after the payment has been made. Prob C §16373(b)(1).

    EXAMPLE▶ If the trustee must make extraordinary repairs, the trustee may pay for the repairs with principal, even though they are normally chargeable to income (Prob C §16370(c)), then repay the principal disbursement by transferring income to principal in several payments made over the period of one or more accounts.

- For payment of capital improvements, or for the construction of new assets, or to pay special assessments. Prob C §16373(b)(2).

- To prepare property for rental, including tenant allowances, leasehold improvements, and broker's commissions. Prob C §16373(b)(3).

- If the amount transferred from income to a depreciation reserve is insufficient to pay the principal payments on an obligation secured by a principal asset, or if the trustee cannot create a depreciation reserve.

PRACTICE TIP▶ Unless the will or the trust requires the trustee to favor one or more beneficiaries, the trustee must exercise the powers granted by §16373 impartially. Prob C §16335(b). In the opinion of some commentators, "charges for capital improvements, construction of a new asset and special assessments should be charged to principal when sufficient cash is available."

Cantrell & Spoor, *Fiduciary Accounting Answer Book,* Q 17:14 (CCH 2015).

As useful as Prob C §16373 is, it does not solve the problems trustees face when the assets they administer produce no trust accounting income. In other words, when there is no cash to pay a principal disbursement, the trustee *may* find a solution in the Uniform Principal and Income Act's adjustment powers. But when there is no income to pay an income disbursement, the trustee either must convert the trust to a unitrust, obviating the distinction between principal and income, or make trust assets productive of income. Alas, no statute solves the problem of the trustee who runs out of cash completely. The adjustment powers may help the trustee who runs out of principal cash by allowing a transfer from income to principal. And the power to convert to a unitrust may help the trustee who has run out of trust accounting income. But the trustee who runs out of cash will find no help in the Act. This trustee must sell assets or borrow money.

VII. ADJUSTMENTS TO OFFSET SHIFTING ECONOMIC INTERESTS OR TAX BENEFITS

§13.18   A. Mandatory Allocation of Prob C §16374

Absent a contrary provision in the trust or will, a trustee must allocate disbursements for certain taxes to income or principal, or partially to both, as required by Prob C §16374. The taxes to which Prob C §16374 applies include all taxes on income, including state and federal income tax, sales tax, excise tax, and estate tax, but not property tax. Application of Prob C §16374, combined with the distribution deduction allowed by IRC §§651 and 661, may shift economic benefits between income beneficiaries and remainder beneficiaries. When this happens, the trustee must adjust income or principal receipts to the extent the trust's taxes are reduced by the distribution deduction. Prob C §16374(d).

When an entity distributes to a trust some, but not all, of the trust's share of the entity's taxable income, the adjustment required by Prob C §16374(d) creates an interrelated calculation.

EXAMPLE▶ ABC Trust receives a K-1 from Partnership reflecting taxable income of $1 million. Partnership distributes to the trust only $500,000, which Partnership represents to be income. (Some would say that the trust also has "phantom income" of $500,000, a reference to the income Partnership withheld from distribution.) The trust is in the 35 percent tax bracket.

In this example, the trust's tax liability would be $350,000, *i.e.,* 35 percent of $1 million, and the Partnership distribution exceeds that liability by $150,000. Thus, at first glance, it appears that the trustee can distribute $150,000 to the income beneficiary, but because the trust can deduct this distribution on its income tax return, the trust's taxes will be reduced. Because the taxes will be reduced by the distribution, the trustee may (or must—for example, in a QTIP trust) distribute more than $150,000 to the beneficiary. A larger distribution, however, will increase the distribution deduction, freeing even more income to be distributed to the beneficiary, resulting in an even larger distribution deduction, and so on.

To calculate the exact amount that may be distributed to the beneficiary, the trustee may use trial and error, or the algebraic formula below.

$$D = (C - (R \times K))/(1 - R)$$

D = Distribution to the income beneficiary
C = Trust's receipt from entity
R = Tax rate on trust income
K = Entity's K-1 taxable income

This formula is necessary only when the entity distributes to the trustee more than is necessary to pay the income tax on the K-1 income, but less than the full amount of that K-1 income. If the entity distributes the full amount of the K-1 income, the trustee may pass through to the beneficiary the entire receipt, eliminating the need for the circular calculation.

§13.19   B. Discretionary Adjustment of Prob C §16375(a)

In certain circumstances, a fiduciary may make adjustments between principal and income to offset the effect of the mandatory allocations of Prob C §16374 or §16375(b), or other tax elections or decisions. Prob C §16375. Examples of when a fiduciary might exercise this adjustment power include the following.

EXAMPLE 1▶ The fiduciary elects to deduct administration expenses that are paid from principal on an income tax return instead of on the estate tax return.

EXAMPLE 2▶ The fiduciary distributes to a trust or another beneficiary a principal asset, which distribution carries out taxable income to the distributee and relieves the person who receives the income from the obligation to pay the tax.

EXAMPLE 3▶ The trustee realizes a capital gain on the sale of a principal asset and pays a large state income tax on the gain, but under applicable federal income tax rules, the trustee may not deduct the state income tax payment from the capital gain in calculating the trust's federal capital gain tax, and the income beneficiary receives the benefit of the deduction for state income tax paid on the capital gain.

See 29 Cal L Rev'n Comm'n Reports 332 (1999), *Proposed Prob C §16375 Background from Uniform Act*.

Other elections which may reduce total income tax paid, but which may shift economic interests between beneficiaries, include:

- The election to treat distributions made within the first 65 days of the beginning of a taxable year as having been made in the prior year (IRC §663(b));

- The election to treat a trust as an estate, or as part of an estate (IRC §645); and

- An election to treat property distributed in kind as if it had been sold to the distributee at fair market value (IRC §643(e)(3)).

On these elections, see Cantrell & Spoor, *Fiduciary Accounting Answer Book*, Q 18:14 (CCH 2015).

§13.20 C. Mandatory Adjustment of Prob C §16375(b)

A fiduciary must allocate income to principal when the following conditions are met (Prob C §16375(b)):

- The fiduciary files an estate tax return on which he or she claims a marital or charitable deduction from the estate tax;
- The fiduciary also files an income tax return, claiming a deduction for amounts paid from principal; and
- As a consequence of claiming the deduction on the income tax return, the estate tax paid from principal is increased and the income tax paid by the decedent's estate, trust, or a beneficiary is reduced.

In the above circumstance, each estate, trust, or beneficiary that benefits from the trustee's election must reimburse the principal from which the increased estate tax was paid. Prob C §16375(b). Section 16375(b) prescribes the amount of reimbursement due to principal as follows:

> The total reimbursement must equal the increase in the estate tax to the extent that the principal used to pay the increase would have qualified for a marital deduction or charitable deduction, but for the payment. The proportionate share of the reimbursement for each estate, trust, or beneficiary whose income taxes are reduced must be the same as its proportionate share of the total decrease in income tax. An estate or trust shall reimburse principal from income.

The mandatory adjustment of Prob C §16375(b) preserves the marital and charitable deduction from the estate tax. As the Comment to §506 of the Uniform Principal and Income Act explains:

> Because a fiduciary will elect to deduct administration expenses for income tax purposes only when the income tax reduction exceeds the estate tax reduction, the effect of this adjustment is that the principal is placed in the same position it would have occupied if the fiduciary had deducted the expenses for estate tax purposes, but the income beneficiaries receive an additional benefit. For example, if the income tax benefit from the deduction is $30,000 and the estate tax benefit would have been $20,000, principal will be reimbursed $20,000 and the net benefit to the income beneficiaries will be $10,000.

14
Conflicts and Litigation

I. INTRODUCTION: GENERAL CONCEPTS §14.1
   A. Protective Court §14.2
   B. Ex Parte Communications §14.3
   C. Attorney Ethics
      1. Removal of an Attorney by the Court §14.4
      2. Attorney Conflicts of Interest §14.5
      3. When the Client Lacks Capacity §14.6
   D. Attorney-Client Privilege §14.7
   E. Fiduciary Obligations and Conflicts of Interest §14.8
   F. Discovery
      1. Beneficiary's Broad Right to Inspect Trustee's Records §14.9
      2. Tax Return Privilege §14.10
   G. Court of General Jurisdiction §14.11
   H. How Probate Court Matters Differ From Other Court Proceedings §14.12
      1. Terminology §14.13
      2. Case Law Applies to All Fiduciaries §14.14
      3. Probate Court Makes Orders, Not Judgments §14.15
      4. Court Has Jurisdiction During Appeal §14.16
      5. No "One Final Judgment" Rule §14.17
      6. Concurrent Cases §14.18
      7. Blended Pleadings §14.19
      8. Right to a Jury Trial §14.20
      9. A Trust Is Not a Legal Entity §14.21

II. FIDUCIARIES, BENEFICIARIES, AND THE DUTY TO ACCOUNT
   A. Fiduciaries Are Personally Accountable §14.22
   B. To Whom an Accounting Is Owed §14.23
   C. Fiduciary Accounting Formats §14.24
   D. Fiduciaries Need Attorneys §14.25

III. ALTERNATIVE DISPUTE RESOLUTION
   A. Overview §14.26
   B. Mediation §14.27
   C. Reference (Appointment of a Referee) §14.28
   D. Private Judging §14.29

IV. REMEDIES §14.30
   A. Appointment of Experts §14.31
   B. Appointment of Attorneys and Guardians ad Litem §14.32
   C. Limiting Powers §14.33
   D. Suspension §14.34
   E. Removal §14.35
   F. Appointing a Replacement §14.36
   G. Contempt §14.37
   H. Surcharging §14.38
   I. Return of Assets §14.39
   J. Fees and Costs §14.40

§14.1 I. INTRODUCTION: GENERAL CONCEPTS

This chapter addresses court proceedings involving fiduciary accountings, both to assist attorneys engaged in those proceedings, and to provide assistance to the judges who are assigned to hear them.

As attorneys experienced in probate matters know, judges given the probate assignment usually have negligible prior experience as attorneys in probate matters. Particularly when appearing before a judge newly assigned to probate, attorneys should remember their roles as officers of the court and help the judge to consider some of the approaches that a more experienced judge would be aware of.

Accountings are at the heart of the responsibility of a fiduciary who is managing assets (as contrasted, *e.g.*, with fiduciaries who are dealing with the care of a person, such as guardians of the person, conservators of the person, and holders of a durable power of attorney for healthcare). As Judge Cardozo succinctly explained in *Meinhard v Salmon* (NY App 1928) 249 NY 458, 164 NE 545, 546:

> Many forms of conduct, permissible in a workaday world

for those acting at arm's length, are forbidden to those bound by fiduciary ties. A trustee is held to something stricter than the morals of the market place. Not honesty alone, but the punctilio of an honor the most sensitive, is then the standard of behavior. As to this there has developed a tradition that is unbending and inveterate.... Only thus has the level of conduct for fiduciaries been kept at a level higher than that trodden by the crowd.

It is easy to recite this classic expression of a fiduciary's obligation, but much more difficult to determine what conduct meets this high standard in practice.

This chapter addresses some general issues, such as jurisdiction. Some extra attention is given to trust matters, because those are usually the ones involving enough money to generate substantial litigation. Other topics that are ordinarily covered in discussing litigation are omitted, such as venue (because usually the venue is obvious, and when it is not, the venue issue is technical and dependent on the type of proceeding).

Probate litigation tends to involve particular misery among the litigants. The litigation is almost always related to a family tragedy, such as the death or incapacity of a parent. There is typically a sense of betrayal because the other parties are family members or trusted friends who were expected to be supportive during this difficult time, not to engage in vicious attacks. Adding to the emotional maelstrom may be pressure from spouses and extended family members. Long simmering sibling rivalries may be reopened. The amount of money usually seems very large to the parties, perhaps being viewed as their only chance to buy a home or have a comfortable retirement. Probate litigation tends to be labor intensive, and thereby shockingly expensive, because it involves peoples' lives, so there is often almost unlimited evidence as to intention, relationships, etc. Lastly, the amounts involved often have an added emotional component because of the feeling that an inheritance is the parents' final expression of love.

§14.2 A. Protective Court

The probate court, a descendant of the chancery court of equity, has a proactive and protective, but somewhat nuanced, role. A court hearing a juvenile dependency matter, while complying with statutes and constitutional protections for all parties, has the clear, primary focus on the protection of children, who cannot be expected to protect themselves. The probate court, in guardianships and conservatorships, has similar clarity. In other matters, sua sponte use of the probate court's equitable powers depends on the situation.

In litigation regarding a multi-million dollar trust, where the parties are all competent and well represented, the court's proactivity may recede to that akin to general civil actions, similar to a baseball umpire simply calling balls and strikes. However, many situations involving estates managed by fiduciaries warrant a more active involvement by the court. The death of a close relative is often so stressful that ordinarily competent people become materially impaired in their ability to act in a businesslike manner and protect their interests in the estate. Beneficiaries of limited means often feel sure that the probate court is protecting their interests, so do not feel the need to retain an attorney, even if they could afford one.

By contrast, "special needs" trusts are established to provide for people with severe disabilities, who typically rely on public benefits. These individuals may be financially or emotionally dependent on the trustee, so their ability to protect their interests is limited. In recognition of these kinds of situations, the probate court is given various abilities to take a more proactive, protective role. For example, the court may order accountings sua sponte, limit fiduciary powers, suspend or remove fiduciaries, and appoint attorneys or guardians ad litem. The specific statutes granting these powers are in the various divisions of the Probate Code. The overall principal, though, is that it is appropriate for the probate court to take an active role in probate matters.

§14.3 B. Ex Parte Communications

In probate court matters, there is a tension between the protective role of the court and the statutory and ethical prohibition against ex parte communications. Probate Code §1051 and Cal Rules of Ct 7.10, *Ex parte communications in proceedings under the Probate Code and certain other proceedings,* make clear that attorneys and others are not supposed to make ex parte communications, and that the court must disclose and follow due process as to any ex parte communications considered. The Code of Judicial Ethics, Canon 3(B), generally precludes courts from considering ex parte communications, and judges commonly have their clerks return such communications without the judge seeing them. However, whether a letter reports that a conservatee is being abused or that an executor is squandering estate assets, the protective role of the probate court is inconsistent with ignoring such communications. Even before the enactment of Prob C §1051 in 2006, many probate judges considered that their statutory responsibility to supervise probate fiduciaries required consideration of those communications.

C. Attorney Ethics

§14.4   1. Removal of an Attorney by the Court

Judges are required to take appropriate corrective action when confronted with unethical behavior by attorneys. Code of Judicial Ethics, Canon 3(d)(2). Although judges have some discretion in whether to report an attorney's unethical behavior to the State Bar, in most probate litigation cases (*e.g.*, accounting disputes) the problem will be a conflict of interest and the court will admonish and remove the attorney. The court's authority to disqualify the attorney "derives from the power inherent in every court '[t]o control in furtherance of justice, the conduct of its ministerial officers.'" *In re Charlisse C.* (2008) 45 C4th 145, 159; CCP §128(a)(2). After such a removal, issues as to what, if any, attorney fees are due the removed attorney are common.

§14.5   2. Attorney Conflicts of Interest

Conflicts of interest often arise in probate proceedings. Sometimes the issue is simple, such as an attorney's representation of co-fiduciaries, when one absconds and the other asks for the attorney's assistance in surcharging the absconder. Other times, the conflict is less obvious.

EXAMPLE 1▶ An attorney drafts a revocable trust, and a successor trustee is appointed because the trustor (also the initial trustee) has become incompetent. The successor seeks to retain the attorney for advice and representation as to the administration of the trust.

In the example above, unless the successor trustee is also the attorney-in-fact under a general durable power of attorney for the trustor, it is probably not possible for the attorney to obtain either a waiver of potential conflict (*e.g.*, if a conflict arises between the successor trustee and the trustor who is also a trust beneficiary) or a waiver of confidentiality on behalf of the trustor. The same problem applies because of the confidences the attorney will have received in the drafting of the trust that would be relevant to the trustee's administration of the trust consistent with the trustor's wishes. If the attorney had a long-established professional relationship with the trustor, the attorney may also harbor feelings that in representing the successor trustee the attorney is really acting for the trustor to make sure the trustor's desires are implemented.

EXAMPLE 2▶ An estate planning attorney seeks to represent the client in a subsequent conservatorship proceeding in which questions about the estate planning are anticipated.

In this second example, the drafting attorney may be viewed as having a conflict between independently representing the principal and defending the attorney's actions in drafting the instrument. When there is a question about the capacity of a principal or proposed conservatee in proceedings under the Probate Code, many judges will expect the attorney to exercise independent judgment, balancing factors that include the principal's best interests, mental capacity, and expressed desires. See Capacity and Undue Influence: Assessing, Challenging, and Defending (Cal CEB Action Guide). Further, the drafting attorney will often be called to testify as a witness regarding the principal's intent and related discussions. If that attorney is to represent any party in the litigation, the client's informed written consent is likewise required before the attorney may proceed. Cal Rules of Prof Cond 5-210.

§14.6 3. When the Client Lacks Capacity

A somewhat circular problem arises whenever an attorney appears in a probate proceeding, claiming to represent a person whose competency is in question. "With the exception of a court appointment, the relationship of lawyer and client is created by contract." *Houston Gen. Ins. Co. v Superior Court* (1980) 108 CA3d 958, 964. If it is later determined that the purported client lacked capacity, then the attorney was never hired.

In proceedings where the court has authority to appoint an attorney, this problem can be avoided by having the court affirm the attorney's representation as a court appointment. Some courts will make an initial determination (subject to due process) as to competency and appoint an attorney as guardian ad litem if the client is found not competent.

§14.7 D. Attorney-Client Privilege

In *Moeller v Superior Court* (1997) 16 C4th 1124, the court held that a successor trustee has a right to discover confidential communications between a predecessor trustee and the predecessor's attorney on matters of trust administration. The court found that the attorney-client privilege belongs to the "office of the trustee" rather than the individual incumbent. The court stated that a trustee seeking advice in a personal capacity in anticipation of possible charges of breach of fiduciary duty may be able to avoid disclosure by personally retaining the attorney as to some issues and paying the attorney from the person's personal funds.

Fiduciaries' personal interests typically deviate from their fiduciary responsibilities in two situations. One is potential litigation by a beneficiary against the fiduciary, *e.g.*, for surcharge or removal. Many fiduciaries are also beneficiaries of the principal's estate plan, so their fiduciary obligations potentially conflict with their individual interests.

In *Wells Fargo Bank v Superior Court (Boltwood)* (2000) 22 C4th 201, the California Supreme Court held that the attorney-client privilege overrides the trustee's obligation of disclosure to the beneficiaries.

The combination of the rules in *Moeller* and *Boltwood* increases the tactical focus on resignation or removal of a person serving as fiduciary because the removed fiduciary loses control of the attorney-client privilege. It is common when there is litigation against a fiduciary for the fiduciary to decide, essentially, "I don't need this," and want to resign. Sometimes getting that resignation is the underlying purpose of the litigation. In some cases, the potential loss of the attorney-client privilege will result in a more tenacious posture.

See also *Eddy v Fields* (2004) 121 CA4th 1543, in which an attorney for two trustees who disclosed files to another attorney representing one of those trustees was held to have waived any work-product privilege that might have applied when files were demanded by the successor trustee.

PRACTICE TIP▶ Many fiduciaries who retain attorneys to advise them will not anticipate the possible loss of the attorney-client privilege unless the attorney takes considerable care in discussing the matter at the beginning of the relationship. It would be prudent to confirm this discussion in writing or include an advisement in the retainer agreement.

When the fiduciary arrangement terminates, the privilege of the fiduciary terminates because there is no longer any fiduciary to hold the privilege. Evid C §954(c). This would leave the communications subject to discovery by any interested party. Under Evid C §§953(c) and 954, the attorney-client privilege of a natural person transfers to the personal representative after the client's death, and the privilege thereafter terminates when there is no personal representative to claim it. The authority conferred in Prob C §9760 complements the grant of authority in Evid C §953(c) to the personal representative to assert or waive the attorney-client privilege while the decedent's estate is being administered. *HLC Props., Ltd. v Superior Court* (2005) 35 C4th 54.

§14.8 E. Fiduciary Obligations and Conflicts of Interest

The rule that fiduciaries must not have a conflict of interest is more nuanced than the rigid and unbending rule applied to an attorney-client relationship. Family members are commonly appointed as attorneys-in-fact, conservators, executors, and successor trustees in situations where their interest in inheritance might be in conflict with their fiduciary position. This alone is insufficient to warrant removal, especially when the choice for the appointment was made by the person whose estate is involved (as conservatee, principal, testator, or trustor). In the usual quiet administration of these situations, no actual conflicts occur that result in an effort to remove the trustee. However, a high level of conflict of interest may warrant suspension or removal of the fiduciary.

These issues are explored in *Getty v Getty* (1988) 205 CA3d 134. Gordon Getty was trustee and a beneficiary of a trust established by his mother, Sarah Getty. The trust estate consisted mainly of approximately 40.2 percent of the then-outstanding capital stock of Getty Oil Company. Gordon Getty was also the largest shareholder. The trust prohibited sale of the Getty Oil Company shares held in the trust, unless necessary "to save the trust estate from a substantial loss." Gordon Getty, individually and as trustee of Sarah Getty's trust, along with the other shareholders, sold the stock of Getty Oil Company to Texaco for over $4 billion. Much civil litigation ensued regarding this sale. Gordon's sisters, also beneficiaries of Sarah Getty's trust, petitioned for Gordon Getty's surcharge and removal as trustee. The trial court concluded that there was sufficiently clear evidence of an actual conflict of interest to warrant suspension and appointment of a temporary trustee, pending trial of the issues. The court of appeal upheld the trial court, holding that the court had the necessary authority, and that the manifest and substantial conflict of interest warranted the court's actions.

F. Discovery

§14.9 1. Beneficiary's Broad Right to Inspect Trustee's Records

In disputes between a beneficiary and the fiduciary as to accountings, the beneficiary's right to full disclosure of records by the trustee expands the scope of permissible disclosure, so it is not limited by the usual standards of civil discovery. In *Strauss v Superior Court* (1950) 36 C2d 396, a beneficiary's subpoena duces tecum to the trustee demanded all "books, documents, and records relating to the creation, existence, and administration" of the trust. The trust had been in existence for almost 15 years. The trial court quashed the subpoena as being overbroad. The Supreme Court reversed, holding that the usual limitations to discovery are inapplicable as between a beneficiary and trustee. The court in *Strauss* stated, "the trustee's records as to the administration of the trust are deemed a part of the trust estate, and the right of the beneficiaries to an inspection of them stems from their common interest in the property along with the trustee." 36 C2d at 400.

On the attorney-client privilege, see §14.7.

§14.10 2. Tax Return Privilege

Another privilege that is often at issue is the tax return privilege. The court in *Webb v Standard Oil Co.* (1957) 49 C2d 509 first articulated the privilege, holding that former Rev & T C §§19282-19283 were intended to preserve the secrecy of tax returns, except in certain enumerated cases. The purpose of the privilege is to facilitate tax enforcement by encouraging a taxpayer to fully disclose information without fear that third parties would be able to obtain the information for other purposes. 49 C2d at 512. No case has addressed whether a probate fiduciary can assert the tax return privilege against a beneficiary's request to inspect and copy it.

The judicially created tax return privilege is not absolute. In *Miller v Superior Court* (1977) 71 CA3d 145, the tax return privilege was asserted in a contempt proceeding brought against a former spouse for failure to pay child support. The court of appeal held that the social policy favoring child support payments outweighed the public policy supporting the tax return privilege.

No court of appeal decision has directly addressed the conflict between the tax return privilege and the trustee's obligation to make available all books and records for inspection by trust beneficiaries. The decision appearing most clearly on point is *Schnabel v Superior Court* (1993) 5 C4th 704. In that case, the court considered a request for disclosure of third party tax returns in a marital dissolution proceeding. The court held that each spouse has a fiduciary duty to the other in managing community property, which includes the obligation to make full disclosure to the other spouse of all material facts and information regarding the existence, characterization, and valuation of all assets in which the community has, or may have, an interest, and to provide equal access to all information, records, and books that pertain to the value and character of those assets and debts, on request. 5 C4th at 715. Because one spouse had access to the corporate records, including tax returns, the other spouse also was entitled to see those returns. The decision discusses extensively factors that must be balanced in the spousal context where third parties' privacy interests are involved. Throughout the decision, it seems clear that there was no question but that the spouses' personal tax returns were discoverable *because of the parties' fiduciary relationship*. Since a trustee has a fiduciary duty to the trust's beneficiaries to disclose records, based on the principles in the *Schnabel* decision it seems most reasonable that the beneficiaries are entitled to see the tax returns of the trust.

The issue of the tax return privilege for trustees is somewhat clouded by the California Supreme Court's decisions in *Moeller v Superior Court* (1997) 16 C4th 1124 and *Wells Fargo Bank v Superior Court (Boltwood)* (2000) 22 C4th 201. In those cases, the court held that trust beneficiaries are not entitled to breach the trustee's attorney-client privilege. The two privileges are essentially different in the public policies they express. A trustee, in working with an attorney, may be addressing issues involving third parties that would harm the trust if disclosed. The communications themselves do not directly affect the trust, although the trust may be affected by the trustee's actions which may be guided by such communications. A trustee may often be subject to personal liability regarding issues discussed with an attorney, so has a greater need to have some privacy in those communications.

In contrast to the advisory nature of attorney-client communications, a trust's tax return is the operative document in transactions with the state and federal governments. These documents commonly result in the requirement of payment of trust funds, or calculation of taxable income which flows through to the beneficiaries (*i.e.,* "distributable net income" (DNI), which is taxable to beneficiaries and may have little to do with the actual cash distributed). No personal interests of the trustee are involved in the tax returns; in contrast, the beneficiaries are personally, directly or indirectly affected. Trusts' tax returns are sometimes subject to ordinary errors, and often show the trustee's characterization of assets or transactions. It does not make sense to require beneficiaries to "reverse engineer" the trust's tax returns by paying an expert to take the trust's records, and then determine what must have been reported in the return to explain the trust's tax payments and flow-through tax liability.

Nothing should be included in a trust's tax return that is not already in the trust's other records that the beneficiaries may inspect. Unlike a trust's tax returns, personal income tax returns may disclose criminal activity (*e.g.,* taxable income for illegal occupations), or highly sensitive personal information (*e.g.,* substantial deductions for medical problems). The tax return privilege protects against these disclosures of sensitive personal information and encourages individuals to file honest returns. No similar policy reasonably justifies denying beneficiaries access to the trust's tax return.

In summary, beneficiaries' property rights in the trust records, the trustee's fiduciary obligation to the beneficiaries, and the effect of trust income tax returns on the beneficiaries create a situation most akin to the issues articulated by the California Supreme Court in the *Schnabel* decision, entitling the beneficiaries to discover the trust tax returns.

§14.11   G. Court of General Jurisdiction

Probate Code §800, which provides that the court in proceedings under the Probate Code is a court of general jurisdiction, was enacted to abrogate the idea that the probate court is a court of "limited jurisdiction." See *Conservatorship of O'Connor* (1996) 48 CA4th

1076, 1090. This seems simple in concept: there is no "probate court," there is only the superior court, sometimes exercising jurisdiction regarding matters governed by the Probate Code. So, for example, there should now be no question that a court can issue a restraining order if warranted in a proceeding under the Probate Code. However, eliminating the former dividing line between general civil actions and special proceedings under the Probate Code has created some procedural complexity and confusion.

§14.12   H. How Probate Court Matters Differ From Other Court Proceedings

Fiduciary accountings and related issues cut broadly across all of the relationships established under the Probate Code. Because of semantic and procedural aspects of probate practice that are different from other court proceedings, probate proceedings can have a slightly surreal feeling to attorneys and judges new to this area. The following sections address some of these aspects.

§14.13   1. Terminology

Fiduciary. "Fiduciary" is a useful collective noun that includes all of the fiduciaries addressed in the Probate Code, including but not limited to guardians, conservators, trust or estate beneficiaries, and principals under powers of attorney.

Beneficiary. Unlike "fiduciary," there is no comparable term that includes all of the persons to whom the fiduciary duty is owed (*e.g.,* wards, conservatees, beneficiaries of estates or trusts). In this chapter, all of those categories are included in the term "beneficiary."

Probate Court. There is no "probate court" in California. There is only the superior court exercising its jurisdiction under the Probate Code. See *Schlyen v Schlyen* (1954) 43 C2d 361. Nonetheless, the verbosity of the phrase "the Superior Court acting in its jurisdiction under the Probate Code" leaves little practical alternative to the casual use of the term "probate court."

"Probate" versus "Probate." The term "probate" has two, unfortunately overlapping meanings. The broader term refers to all of the matters handled by the probate court, *i.e.,* the Probate Code. There are many fiduciary arrangements not addressed by the Probate Code, so the term "probate fiduciary" may be used.

The more narrowly defined term "probate" refers to the formal, court-supervised administration of a decedent's estate under Division 7 of the Probate Code. Under this meaning, "probate" can be a verb (*e.g.*, to probate an estate) or a noun (*e.g.*, doing a probate). This is the dreaded probate so widely vilified by those selling living trusts. To distinguish the two meanings concisely, this narrower meaning of "probate" is sometimes called simply a "formal probate" (although it is no more formal than guardianships or conservatorships).

§14.14   2. Case Law Applies to All Fiduciaries

Appellate decisions that involve the law governing fiduciaries address the particular case before the court (*e.g.*, guardianship, conservatorship, trusts). It is, however, generally accepted that decisions based on principles that are woven through all probate fiduciary roles apply to all fiduciaries. For example, the California Supreme Court issued seminal decisions, commonly referenced as *Moeller/Boltwood*, regarding the holder of a trustee's attorney-client privilege. These decisions were not based on provisions in the Probate Code or principles only applicable to trusts. The *Moeller/Boltwood* principles are applied across the board to other probate fiduciaries. Sometimes these cases will refer to statutes that are applicable only to the specific subject matter (*e.g.*, trusts), but there is much redundancy in the Probate Code, so further exploration will usually find comparable statutes or applicable common law principals for other probate fiduciaries.

§14.15   3. Probate Court Makes Orders, Not Judgments

The rulings of the court in Probate Code proceedings are orders, not judgments or decrees, even though "judgment" and "decree" are commonly stated in the caption of papers prepared by attorneys for judges' signatures. The caption rarely matters, but there are important procedural distinctions between orders and judgments. See *Estate of Stoddart* (2004) 115 CA4th 1118. Notably, the statutory provisions in the Probate Code regarding appeals (Prob C §§1300–1304) consistently refer to "order."

§14.16   4. Court Has Jurisdiction During Appeal

The probate court is not divested of all jurisdiction during an appeal, unlike general civil actions. When a final judgment is appealed in a civil action, that divests the trial court of jurisdiction to make further rulings in the case. However, as noted in §14.15, probate courts issue orders, not judgments. Because the fiduciary relationship usually is ongoing during an appeal, it is essential that the probate court be able to deal promptly with further issues that develop. So, for example, if a court finds that a fiduciary has engaged in serious willful misconduct and orders that the fiduciary should be permanently removed, it would be terrible and absurd to allow the fiduciary to continue to act for the months or years that can be involved in an appeal. In such a case, if the court had not previously suspended the fiduciary and, perhaps, appointed a temporary replacement, the court could do so at the end of the trial, or when the notice of appeal is filed. See Prob C §§1310–1312.

§14.17   5. No "One Final Judgment" Rule

Probate court orders are not subject to the general rule in civil actions that there must be only one judgment. It is common practice for probate courts to resolve petitions piecemeal. A common example would be the court ordering an accounting to be filed, as prayed for in a petition also seeking the fiduciary's removal and surcharge, deferring the other issues until the accounting has been reviewed. Many of these piecemeal orders may be appealable directly. Prob C §§1300–1304. This can be a trap for general civil litigators who are accustomed to waiting until a final judgment is rendered before deciding whether to file an appeal.

§14.18   6. Concurrent Cases

It is common for multiple court files to be open in litigation regarding essentially the same facts. Allegations of financial elder abuse may involve:

- A conservatorship;
- The conservatee's trust;
- An Elder Abuse Restraining Order; and
- A general civil and elder abuse action brought under the Elder Abuse and Dependent Adult Civil Protection Act (EADACPA) (Welf & I C §§15600–15675).

These will all address substantially the same alleged actions or events.

Often, these proceedings should be heard together to save court time and avoid conflicting court decisions.

Because proceedings under the Probate Code are in rem, the files should not be consolidated. Instead, the court should order the files "consolidated for trial" to avoid the obviously inefficient potential for multiple trials or unnecessary arguments about the extent to which a finding in one of these proceedings may be applicable to collaterally estop the litigation in another of the files.

Because of the probate court's authority to make interim orders as needed, and because the procedures for probate proceedings are less familiar to many judges, it may make sense for the cases to be consolidated for hearing and transferred to a judge of the probate department to manage them all and get them resolved. For example, civil cases do not appear on the court's calendar until some later hearing is set. Jurisdiction in probate cases depends on notice of the hearing, so courts keep continuing the hearing until the matter goes to trial, to avoid "breaking the string" and losing jurisdiction.

§14.19   7. Blended Pleadings

Sometimes attorneys file a blended pleading, in which a civil cause of action (*e.g.*, for elder abuse) is included in a probate petition for accounting or removal of the fiduciary. Some courts view this approach with disfavor. When attorneys file a blended pleading, they will often try to elect one set of procedures as controlling. For example, an attorney who usually appears in the probate court is likely to mail the notices as required by the Probate Code. An attorney who generally does civil litigation may apply just those procedures, having summonses issued and served. However, there is no authority for disregarding the applicable procedures for either the Code of Civil Procedure or the Probate Code just because the pleadings have been blended into a single document. That is, for a blended pleading, both the civil procedure (summons and complaint) and the probate procedure (notices of hearing) must be followed for the court to have jurisdiction to proceed. It can be a problem for the court's legal process clerks, who know the procedures for probate and for civil actions, to be told to apply both sets of procedures to the same pleading (*e.g.*, issue summons and set the pleading for a noticed hearing in the probate department).

§14.20 8. Right to a Jury Trial

A general civil action (*i.e.*, a civil complaint for money damages) would entitle the plaintiff to a jury trial on causes of action such as negligence, breach of contract, or conversion. However, jury trials are generally not available for petitions in the probate court. Prob C §825. To the extent that civil pleadings and probate petitions are brought in the same action or proceeding, there might be a right to a jury trial on some of the issues but not others. In this situation, usually a court will first resolve the issues that may be heard without a jury; often, the resolution of those issues will avoid the need for a jury trial concerning the remaining issues because the court's findings will be res judicata as to the other issues.

§14.21 9. A Trust Is Not a Legal Entity

Although a decedent's estate (sometimes referred to as a "probate estate" or "formal probate") is a legal entity, a trust is not an entity which exists separate from its trustees. Rather, a trust is a fiduciary relationship in which legal title to property is held by the trustee for the benefit of another. A trust cannot be sued, and a judgment against a trust, rather than against its trustees, is not enforceable. *Portico Mgmt. Group, LLC v Harrison* (2011) 202 CA4th 464. Thus, "the proper procedure for one who wishes to ensure that trust property will be available to satisfy a judgment ... [is to] sue the trustee in his or her representative capacity." *Greenspan v LADT LLC* (2010) 191 CA4th 486, 522.

However, trusts are often named, even in the trust documents, as if they were legal entities. One difficulty in identifying a trust is that trust documents are generally private; they are not formally registered anywhere. Adding a name does facilitate identifying the specific trust that is involved. Referring to a trust by its name feels compelling when the alternative is constantly referencing it, *e.g.*, as "John Doe as trustee of that certain trust executed on January 1, 2000 in Los Angeles, California, between Jane Roe and James Roe, as settlors and trustees thereof." That mouthful makes "The Jane and James Roe Family Revocable Trust" seem elegantly concise by comparison.

> **NOTE▶** Likewise, guardianships, conservatorships, and powers of attorney are not legal entities—they are just proceedings involving the ward, conservatee, or principal.

Adding to the potential for confusion, under the Internal Revenue Code, both trusts and decedents' estates are treated as separate legal entities, with obligations to secure a taxpayer identification number separate from the Social Security number of the person involved.

II. FIDUCIARIES, BENEFICIARIES, AND THE DUTY TO ACCOUNT

§14.22   A. Fiduciaries Are Personally Accountable

The connection between a fiduciary's accountability and the accounting itself is simple and direct. The fiduciary is accountable to the beneficiary, and is required to provide an accounting from which the fiduciary's performance can be judged.

Occasionally, the court will be presented with a successor fiduciary's accounting for the period when a predecessor fiduciary served instead. This cannot be accepted as the predecessor's accounting because it is not the predecessor's accounting. If an accounting by, or on behalf of, the predecessor cannot be secured, the successor's "accounting" may be viewed as a petition for instruction (to determine that nothing further can reasonably be done about the missing accounting) or as a petition to surcharge the predecessor fiduciary for defalcations demonstrated in the successor's "accounting."

In a formal probate, Prob C §10953 authorizes compelling the personal representative's attorneys or personal representative to prepare and file an accounting. There is no analogous case or statute as to other fiduciaries.

§14.23   B. To Whom an Accounting Is Owed

Parties often assume that contingent beneficiaries of a trust are of lesser importance, or even that they are not "real" beneficiaries; however, contingent beneficiaries of a trust generally have the same right to review trust records as a beneficiary receiving benefits currently. "[A] trustee owes the same fiduciary duty to a contingent beneficiary as to one with a vested interest in so far as necessary for the protection of the contingent beneficiary's rights in the trust property." *Kenny v Citizens Nat. Trust & Sav. Bank of L.A.* (1954) 269 P2d 641, 649.

Most trusts have a "disaster clause" providing for nearly unlimited contingent beneficiaries, recognizing the remote possibility of some disaster resulting in the primary beneficiaries dying before the trust is distributed. It can seem irrational, considering that a beneficiary might have only a 0.01 percent possibility of ever receiving something, that the beneficiary is entitled to review all the trust books and records, but having trustees decide what records some beneficiaries can and cannot see would be a dangerous path.

§14.24   C. Fiduciary Accounting Formats

Not all fiduciary accountings are in the same format. Most trust accountings do not require court approval and are provided directly to the beneficiaries. All that is required for a non-court accounting is for all of the necessary information, including financial transactions, to be presented. By contrast, accountings submitted for court approval must be in the format specified in Prob C §§1060–1064. The rationale for this distinction is the legislature's recognition that it is simply too burdensome for courts to have to sift through unfamiliar formats to review accountings.

However, sometimes a court has to address whether a non-court accounting previously provided was sufficient to start laches or the statute of limitations running as to the beneficiary's right to challenge the accounting. In that situation, though, the litigation will likely focus on some particular aspect of the accounting regarding some particular transaction, and the court will not be expected to review the entire accounting.

§14.25   D. Fiduciaries Need Attorneys

Unfortunately, people who serve as fiduciaries often fail to consult with attorneys. Serving as a fiduciary involves heavy responsibilities, and ignorance of those responsibilities can have severe consequences. The usual reasons people fail to consult with attorneys are cost and overconfidence. Those who sell self-help legal books and books on revocable trusts and durable powers of attorney often make a big deal about how they avoid the need for court involvement. Unfortunately, this concept becomes oversimplified in the minds of customers and their family and friends, leading to a simplistic belief that no court involvement will ever occur and no attorney services or fees will be needed. Much of the litigation related to fiduciary accountings results from this misconception.

III. ALTERNATIVE DISPUTE RESOLUTION

§14.26   A. Overview

Alternative dispute resolution (ADR) is particularly useful in litigation regarding accountings, both because of the extraordinary amount of court time and attorney fees that can be incurred in litigating these issues under the normal civil litigation model, and because the parties often bring a level of emotion to these disputes. In many cases, the parties' underlying motivation is primarily emotional, particularly in family law proceedings.

Despite the fact that accountings are central to a fiduciary's responsibility to manage assets, most accounting disputes are ill suited for resolution through the normal civil litigation process. Small claims court exists in recognition of the truth that neither attorney fees nor the resources of the superior court work well in resolving relatively small amounts in dispute. Most accounting litigation does not focus on a few large transactions of the kind that the superior court litigation process works well to resolve. Instead, accounting disputes commonly present an extensive list of individual items, each of which would be well within the amount ordinarily heard in a small claims court. The fact that the total amount in dispute might qualify a case for superior court resolution does not necessarily mean it is the best forum for doing so.

Accounting disputes are usually paired, concurrently or sequentially, with an attorney fee dispute. Although these may involve large amounts, the detailed work involved to resolve the conflicts can take inordinate amounts of court time, and strikingly increase the amount of attorney fees.

Because of these emotional undertones, judicial settlement conferences are less effective than in other civil actions. Courts generally have neither the time nor the inclination to spend hours hearing about grievances that have no nexus to the legal issues before the court.

When considering ADR, the court should also consider appointment of an expert under Evid C §730. Although, as a matter of law, testimony of a court-appointed expert is entitled to no greater weight than any other expert, in practice the parties recognize that the court's expert is not paid for to secure a beneficial result for either party.

§14.27 B. Mediation

Mediation is particularly well suited to resolving fiduciary accounting disputes for two reasons:

- Probate proceedings often involve emotional components, motivating or exacerbating the conflict, that are either irrelevant or merely tangential to the legal issues. This is particularly true in accounting disputes, where the focus is usually on the sufficiency of documentation and whether the fiduciary's action was prudent. Mediators typically explore and uncover these emotional issues with the parties (sometimes with imperfectly disguised eye-rolling by the attorneys, who are tired of their clients trying to raise these old family tensions and see them as irrelevant to "the issues"). What mediators commonly observe, however, is that when people have had an opportunity "to be heard" concerning what they care about, they are then often better able to resolve the legal issues.

- Fiduciary accounting disputes commonly involve multiple small transactions that would be funneled by the legal system into small claims court for resolution by the parties without counsel. Although the cumulative amount in dispute often is substantial, each transaction must be considered independently. This can be very labor intensive and often results in attorney fees that seem disproportionate. Mediation helps the parties see the problem from a broader perspective and allows them to find a settlement they can live with. Mediation helps avoid the extraordinarily expensive alternative of having attorneys litigate all of the transactions, with professional obligations and judicial expectations for thorough preparation and presentation as to each item.

NOTE▶ The disputes about fiduciary and attorney fees that so commonly accompany accounting disputes have the same issue. The analysis and preparation required to present evidence regarding numerous timesheet entries can easily take more time than the work which is the subject of the dispute.

Probate courts have generally recognized that mediation is highly desirable, and have developed various strategies to promote the process. One approach is to simply order the parties to participate in mediation. The problem with this approach is well articulated in

Jeld-Wen, Inc. v Superior Court (2007) 146 CA4th 536, often cited for the proposition that "courts cannot order mediation" (except for statutory provisions not relevant here, such as family law cases and small civil actions under CCP §§1775-1775.15).

In the *Jeld-Wen* case, the trial court's order for the parties to participate in mediation was reversed. The decision included two holdings. First, the court cannot order the parties to pay the mediator. Second, if mediation is used in place of a judicial settlement conference, it cannot be ordered more than once. (In the *Jeld-Wen* case, the court ordered the parties to participate in multiple mediations and to pay for the mediations.)

These two holdings are not necessarily an impenetrable barrier to ordering mediation. A court may have a mediation program (although their use is somewhat controversial) in which the mediators agree to provide some of their time (*e.g.,* 2 hours in Contra Costa County) without charge. The court may order the parties to participate in a mediation for at least the period of time available without charge through the court's program. The parties are not required to use the court's mediation program, but having it available as an option should meet the test of not requiring the parties to pay for the mediation. In ordering the mediation, the court may make an express finding that the mediation is ordered instead of a mandatory settlement conference.

When ordering mediation, it is tempting to order the parties' participation in good faith. This should be avoided because the order is inherently unenforceable, since mediation is confidential. See Evid C §§1115-1128. Theoretically, parties could spend the 2 hours with their fingers in their ears, yelling "blah, blah, blah." In reality, this would obviously never occur. Instead, the attorneys will likely quietly favor an order to participate in mediation, knowing the benefits of mediation despite their clients' reluctance.

Although some people feel strongly that mediation should only be used if voluntary, the reality is that litigation mediation is almost always coerced, one way or another. The parties may be strongly encouraged by the court to participate in mediation, and fear judicial displeasure. The courts' budget cutbacks may have resulted in long waits for judicial settlement conferences, or long waits until a matter can go to trial. The parties may come to realize that the legal fees are mounting rapidly and become desperate to stop the financial hemorrhaging. Or they may finally realize that there is no "sure thing" in litigation, and the possible benefit of a complete win in court is not as great as the possible disaster of a complete loss.

Although the mediation privilege is very broad, some information may be disclosed, such as how long the mediation lasted, and whether it was successful. Although not directly applicable to mediations in probate proceedings, the Statement of Agreement or Nonagreement (Judicial Council Form ADR-100) allows a mediator to report this kind of information, which is not covered by the mediation privilege. A written settlement agreement is intended to be used outside of the mediation, so it also is not privileged.

PRACTICE TIP▶ If a case does settle in mediation, counsel should expressly state in the settlement agreement that the agreement is admissible and enforceable, even if the agreement is prepared after the mediation. Evid C §1122.

§14.28 C. Reference (Appointment of a Referee)

"A referee is a person who is appointed to exercise judicial powers, to take testimony, to hear the parties, and report . . . findings." *Department of Motor Vehicles v Superior Court* (1969) 271 CA2d 770, 774.

Although a court may choose to spend the time in trial to review an accounting (*Ideal Packing Co. v Brice* (1955) 132 CA2d 582, 584), courts will commonly decide to refer the matter to a referee under CCP §638 (voluntary reference) or CCP §639 (involuntary reference). These appointments are particularly appropriate when dealing with accounting disputes because the careful and thorough process of civil trials in California becomes very cumbersome when addressing multiple issues, each of which would otherwise be handled in small claims court. As severe cuts in court budgets result in longer and longer delays to get a matter to trial, the use of referees in appropriate cases may be increasing. The fee disputes that so often accompany fiduciary accounting litigation, and that similarly can involve a large amount of court time dealing with relatively small items, are likewise well suited to referral to a referee.

When the parties agree, the reference may include all issues in dispute (a "general reference"). All other voluntary and involuntary appointments of a referee are "special references."

Special references typically must be specific as to the issues of fact to be decided by the referee. See *Settlemire v Superior Court*

(2003) 105 CA4th 666; CCP §639(a)(3). However, CCP §639(a)(1) allows an involuntary reference for "the examination of a long account ... in which case the referees may be directed to hear and *decide the whole issue,* or report upon any specific question of fact involved therein." (Emphasis added.)

An involuntary reference can also be made under CCP §639(a)(2), "[w]hen the taking of an account is necessary." This would be the situation when no fiduciary accounting can be secured, but the court must determine what amount, if any, should be imposed as a surcharge for numerous transactions.

Code of Civil Procedure §639(a)(4) allows the court to appoint a referee "[w]hen it is necessary for the information of the court in a special proceeding." Probate proceedings are special proceedings. CCP §§1, 21-23; *Robinson v Fair* (1888) 128 US 53; *Estate of Roberts* (1942) 49 CA2d 71; *Estate of Quinn* (1955) 43 C2d 785. No published case has addressed whether, as in CCP §639(a)(1), this allows all issues to be referred (if brought under the Probate Code and not, *e.g.,* a general civil action for damages).

Code of Civil Procedure §639(a)(5) provides for appointment of a referee to address discovery issues. This reference can be particularly helpful to the court in an accounting or fee dispute because there may be a large number of relatively small issues being addressed with great volumes of paper and potential testimony.

When all issues are referred, pursuant to CCP §638, the findings of the referee are treated as the findings of the court, and all that remains for the trial court to do is to issue an order or judgment to implement the referee's decision. CCP §645.

For all other references (*i.e.,* special references under CCP §638 and all references under CCP §639), the referee's report is merely advisory. CCP §640(b). Great weight is given by the court to the referee's factual findings because the referee was able to evaluate the witnesses' credibility. *Borre v State Bar* (1991) 52 C3d 1047, 1051. The court generally will not rehear the evidence, but may review the record to determine whether there is sufficient evidence to support the referee's factual findings. Any party who disagrees with some or all of the referee's report may file a motion stating exceptions to the report, which will then be considered by the court. The objector has the burden of proof to show that a referee's report is not supported by the record. See *Van Sloten v State Bar* (1989) 48 C3d 921, 931.

Any party may initiate appointment of a referee by filing a Stipulation or Motion for Order Appointing Referee (Judicial Council Form ADR-109), used for both voluntary and involuntary appointments. The form is not required when the court is considering appointment of a referee sua sponte.

An Order Appointing Referee (Judicial Council Form ADR-110) is used to appoint a referee. Cal Rules of Ct 3.922, *Form and contents of order appointing referee,* has an apparent anomaly in subdivision (e), providing:

> **(e) Authority of discovery referee**
> If the referee is appointed under [CCP §639(a)(5)] to hear and determine discovery motions and disputes relevant to discovery, the order must state that the referee is authorized to set the date, time, and place for all hearings determined by the referee to be necessary; direct the issuance of subpoenas; preside over hearings; take evidence; and rule on objections, motions, and other requests made during the course of the hearing.

Although Form ADR-110 specially addresses discovery referees, the form does not contain the language of Cal Rules of Ct 3.922. Furthermore, it seems this language should appear in substantially all orders appointing a referee, as these powers are necessary for a referee to make the findings of fact that are the essence of a reference. Particularly when dealing with persons who are not parties to the litigation (*e.g.,* witnesses), it would be helpful to have these powers expressed in the order to clarify the scope of the referee's authority.

The hearings before the referee must be made open to the public (Cal Rules of Ct 3.907 and 3.931), but courts rarely make court facilities available for these hearings.

Referee fees are determined and allocated among the parties by the court, unless the parties agree otherwise. CCP §645.1. It is theoretically possible that the expense would be borne by the court, or a referee would accept appointment pro bono, but this would be exceptional.

NOTE➤ This discussion addresses the use of referees appointed by the court pursuant to CCP §§638-645.2 to make findings of fact as to contested issues. This section does not address the appointment or services of "probate referees" who are, essentially, appraisers designated by the State Controller then appointed by the court. See Prob C §§400-453. This confusion may be enhanced by the provisions in the Probate Code allowing a probate referee to, *e.g.*, issue subpoenas and take testimony. There appears to be no reason why a probate referee could not also be appointed by the court as a referee under CCP §§638-642.5, but in practice this is rare, if it occurs at all.

§14.29   D. Private Judging

Article VI, §21 of the California Constitution provides:

> On stipulation of the parties litigant the court may order a cause to be tried by a temporary judge who is a member of the State Bar, sworn and empowered to act until final determination of the cause.

In choosing a private judge, it is common to hire a retired judge of the superior court, although that is not required.

In the author's experience, there is something offensive to many people about leaving the California trial court system to hire a private judge. Nonetheless, private judging is clearly established as an option in California, and provides many benefits. One benefit is that private judges provide some relief for the trial courts. The cases in which the parties hire a private judge are typically difficult cases that would otherwise consume much court time.

Using a private judge lets the parties ensure that they have a judge who is familiar with the particular subject matter (*e.g.*, fiduciary accountings and disputes). Although the fees paid to the private judge are often substantial, there nevertheless may be substantial savings for the parties as well. Hearings, briefing, etc., can be arranged much more easily and conveniently, saving time for the also expensive attorneys involved in the case. With a judge known to be familiar with the subject area, much less briefing may be required.

An important distinction between a private judge and a consensual reference under CCP §638, is that the judge can sign orders directly. This is more efficient than a referee preparing a report and a proposed order, then submitting the papers to the court for signature by a judge.

A private judge also has somewhat broader powers than a referee. For example, a referee does not have the power to deal with contempt (*e.g.*, if a discovery order is being ignored), so that matter must then be brought back to the trial court for resolution.

There is no Judicial Council form for private judging. Once a private judge has been retained and the order for appointment has been secured from the superior court, all further involvement with the superior court is generally terminated, except for the work of the legal process clerks in filing the papers. Private judging is not truly private—the pleadings are publicly filed, as in other cases. The hearings must be available to the public. It may be more difficult for third parties to find out when and where the hearings are, since they are not included in the court's calendaring system, but any appeals follow the usual public process.

It is possible to file an application or motion to withdraw a stipulation for the appointment of a temporary judge under Cal Rules of Ct 2.816(e), but this is rarely done and rarely successful.

§14.30   IV. REMEDIES

Detailed treatment of all the legal remedies available as part of, or concurrently with, fiduciary accountings is beyond the scope of this chapter. Rather, this section of the chapter reviews various tools and alternatives available to courts to address some of the common and difficult issues in fiduciary accounting litigation.

Dealing with accountings in probate proceedings can tax the patience and creativity of the court. Courts commonly issue orders for accountings to be filed. Not infrequently, there is a lack of compliance with the order. Particularly common are failures to appear at a hearing as ordered, and failure to file an accounting that complies with the requirements of the Probate Code and applicable rules. A wide range of responses by the court is possible when orders are violated, but often these will cost the court more time and effort than seems warranted.

It is never good for the court to be seen as tolerating a violation of its orders. This situation commonly arises in a courtroom crowded with other probate matters, so the court must also be mindful that having court orders taken seriously is important both to maintain general respect for the courts and to discourage others in the courtroom from feeling emboldened to violate court orders in their cases.

PRACTICE TIP➤ There is no authority for the court to appoint a successor in disputes involving attorneys-in-fact. If no successor is available under the terms of the power of attorney, and some actions are needed on behalf of the principal, it may be necessary to initiate a conservatorship. This may be done by the court's appointment of a guardian ad litem with express authority to initiate that proceeding.

§14.31 A. Appointment of Experts

A court may appoint one or more experts, when necessary, and impose the expense on the parties. Evid C §§730, 731(c). In fiduciary accounting litigation, various situations may call for the use of Evid C §730. The parties may be disputing the reasonableness of a decision by a fiduciary in some transaction, relying only on their deeply felt opinions, perhaps because each side believes their position is obviously correct, or perhaps because they simply wish to avoid the expense of securing expert testimony. After hearing this testimony, the court may feel a profound lack of any rational basis for deciding the matter in either party's favor and may then appoint an independent expert of the court's own choosing to provide more reliable information.

Alternatively, the court may be presented with an uncontested petition for approval of an accounting, and realize that the beneficiary is unable to effectively evaluate the information presented. This would commonly be the case with a special needs trust for a seriously disabled beneficiary. Also, when a revocable trust is used as a conservatorship substitute and the trustor has become incapacitated, to approve an accounting based only on the information typed on the pages really provides no protection for the beneficiary. So, when the accounting presented to the court seems analogous to a conservatorship of the estate, the court may wish to have the court investigator look into the matter, as would be done in a conservatorship. There might be an objection to this, however, as the Probate Code only provides for use of a court investigator in guardianship and conservatorship investigations. Evidence Code §730 provides the authority for a court to have a court investigator look into the matter.

The court may also choose to appoint an investigator to assist with evaluation of the trustee or attorney fees. Reversing the trial court's award of attorney fees, the court in *Donahue v Donahue* (2010) 182 CA4th 259, 276 stated:

> It is true that judges themselves are deemed to be experts on the value of legal services, and may rely on their own experience about reasonable and proper fees, without resort to expert testimony. "In many cases the trial court will be aware of the nature and extent of the attorney's services from its observation

of the trial proceedings and the pretrial and discovery proceedings reflected in the file."

But a judge's litigation experience may not extend to many critical aspects of fee awards pertaining to prudent trust administration, including management of complex litigation, legal auditing, and legal cost control.

In this area, the testimony or declaration of fee experts may assist the trial court, on remand, in determining the appropriate amount. . . . It is no insult to the judiciary to admit that a court's expertise is rarely at its most formidable in the evaluation of counsel fees.

§14.32 B. Appointment of Attorneys and Guardians ad Litem

Probate courts are often confronted with adults whose interests are being materially affected, but who seem unable to represent themselves. Because appointment of attorneys for minors and conservatees is common, and the courts are given wide latitude in making those appointments, probate judges are sometimes inclined to appoint attorneys to represent others in probate proceedings. It is important to note that appointing an attorney for someone is only available where statutorily authorized, and in probate proceedings that is limited to guardianships and conservatorships.

PRACTICE TIP▶ In conservatorship proceedings, some courts are inclined to appoint both an attorney and a guardian ad litem, intending the attorney's role to be vigorous advocacy for whatever desires the conservatee is able to express, and the guardian ad litem's role to be acting in the conservatee's best interest. Some courts view an attorney's role as including a protective function, so rarely, if ever, would the court make both appointments.

The court, on its own motion or the request of any interested person, may appoint a guardian ad litem to represent a minor, an incapacitated person, or others whose identity or whereabouts is unknown. Prob C §1003. Probate courts commonly appoint attorneys as guardians ad litem sua sponte as needed, when no other acceptable applicant appears. Because guardians ad litem who are not attorneys may not appear in pro per (*Torres v Friedman* (1985) 169 CA3d 880), appointing an attorney as guardian ad litem does not substantially increase the expense.

Appointing someone other than an independent attorney as guardian ad litem commonly raises conflict-of-interest issues because the other parties usually have a personal stake in the outcome of the litigation. The court may also take into consideration any conflict of interest for the person nominating the guardian ad litem. *Williams v Superior Court* (2007) 147 CA4th 36.

Appointment of guardians ad litem has commonly been done ex parte. However, appointment of a guardian ad litem involves a finding of incapacity. For minors, the finding is inherent in their minority. For adults, this requires notice and an opportunity to be heard. *In re James F.* (2008) 42 C4th 901, 910. The effect of the guardian ad litem's appointment is to transfer direction and control of the litigation from the person to the guardian ad litem, who may waive the person's right to a contested hearing. Before appointing a guardian ad litem for a person in a dependency proceeding, the court must hold a hearing at which the person has an opportunity to be heard.

CAUTION▶ Use of Petition for Appointment of Guardian Ad Litem—Probate Code (Judicial Council Form DE-350/GC-100) and Order Appointing Guardian Ad Litem—Probate (Judicial Council Form DE-351/GC-101) is mandatory.

§14.33 C. Limiting Powers

In addition to the ability to suspend probate fiduciaries (and appoint temporary successors) pending resolution of the litigation, courts can also impose temporary limitations on the powers of a fiduciary.

It is tempting for a court, because of the court's responsibility to supervise fiduciaries, to make interim orders for the fiduciaries to take certain actions (*e.g.,* sell real property or make interim distributions). There is scant authority for such actions; however, when it is clear to the court that some such action should be taken, if the fiduciary is recalcitrant, then the court may suspend the fiduciary's authority to address that issue (see §14.34) and appoint a temporary fiduciary with authority to take the action. When this is explained to the fiduciary, commonly there will be no need to bring in a temporary fiduciary.

Limiting powers also can be used when a fiduciary is spending large amounts of attorney fees to defend actions that appear indefensible. Although, of course, the fiduciary is entitled to a trial on the underlying issue, in such a situation it is reasonable for a court to suspend the fiduciary's authority to pay litigation expenses from the estate, pending resolution of the underlying conflict. When it is finally determined that a fiduciary has committed substantial wrongdoing, it is often difficult, or impossible, to make the beneficiary whole, much less to recover any of the estate's funds the fiduciary expended in supporting the wrongful conduct.

§14.34 D. Suspension

Suspending a fiduciary pendente lite may be the only way for a court to prevent substantial harm as the litigation, particularly fiduciary accounting disputes, lingers. It is important in this situation to make a clear record of the reasons for the court's interference, since the fiduciary's prior appointment must be given great weight. The court's preference, of course, will be to await final resolution of the conflicts before determining whether alleged malfeasance warrants further intervention by the court, such as removal of the fiduciary.

One situation that likely warrants suspension and replacement of a fiduciary pendente lite is when it becomes clear that the fiduciary's personal interest is interfering with proper fiduciary activities. For example, if it becomes apparent that a conservator is limiting care and medical expenditures for a conservatee because of the conservator's concern about maximizing the inheritance the conservator expects to receive on the conservatee's death, suspension and appointment of a temporary replacement may actually be a matter of the conservatee's life or death.

§14.35 E. Removal

Removal of a fiduciary is done cautiously because it usually cannot be undone, if that should later appear warranted. For example, wills and trusts commonly contain provisions for appointing a line of successors as fiduciary. If one is removed, the next in line may accept appointment. If it later appears that the fiduciary's actions did not warrant removal, the court is not allowed to remove the successor then in place.

A fiduciary may be removed when the fiduciary's personal interests are in conflict with the interests of the estate. In *Estate of Hammer* (1993) 19 CA4th 1621, it was held that a fiduciary's litigation against a beneficiary, although completely unrelated to the fiduciary relationship, nonetheless warranted removal.

§14.36   F. Appointing a Replacement

Choosing a replacement for a fiduciary may be as simple as looking at the operative document to see who is named as successor. Otherwise, the choice may be more difficult. Appointment of a bank as fiduciary is comforting because there is practical certainty that any malfeasance can be remedied (*i.e.*, there is a very deep pocket). Appointment of anyone else, whether a relative of the beneficiary or a private professional fiduciary, will generally warrant conditioning the appointment on the posting of a bond covering the entire amount of the estate. (A common sentiment among experienced probate judges is, "I have never regretted ordering that a bond be posted. I have greatly regretted having no bond posted.") One way a court may limit the amount of the bond is to limit, expressly, the powers of the replacement fiduciary, so that no one dealing with the replacement could reasonably believe that the replacement has authority, for example, to sell or encumber real property.

It is often tempting for a court to suspend a fiduciary during bitterly contested litigation regarding an accounting, and bring in a professional fiduciary who can be expected to manage the estate competently, in a businesslike fashion, with no seething, underlying family tensions. However, before doing this, the court must clearly articulate the justification for the intervention. *Conservatorship of Ramirez* (2001) 90 CA4th 390.

§14.37   G. Contempt

The superior court has contempt powers to apply when court orders are violated. In probate courts, this power is rarely used because it is so cumbersome. Because contempt proceedings are quasi-criminal, a person charged with contempt has a right to legal representation, and the right not to be compelled to testify. Proceedings such as accounting disputes are long enough without having to address these additional issues.

One important aspect of the court's contempt powers, however, is the ability to have someone incarcerated for continuing contempt. As a last resort against a fiduciary who simply willfully refuses to file an accounting, for example, the court could have the person incarcerated until the accounting is filed.

Code of Civil Procedure §177.5. Civil fines provide a relatively simple and practical alternative to the threat of contempt for violation of court orders. A party against whom such sanctions are sought is entitled to adequate notice and a hearing, but not to appointment of counsel. *People v Hundal* (2008) 168 CA4th 965. The potential fine of $1500 is, somewhat surprisingly, 50 percent higher than the maximum $1000 fine for contempt.

It is never good for the court to be seen as tolerating violations of its orders. See discussion in §14.30. Most people will see that the court is taking the matter seriously when a $1500 fine is imposed, payable to the court.

Cal Rules of Court 2.30; *Sanctions for rules violations in civil cases.* Another option that can be helpful when a party fails to comply with a California Rule of Court is imposing sanctions under Cal Rules of Ct 2.30. Unlike CCP §177.5, Cal Rules of Ct 2.30 has no cap on the amount that may be imposed. Sanctions may be paid to an aggrieved party or the court, and may include the attorney fees incurred in securing the sanction.

§14.38   H. Surcharging

Surcharging is the court's primary redress against fiduciaries who fail to perform their duties. The surcharge order must be specific as to items and calculations, rather than simply providing a total amount. The decision in *Estate of Gerber* (1977) 73 CA3d 96, 119, illustrates the complexity that can be involved. The court must decide between surcharge based on the loss to the estate, or based on the gain (if any) of the fiduciary. A fiduciary may not be surcharged for attorney fees to impose the surcharge, but only for the fees incurred in straightening out the mess. 73 CA3d at 119.

When the issue of a potential surcharge is raised, it is important to ensure that notice has been given to the bond company, if any, for the fiduciary, under Prob C §1213. This will allow the bond company to participate directly in the determination of any amount of surcharge. Otherwise, ordinary due process will entitle the bond company to collaterally attack the surcharge amount when, as is often the case, the fiduciary is unable to pay the surcharge amount. This notice is easy to accidentally overlook, since the surcharge may be made directly on an accounting filed by the fiduciary, who was certainly not pleading that there should be a surcharge.

§14.39 I. Return of Assets

As part of the appointment of a successor fiduciary, even a temporary one, the court may require all assets of the estate to be transferred by the suspended or removed fiduciary. Since those assets include the books and records, this means the books and records go to the successor. That is problematic for the former fiduciary if an accounting is required or there is other litigation. Among the court's options is the option to allow the former fiduciary to have copies made, at the former fiduciary's expense. Alternatively, the court may simply order the successor to make the books and records available to the former fiduciary at reasonable times and on reasonable notice.

§14.40 J. Fees and Costs

Fiduciaries are generally entitled to reasonable fees for their services. A fiduciary's attorney fee is usually an expense to be paid from, or reimbursed to, the estate managed by the fiduciary. This does not mean that all of the fiduciary's attorney fees are necessarily payable from the estate. Only reasonable attorney fees are reimbursable. To the extent that the fees are incurred defending acts determined to be wrongful, such as improper expenditures as shown in the accounting, those attorney fears are generally not payable from the estate.

Sometimes the fees can be disallowed in large blocks. For example, if $10,000 of fees are incurred related to a sale of real property, and the court determines the sale was improperly concluded for the trustee's own benefit, then the entire amount could be summarily disallowed. Much more commonly, the conflict involves a challenge to a large number of fee entries, both as to the nature and quality of the services provided.

To the extent that the fiduciary's acts are determined to be proper, the fiduciary should be entitled to use the estate's funds to pay for legal fees and costs incurred. Even the fees incurred in defending the amount of the fees charged by the fiduciary or the principal may be payable from the principal's estate. See, by analogy, *Estate of Trynin* (1989) 49 C3d 868.

Probate Code §1002 provides that the costs may be ordered paid "by any party to the proceedings or out of the assets of the estate, as justice may require." Thus, if an interested party successfully secures removal of the fiduciary, the petitioner's costs would probably be payable from the removed fiduciary's assets, but might be ordered paid from the estate, if the removed fiduciary is unable to pay them.

15
Project Management; Useful Miscellanea; a Word to CPAs

I. INTRODUCTION §15.1

II. THE ENGAGEMENT LETTER §15.2
   A. Define the Scope of the Engagement §15.3
   B. Avoid Hyperbole §15.4
   C. Specify Responsibility for Appraising Assets §15.5
   D. Define Fiduciary's Responsibility §15.6
   E. Be Realistic About Deadlines §15.7
   F. Ask for a Broad Array of Documents §15.8
   G. Fee Structure
      1. Hourly Billing §15.9
      2. Flat-Fee Billing §15.10
   H. Deposit for Future Services §15.11
   I. Record Retention Policy §15.12
   J. Termination Clause §15.13
   K. Wait! §15.14

III. TIPS FOR THE ACCOUNTANT
   A. Help Fiduciary Manage Documents §15.15
   B. Security Measures §15.16
   C. Powers of Attorney §15.17
   D. Software §15.18

IV. FOR ATTORNEYS: USING FIDUCIARY ACCOUNTINGS AS A CLIENT MANAGEMENT TOOL
   A. Start Early §15.19
   B. Schedule Face-to-Face Meetings §15.20

V. A WORD TO CERTIFIED PUBLIC ACCOUNTANTS
   A. The General Rule §15.21
   B. If Fiduciary Accounting Is Not a Financial Statement §15.22
   C. Accounting for Presentation to the Court §15.23

D. Management-Use-Only Reports §15.24
   E. Accounting for Trustees Who Will Not Seek the Court's Approval §15.25
   F. Countering the Beneficiary's Dismay §15.26

VI. SAMPLE ENGAGEMENT LETTER §15.27

VII. LIST OF DOCUMENTS NEEDED TO PREPARE FIDUCIARY ACCOUNTING §15.28

VIII. CHART: ALLOCATION OF RECEIPTS AND DISBURSEMENTS UNDER CALIFORNIA UNIFORM PRINCIPAL AND INCOME ACT §15.29

§15.1   I. INTRODUCTION

As mentioned in the preface, in this book the word "accountant" is defined as any person who prepares a fiduciary accounting, whether or not that person is a certified public accountant. The accountant might be an attorney, a paralegal, a bookkeeper, the fiduciary himself or herself, or one of the small number of people who specialize in the preparation of fiduciary accountings. Until this chapter, this book has spoken to all readers without regard to the reader's professional license or lack thereof.

In this chapter, for the first time, the reader's profession matters. This chapter recommends that anyone who prepares a fiduciary accounting (the accountant), who himself or herself is not the fiduciary, begin the relationship with the fiduciary by entering into a contract. Called an engagement letter, that contract communicates the duties the accountant will perform during the course of the accountant's engagement with the fiduciary. These duties will vary, depending on the accountant's profession. Attorneys owe their clients those duties codified in Bus & P C §6069, and attorneys are regulated in their performance of these duties by the California State Bar Rules of Professional Conduct. See http://rules.calbar.ca.gov/Rules/RulesofProfessionalConduct/CurrentRules.aspx. Certified Public Accountants (CPAs) may owe duties not just to the people who hire them, and CPAs are regulated by the California Board of Accountancy. The regulations that govern attorneys and CPAs will have implications throughout the attorney's or CPA's engagement with the fiduciary and in the years that follow.

Professional regulations may affect the accountant's record retention and certainly they affect the limitations period on actions against the professional. Accountants who are also regulated professionals must take into consideration the strictures of their professions when drafting an engagement letter and, as a consequence, these professionals cannot rely solely on this chapter when preparing their engagement letters.

Certified public accountants face a dilemma unique to their profession, defining what CPAs call the "level of service" required by the engagement. This topic is addressed at the end of this chapter, in a section directed to CPAs.

§15.2 II. THE ENGAGEMENT LETTER

Every accountant who prepares an accounting for a fiduciary should have an engagement letter that clearly states, on the one hand, the accountant's obligations and, on the other, the fiduciary's. If the accountant is an attorney, or if the accounting will be prepared by a paralegal in the attorney's office, preparation of the accounting will be just one part of the legal services the client will expect. For these clients, attorneys may wish to incorporate into the engagement letter some of the suggestions made below. (For a complete discussion of attorney-client fee agreements, see Fee Agreement Forms Manual (2d ed Cal CEB).)

If the accountant is a certified public accountant, the accountant should follow the recommendations of the American Institute of Certified Public Accountants (AICPA) and those practice guides that provide sample engagement letters vetted by the bodies that insure and regulate public accountants. The following material suggests ways in which the CPA may wish to augment the sample forms provided elsewhere in this book. For the accountant who is not an attorney or CPA, a sample engagement letter is provided at the end of this chapter.

§15.3 A. Define the Scope of the Engagement

The first paragraph of the letter should identify the parties to the contract, should say that the fiduciary is engaging the accountant to prepare a fiduciary accounting for a defined period of time, and that the accounting will be prepared in a format acceptable to the probate court. This activity is at the heart of the contractual relationship and the engagement letter is where the accountant will define what the fiduciary may and may not expect from that relationship. Each relationship will be unique and the fiduciary should tailor his or her standard form engagement letter for each new engagement.

The contract should identify the fiduciary by name and by role—for example, "Sally Cash, trustee of the April Cash Trust," or "Prudence Smith, conservator of the estate of Jezebel Mudd." After introducing the parties, they may be given labels, for example "Accountant" and "Fiduciary," to enable the accountant to use a standard contract for most engagements, rather than reinventing the engagement letter each time.

The introductory portion of the letter should remind the fiduciary that the letter is a contract and should advise the fiduciary to read the contract carefully before signing. If the fiduciary has an attorney, the accountant may wish to mention that person by name and suggest that the attorney review the contract before the fiduciary signs it. If the fiduciary plans to look to an enrolled agent or CPA for the preparation of income tax or estate tax returns, the introductory paragraphs of the engagement letter should say this as well.

§15.4 B. Avoid Hyperbole

The engagement letter should be limited to describing the terms of the engagement. In the letter, one should not advertise his or her services with language that might expand the scope of the engagement. For example, words like "exhaustive" and "thorough" should be avoided. Additionally, the engagement letter is not the place to communicate with the client about matters extraneous to the contract. Avoid friendly mention of social ties, avoid mentioning other shared endeavors, and never mention in an engagement letter persons who are strangers to the fiduciary relationship that is the subject of the engagement. For example, in a letter to a professional trustee regarding the Smith Family Trust, do not mention the services earlier provided to the addressee while he was serving as trustee of the Brown Trust.

§15.5 C. Specify Responsibility for Appraising Assets

Lay persons often naively assume that the person preparing the fiduciary accounting will also volunteer opinions of the value of the estate's or trust's assets. To avoid this misunderstanding, the engagement letter should clearly state that for assets for which there is no readily available market value, the accountant will rely on the fiduciary's opinion of value or on appraisals obtained by the fiduciary, as the case may be. In the alternative, if the accountant is competent and willing to give an opinion on the value of an asset, the engagement letter should clearly specify the scope of that engagement. Indeed, if the accountant will also appraise assets, the accountant should consider using a separate engagement letter for the appraisal. This practice allows the accountant to say in the fiduciary-accounting engagement letter, that **"except as provided in our separate agreement regarding the _ _[name of asset]_ _ ..., we agree that I shall not provide an opinion of the value of the estate's assets."**

§15.6   D. Define Fiduciary's Responsibility

It is impossible to prepare a good accounting for the fiduciary who has kept poor records. The engagement letter therefore should make clear that keeping good records is the fiduciary's responsibility. Under separate cover, or enclosed in the engagement letter, the accountant should provide a list of the records needed to prepare the accounting. See §15.28.

Some accountants, knowing they will prepare a fiduciary's accounting year after year, ask to receive duplicate bank and brokerage account statements directly from the institution. It is questionable whether an attorney should do this, however, unless the attorney intends to inspect those statements as they arrive, because bank and brokerage account statements may reveal breaches of fiduciary duties the attorney ignores at his or her peril. In *Stine v Dell'Osso* (2014) 230 CA4th 834, David B. Davis III served as conservator of his mother's person and estate. Allegedly, he told the court that all of his mother's assets were held in trust and, consequently, he inventoried and accounted for nothing. Neither did he post a bond. After several years, he was removed as conservator for allegedly converting $1 million of his mother's assets. After Davis's removal, the successor conservator sued Davis's attorneys, alleging that they had known of the unreported assets and committed malpractice by failing to report the assets to the court and seek a bond. The trial court granted the attorneys' demurrer without leave to amend, but the court of appeal reversed and allowed the successor conservator's malpractice action to proceed. The attorneys in *Stine* may in fact have been ignorant of their client's malfeasance and the opinion in *Stine* does not mention what information the attorneys allegedly possessed that should have put them on notice that something was wrong. *Stine* warns us, however, that the attorney who receives statements from a client must scrutinize the statements or ask the client to stop sending them.

Unless the accountant is an attorney, the engagement letter also should clearly state that the account preparer will give no advice on the exercise of the fiduciary's discretionary powers. Regarding allocation of receipts and disbursements between principal and income, the best practice is to examine the will or the trust document, locate the provisions regarding principal and income, and quote them in the engagement letter. (See chap 13 about allocations between principal and income.) Then state that for advice regarding the exercise of any discretionary powers, the fiduciary should consult an attorney. Clients may rely on their attorneys to know the codified and judge-made laws that govern the fiduciary relationship, but the same cannot be said of the other professionals who prepare fiduciary accountings. These professionals may be quite knowledgeable, but the fiduciary who relies for legal advice on a person not licensed to practice law may have no recourse if that "legal" advice proves unreliable. More to the point, questions regarding the exercise of a fiduciary power are legal questions and should be posed to a lawyer.

If the accountant is a CPA, but wishes to limit the engagement to the preparation of the fiduciary accounting, the accountant must say so plainly. The best practice would be to mention by name the person who is responsible for the other work the fiduciary might need—for example, the preparation of tax returns, or an accounting for a business accounted for separately (see chap 13).

§15.7   E. Be Realistic About Deadlines

If the accountant promises to finish the fiduciary accounting within a certain time, the engagement letter should say this, but cautiously. When preparing a fiduciary accounting, the biggest challenge is collecting a complete data set. Unless the fiduciary is remarkably organized, the project will be delayed while the accountant waits for documents. Use the engagement letter to clarify the effect such delays will have on the agreed-on deadlines and consider using language such as the following:

> **Within 7 business days of receipt of your retainer of $__[dollar amount]__ and the materials requested below, Accountant will identify any documents Fiduciary must yet provide. For example, if Accountant requests "all bank statements for Bank of America account XXXXXX-6789," and Fiduciary provides all but the September statement, Accountant will tell Fiduciary this within the 7 business days mentioned above.**

Comparable language can be found in the sample engagement letter in §15.27.

Once the accountant has all of the above materials, he or she will produce a first draft of the fiduciary accounting for the fiduciary's review, according to the schedule below. Tax accountants who also prepare fiduciary accountings should consider promising a quick turnaround if the client produces all the documents in the slow season and should build in additional time for projects that arrive during tax season. The accountant in this situation might provide several pairs of dates in the engagement letter, as in the following example:

Documents Delivered By Account	Date Accountant Will Deliver Draft
December 1, 2014	December 15, 2014
December 15, 2014	January 15, 2015
January 1, 2015	January 30, 2015
February 28, 2015	March 30, 2015
April 1, 2015	April 30, 2015

If the fiduciary has given the accountant all the information the accountant has requested, and any additional information the accountant may request during the course of the project, it is likely that the first draft will differ very little from the final draft. However, if the fiduciary has not provided all the requested information, the first draft may be missing descriptions of the purpose of some disbursements, the payor of certain receipts, and other such information. If this is the case, when the accountant delivers the first draft, he or she must request the additional information. When the fiduciary provides the additional information, the accountant must complete the second draft of the accounting within an agreed-on number of days of receipt of that information. If the fiduciary has provided all the information requested, the second draft should be the final draft.

§15.8   F. Ask for a Broad Array of Documents

The sample engagement letter in §15.27 refers to a list of documents the accountant will need to prepare the accounting—a list which is enclosed with the engagement letter. Accountants who adopt the practice of asking for documents in the engagement letter must necessarily provide a long list, which may include categories of documents irrelevant to the particular accountant-fiduciary relationship. Alternatively, the accountant may ask for documents in a letter separate from the engagement letter, which allows the accountant to first review recent income tax returns in order to gather information about known assets. Every request for assets should include an omnibus clause that asks for **"any other documents relevant to the assets on hand when you took office as** _ _[*guardian/conservator/personal representative/trustee*]_ _ **or relevant to your financial transactions while in office."**

G. Fee Structure

§15.9   1. Hourly Billing

If the accountant bills for projects by the hour, the engagement letter must identify each person who may work on the matter and the person's hourly rate. The letter also should state the policy on fee increases. If billing rates are adjusted periodically, the letter should say so, and if increases are subject to any rules of professional responsibility, the accountant should be certain to follow those rules. If billing rates are adjusted on an irregular basis, the best practice is to state in the engagement letter the date of the last adjustment and the policy for future adjustments. For example, the letter might say, **"We last increased our rates on January 1, 2014 and we will give you 60 days' written notice of any future increases."**

§15.10   2. Flat-Fee Billing

Clients who have never paid by the hour for professional services may think they are purchasing a product—the fiduciary accounting—

instead of hiring services. These clients may prefer to pay a flat fee for the preparation of the accounting, instead of paying for services by the hour. This preference is understandable, but the authors know of no accountants willing to prepare a fiduciary accounting on a flat-fee basis. As a rule, they are keenly aware of the dangers of promising to deliver a completed product for a fixed price.

The problem with flat-fee billing is that the accountant must quote the flat fee at the beginning of the engagement, when the accountant knows almost nothing about the fiduciary's administration of the estate. At this time, the fiduciary may have a complete and nuanced recollection of his or her administration and, because the details are clear in the mind of the fiduciary, he or she may think it will be easy to prepare the accounting. By contrast, the accountant knows nothing about the fiduciary's activities. Neither does the accountant know anything about the fiduciary's attention to detail or record-keeping ability. When quoting a price for the accounting, the accountant dare not rely on the fiduciary's conviction that "this will be easy," and should not assume that accounting for an estate with just a few assets will be simple. This uncertainty makes it exceedingly difficult to set a price that is fair to both the fiduciary and the accountant, which is probably why the authors are aware of no accountants charging flat fees for fiduciary accountings.

§15.11   H. Deposit for Future Services

At the beginning of the accountant-fiduciary relationship, the accountant may wish to ask the fiduciary to pay a deposit toward future accounting fees. The deposit may be used in one of several ways, described below.

> **PRACTICE TIP▶** Attorneys who obtain from their clients a deposit toward future services must strictly adhere to the California State Bar Rules of Professional Conduct and the Business and Professions Code rules. See Fee Agreement Forms Manual, chap 1 (2d ed Cal CEB).

Some accountants ask for a deposit, in the nature of last-month's rent, before beginning their work. In their engagement letters, these accountants explain that the fiduciary will receive monthly (or less frequent) invoices and must pay the invoice on receipt or within a specified period of time—for example, within 30 days. If the fiduciary fails to pay as agreed, the accountant will cease working on the accounting, will apply the deposit to the unpaid invoice, and will resume work only when the deposit is replenished. When the accounting is finished, the fiduciary will apply the deposit to the final invoice and will refund to the fiduciary the unused portion of the deposit. This model protects the accountant from nonpayment, provided the accountant has the self discipline to stop working if an invoice is not paid, and does not require the fiduciary to give a large deposit. The deposit need not be any larger than the largest invoice the accountant is likely to send.

Another type of deposit might be called the "half up front, half on completion" model. Accountants who use this model first estimate the amount it will cost to complete the fiduciary accounting, then ask for half of the estimate before beginning the project. The accountant then bills hourly for his or her time and when the accountant has billed the full amount of the deposit, the accountant pays himself or herself for the work completed to date. The accountant will finish the project with the expectation of being paid in full when the fiduciary accounting is finished. This model provides accountants with some protection from nonpayment and does not require the fiduciary to pay the full amount up front.

A third type of deposit is called the "evergreen" deposit. Accountants who use this model ask for a deposit sufficient to cover several invoices. Each invoice is paid from the deposit until the deposit drops below an agreed-on threshold, at which point the fiduciary must replenish the deposit. For example, the accountant might ask for a deposit of $6000 and require the fiduciary to replenish the deposit whenever the balance drops below $2500. This model costs fiduciaries the most up front, but when the deposit is sufficiently large, provides accountants with the best protection against nonpayment.

Whichever model of deposit the accountant uses, the authors recommend administering it according to the following set of best practices. On accepting the deposit, the accountant should segregate it from his or her operating funds. This may be done with bookkeeping entries, if the accountant's profession otherwise allows this practice. Attorneys, however, must segregate the deposits they collect in a separate account. See Fee Agreement Forms Manual, chap 1 (2d ed Cal CEB). Other professionals may wish to adopt this practice also. After performing the services for which he or she expects payment, the accountant should send the fiduciary an invoice describing those services. The accountant should give the fiduciary a period of time to consider the invoice, and only after this period has elapsed, should the accountant pay himself or herself from the deposit. This delay allows the fiduciary time to complain about the invoice and possibly obtain an adjustment, before the accountant takes his or her payment.

§15.12   I. Record Retention Policy

An engagement letter should state the accountant's record retention policy. Retaining client files provides a benefit to the client, and a measure of protection to the accountant, but each profession has developed its own set of rules regarding record retention and a complete discussion of those rules is beyond the scope of this book. What follows are general guidelines that the accountant should consider in conjunction with the rules of his or her profession.

If the accounting will be submitted to the court for approval, the accountant may wish to keep the records used to prepare the accounting until the fiduciary has obtained that approval. Once the court has approved the accounting, the accountant may wish to return the records to the fiduciary. When doing this, the accountant should either advise the fiduciary of the date the records may be safely destroyed, or advise the fiduciary to seek an opinion from his or her attorney regarding the destruction date. This date will depend on the nature of the documents used to prepare the accounting. Bank records and the like do not need to be kept in perpetuity, but many believe tax returns should be preserved for the lifetime of the entity, plus 7 years. For suggestions on which records to keep permanently, see California Decedent Estate Practice §24.24 (2d ed Cal CEB).

For trust accountings not submitted to the court, records must be kept at least until the statute of limitations has run on claims against the trustee for actions taken during the account period, and the authors recommend keeping the records for an even longer period. Probate Code §16460 bars claims against a trustee more than 3 years after a beneficiary receives an accounting that "adequately discloses" the existence of the claim (Prob C §16460), but that statement is not as reassuring in practice as it sounds in print. Consider the following example. A trustee served his accounting on all persons entitled to it and obtained proof that each beneficiary had received it. The accounting was for the calendar year 2009 and each beneficiary received his or her copy 3 months after the end of the year, on March 31, 2010. The accounting was accompanied by the warning required in Prob C §16063(a)(6): "[C]laims against the trustee for breach of trust may not be made after the expiration of three years from the date the beneficiary receives an account or report disclosing facts giving rise to the claim." One of the beneficiaries, a spendthrift, quickly spent the distributions she received in 2009. Early in 2013, she learned that her siblings, the other beneficiaries, still owned the property distributed to them at the same time she got her 2009 distribution. She quickly jumped to the conclusion that her siblings had received more than their due and became suspicious that the trustee, also a sibling, had breached the trust. In early April 2013, she persuaded an attorney of her theory and, on her behalf, he filed suit on April 15, 2013. If the trustee's 2009 accounting adequately reveals the facts of his administration, the trustee's attorney will move for summary judgment or judgment on the pleadings, arguing that the beneficiary's claim is barred by Prob C §16460. The beneficiary's attorney should be expected to argue that the facts giving rise to the beneficiary's claim were not adequately disclosed, thus the statute of limitations has not begun to run. If this argument is persuasive, the judge might not dismiss the case, or might not dismiss it until the trial. Trustees have the burden of proof on every element of their accounts (*Estate of McLaughlin* (1954) 43 C2d 462, 465), and the trustee who finds himself or herself in this situation will make that proof with the trust records used to prepare the accounting. For that reason, the authors recommend that trustees preserve the records of their administration for several years after the 3-year statute has run.

Finally, and unfortunately, whether the fiduciary is court-supervised or not, the accountant also must consider any applicable statutes of limitations on the fiduciary's claims of malpractice against the accountant. Depending on the nature of the matter, these limitation periods may be longer than the period during which the fiduciary might be sued by the person to whom he or she owes duties. Fortunately, the fiduciary-accountant relationship is often characterized by a measure of trust and gratitude not found in the fiduciary-beneficiary relationship, and accountants often will feel comfortable telling their clients, for example, "Take these documents home, store them for 7 years, then destroy them without ever looking at them again." In a more uneasy fiduciary-accountant relationship, the accountant must retain a copy of all documents necessary to protect himself or herself in the event the fiduciary makes a claim of malpractice.

§15.13   J. Termination Clause

The accountant should reserve the right to terminate the engagement if the fiduciary does not provide the documents requested or if continuing the engagement would compromise the accountant's professional standards. The language below is commonly found in attorney-client engagement letters. Each professional who prepares fiduciary accountings should consider the rules of his or her profession before relying on this example.

> **We may withdraw from representing you with your consent or for good cause. Good cause includes your breach of this contract, including failure to timely pay our fees or make additional deposits to the client trust account. Good cause also includes your refusal to cooperate with us, your refusal to follow our advice on a material matter, or the discovery of any fact or circumstance that would make our representation of you unethical or unlawful. If we withdraw, you will remain obligated to pay for services provided through the date of the withdrawal and for any costs we advance on your behalf.**

§15.14   K. Wait!

An engagement letter should end with a warning that the accountant will not begin providing services until the fiduciary has signed and returned the engagement letter. If the accountant requests a deposit, the letter also should say that the accountant will not begin work until the deposit has been received. Finally, the engagement letter should say that the accountant will provide no services until the fiduciary has provided the documents requested in the letter, or under separate cover.

After making these statements, the accountant should abide by them. The accountant who begins working before receiving the signed engagement letter, any deposit, and a complete set of financial records teaches the fiduciary that the accountant does not mean what he or she says. Later in the relationship, if this accountant must threaten a work stoppage in order to get more information from the fiduciary, the fiduciary may not take the threat seriously and the accountant may find himself or herself working against a deadline that cannot be met.

III. TIPS FOR THE ACCOUNTANT

§15.15 A. Help Fiduciary Manage Documents

Most fiduciaries are lay people and have never before administered a trust or estate. If the fiduciary is a lay person and is administering the estate of a deceased loved one, grief and a host of other emotions may hinder the fiduciary's performance of his or her duties. In this situation, the accountant can help the fiduciary identify the scope of his or her responsibility by examining the decedent's prior tax returns and listing each income-producing asset and each parcel of real property for which property tax was paid. To this list, the accountant should add a category for assets the existence of which are not revealed by the tax return. The list should also include all property specifically identified in the governing document, including tangible personal property. The accountant should then sort the list into two categories:

- Those assets that are subject to the fiduciary relationship; and
- Those for which the fiduciary bears no responsibility.

Next, the accountant can help the fiduciary collect the necessary data by making the process as concrete as possible. For example, some accountants create a file folder for each asset subject to administration and another set of folders for each asset *not* subject to administration, regarding which the fiduciary may nevertheless receive information. These accountants augment the collection of asset files with files for the likely categories of disbursements—for example, debts of the decedent, administration of the decedent's residence prior to sale, and expenses of administration. Finally, the accountants provide folders for the other information relevant to the fiduciary's duties. A representative list of folders is provided below.

1. Governing document
    a. If the governing instrument is a will, this folder will hold all of the following:
        i. The will itself (and all codicils)
        ii. The order for probate

iii. Letters testamentary

iv. The petition for probate, which shows the persons entitled to notice (optional)

b. If the governing instrument is a trust, this folder will hold all of the following:

i. The trust instrument

ii. Any operative amendments

iii. Proof of service of the trustee notification, which shows the persons interested in the trust estate (optional)

iv. A marked-up copy of the trust and amendments, charting the effect the amendments have had on the original document and flagging provisions thought to be important to the trust administration (optional)

2. Intestate decedents

a. The order for probate

b. Letters of administration

c. The petition for probate, which shows the persons entitled to notice (optional)

3. A folder for each financial institution
4. A folder for each parcel of real property
5. Paid bills and invoices
6. Purchases, sales, other business transactions
7. Contact information
   a. For client
   b. For client's attorney
   c. For all accountants involved in decedent's or trustor's life
8. Historic tax returns
9. Recent tax returns
10. Other assets
11. Correspondence
12. Timesheets
13. Miscellaneous

Fiduciaries find these accountant-provided folders most useful when they are labeled as specifically as possible, for example, "Bank of America account no. XXXXXX-6789," is more useful than "Bank Statements." Additionally, the accountant should give the fiduciary instructions for using the folders. For example, the accountant might say "put all the documents relevant to Bank of America account no. XXXXXX-6789 in this file and put all the invoices you pay into this other file."

A complete list of the documents that might be needed to prepare a fiduciary accounting is found in §15.28.

§15.16   B. Security Measures

Preparing a fiduciary accounting necessarily requires the accountant to collect a lot of sensitive information which, in the hands of the wrong person, could be used to defraud the fiduciary. Knowing this, the accountant should gather information carefully. For example, if the accountant will not need Social Security numbers, the accountant should not collect them. And when the accountant asks for those records essential to the project, the accountant also may wish to ask the fiduciary to redact all but the last four numerals from each account number, before the fiduciary transmits the account statement to the accountant. If information is transmitted and stored electronically, the accountant must be sure that his or her computer security system is up-to-date and working. A safer practice may be to store sensitive information only on paper, in a locked file cabinet or behind a locked door.

§15.17   C. Powers of Attorney

Some accountants ask their clients for a very limited power of attorney. The power given is limited to demanding documents from financial institutions. Such a power of attorney allows the accountant to bypass the fiduciary and seek financial records directly from, for example, a bank.

§15.18   D. Software

To prepare their fiduciary accountings, the authors recommend that accountants use a spreadsheet program such as Excel. Although several companies have produced software specifically for the preparation of fiduciary accountings, the weaknesses of these programs make them ill suited to some projects. For example, one of the better known trust accounting software programs aggregates gains and losses on one schedule. In many states, this is acceptable, but for court accountings in California it is not. In California, gains are charges and losses are credits and they must be accounted for on separate schedules. Prob C §§1060-1061. Another program integrates liabilities into the schedules of accounts, thereby reducing the fiduciary's charges, a practice not allowed in California court accountings, where liabilities are reported on an auxiliary schedule. Prob C §1063(g).

The programs produced exclusively for the California market have their strengths, but none of them offer the accountant much flexibility. For example, consider the challenge of accounting for a trustee who administers three trusts—the Survivor's Trust, the Bypass Trust, and the QTIP Trust—but who has paid the expenses of all three trusts solely from the Survivor's Trust. This trustee should prepare three separate accounts, one for each trust. All the disbursements will be reported in the accounting for the Survivor's Trust, which will have an auxiliary schedule on which the accountant apportions the disbursements amongst the three trusts as they should be apportioned. At the end of the account period, the Survivor's Trust will carry two receivables, one from the Bypass Trust and one from the QTIP Trust. These receivables will tie to the auxiliary schedule on which the apportionment was calculated. Concomitantly, the Bypass Trust and QTIP Trust will list on their schedules of liabilities the debts owed to the Survivor's Trust. The challenge of accounting for a trustee who has behaved as did this trustee is not uncommon, but no fiduciary accounting program handles this challenge adroitly. Only on a spreadsheet can the accountant accurately model the many predicaments fiduciaries encounter or create for themselves.

IV. FOR ATTORNEYS: USING FIDUCIARY ACCOUNTINGS AS A CLIENT MANAGEMENT TOOL

§15.19   A. Start Early

Attorneys may wish to encourage their fiduciary clients to begin preparing their accountings far in advance of the date the account period ends. Starting early helps guardians, conservators, and personal representatives identify any assets inadvertently omitted from their inventories, and helps trustees identify the assets comprising the trust estate. Starting early also helps the fiduciary understand which records are necessary for the preparation of the accounting and leads the fiduciary to keep good records. If the attorney examines the fiduciary's accounting (for example, after 6 months of the fiduciary's administration), the attorney may identify actions the fiduciary should curtail and breaches that may be remedied. This practice also alerts the fiduciary to just how carefully his or her actions may be scrutinized.

§15.20 B. Schedule Face-to-Face Meetings

Meeting with clients personally strengthens the client relationship and will elevate the client's commitment to the project. Consider scheduling a series of meetings, with well-defined deliverables due at each. At the first meeting, early in the attorney-client relationship, the attorney should obtain the information necessary to prepare the inventory—or for a trustee, the schedule Assets on Hand—Beginning of Period. At the second meeting, the attorney might examine the fiduciary's record-keeping system and show the fiduciary a sample accounting. At this meeting, the fiduciary might decide to hire assistance with the accounting, but if the fiduciary is determined to prepare his or her own accounting, the attorney might want to schedule a third meeting. At this meeting, the attorney can evaluate the fiduciary's progress on the accounting and, if advisable, again recommend hiring someone to help prepare the accounting.

V. A WORD TO CERTIFIED PUBLIC ACCOUNTANTS

§15.21 A. The General Rule

As a general rule, when an accountant in public practice (a certified public accountant, or CPA) prepares a financial statement, the accountant will be governed by the Statements on Standards for Accounting and Review Services (SSARS). See http://www.aicpa.org/Research/Standards/Pages/default.aspx. The American Institute of Certified Public Accountants (AICPA) Code of Professional Conduct defines the practice of public accountancy as follows:

> The practice of public accounting consists of the performance for a client, by a member or a member's firm, while holding out as CPA(s), of the professional services of accounting, tax, personal financial planning, litigation support services, and those professional services for which standards are promulgated by bodies designated by Council, such as Statements of Financial Accounting Standards, Statements on Auditing Standards, Statement on Standards for Accounting and Review Services (SSARS), Statements on Standards for Consulting Services, Statement of Governmental Accounting Standards, and Statement on Standards for Attestation Engagements.

If the accountant is practicing public accounting and the accountant prepares a financial statement, unless an exception applies, at a minimum the accountant must prepare a compilation report. See Barnhill et al., *Accounting and Reporting for Estates and Trusts* §§501.1-501.11 (Thompson/PPC 7th ed 2013). This implies the question whether a fiduciary accounting is a financial statement.

§15.22   B. If Fiduciary Accounting Is Not a Financial Statement

The authors assume the CPA has not been hired to "audit" a fiduciary account, as that term is used when describing services under the Statements on Auditing Standards (SAS). This book also does not address the level of service required when a CPA is hired to "review" a fiduciary accounting, as that term is used in the Statement on Standards for Accounting and Review Services (SSARS). Although a CPA might be hired to audit or review a fiduciary accounting, such engagements are rare and the level of service required in such an engagement is far beyond the scope of this book.

Only one readily available text discusses whether a fiduciary account is a financial statement. See Barnhill et al., *Accounting and Reporting for Estates and Trusts* §§501.7–501.15 (Thompson/PPC 7th ed 2013). The discussion there begins with a definition of "financial statement" broad enough to encompass fiduciary accounting (§501.7):

> The SSARS (AR 60.04) defines a financial statement as a "structured representation of historical financial information, including related notes, intended to communicate an entity's economic resources and obligations at a point in time, or the changes therein for a period of time, in accordance with a financial reporting framework."

Barnhill and his coauthors "believe the most common [fiduciary] accountings represent financial statements" (§501.10); nevertheless, many CPAs believe fiduciary accountings are not financial statements. The majority opinion, however, is that fiduciary accountings are financial statements, and until the published opinions say otherwise, it would be prudent for CPAs to treat them as such. Thus, absent an agreement to provide a higher level of service and absent some other exception, the CPA hired to prepare a fiduciary accounting should assume that the report required is a compilation report.

§15.23 C. Accounting for Presentation to the Court

An exception lies when the CPA is hired to prepare a fiduciary accounting that will be presented to the court. Even if a fiduciary accounting is a financial statement, if it is prepared for presentation to the court, SSARS will not dictate the report the CPA should prepare. SSARS AR §9080.17-29. The California Probate Code, California's Rules of Court, and the Local Rules of each county, court, or court department govern the type of report that must accompany an accounting a fiduciary submits to the court. Because the court specifies the form of the report that must accompany such accountings, in a court accounting, SSARS do not apply (SSARS AR §9080.17-20):

> SSARS do not apply to financial statements submitted in conjunction with litigation services that involve pending or potential formal legal or regulatory proceedings before a "trier of fact" in connection with the resolution of a dispute between two or more parties when the accountant's work under the rules of the proceedings is subject to detailed analysis and challenge by each party to the dispute.

All of the following are prepared for presentation to the court:

- Accounting for decedent's estate (probate);
- Guardianship accounting;
- Conservatorship accounting; and
- Trust accounting in a litigated dispute.

Additionally, a trustee who is not yet involved in litigation may seek the preparation of an accounting, intending to file it with the court and seek the court's approval. Prob C §17200.

A CPA would not sign the accounting prepared for submission to the court and, in all likelihood (unless the CPA is also an attorney), would not prepare the report that would accompany that submission. Most often, the CPA would present the accounting to the fiduciary or his or her attorney and the attorney would prepare the report. In that case, a CPA should present the accounting with a statement that the accounting has been prepared as agreed on in the engagement letter.

§15.24 D. Management-Use-Only Reports

Although CPAs may provide clients with management-use-only financial statements without issuing a compilation report (SSARS AR No. 8), it is doubtful a fiduciary accounting would ever be "management use only." Certainly, the trustee would be considered a manager, but unless the trustee's legal advisor were a co-trustee, that advisor would not be management and nor would the beneficiaries. See Barnhill et al., *Accounting and Reporting for Estates and Trusts* §§507.3-507.11 (Thompson/PPC 7th ed 2013).

§15.25 E. Accounting for Trustees Who Will Not Seek the Court's Approval

Trustees and agents under powers of attorney are the only Probate Code fiduciaries not required to submit their accountings to the court for its approval. See Prob C §2620 (guardians and conservators); Prob C §§10950-10951 (personal representatives, except when accounting is waived (Prob C §10954), in which case, no accounting will be prepared). Agents so rarely prepare formal accountings, that when discussing those fiduciaries who need not present their accountings to the court, this text speaks only of trustees.

The CPA who prepares a fiduciary accounting for a trustee who will not seek court approval must apply SSARS if the accounting is a financial statement. Generally, fiduciary accountings are compiled from information provided by the trustee, and the CPA would therefore make a compilation report. The gist of the compilation report would be as follows:

> I have compiled the accompanying trust accounting of [trustee of the _____ Trust] and the related [statements or auxiliary schedules] for the [period of account], in accordance with Statements on Standards for Accounting and Review Services issued by the American Institute of Certified Public Accountants.
>
> A compilation is limited to presenting in the form of financial statements information that is the representation of the trustee. I have not audited or reviewed the accompanying financial statements and, accordingly, do not express an opinion or any other form of assurance on them.

This report is appropriate in any CPA-prepared trust accounting that will not be presented to the court because in the preparation of a trust accounting the CPA does not provide the level of service

§15.25

required by an audit or a review. A well-prepared trust accounting will, however, compile all the information required by California Trust Law and recommended by the Committee on National Fiduciary Accounting Standards. Certainly, an accounting prepared as described in this book meets those standards. Nevertheless, some CPAs distance themselves even further from the information reported in the trust accountings they prepare by adding to their compilation reports a sentence like the following:

> The trustee has elected to omit substantially all disclosures ordinarily included in trust financial statements prepared in conformity with the basis of accounting recommended by the Report of the Committee on National Fiduciary Accounting Standards and as prescribed by the California Probate Code.

The authors have seen this statement in countless compilation reports and know with certainty that it is frequently untrue. Accountants more familiar with financial and tax accounting than with fiduciary accounting often make mistakes when they prepare trust accountings, but their mistakes are rarely those of omission. Typically, accountants understand the "follow the penny" nature of fiduciary accountings and prepare their trustee-clients' accountings accordingly, disclosing everything that can be found on the bank and brokerage account statements, the escrow closing statements, the receipts from sales, and the trust's other financial records. These disclosures are sufficient to meet the standards of California Trust Law and those of the Committee on National Fiduciary Accounting Standards, and CPAs who routinely include the above statement in their compilation report do so mistakenly.

This mistake may have serious consequences for the trustee. The statute of limitations on breaches of trust begins to run when a beneficiary receives an account that adequately discloses the existence of a claim. Prob C §16460. Thus, a trustee's accounting fulfills its purpose only if it makes all the disclosures ordinarily included in fiduciary accountings. If the trustee's accounting makes all the necessary disclosures, but the attached report says that the accounting "omits substantially all disclosures ordinarily included in trust financial statements . . . ," the beneficiary who sues the trustee late will have little difficulty persuading a judge that the accounting failed to disclose facts material to the beneficiary's claim and that the statute of limitations therefore has not yet run. In such a case, the trustee may find himself or herself defending an accounting long after the trustee should have been protected by the statute of limitations.

Certified public accountants who prepare their client's trust accountings in the manner recommended by this book may report on those accountings confident they have disclosed everything required by the Report of the Committee on National Fiduciary Accounting Standards and California's Probate Code. These CPAs should not report that their trustee clients have elected to "omit substantially all disclosures ordinarily included in trust financial statements." Instead, these accountants should report as if they have examined all the records necessary to prepare a fiduciary accounting, without forming an opinion on, or offering any assurance as to, whether the trustee has invested in accordance with California's Uniform Prudent Investor Act (Prob C §§16002(a), 16003, 16045-16054). If the accounting is prepared as recommended in this book, such a report would accurately state the level of service provided without offering the parties any assurance of the quality of the trust's economic resources. Moreover, such a report should not delay the running of the statute of limitations on claims against the trustee.

§15.26 F. Countering the Beneficiary's Dismay

Even if the CPA's report does not include the "omits substantially all disclosure" language (see §15.25), unsophisticated beneficiaries who receive accountings accompanied by a compilation report are often shocked and dismayed that the CPA has offered no assurance that the accounting is reliable, true, or accurate. Understanding nothing about the public accountant's duties of professional responsibility, some unsophisticated beneficiaries read the compilation report to mean that the CPA is distancing himself or herself from the accounting because it presents a false picture of the trust administration. To counter this tendency, the fiduciary should deliver the accounting to beneficiaries accompanied by an explanation. Better yet, the fiduciary's attorney may offer an explanation.

Additionally, the fiduciary or his or her attorney should describe the information on which the accountant relied. By so doing, the fiduciary can eliminate the beneficiary's fear that the accountant relied on inadequate information. The authors recommend telling beneficiaries the following:

The accounting of _ _[trustee]_ _ for the period _ _[dates]_ _ was prepared by a Certified Public Accountant who was given, and who relied on, the following information provided by the trustee [for example]:

- Appraisal of _ _[real property, identified by address]_ _ prepared by _ _[appraiser, identified by name]_ _;

- Bank statements from _ _[bank]_ _ for the period beginning _ _[date]_ _ and ending _ _[date]_ _;

- Brokerage account statements from _ _[brokerage]_ _ for the period beginning _ _[date]_ _ and ending _ _[date]_ _;

- Seller's Final Closing Statement dated _ _[date]_ _ for sale of real property commonly known as _ _[address]_ _.

Providing the above information will go a long way toward assuaging the beneficiaries' suspicions, and will not give the beneficiaries information to which they are not already entitled. Trustees and beneficiaries have a common interest in the trust's books and records; these records are deemed a part of the trust estate and "the right of the beneficiaries to an inspection of them stems from their common interest in the property along with the trustee." *Strauss v Superior Court* (1950) 36 C2d 396, 402.

§15.27 VI. SAMPLE ENGAGEMENT LETTER

_ _[Date]_ _

_ _[Name and title]_ _

_ _[Address]_ _

Dear _ _[name]_ _ :

Enclosed are the following:

1. A copy of this letter; and

2. A list of the documents the Fiduciary Accounting Specialist must have before work may begin on the project that is the subject of this letter.

Nature of Agreement

This letter states the terms under which the Fiduciary Accounting Specialist (Accountant) will prepare for _ _[identify the client by name and fiduciary position]_ _ (Fiduciary) a fiduciary accounting for the period beginning _ _[date]_ _ and ending _ _[date]_ _, which accounting will be prepared in a format acceptable to the probate court of _ _[specify]_ _ County. When signed by Fiduciary, this letter will be the contract between Accountant and Fiduciary.

Fiduciary _ _[describe nature of fiduciary role]_ _

EXAMPLE: Fiduciary is the trustee of the April Cash Trust, a trust that became irrevocable on January 1, 2013. Fiduciary is accounting to the Alameda County probate court for the period beginning on that date and ending on June 30, 2013.

Scope of Engagement

From the information Fiduciary will provide, Accountant will (1) organize the data provided, (2) request any data obviously missing, (3) seek clarification of transactions from Fiduciary, and (4) prepare the schedules of account required by Probate Code §§1060–1063, for the period identified above. When the schedules of account are completed, Fiduciary is responsible for reviewing them for accuracy and completeness. The additional services included in this agreement are limited to the following: communications with Fiduciary, and with Fiduciary's attorney and tax or financial accountants; responding to subpoenas for records and/or testimony; and testifying as a material witness if subpoenaed to do so.

Reliance on Fiduciary's Documents and Information

Fiduciary will provide accurate and complete records of all financial transactions for which Fiduciary must account. Fiduciary understands that Accountant will rely on these records to produce the fiduciary accounting. Accountant has no obligation to investigate any financial transaction reported by Fiduciary and no obligation to investigate whether Fiduciary has reported all financial transactions for which Fiduciary is accountable. Accountant will not independently verify the transactions accounted for, but may ask Fiduciary for clarification and additional information, which Fiduciary agrees to promptly provide.

Fiduciary will provide Accountant only with copies of Fiduciary's financial records. Fiduciary will not provide Accountant with the *only* copy of any document. Accountant is not a repository for the books and records Fiduciary may be required to keep, and Fiduciary will not ask Accountant to serve as such.

Time to Completion of Accounting

Within _ _[number of weeks]_ _ of receiving the documents and information requested of Fiduciary, Accountant will review the documents and information and notify Fiduciary of all information that is obviously still missing. Within _ _[number of weeks]_ _ of the date Fiduciary delivers to Accountant the requested missing information, if any, Accountant will complete the first draft of the fiduciary accounting, provided, however, that this deadline may be extended by Accountant's later discovery that information is still missing.

Fiduciary understands that it is Fiduciary's obligation to provide the documents necessary for the preparation of the accounting. Fiduciary further understands that without these documents, Accountant may be unable to start Accountant's work and certainly cannot finish that work. Fiduciary therefore agrees that if Fiduciary delays providing to Accountant the information requested in this letter or any information later requested, Accountant may delay completion of the project that is the subject of this agreement.

Fees and Deposit

For the services covered by this agreement, Accountant will bill in one-quarter-hour increments and Fiduciary will pay, according to the rate schedule below.

Timekeeper 1 (*e.g.*, attorney)	$_ _[amount]_ _
Timekeeper 2 (*e.g.*, paralegal)	$_ _[amount]_ _

Accountant will increase the above rates on January 1 of each year by 3 percent. Fiduciary agrees to pay the increased rates, without prior notice.

Fiduciary will deposit $1500 with Accountant and Accountant will hold this amount for payment of Accountant's final invoice. Accountant will invoice Fiduciary after the close of any month in which Accountant has provided Fiduciary with services. All invoices are due on receipt. If Fiduciary has not paid an invoice within 30 days of the date it was mailed to Fiduciary, Accountant may apply the deposit to the invoice and cease working on Fiduciary's behalf. In the event of such a work stoppage, Accountant will resume work only after Fiduciary has replenished the deposit and paid any amount of the invoice still outstanding. When Accountant has finished the services required by this agreement, Accountant will send Fiduciary a final invoice, wait 10 days for Fiduciary to review the invoice, then apply the deposit to the invoice and refund to Fiduciary the excess of the deposit over the invoice. If the deposit is smaller than Accountant's final invoice, Fiduciary shall pay Accountant the difference between the final invoice and the deposit.

Limits on Engagement

In a fiduciary accounting that will be submitted to the court for approval, Fiduciary must state the market value of the assets on hand at the end of the accounting period. (Probate Code §1063(a).) Except for cash, cash equivalents, and those securities for which market values are readily available, Accountant will obtain from Fiduciary the market values of each asset on hand at the end of the accounting period. It is Fiduciary's responsibility to obtain appraisals of assets for which an appraisal is required.

Accountant will not contact any financial institutions on Fiduciary's behalf and is not responsible for collecting data from any source other than Fiduciary.

This agreement is not an agreement to serve as an expert witness and if Fiduciary's attorney wishes to hire Accountant for such services, a separate agreement would be required.

Accountant is not a certified public accountant and Fiduciary has not engaged Accountant to audit, review, or compile a financial statement. Neither has Fiduciary engaged Accountant to prepare any tax returns. For the preparation of tax returns, Accountant will engage _ _[name]_ _, or such other person as Accountant may choose.

Accountant is not an attorney and Fiduciary has not engaged Accountant to provide legal advice. If Fiduciary has powers exercisable in Fiduciary's discretion, for guidance regarding the exercise of these powers, Fiduciary will rely on the advice of _ _[name of attorney]_ _, or on the advice of another attorney of Fiduciary's choosing. Similarly, if Fiduciary seeks guidance regarding the performance of any duties, or regarding liability for the exercise of any powers, Fiduciary will seek the counsel of a person licensed to practice law by the State Bar of California.

Termination

Fiduciary may terminate this engagement at any time and for any or no reason, by notifying Accountant of the termination in writing. On termination, Fiduciary will pay for all services rendered by Accountant and will reimburse Accountant for any expenses incurred by Accountant, through the date and time Accountant receives notice of the termination.

Accountant may terminate this engagement for cause, including Fiduciary's failure to provide Accountant with the information necessary for the performance of this contract. Fiduciary's failure to pay fees and reimburse expenses is also cause for Accountant to terminate this engagement.

File Retention

Accountant will retain a copy of the completed fiduciary accounting for _ _[number of years]_ _ and then will destroy the accounting in Accountant's regular course of business. Accountant, at Accountant's discretion, may or may not retain the documents Accountant will rely on to prepare the fiduciary accounting. Fiduciary is not relying on Accountant to preserve these documents and understands that Accountant may destroy them in the regular course of business. When Accountant destroys the completed fiduciary accounting and any related documents, Accountant will do so without first contacting Fiduciary. Knowing this, Fiduciary will not rely on Accountant to preserve those records Fiduciary might later need.

Communication With Others

Fiduciary agrees that Accountant may discuss Accountant's work, the Fiduciary's books and records, and information gathered in the process of preparing the accounting with the following people: Fiduciary's attorney, Fiduciary's tax accountant, Fiduciary's certified public accountant.

Conclusion

Fiduciary is reminded that this is a contract and is encouraged to discuss its terms with his or her attorney. This letter should be read carefully before Fiduciary signs it. Accountant will not perform any services for Fiduciary until Fiduciary returns the signed contract, pays to Accountant the deposit identified above, and provides Accountant with the documents identified on the list enclosed with this letter.

Very truly yours,

ACCOUNTANT

I agree to the terms of this contract.

Date: _ _ _ _ _ _   __[Signature]__
                             _ _[Typed name]_ _
                             FIDUCIARY

§15.28 VII. LIST OF DOCUMENTS NEEDED TO PREPARE FIDUCIARY ACCOUNTING

The following is a list of documents needed to prepare a fiduciary accounting:

- Every bank statement for every bank account, beginning the month before the beginning date of the fiduciary accounting;
- Every brokerage account statement for every brokerage account, beginning the month before the beginning date of the fiduciary accounting;
- Copies of all canceled checks that cleared any fiduciary account during the account period;

- The income tax return for the period before the period accounted for;
- Any tax returns filed during the period of the fiduciary accounting;
- All confirmations of sales and purchases of financial assets during the account period;
- Copies of all bills, invoices, and receipts;
- Deposit records, including the following information for each deposit:
  - The payor;
  - The purpose of each payment deposited;
  - The amount of each deposit; and
  - The date of the deposit;

  NOTE▶ If multiple items are deposited simultaneously, the fiduciary must be able to identify each individual deposit with the particularity described just above.
- A list of every asset administered;
- A description of all transactions the purpose of which, and the parties thereto, would not be obvious from the financial paperwork; and
- All other statements of financial activity during the period of the account.

§15.29 VIII. CHART: ALLOCATION OF RECEIPTS AND DISBURSEMENTS UNDER CALIFORNIA UNIFORM PRINCIPAL AND INCOME ACT

Description	Probate Code Section	Principal	Income
RECEIPTS			
From Entities:			
Money, except as otherwise provided in Prob C §16350(c)–(f) (see below)	16350(b)		100%
Property other than money	16350(c)(1)	100%	
Money received for interest in entity	16350(c)–(d)	100%	
Interest	16357		100%
Dividends accrued before death	16346(a)	100%	
Dividends after death	16346(b)		100%
Capital gain dividends from regulated investment companies or real estate investment trusts	16350(b)(4)	100%	
Sales proceeds, including capital gains	16355(b)	100%	
Debt Instruments:			
Amount received for prepaying principal	16357(a)		100%
On obligations maturing after 1 year, sales amount received, including premium over value	16357(b)	100%	
On obligations maturing within 1 year, difference between cost and maturity	16357(b)		100%
Interest accrued before death	16346(a)	100%	
Interest after death	16346(b), 16357(a)		100%
Derivatives:			
Rights	16366(b)	100%	
Options	16366(c)	100%	

Description	Probate Code Section	Principal	Income
Payments from "Separate Fund" (annuity, IRA, or pension, profit sharing, stock bonus or stock ownership plan):			
Note: If the allocation between income and principal under §16361 is insubstantial, all may be allocated to principal. Prob C §16360.			
Payments to marital deduction qualifying trust (QTIP trust) other than payments from qualified survivor annuities if trust would not qualify under §16361(b)–(c):	16361(d) 16361(e)		
If documentation from payor reflects internal income of separate fund	16361(f)	Balance	Amount of internal income
If no documentation from payor reflects internal income of separate fund	16361(g)		4% of fund value; or product of interest rate and present value of future payments per IRC §7520
Payments not to marital deduction qualifying trust from separate fund and all other payments:	16361(a)		
Portion of payment characterized as interest or dividends, or in lieu thereof	16361(b)	Balance	100% of such portion
No part of payment characterized as interest or dividend or equivalent payment:			
When all or part of payment is required to be made	16361(c)	90%	10%
When no part of payment is required to be made	16361(c)	100%	

Description	Probate Code Section	Principal	Income
When payment is entire amount to which trustee is entitled	16361(c)	100%	
Mineral & Natural Resources Interests:			
Nominal rental	16363(a)(1)		100%
Production payment (no factor for interest)	16363(a)(2)	100%	
Royalty (more than nominal)	16363(a)(3)	90%	10%
Other mineral payment	16363(a)(4)	90%	10%
Water:			
Payment for renewable water interest	16363(b)		100%
Payment for nonrenewable water interest	16363(b)	90%	10%
Timber:			
Payments for renewal timber	16364(a)(1)		100%
Payments for timber exceeding growth rate	16364(a)(2)	100%	
Real Estate (not accounted for as a business):			
Rents	16356		100%
Amount received for cancellation or renewal of lease	16356		100%
Rental deposits	16356	100%	
Eminent domain proceeds	16355(d)	100%	
Insurance Policies:			
Dividends if premiums paid from principal	16358(a)	100%	
Dividends if premiums paid from income	16358(a)		100%
Proceeds of insurance policies in general	16358(a)	100%	
Proceeds of insurance policies insuring against loss of occupancy or use by income beneficiary, loss of income, or loss of profits (if not accounted for separately as business)	16358(b)		100%

Description	Probate Code Section	Principal	Income
Other Receipts:			
Reimbursement not based on lost income	16355(c)	100%	
Net income if there is no income beneficiary	16355(e)	100%	
Liquidating assets (if no reserve)	16362	90%	10%
DISBURSEMENTS			
Administration Expenses:			
Investment advisor fees	16370(a), 16371(a)(1)	50%	50%
Custody fees	16370(a), 16371(a)(1)	50%	50%
Accounting fees	16370(b), 16371(a)(1)	50%	50%
Proceedings affecting both income and principal	16370(b), 16371(a)(1)	50%	50%
Proceedings and matters primarily concerning income	16370(c)		100%
Proceedings and matters primarily concerning principal, including proceedings construing or protecting trust	16371(a)(4)	100%	
Taxes:			
Tax on income	16374(a)		100%
Tax on gain	16374(b)	100%	
Estate tax and penalties	16371(a)(6)	100%	
Regularly recurring taxes assessed against principal	16370(c)		100%
Real Estate-Related Expenses:			
Sales expenses	16371(a)(2)	100%	
Ordinary repairs	16370(c)		100%
Principal portion of mortgage payments	16371(a)(3)	100%	
Interest portion of mortgage payments	16370(c)	100%	

Description	Probate Code Section	Principal	Income
Casualty insurance premiums	16370(d)		100%
Contamination-related expenses	16371(a)(7)	100%	
Property taxes	16370(c)	100%	

NOTE▶ Discretionary adjustments between principal and income may be possible if all provisions of Prob C §16336 are complied with. Examples of other transfers from income to principal are for assets subject to depreciation (see Prob C §16372) and capital improvements (see Prob C §16373).

Table of Statutes, Regulations, and Rules

CALIFORNIA

Constitution

Art VI
   21: §14.29

Statutes

BUSINESS AND PROFESSIONS CODE
   6069: §15.1

CODE OF CIVIL PROCEDURE
   1: §14.28
   21–23: §14.28
   128(a)(2): §14.4
   177.5: §14.37
   638: §§14.28–14.29
   638–642.5: §14.28
   638–645.2: §14.28
   639: §14.28
   639(a)(1): §14.28
   639(a)(2): §14.28
   639(a)(3): §14.28
   639(a)(4): §14.28
   639(a)(5): §14.28
   640(b): §14.28
   645: §14.28
   645.1: §14.28
   685.010: §9.32
   1775–1775.15: §14.27
   2016.010–2036.050: §2.53
   2084 (former): §2.53

EVIDENCE CODE
   730: §§14.26, 14.31
   731(c): §14.31
   953(c): §14.7
   954: §14.7
   954(c): §14.7
   1115–1128: §14.27
   1122: §14.27

FAMILY CODE
   297.5: §9.23
   297.5(c): §§9.8, 9.23, 9.25

PROBATE CODE
   Art 5.1: §6.8
   Art 5.2: §6.8
      Chap 2, Pt 4, Div 9: §6.16
   Art 5.3: §6.8
   Chap 2, Pt 6, Div 11: §9.23
   Chap 3, Pt 4, Div 9: §6.16
   Chap 8, Pt 10, Div 7: §9.32
   Pt 4, Div 9: §9.8
   Pt 4, Div 11: §§9.8, 9.17, 9.29
   Pt 6, Div 11: §9.8
   Div 7: §4.6
   Div 8: §4.6
   Div 10: §§8.13, 9.8, 9.22, 9.33
   4: §8.17
   24: §2.44
   58: §2.6
   84: §2.45
   249.5: §9.16
   249.5(c): §9.16
   400–453: §14.28
   800: §14.11
   812: §2.61
   825: §14.20
   850(a)(1)(D): §2.3
   1002: §14.40
   1003: §14.32
   1051: §14.3
   1060: §§2.72, 4.11, 4.15, 7.5
   1060–1061: §15.18
   1060–1063: §§2.22, 15.27
   1060–1064: §§2.16, 2.62, 2.66, 2.71, 4.5, 6.16, 14.24
   1060(a): §4.15
   1060(a)(1): §§2.30, 4.15
   1061: §§5.1, 6.1
   1061–1062: §§6.3, 8.1, 8.26
   1061–1064: §§2.72, 4.15, 7.5
   1061(a)(1): §§2.9, 4.4–4.5, 4.11, 4.15–4.16, 4.31, 5.5
   1061(a)(2): §5.7

1061(a)(3): §6.1
1061(a)(4): §13.4
1061(a)(8): §13.4
1061(a)(10): §§4.1, 4.15-4.16, 4.31, 10.10, 12.4, 12.7
1061(b): §§7.2, 12.2
1061(c): §§1.1, 12.1
1062: §§4.10, 12.2
1062(a): §§2.71, 6.1-6.3
1062(b): §§2.72, 8.6
1062(d): §6.2
1062(e): §§2.72, 9.4
1062(f): §7.5
1063: §§2.72, 4.17, 11.1, 12.2
1063(a): §§10.10, 11.2, 15.27
1063(b): §§3.8, 4.28, 6.52, 8.28, 11.3, 11.16
1063(c): §11.6
1063(d): §11.7
1063(e): §11.8
1063(f): §11.5
1063(g): §§4.22, 11.9, 15.18
1063(h): §§2.9, 6.49, 11.10
1064: §2.22
1213: §14.38
1220: §2.41
1300-1304: §§14.15-4.17
1310-1312: §14.16
1460: §2.25
1500: §2.2
1501: §2.2
1510: §2.2
1514: §2.2
1514(c): §2.2
1514(d): §2.2
1600(a): §§2.15, 10.2
1601: §10.2
1800.3: §2.3
1821: §2.3
1860: §10.2
1860(a): §2.15
1870-1871: §2.3
2255(a): §2.10
2255(b): §2.10
2256: §2.14
2300: §4.4
2310: §4.4
2400-2595: §2.3
2401: §4.26
2420-2423: §2.3
2457: §2.3
2459: §2.3

2462: §2.3
2467: §2.15
2580: §2.3
2600(b): §2.9
2610: §§2.9, 4.9, 4.15
2610(a): §§2.9, 4.4, 4.15
2610(c): §4.13
2620: §§2.24-2.25, 2.72, 15.25
2620(a): §§2.11-2.12, 2.17, 10.2
2620(b): §§2.15, 10.2
2620(c)(2): §2.23
2620(c)(3): §2.23
2620(c)(4)-(5): §2.23
2620.2: §2.24
2621: §§2.3, 2.25
2622: §2.25
2622.5: §8.7
2627: §10.2
2628(b): §2.26
2630: §10.2
2632(b): §2.13
2632(c): §2.13
2828(a): §2.26
4230: §2.4
4236: §2.4
4236(b): §2.4
6042(c): §9.16
6335: §13.16
6401-6402: §9.16
6401(a): §9.16
6402(a): §9.16
6402(b): §9.16
6402(c): §9.16
6402(d): §9.16
6402(e): §9.16
6402(f): §9.16
6406: §9.16
6407: §9.16
6450(a): §9.16
6451: §9.16
7000: §4.18
7000-7001: §6.46
7001: §2.5
8540: §2.6
8545: §2.6
8546(c): §2.30
8800: §§2.30, 4.9
8800-8802: §4.5
8800(b): §2.6
8802: §4.15
8850: §2.30
8850-8873: §2.31

8850(a): §2.30
8901: §§2.30, 4.13
8902: §4.13
8940(b): §2.30
9650: §4.26
9650(c): §§9.1, 11.5
9760: §14.7
10800(b): §§1.7, 8.28, 11.16
10810(b): §§2.40, 3.8
10900: §4.5
10901: §2.37
10902: §§2.31, 4.5
10950: §2.33
10950-10951: §15.25
10950-10954: §2.38
10951: §2.32
10951-10953: §2.72
10952: §§2.34, 10.3
10953: §14.22
10953(b): §2.35
10953(c): §§2.35-2.36
10954: §§2.39, 15.25
10954(c): §2.40
10954(c)(1): §2.40
11000: §§2.5, 2.41
11003(b): §8.7
11051(a): §2.38
11051(b): §2.38
11700: §9.8
11754: §8.2
12000: §§9.26, 9.32
12000-12007: §§9.26, 9.32, 9.36
12002: §§9.27, 9.29, 9.31, 11.7
12002(b): §9.27
12002(c): §§9.29-9.30
12003: §§9.32, 9.36, 11.8
12003-12005: §11.8
12004: §11.8
12005: §11.8
13000-13660: §10.2
15200: §4.6
15202: §4.6
15206: §4.6
15209: §2.8
15600: §4.8
15644: §2.55
15800: §§2.43, 2.69
15800(b): §§2.67-2.68
16000: §§1.9, 2.45, 2.48, 2.50
16000-16015: §9.8
16002: §2.48
16002(a): §§2.43, 8.6, 15.25

16003: §§1.9, 2.48, 13.5, 15.25
16004: §2.48
16004(a): §§4.27, 8.6
16004.5: §2.63
16004.5(b)(1): §2.63
16005: §2.48
16006: §§2.48, 4.10, 4.15, 4.28, 8.6
16007: §§2.48, 4.10
16009: §§1.9, 2.48, 2.55, 4.10
16010: §§2.48, 4.26-4.27
16011: §2.48
16012: §2.48
16014: §2.48
16045-16054: §§2.48, 7.16, 8.8, 13.5, 15.25
16047(b): §7.16
16060: §§2.44, 2.48, 2.52, 4.10
  Comment: §2.52
16060-16064: §2.45
16060-16105: §4.8
16061: §§2.44, 2.46, 2.51, 4.10
  Comment: §2.51
16061(a)(5): §§7.5-7.6
16061(c): §§7.5-7.6
16062: §§2.45-2.46, 2.50, 2.68, 6.50
16062(a): §§2.44, 2.50, 2.68, 10.4
16062(e): §9.35
16063: §§2.71-2.72, 4.10, 7.5-7.6
16063(a): §§2.56, 8.1, 8.6
16063(a)(1): §§2.71, 4.22, 6.1
16063(a)(2): §§2.65, 2.71
16063(a)(3): §§2.65, 2.71
16063(a)(4): §§2.65, 2.71
16063(a)(5): §§2.65, 2.71
16063(a)(6): §§2.57, 2.65, 2.71, 15.12
16063(b): §2.66
16064(a): §2.47
16064(b): §§2.48, 2.68
16068(b): §2.51
16069: §2.56
16069(b): §2.45
16226: §7.16
16247: §2.72
16312(b)(2): §13.16
16312(b)(11): §13.16
16320: §5.7
16320-16375: §§1.1, 2.4, 2.56, 2.72, 4.6, 4.20, 5.7, 6.8, 6.10-6.11, 6.16, 6.31, 6.38, 6.41, 7.8, 7.16, 8.12, 9.2, 9.26-9.27, 9.31, 9.34, 10.4, 11.12, 13.1, 13.5

16322: §§2.56, 7.14, 10.4
16324: §§2.56, 6.8, 13.16
16325: §11.6
16328: §2.56
16335: §§5.7, 6.8, 9.2, 13.1
16335(a)(3): §2.56
16335(b): §§6.44, 13.1, 13.17
16336: §§1.1, 6.44, 7.16, 13.7-13.9, 13.11, 15.29
16336(a): §§13.1, 13.12
16336(a)(1)-(2): §6.44
16336(a)(1)-(3): §13.6
16336(a)(3): §§6.44, 13.6
16336(b): §6.27
16336(b)(1): §13.7
16336(b)(2): §13.7
16336(b)(3): §13.7
16336(b)(4): §13.7
16336(b)(5): §13.7
16336(b)(6): §13.7
16336(b)(7): §13.7
16336(b)(8): §13.7
16336(c): §13.7
16336(g): §13.8
16336(h): §13.8
16336.4: §13.7
16336.4-16336.6: §7.16
16336.4(b)(1): §13.1
16336.4(e)(2): §13.1
16336.5: §13.7
16336.6: §13.1
16337: §13.9
16338: §13.9
16339: §§4.18, 5.7
16340: §§8.8, 8.16, 9.26-9.27, 9.31, 9.36
  Comment: §§4.7, 8.15, 9.31
16340(a): §§6.45, 9.27, 9.33
16340(a)(1): §§9.27-9.28
16340(a)(2): §9.31
16340(b): §§9.26, 9.32-9.33, 9.36
16340(c): §8.15
16340(c)(1): §9.33
16340(c)(2): §§1.30, 8.13-8.14, 8.20, 9.33
16340(c)(2)-(3): §§1.30, 8.13
16340(c)(3): §9.33
16340(d): §11.8
16340(f): §9.27
16341(a): §9.33
16341(b): §9.33
16341(c): §9.33

16345: §§1.1, 4.6-4.7, 4.20
16345(b): §§4.20, 5.7
16345(b)(1): §4.6
16345(b)(2): §5.4
16345(b)(3): §4.6
16345(c): §§4.6, 4.20, 10.4
16345(d): §4.20
16346: §4.28
16346(a): §§4.20, 15.29
16346(b): §15.29
16347: §4.21
16350: §§4.20, 6.8, 6.42, 6.44
  Comment: §6.11
16350-16367: §6.16
16350(a)(1): §6.9
16350(b): §§6.9, 13.2, 15.29
16350(b)(4): §15.29
16350(c): §6.9
16350(c)-(d): §15.29
16350(c)-(f): §15.29
16350(c)(1): §§6.10, 15.29
16350(c)(2): §6.10
16350(c)(3): §6.10
16350(c)(4): §§6.10-6.11
16350(d): §6.10
16351: §§4.18, 5.7, 6.13
16352: §§6.21, 13.2, 13.4, 13.14
16352(b): §§6.14, 13.4
16352(c): §§6.34, 13.3
16352(c)(7): §6.42
16353-16358: §6.16
16355: §7.9
16355(a): §§4.18, 6.16
16355(b): §§6.16, 7.8-7.9, 7.12, 11.13, 15.29
16355(c): §§6.16, 15.29
16355(d): §§6.16, 15.29
16355(e): §§6.16, 15.29
16355(f): §6.16
16356: §§1.27, 4.18, 4.29, 6.17, 13.2, 15.29
16357: §§6.6, 6.21, 7.10, 7.12, 13.5, 15.29
  Comment: §§6.19, 7.10
16357(a): §§4.19, 6.18, 6.25, 15.29
16357(b): §§7.11, 15.29
16357(c): §§6.20, 7.10
16358: §§4.18-4.19, 6.21, 6.24-6.26, 7.15
16358(a): §15.29
16358(b): §15.29
16358(c): §6.21

16360: §§6.8, 6.27, 15.29
  Comment: §6.27
16360-16367: §6.16
16361: §§6.20-6.21, 6.27-6.30, 6.33, 7.10, 15.29
16361(a): §15.29
16361(b): §§6.29, 15.29
16361(b)-(c): §15.29
16361(c): §§6.29-6.30, 15.29
16361(d): §15.29
16361(e): §§6.30, 15.29
16361(f): §§6.30, 6.31, 15.29
16361(g): §§6.32, 15.29
16362: §§6.20, 6.27, 6.33, 7.10, 15.29
16362(a): §6.33
16362(b): §6.33
16363: §§6.20, 6.27, 6.33-6.34, 7.10
  Comment: §6.34
16363-16364: §7.9
16363(a)(1): §§6.35, 6.37, 15.29
16363(a)(2): §§6.36-6.37, 15.29
16363(a)(3): §§6.37, 15.29
16363(a)(4): §§6.37, 15.29
16363(b): §§6.35, 6.37, 15.29
16363(d): §§6.38, 6.41
16364: §§6.20, 6.27, 6.39, 7.10
16364(a): §6.39
16364(a)(1): §§6.40, 15.29
16364(a)(2): §§6.40, 15.29
16364(a)(3): §6.40
16364(b): §6.39
16364(c): §6.39
16365: §§7.16, 13.10-13.12
16366: §§6.20, 6.42, 7.10
16366-16367: §6.15
16366(b): §15.29
16366(c): §§7.13, 11.12, 15.29
16367: §§6.20, 6.27, 7.10
16367(b): §6.43
16367(c): §§6.43, 7.14
16370: §9.31
16370-16371: §§8.15, 8.17
16370(a): §§8.17, 15.29
16370(b): §§8.17, 15.29
16370(c): §§8.15, 8.19, 8.21, 8.23-8.24, 13.17, 15.29
16370(d): §§8.18, 8.23, 15.29
16371: §9.31
16371(a)(1): §§8.17, 15.29
16371(a)(2): §§8.18, 8.23, 15.29
16371(a)(3): §§8.23-8.24, 15.29
16371(a)(4): §§8.18, 8.23, 15.29
16371(a)(5): §8.18
16371(a)(6): §§8.13, 8.20, 15.29
16371(a)(7): §§8.23, 15.29
16372: §§13.13, 15.29
16372(a): §13.14
16372(b): §§13.14-13.15
16372(b)-(c): §13.15
16373: §§13.15, 13.17, 15.29
16373(a): §13.17
16373(b): §13.17
16373(b)(1): §13.17
16373(b)(2): §13.17
16373(b)(3): §13.17
16374: §§8.22, 13.18-13.19
16374(a): §15.29
16374(b): §15.29
16374(c): §8.22
16374(c)(4): §8.22
16374(d): §13.18
16374.5: §§9.2, 9.34
16374.9(d): §9.34
16375: §§1.1, 9.34, 13.19
16375(a): §§8.22, 13.19
16375(b): §§13.19-13.20
16400: §2.55
16403: §4.8
16430: §9.31
16440: §2.55
16460: §§2.57, 2.70, 2.72, 15.12, 15.25
16460(a): §2.68
16460(b)(2): §2.68
16461: §2.58
16461(c): §2.58
16461(c)-(d): §2.58
16461(d): §2.58
16464: §§2.60, 2.63
16464(b): §2.60
16464(b)(1): §2.61
16464(b)(2): §§2.60, 2.62
16464(b)(4): §2.64
16500-16504: §13.9
16503(b): §13.9
17200: §§2.3, 2.65, 2.71, 13.9, 15.23
17200(a)(4): §9.8
17200(a)(7)(B): §2.51
17200(b)(5): §§2.59, 2.66
17200(b)(7): §2.46
17200(b)(7)(A): §2.46

17200(b)(7)(C): §§2.46, 2.50
17202: §2.66
17203: §2.59
17211: §8.7
20100: §9.33
20100-20225: §§9.8, 9.22
20110: §9.22
20210: §9.22
21043: §9.39
21111
   Comment: §9.18
21111(b): §9.18
21117(a): §9.10
21117(b): §9.11
21117(c): §9.12
21117(d): §9.13
21117(e): §9.14
21117(f): §9.15
21118: §9.13
21120: §9.15
21131: §9.20
21134: §9.20
21350.5: §2.47
21380: §2.65
21380(a)(1)-(4): §2.47
21380(a)(1)-(a)(4): §2.47
21400: §§9.8, 9.19-9.20, 9.29
21400-21401: §9.9
21400-21406: §§9.8, 9.17, 9.19, 9.26, 9.29, 9.31
21401: §§9.29, 9.32
21402(a)(2): §9.19
21402(a)(3): §§9.19, 9.32
21402(a)(4): §9.19
21402(a)(5): §9.19
21402(a)(6): §9.19
21402(b): §9.16
21403: §9.19
21403(b): §9.19
21404: §9.20
21405: §9.19
21405(a): §§9.19, 9.21
21405(b): §9.21
21600-21623: §9.23
21600-21700: §9.8
21610: §9.23
21610-21623: §§9.8, 9.23
21612(a): §9.25
21612(b): §9.25
21620-21623: §9.24
21623(a): §9.25
21623(b): §9.25

REVENUE AND TAXATION CODE
19282-19283 (former): §14.10

WELFARE AND INSTITUTIONS CODE
15600-15675: §14.18

ACTS BY POPULAR NAME
Civil Discovery Act: §2.53
Elder Abuse and Dependent Adult Civil Protection Act (EADACPA): §14.18
Uniform Principal and Income Act (UPAIA): §§1.1, 1.30, 2.4, 2.56, 4.6-4.7, 4.20, 5.7, 6.8, 6.10-6.11, 6.16, 6.20, 6.31, 6.38, 6.41, 7.9, 7.14, 7.16, 8.12, 8.22, 9.2, 9.27-9.29, 9.31, 9.34, 10.4, 11.12, 13.1, 13.5, 13.17
   Art 5.1: §7.8
   Art 5.2: §7.8
   Art 5.3: §7.8
Uniform Prudent Investor Act (UPIA): §§2.48, 2.54, 7.16, 15.25

SESSION LAWS
Stats 2010, ch 621, §11: §2.46

Rules

CALIFORNIA RULES OF COURT
2.30: §14.37
2.816(e): §14.29
3.907: §14.28
3.922: §14.28
3.931: §14.28
7.10: §14.3
7.101(a): §4.9
7.575(b): §2.18
7.575(b)(3): §2.21
7.575(b)(4): §2.21
7.575(e)(2): §2.20
7.575(f): §2.22
7.757(e)(2)(A): §2.20
7.757(e)(2)(B): §2.20
7.757(e)(2)(C): §2.20
7.902: §2.66
7.1007: §2.27

CALIFORNIA RULES OF PROFESSIONAL CONDUCT
5-210: §14.5

CODE OF JUDICIAL ETHICS
Canon 3(B): §14.3
Canon 3(d)(2): §14.4

Local Court Rules

ALAMEDA COURT RULES
7.780(a): §2.11

CONTRA COSTA COURT RULES
806(b): §10.2
825.A: §2.11

UNITED STATES

Statutes

INTERNAL REVENUE CODE
643(e)(3): §13.19
645: §13.19
651: §13.18
661: §13.18
663(b): §13.19
2056: §7.16
2056(b): §13.10
2056(b)(5): §§6.28–6.30
2056(b)(7): §§6.28–6.30
7520: §§6.32, 15.29

ACTS BY POPULAR NAME
Uniform Principal and Income Act (UPAIA): §§7.16, 9.31
§506
    Comment: §13.20
Uniform Principal and Income Act of 1997
§201: §9.31
Uniform Principal and Income Act of 1962
§12: §7.16
Uniform Principal and Income Act of 1931
§11: §7.16

Regulations

TREASURY REGULATIONS
1.661(a)-2(f): §9.6
20.2056(b)-5(f)(4): §§7.16, 13.10
20.2056(c)-2(b)(1)(iii): §7.16

Table of Cases

A

Arluk Medical Center Industrial Group v Dobler (2004) 116 CA4th 1324: §2.43

B

Barnes, Estate of (1965) 63 C2d 580: §9.15
Beach, Estate of (1975) 15 C3d 623: §2.5
Bissinger, Estate of (1964) 60 C2d 756: §2.57
Borre v State Bar (1991) 52 C3d 1047: §14.28

C

Charlisse C., In re (2008) 45 C4th 145: §14.4
Coberly v Superior Court (1965) 231 CA2d 685: §2.57
Conservatorship of Hume (2006) 139 CA4th 393: §§2.9, 5.6
Conservatorship of Lefkowitz (1996) 50 CA4th 1310: §2.5
Conservatorship of O'Connor (1996) 48 C4th 1076: §14.11
Conservatorship of Ramirez (2001) 90 CA4th 390: §14.36

D

Department of Motor Vehicles v Superior Court (1969) 271 CA2d 770: §14.28
Donahue v Donahue (2010) 182 CA4th 259: §14.31

E

Eddy v Fields (2004) 121 CA4th 1543: §14.7
Esslinger v Cummins (2006) 144 CA4th 517: §§2.46, 2.50-2.51
Estate of _____ (see name of party)

G

Gerber, Estate of (1977) 73 CA3d 96: §14.38
Getty v Getty (1988) 205 CA3d 134: §14.8
Giraldin, Estate of (2012) 55 C4th 1058: §§2.67-2.69
Giraldin, Estate of (2011) 199 CA4th 577: §2.69
Greenspan v LADT LLC (2010) 191 CA4th 486: §14.21
Grothe v Cortlandt (1992) 11 CA4th 1313: §9.42
Gunter v Janes (1858) 9 C 643: §§2.55, 6.50

H

HLC Properties, Ltd. v Superior Court (2005) 35 C4th 54: §14.7
Hammer, Estate of (1993) 19 CA4th 1621: §14.35
Hasso v Hasso (2007) 148 CA4th 329: §6.10
Houston Gen. Ins. Co. v Superior Court (1980) 108 CA3d 958: §14.6
Hume, Conservatorship of (2006) 139 CA4th 393: §§2.9, 5.6
Hundal, People v (2008) 168 CA4th 965: §14.37

I

Ideal Packing Co. v Brice (1944) 132 CA2d 582: §14.28
In re Charlisse C. (2008) 45 C4th 145: §14.4
In re James F. (2008) 42 C4th 901: §14.32

J

James F., In re (2008) 42 C4th 901: §14.32
Jeld-Wen, Inc. v Superior Court (2007) 146 C4th 536: §14.27
Johnson v Kotyck (1999) 76 CA4th 83: §§2.67, 2.70

K

Kasperbauer v Fairfield (2009) 171 CA4th 229: §2.57
Kenan v Commissioner (2d Cir 1940) 114 F2d 217: §9.6
Kenny v Citizens Nat. Trust & Sav. Bank of L.A. (1954) 269 P2d 641: §14.23
Kobida v Hinkelmann (1942) 53 CA2d 186: §§2.55, 4.30

L

Lefkowitz, Conservatorship of (1996) 50 CA4th 1310: §2.5

M

Manson v Shepherd (2010) 188 CA4th 1244: §6.10
McLaughlin, Estate of (1954) 43 C2d 462: §15.12
Meinhard v Salmon (NY App 1928) 249 NY 458, 164 NE 545: §14.1
Miller v Superior Court (1977) 71 CA3d 145: §14.10
Moeller v Superior Court (1997) 16 C4th 1124: §§14.7, 14.10

O

O'Connor, Conservatorship of (1996) 48 C4th 1076: §14.11

P

People v Hundal (2008) 168 CA4th 965: §14.37
Plumer, Estate of (1958) 159 CA2d 389: §9.15
Portico Mgmt. Group, LLC v Harrison (2011) 202 CA4th 464: §14.21

Q

Quinn, Estate of (1955) 43 C2d 785: §14.28

R

Ramirez, Conservatorship of (2001) 90 CA4th 390: §14.36
Roberts, Estate of (1942) 49 CA2d 71: §14.28
Robinson v Fair (1888) 128 US 53: §14.28
Russell, Estate of (1968) 69 C2d 200: §9.15

S

Salter v Lerner (2009) 176 CA4th 1184: §2.52
Schlyen v Schlyen (1954) 43 C2d 361: §14.13
Schnabel v Superior Court (1993) 5 C4th 704: §14.10
Schwartz v Labow (2008) 164 CA4th 417: §2.66
Settlemire v Superior Court (2003) 105 CA4th 666: §14.28
Stahl v Wells Fargo Bank (1998) 63 CA4th 396: §13.16
Stauffer, Estate of (1959) 53 C2d 124: §9.18
Stine v Dell'Osso (2014) 230 CA4th 834: §15.6
Stoddart, Estate of (2004) 115 C4th 1118: §14.15
Strauss v Superior Court (1950) 36 C2d 396: §§2.53, 2.55, 14.9, 15.26

T

Torres v Friedman (1985) 169 CA3d 880: §14.32
Trynin, Estate of (1989) 49 C3d 868: §14.40

V

Van Sloten v State Bar (1989) 48 C3d 921: §14.28

W

Webb v Standard Oil Co. (1957) 49 C2d 509: §14.10
Wells Fargo Bank v Superior Court (Boltwood) (2000) 22 C4th 201: §§2.54, 14.7, 14.10
Williams v Superior Court (2007) 147 CA4th 36: §14.32

Z

Ziegler v Bonnell (1942) 52 CA2d 217: §9.42

Table of Forms

Additions to trust schedule, 5.8
Assets on hand at beginning of account period
    Failing to recognize thing is an asset, 4.34
    Using negative numbers, 4.33
Assets on hand at end of account period
    Sample assets on hand—end of period schedule (cash, equities, corporate bonds, mutual funds, a limited partnership, and personal property), 10.12
    Sample assets on hand—end of period schedule (cash, real estate, and receivables), 10.11
Auxiliary schedules
    Spreadsheet illustrating sale price equal to asset's carry value, 11.17
    Spreadsheet showing payments of principal from a debtor to trust, 11.18
    Spreadsheets showing liabilities
        Spreadsheet accounting for tenant security deposit, 11.21
        Spreadsheet showing increase in liabilities, 11.22
    Spreadsheets showing transactions affecting an asset's carry value
        Disbursement of funds to improve real property, 11.20
        Purchase of bond and reinvestment of dividends, 11.19
Disbursements
    Amounts disbursed in escrow, 8.30
    Debts associated with a decedent's death paid from principal, 8.31
    Disbursement of funds to improve real property, 11.20
    Expenses associated with real property, 8.32
    Loan payments, payments on trust debts, 8.33
    Receipts related to real property, 8.29
    Sample complete disbursement schedules
        Disbursements from the cash trust, 8.4
        Disbursements from the real estate trust, 8.5
Distributions
    Accounting for the accrual of interest on a general pecuniary gift, 9.44
    Expenses and receipts applicable to a specific gift, 9.43
Engagement letter (sample), 15.27
Gains and losses
    Gains on sales or other dispositions, 7.19
    Insurance proceeds, 7.20
    Sales in which expenses were paid in course of sale, 7.21
Preparing accounting
    Spreadsheet for checking account, 3.51
    Spreadsheet for investment account, 3.52
    Spreadsheet for personal property, 3.54
    Spreadsheet for real property, 3.53
    Summary of account, 3.57
    Summary reconciliation spreadsheet, 3.56
    Third pass spreadsheet, 3.55
Receipts
    Assets listed in Prob C §16357(c), 6.59
    Bank account interest, 6.57
    Dividend reinvestment programs, 6.60

Dividends and capital gains, 6.55
Entities, receipts from, 6.54
Interest on bonds owed to trustee, 6.58
Rental properties, receipts from, 6.56
Schedule, 6.53

Index

The symbol "f" after a section number indicates that a form appears in the section.

Abatement
  Distributions. See **Distributions**
Additional Property Received During Period of Account
  Generally, 4.6, 5.1, 6.46
  Additions to trust schedule, sample, 1.16, 5.8f
  Appearance of schedule, 5.3
  Carry value, 5.2, 5.4
  First account, preparing schedule for, 5.4
  Life insurance proceeds, 6.25
  Preparing schedule, 3.40
  Principal and income, receipts from decedent's estates and other trusts, 1.6, 5.7
  Prior period of administration, accounting for assets received at end of, 4.18
  Second and subsequent accounts, preparing schedule for, 5.5
  Supplemental inventory, 5.6
Administrators of Estate. See **Personal Representatives**
Adoption
  Distributions, effect of adoption on, 9.16
ADR. See **Alternative Dispute Resolution (ADR)**
Affidavits and Declarations
  Trust, declaration of, 2.45
Agents and Agency
  Irrevocable trust, disclosure of agents hired by trustee of, 2.65
  Powers of attorney, agents under. See **Powers of Attorney**
Agreements
  Engagement letter. See **Engagement Letter**
  Mineral and water interests, production payments under agreement that provides for interest or its equivalent, 6.36
  Qualified personal residence trust (QPRT), effect of third-party trustee's written agreement to administer property, 4.6
Alternative Dispute Resolution (ADR)
  Generally, 14.26
  Experts, appointment of, 14.26
  Mediation, 14.27
  Private judging, 14.29
  Reference (appointment of referee), 14.28–14.29
Amendments and Modifications
  Conservator's powers
    Insurance, conservator's power to renew, modify, and terminate, 2.3
    Trusts, limits on conservator's power to amend and revoke, 2.3
Annuities
  Defined, 9.14
  Distributions, 9.14, 9.19, 9.32
  Interest on bequests, gifts of annuities, or gifts for maintenance, 9.32, 9.36, 11.8
  Receipts from annuities, rules governing, 6.28
Appeals
  Probate court retaining jurisdiction during appeal, 14.16
Appearance in Court
  Personal representative ordered to appear and show cause for failure to file account, 2.38
Appearance of Schedule
  Additional property received during period of account, 5.3
  Assets on hand at beginning of account period, 4.3
  Disbursements. See **Disbursements**
  Distributions. See **Distributions**
  Gains and losses. See **Gains and Losses**
  Receipts, 6.2, 6.53f

Appearance of Schedule—*cont.*
   Summary of account. See **Summary of Account**
Appraisal. See **Inventory and Appraisal**
Appreciation and Depreciation
   Definition of depreciation, 13.14
   Depreciation reserve
      Creating depreciation reserve, instructions for, 13.15
      Limits on creating depreciation reserve, 13.14
      Recharacterization of cash in depreciation reserve prohibited, 13.16
      Trustee's discretion to create depreciation reserve, 13.13
   Distributions of appreciated and depreciated assets, examples of, 9.5–9.6
Approval of Accounting
   Conservators. See **Conservators and Conservatorships**
   Guardians. See **Guardians and Guardianships**
   Personal representatives. See **Personal Representatives**
   Petition for. See **Approval of Accounting, Petition for**
   Trust accounting not submitted for court approval distinguished, 2.71
Approval of Accounting, Petition for
   Guardian or conservator, petition for approval by, 2.22
   Inventories reconsidered prior to petitioning court for approval, 4.23
   Trustee's petition for court approval of account, 2.59, 2.66, 2.70
Assets on Hand at Beginning of Account Period
   Generally, 4.1
   Appearance of schedule, 4.3
   Auxiliary schedules, use of. See **Auxiliary Schedules**
   Best practices for presentation of assets, 4.17, 4.23
   Carry value
      Adjusting carry values to make account balance as common mistake, 4.30
      Defined, 4.12

Carry value—*cont.*
   Net value or market value distinguished from carry value, 4.31
   Stating carry value of each item of property (see Step three: stating carry value of each item of property, below)
Chose in action, including, 4.26
Commingled funds, omitting, 4.30
Common mistakes
   Adjusting carry value to make account balance, 4.30
   Commingled funds, omitting, 4.30
   Confusing notion of wealth with notion of responsibility, 4.29
   Excluding assets for which fiduciary has responsibility, 4.25
   Failing to recognize thing as asset, 4.26, 4.34*f*
   Failure to inventory asset for which fiduciary responsible, 4.23
   Including assets for which fiduciary has no responsibility, 4.24
   Negative numbers, using, 4.22, 4.33*f*
   Net value or market value confused with carry value, 4.31
   Responsibility to collect asset, failure or refusal to recognize, 4.27
   Responsibility to collect asset, failure to recognize commencement of, 4.28
   Securities accounts, treating as single property, 4.32
   Source of receipt, omitting, 6.49
Conservators (see Guardians and conservators, below)
Failing to recognize thing as asset, effect of, 4.26, 4.34*f*
First accounts. See **First Accounts**
Guardians and conservators
   Beginning date, identifying, 4.4
   Best practices for presentation of assets, 4.17
   Carry value, 4.12–4.13, 4.15–4.16
   Common mistakes (see Common mistakes, above)
   Preparing schedule (see Preparing schedule, below)

Assets on Hand at Beginning of Account Period—*cont.*
Guardians and conservators—*cont.*
  Property for which guardian or conservator accountable, identifying, 4.9
  Second and subsequent accounts, identifying property for which all fiduciaries responsible, 4.11
Income (see Principal and income, below)
Interest
  Beginning date for income interest, determining, 4.6
  Ending date for income interest, determining, 4.7
  Mandatory income interest, 4.21
Inventory of asset for which fiduciary responsible, effect of failure to include, 4.23
Life insurance proceeds, 4.18–4.19, 6.25
Negative numbers, using, 4.22, 4.33*f*
Organizing accounts to include on schedule, 3.2
Personal representatives
  Beginning date, identifying, 4.5
  Best practices for presentation of assets, 4.17
  Carry value, 4.12–4.13, 4.15–4.16
  Common mistakes (see Common mistakes, above)
  Preparing schedule (see Preparing schedule, below)
  Principal and income, accounting for, 4.18
  Property for which personal representative accountable, identifying, 4.9
  Second and subsequent accounts, identifying property for which all fiduciaries responsible, 4.11
Preparing schedule
  Generally, 4.2
  Step one (see Step one: identify the beginning date, below)
  Step three: stating carry value of each item of property (see Step three: stating carry value of each item of property, below)

Preparing schedule—*cont.*
  Step two: identify all property for which fiduciary accountable (see Step two: identify all property for which fiduciary accountable, below)
Principal and income
  Disbursements, allocation or apportionment to income or principal, 4.20
  List of assets allocated to principal, 4.18
  Mandatory income interest, 4.21
  Receipts, allocation or apportionment to income or principal, 4.20
  Trustees (see Trustees, below)
Receipts. See **Receipts**
Responsibility to collect asset, failure or refusal to recognize, 4.27
Responsibility to collect asset, failure to recognize commencement of, 4.28
Samples, 1.15, 1.41, 4.3
Second and subsequent accounts, 4.11, 4.16
Securities accounts treated as single property as common mistake, 4.32
Security deposits, 4.29
Step one: identify the beginning date
  Guardians and conservators, 4.4
  Personal representatives, 4.5
  Trustees (see Trustees, below)
Step three: stating carry value of each item of property
  Definition of carry value, 4.12
  Guardians, conservators, and personal representatives, carry value stated in accounts, 4.13, 4.15–4.16
  Trustees, carry value in accounts of, 4.12, 4.14–4.16
Step two: identify all property for which fiduciary accountable
  First account by trustee, 4.10
  Guardians and conservators, 4.9
  Personal representatives, 4.9
  Second and subsequent accounts, property for which all fiduciaries responsible, 4.11

Assets on Hand at Beginning of Account Period—*cont.*
Trustees
Best practices for presentation of assets, 4.17
Carry value, 4.12, 4.14–4.16
Common mistakes (see Common mistakes, above)
First account, identifying property for which trustees responsible, 4.10
Income interest, determining beginning date for, 4.6
Income interest, determining ending date for, 4.7
List of assets allocated to principal, 4.18
Preparing schedule (see Preparing schedule, above)
Second and subsequent accounts, identifying property for which all fiduciaries responsible, 4.11
Vacancy, effect of trustee starting after, 4.8

Assets on Hand at End of Account Period
Generally, 10.1, 10.5
Auxiliary schedules, use of, 4.17, 11.2
Best practices
Check beginning schedules, 10.6
Personal representatives checking inventories and appraisals, 10.7
Carry value
First account period, 10.1
Market value substituted for carry value as common mistake, 10.10
Second and subsequent account period, 10.1
Common mistakes
Assets not inventoried, 10.7, 10.9
Market value substituted for carry value, 10.10
Source of receipt, omitting, 6.49
Conservators (see Guardians and conservators, below)
Guardians and conservators
Best practices (see Best practices, above)
Common mistakes (see Common mistakes, above)
Preparing schedule, 10.2

Income (see Principal and income, below)
Inventory of asset for which fiduciary responsible, effect of failure to include, 10.7, 10.9
Personal representatives
Best practices (see Best practices, above)
Checking inventories and appraisals, 10.7
Common mistakes (see Common mistakes, above)
Preparing schedule, 10.3
Preparing schedule
Generally, 3.44
Guardians and conservators, 10.2
Personal representatives, 10.3
Trustees, 10.4
Principal and income
Generally, 10.8
No income beneficiary, accounting for principal and income during accounting period with, 6.16
Sample schedules
Cash, equities, corporate bonds, mutual funds, limited partnership, and personal property, 1.22, 10.12*f*
Cash, real estate, and receivables, 1.47, 10.11*f*
Trustees
Best practices (see Best practices, above)
Common mistakes (see Common mistakes, above)
Preparing schedule, 10.4

Attorney-Client Privilege, 14.7, 14.10, 14.14

Attorneys
Absconding guardian or conservator, attorney's duty to account in place of, 2.13
Absconding personal representative, court compelling attorney to account for, 2.36
Appointment by probate court, 14.32
Attorney-client privilege, 14.7, 14.10, 14.14

Attorneys—cont.
  Client management tool, attorneys using fiduciary accountings as
    Advance preparation of accountings, encouraging, 15.19
    Face-to-face meetings, scheduling, 15.20
  Duties owed to clients
    Generally, 15.1
    Engagement letter including duties. See **Engagement Letter**
  Engagement letter. See **Engagement Letter**
  Ethics. See **Legal Ethics**
  Fees. See **Attorneys' Fees**
  Inventory and appraisal. See **Inventory and Appraisal**
  Litigation. See **Litigation**
  Removal of attorney by probate court, 14.4
  Work-product privilege, 14.7
Attorneys' Fees
  Alternative dispute resolution used to resolve attorney fee disputes, 14.26
  Bad faith opposition to objection to account, fiduciary's payment of objector's attorney fees for, 8.7
  Engagement letter, fee structure included in. See **Engagement Letter**
  Investigator appointed by court to assist with evaluation of attorney fees, 14.31
  Reimbursement of fiduciary's attorney fees, 14.40
Audit
  Personal representative's account, inspection and audit of supporting documents, 2.37
Auxiliary Schedules
  Generally, 11.1
  Allocation of receipts and disbursements between principal and income, 2.56, 3.49, 4.20, 11.4, 11.6, 15.29
  Assets on hand at beginning of account period
    Liabilities accounted for on separate auxiliary schedule, 4.22

Assets on hand at beginning of account period—cont.
  Market value of assets on hand at beginning of account period, 4.17
Assets on hand at end of account period, market value of, 4.17, 11.2
Changes in form of assets. See **Changes in Form of Assets**
Disbursements. See **Disbursements**
Distributions. See **Distributions**
Liabilities. See **Liabilities**
Proposed distributions. See **Distributions**
Real property located in foreign jurisdiction, 2.9, 6.49, 11.10
Receipts. See **Receipts**
Specifically devised property, 6.45, 8.25, 11.7
Bad Faith
  Fiduciary's payment of objector's attorney fees for bad faith opposition to objection to account, 8.7
Banks and Banking
  Appointment of bank as fiduciary, 14.36
  Checking and savings accounts, gathering and organizing information regarding. See **Preparation of Fiduciary Accounting**
  Financial statements. See **Financial Statements**
  Qualified terminable interest property (QTIP) trust, bank as successor trustee for, 4.8
  Receipts schedule, allocation of bank account interest owed to trustee on, 6.18, 6.57f, 11.14
Basis
  Carry value distinguished, 4.12
Beneficiaries
  Absconding beneficiary, 1.38
  Defined, 2.7, 2.44
  Distributions. See **Distributions**
  Income beneficiary defined, 11.6
  Irrevocable trusts, duties owed by trustee to beneficiaries of. See **Irrevocable Trusts, Trustees of**
Bequest. See **Gift, Bequest, or Devise**

Bonds
Accrued interest, purchase of bond with, 1.7
Assets on hand at end of account period, sample schedule, 1.22, 10.12f
Purchase of bond and reinvestment of dividends, sample spreadsheet, 11.19f
Receipts schedule, allocation of interest on bonds owed to trustee on, 6.19, 6.58f
Samples
Assets on hand at end of account period, sample schedule, 1.22, 10.12f
Purchase of bond and reinvestment of dividends, sample spreadsheet, 11.19f

Breach of Trust
Distributions in breach of trust, examples of, 1.9
Failure to collect debt owed to trust as breach, 4.27
Irrevocable trusts, trustees of
Generally, 2.47–2.48
Commingling of funds as breach of trust, 2.55
Release precluding beneficiary from suing for breach of trust, 2.60
3-year statute of limitations on actions by beneficiaries against trustees for breach of trust, 2.57, 2.59
Revocable trusts, breach of duty to account by trustees of, 2.70
Statute of limitations, disclosure of potential breaches of trust triggering running of, 8.6, 15.25

Brokerage Accounts. See **Securities**

Burden of Proof
Trustees' burden of proof on every element of accounts, 15.12

Business Owned by Trust, Accounting Separately for. See **Trade or Business Owned by Trust, Accounting Separately for**

Capacity
Guardian ad litem appointed for incapacitated person. See **Guardians Ad Litem**

Probate proceedings, effect of principal's or proposed conservatee's capacity in, 14.5–14.6, 14.30–14.31

Capital Gains and Losses. See **Gains and Losses**

Carry Value
Generally, 4.1
Adjusting carry values to make account balance as common mistake of fiduciaries, 4.30
Assets on hand at beginning of account period, schedule for. See **Assets on Hand at Beginning of Account Period**
Assets on hand at end of account period, schedule for. See **Assets on Hand at End of Account Period**
Basis distinguished, 4.12
Bonds owed to trustee, carry value of, 6.19
Changes in form of asset schedule, reporting carry value on. See **Changes in Form of Assets**
Condemned assets, carry value of, 6.16
Defined, 4.12, 5.2, 9.4
Distributions. See **Distributions**
Gross fair market value of property received exceeding carry value of property exchanged, transaction characterized as gain if, 7.1
Gross fair market value of property received less than asset's carry value, transaction characterized as loss if, 7.1
Net value or market value distinguished from carry value, 4.31, 9.5
Preparing fiduciary accounting, reconciling assets when. See **Preparation of Fiduciary Accounting**
Summary of account, use of carry value on, 12.7

Cash
Assets on hand at end of account period, sample schedules, 1.22, 1.47, 10.11f–10.12f
Definition of cash items, 3.3, 4.13

Cash—*cont.*
Inventory and appraisal, including cash assets on, 2.20
Recharacterization of cash in depreciation reserve prohibited, 13.16
Reconciling cash in each account to be included in accounting. See **Preparation of Fiduciary Accounting**
Securities account, reporting of cash held in, 4.32

Categorized Accounting. See Standard Accounting

Certified Public Accountants (CPAs)
Definition of public accountancy, 15.21
Duties owed to clients
Generally, 15.1
Engagement letter including duties. See **Engagement Letter**
Engagement letter. See **Engagement Letter**
Limits on level of service provided, statements regarding, 15.25–15.26
Management-use-only reports, 15.24
Presentation to court, accounting for, 15.23
Regulations governing CPAs, 15.1
Statements on Standards for Accounting and Review Services (SSARS), applicability of, 15.21–15.23, 15.25
Trustee not seeking court approval, CPA preparing accounting for, 15.25

Changes in Form of Assets
Generally, 11.11
Carry value
Condemned assets, carry value of, 6.16
Sale of property for carry value, generally, 11.3, 11.11
Sale price equal to asset's carry value, 11.13, 11.17*f*
Transactions affecting asset's carry value, 1.48, 11.15, 11.19*f*–11.20*f*
Condemned assets, proceeds from, 6.16
Depreciation reserve, 13.15
Disbursements and exchanges distinguished, 11.12
Life insurance proceeds, accounting for, 1.23, 6.25
Name changes, 3.27
Payments of principal from debtor to trust, 11.14, 11.18*f*
Preparing schedule, 3.45
Prob C §16357(c), special rules for assets listed in, 6.20, 6.59*f*
Purchase of assets, reporting, 11.3, 11.11, 11.19*f*
Sales proceeds, reporting
Generally, 6.47
Carry value, sale of property for (see Carry value, above)
Sample spreadsheets
Disbursement of funds to improve real property, 1.48, 11.20*f*
Payments of principal from debtor to trust, 11.14, 11.18*f*
Purchase of bond and reinvestment of dividends, 11.19*f*
Sale price equal to asset's carry value, 1.23, 1.48, 11.13, 11.17*f*
Transfers between accounts, 11.3, 11.16

Charts, Checklists, Questionnaires, and Tables
Allocation of receipts and disbursements under California Uniform Principal and Income Act, chart, 15.29
Sample accountings. See **Sample Accountings**

Checking Accounts, Gathering and Organizing Information Regarding. See Preparation of Fiduciary Accounting

Children. See Minors

Chose in Action
Defined, 4.26

Commingled Funds
Omitting commingled funds from schedules of assets as common mistake by fiduciary, 4.30
Receipts. See **Receipts**
Trustee's duty to avoid commingling trust with other property, 2.48, 2.55

Common Mistakes
   Assets on hand at beginning of account period. See **Assets on Hand at Beginning of Account Period**
   Assets on hand at end of account period. See **Assets on Hand at End of Account Period**
   Disbursements. See **Disbursements**
   Distributions, failure to use carry value as common mistake in reporting, 9.35
   Gains and losses. See **Gains and Losses**
   Receipts. See **Receipts**
   Summary of account, avoiding common mistakes on, 12.7

Compensation. See **Salaries and Compensation**

Competency. See **Capacity**

Computers and Computer Software
   Generally, 15.18
   Spreadsheets. See **Spreadsheets**
   Websites. See **Websites**

Condemned Assets, 6.16

Confidentiality
   Attorney-client privilege, 14.7, 14.10, 14.14
   Mediation, confidentiality of, 14.27
   Private professional fiduciary's duty to preserve confidences of clients, 2.70
   Security measures to protect sensitive information, 15.16
   Waiver of confidentiality, 14.5

Conflicts of Interest
   Generally, 14.7–14.8
   Attorney's conflicts of interest, 14.4–14.5
   Guardian ad litem, 14.32
   Litigation. See **Litigation**
   Trustee's duty to avoid conflicts of interest, 2.48
   Waiver of potential conflict, 14.5

Conservators and Conservatorships
   Generally, 2.3
   Absconding conservator, effect of, 2.13
   Appointment of conservator, generally, 2.3, 4.4
   Approval of accounts
      Auxiliary schedule of assets on hand at beginning and end of account period, conservator providing, 4.17, 11.2
      Noticed hearing, obtaining approval of accounts at, 2.25
      Petition for approval, 2.22
   Assets on hand at beginning of account period. See **Assets on Hand at Beginning of Account Period**
   Assets on hand at end of account period. See **Assets on Hand at End of Account Period**
   Auxiliary schedules. See **Auxiliary Schedules**
   Carry value, 4.12–4.13, 4.15–4.16
   Court investigators, use of, 14.31
   Court supervision, generally, 2.3
   Death of conservatee, effect of, 2.3, 2.31, 4.5, 10.2
   Death of conservator, effect of, 2.13
   Disbursements. See **Disbursements**
   Distributions. See **Distributions**
   Duration of conservatorship, 2.3
   Duties of conservator
      Generally, 2.3
      Final accounting, 2.15, 10.2
      Inventory and appraisal, duty to file. See **Inventory and Appraisal**
      Periodic accounting. See **Periodic Accounting**
   Final account, 2.15, 10.2
   First accounts. See **First Accounts**
   Gains and losses, reporting. See **Gains and Losses**
   Guardian ad litem, appointment of, 14.6, 14.30, 14.32
   Hearing, notice of
      Approval of accounts obtained at noticed hearing, 2.25
      Heirs or beneficiaries of conservatee entitled to notice of hearing of conservator's account, 2.3
      Persons entitled to notice of hearing, 2.3, 2.25
   Inventory and appraisal. See **Inventory and Appraisal**
   Legal entity, conservatorships not constituting, 14.21

Conservators and Conservatorships—*cont.*
Letters of conservatorship, powers created by, 2.3
Notice
  Failure to file accounting, notice of, 2.24
  Hearing, notice of (see Hearing, notice of, above)
Objections to accounting, 2.25
Original account statements, filing of, 2.23
Penalties for late accounts, 2.24
Periodic accounting. See **Periodic Accounting**
Petition for approval of accounting, 2.22
Powers of conservator, 2.3, 2.70
Prior court approval required for conservator to exercise specified rights, 2.3
Receipts. See **Receipts**
Schedules, preparing. See **Schedules**
Second and subsequent accounts. See **Second and Subsequent Accounts**
Simplified accounting. See **Simplified Accounting**
Standard accounting. See **Standard Accounting**
Substituted judgment used to revoke trusts, 2.70
Summary of account. See **Summary of Account**
Temporary conservators
  Compensation, 2.24
  Inventory and appraisal, filing requirements for, 2.10
  Periodic accounting by, 2.14
Time. See **Time**
Waiver of account, 2.26

Constitutional Law
Jury trial, right to, 14.20

Construction and Interpretation
See also **Definitions**
90:10 rule of Prob C §16361(c), effect of, 6.30
"One final judgment" rule, 14.17
Will provision's broad and liberal interpretation to avoid intestacy, 9.15

Contempt
Guardian or conservator, contempt of court for failure to timely file accounting, 2.24
Personal representative's failure to account, contempt of court for, 2.38
Probate court's contempt powers, 14.37

Contracts. See **Agreements**

Corporations
Receipts from entities. See **Receipts**
S corporations. See **S Corporations**

Costs
See also **Expenses and Expenditures; Fees**
Expense of administration, cost of court accounting as, 2.72
Litigation costs, 14.40

CPAs. See **Certified Public Accountants (CPAs)**

Crimes and Criminal Law
Absconding beneficiary, effect on proposed distribution, 1.38
Absconding guardian or conservator, attorney's duty to account in place of, 2.13
Absconding personal representative, court compelling attorney to account for, 2.36

Death
Conservatee's death, effect of, 2.3, 2.31, 4.5, 10.2
Conservator's death, effect of, 2.13
Disbursements, payment of debts and expenses associated with decedent's death. See **Disbursements**
Distributions after decedent's death. See **Distributions**
Guardian, effect of death of, 2.13
Minor's estate as consequence of death of intestate decedent, 2.2
Personal representative's death, effect of, 2.35
Ward's death, effect of, 2.31, 4.5, 10.2

Declarations. See **Affidavits and Declarations**

Deeds of Trust. See **Mortgages and Deeds of Trust**

Definitions
See also **Construction and Interpretation**
Accountant, 3.1, 15.1
Administrator, 2.6
Administrator with will annexed, 2.6
Agent, 2.4
Annuity, 9.14
Assets, 3.3
Attorney-in-fact, 2.4
Beneficiary, 2.7, 2.44
Carry value, 4.12, 5.2, 9.4
Cash items, 3.3, 4.13
Chose in action, 4.26
Collateral-backed securities, 6.43
Date of distribution, 9.1
Demonstrative gifts, 9.12
Depreciation, 13.14
Disbursements, 8.2, 11.12
Disbursements during administration, 8.12
Distributable net income (DNI), 14.10
Distribution, 8.2, 9.1
Engagement letter, 15.1
Entity, 6.9
Exchanges, 11.12
Executor, 2.6
Expenses attributable to property, 9.27
Fiduciary, 14.13
Financial statement, 15.22
General gifts, 9.11
General pecuniary gifts, 9.13
General reference, 14.28
Income, 1.10, 2.56, 6.8, 13.1
Income beneficiary, 11.6
Involuntary reference, 14.28
Liquidating assets, 6.33
Mandatory income interest, 4.21
Partial liquidations, 6.10
Personal representative, 2.6
Posthumously-conceived child, 9.16
Power of attorney, 2.4
Principal, 2.4
Probate, 4.6, 14.13
Probate court, 14.13
Professional appraiser, 6.10
Public accountancy, 15.21
Receipts, 6.1
Referee, 14.28
Res, 8.26
Residuary gift, 9.15
Settlor, 2.7
Special administrator, 2.6
Special reference, 14.28
Specific gifts, 9.10
Stub account, 2.15
Summary of account, 12.1
Trustee, 2.7
Uniform Principal and Income Act (UPAIA) terminology. See **Uniform Principal and Income Act (UPAIA)**
Voluntary reference, 14.28

Deposits
Engagement letter specifying deposit for future services, 15.11, 15.14
Security deposits. See **Security Deposits**

Depreciation. See **Appreciation and Depreciation**

Devise. See **Gift, Bequest, or Devise**

Disabled Persons
Special needs trusts, 14.2, 14.31

Disbursements
See also **Distributions; Receipts**
Generally, 8.2
Administration, payment of expenses of
 Generally, 8.16
 Equal allocation between income and principal, 8.17
 100 percent from income, 8.19
 100 percent from principal, 8.18
Allocation or apportionment of receipts and disbursements between principal and income, 2.56, 3.49, 4.20, 11.4, 11.6, 15.29
Appearance of schedule
 Sample complete disbursements schedules (see Samples, below)
 Type of fiduciaries, requirements based on, 8.3
Asset purchases not constituting disbursements, 8.27
Best practices
 Disclose, explain, and atone for mistakes, 8.7
 Escrow, separate category for amounts disbursed in, 8.10, 8.30f
 Presentation of disbursements, categories and order of, 8.8

Disbursements—cont.
  Best practices—cont.
    Separate categories for each real property and business enterprise, 8.9, 8.29f
    Subtotals, use of, 8.11
  Common mistakes
    Asset purchases not constituting disbursements, 8.27
    Payments from sources other than res, 8.26
    Transfers between accounts not constituting disbursements, 3.8, 8.28
  Complete disbursements schedules, samples of (see Samples, below)
  Conservatee or ward, expenses paid for benefit of, 8.2
  Contents of disbursements schedule, 8.1
  Creditor's claim for funeral expenses, payment of, 1.30, 8.2
  Debts and expenses associated with decedent's death or termination of income interest
    Generally, 8.12
    Discretion to pay from either income or principal, 8.14
    Equal payment from income and principal, 8.15
    Funeral expenses, 1.30, 8.2
    Payments from principal, 8.13, 8.31f
  Defined, 8.2, 11.12
  Depreciation reserve used for principal disbursements related to property, 13.15
  Disclosure
    Improper disbursements, disclosure of, 8.7
    Statute of limitations, disclosure of potential breaches of trust triggering running of, 8.6
  Distributions distinguished, 8.2, 9.2
  Environmental matters, amounts recovered from third parties to reimburse trust for disbursements related to, 6.16

Escrow
  Examples of transactions conducted through escrow, 1.35, 1.44, 6.5
  Separate category for amounts disbursed in escrow, 8.10, 8.30f
Exchanges distinguished, 11.12
Expenses
  Administration, expenses of (see Administration, payment of expenses of, above)
  Decedent's death or termination of income interest, expenses associated with (see Debts and expenses associated with decedent's death or termination of income interest, above)
  Income (see Principal and income, below)
  Judicial Council form for standard and simplified accounts, categories for receipts and disbursements on, 2.20
  Loan payments and payments on trust debts, 8.24, 8.33f
  Payments from sources other than res, 8.26
  Preparing schedule, minimum requirements for, 3.41, 8.6
  Presentation of disbursements, categories and order of, 8.8
  Principal and income
    Administration, expenses of (see Administration, payment of expenses of, above)
    Depreciation reserve used for principal disbursements related to property, 13.15
    Loan payments and payments on trust debts, 8.24, 8.33f
    Mandatory allocation of Prob C §16374, 13.18
    Real property, payment of expenses of administering, 8.23, 8.32f
    Specifically gifted property, 8.25
    Taxes, payment of (see Taxes, payment of, below)

Disbursements—*cont.*
　Principal and income—*cont.*
　　Termination of income interest (see
　　　Debts and expenses associated
　　　with decedent's death or
　　　termination of income interest,
　　　above)
　　Transfers from income to principal
　　　in anticipation of principal
　　　disbursement, 13.17
　Real property
　　Expenses of administering real
　　　property, payment of, 8.23,
　　　8.32*f*
　　Improvement of real property,
　　　sample spreadsheet illustrating
　　　disbursement of funds for, 1.48,
　　　11.20*f*
　　Real estate trust, disbursements
　　　from, 1.35, 1.44, 8.5*f*
　　Receipts related to real property,
　　　8.29*f*
　　Rent payments, 8.2, 8.6
　　Separate categories for each real
　　　property and business
　　　enterprise, 8.9, 8.29*f*
　Rent payments, 8.2, 8.6
　Samples
　　Cash trust, disbursements from,
　　　1.19, 8.4*f*
　　Improvement of real property,
　　　sample spreadsheet illustrating
　　　disbursement of funds for, 1.48,
　　　11.20*f*
　　Real estate trust, disbursements
　　　from, 1.35, 1.44, 8.5*f*
　　Simplified accounting, listing of
　　　receipts and disbursements for,
　　　2.20–2.21
　Specifically gifted property, 8.25
　Standard accounting, categories for
　　　receipts and disbursements,
　　　2.20
　Subtotals, use of, 8.11
　Taxes, payment of
　　Gift, estate, inheritance, and similar
　　　taxes, 8.20
　　Income and capital gain tax, 8.22
　　Property taxes, 8.21

　Termination of income interest (see
　　　Debts and expenses associated
　　　with decedent's death or
　　　termination of income interest,
　　　above)
　Transfers between accounts not
　　　constituting disbursements, 3.8,
　　　8.28
　Trustee fees, 8.2
　Ward or conservatee, expenses paid
　　　for benefit of, 8.2
Disclosure
　Disbursements. See **Disbursements**
　Existence of potential claims,
　　　disclosure of, 2.72
　Irrevocable trust, disclosures made in
　　　accounting. See **Irrevocable
　　　Trusts, Trustees of**
　Preparation of trust account, including
　　　disclosures as if preparing for
　　　court review, 2.72
　Receipts schedule, disclosing mistake
　　　on, 6.6
　Revocable trust, disclosures made by
　　　trustee of, 2.70
　Statute of limitations, disclosure of
　　　potential breaches of trust
　　　triggering running of, 8.6, 15.25
Discovery
　Beneficiary's right to inspect trustee's
　　　records, 14.9–14.10
　Referee appointed to address
　　　discovery issues, 14.28
　Tax return privilege, 14.10
Discretion of Court
　Conservator, appointment of, 2.3
　Guardian, appointment of, 2.2
Distributable Net Income (DNI), 14.10
Distributions
　　See also **Disbursements**
　Generally, 9.1
　Abatement
　　Generally, 9.9
　　Categorization of gifts (see
　　　Categorization of gifts, below)
　　Categorization of people, 9.16
　　Examples of abatement in action
　　　(see Abatement in action,
　　　examples of, below)
　　Mortgage, deed of trust, or other
　　　lien, gift exonerated from, 9.20

Distributions—*cont.*
  Abatement—*cont.*
    Rules of abatement (see Rules of abatement, below)
    Abatement in action, examples of
      Generally, 9.21
      Example five and self-test, 9.41
      Example four and self-test, 9.40
      Example one and self-test, 9.37
      Example six and self-test, 9.42
      Example three and self-test, 9.39
      Example two and self-test, 9.38
  Adoption, effect of, 9.16
  Allocation of income after decedent's death or after income interest in trust ends
    General pecuniary gifts, annuities, and gifts of maintenance, 9.32
    Net income distributable to residuary beneficiaries, 9.33
    Specific gifts (see Specific gifts, below)
  Annuities, 9.14, 9.19, 9.32, 11.8
  Appearance of schedule
    Categorization of gifts (see Categorization of gifts, below)
    Examples, 9.3
  Carry value, accounting for distributions using
    Generally, 9.4
    Common mistake, failure to use carry value as, 9.35
    Example one: distribution of depreciated asset, 9.5
    Example two: distribution of appreciated asset, 9.6
  Categorization of gifts
    Generally, 9.7
    Annuity, 9.14, 9.19
    Demonstrative gifts, 9.12, 9.19
    General gifts, 9.11, 9.19
    General pecuniary gifts, 9.13, 9.32, 9.44*f*
    Property not distributed by instrument, 9.15
    Residuary gifts, 9.15
    Specific gifts (see Specific gifts, below)
  Categorization of people, 9.16
  Common mistake, reporting distributions using carry value as, 9.35
  Date of distribution, determining, 9.1
  Death, allocation of income after decedent's (see Allocation of income after decedent's death or after income interest in trust ends, above)
  Defined, 8.2, 9.1
  Demonstrative gifts, 9.12, 9.19
  Disbursements distinguished, 8.2, 9.2
  Expenses and receipts attributable to specific gifts
    Generally, 9.27
    Example, 9.43*f*
    Receipts and disbursements, at beginning, 9.28
    Receipts and disbursements, at end, 9.30
    Receipts and disbursements, during administration, 9.29
  Final distribution, petition for. See **Final Distribution, Petition for**
  General gifts, 9.11, 9.19
  General pecuniary gifts, 9.13, 9.32, 9.44*f*
  Income
    Generally (see Principal and income, below)
    Allocation of income after decedent's death or after income interest in trust ends (see Allocation of income after decedent's death or after income interest in trust ends, above)
  Interest
    Bequests, gifts of annuities, or gifts for maintenance, interest on, 9.32, 9.36, 11.8
    General pecuniary gift, accounting for accrual of interest on, 9.44*f*
  Intervals for distributions, 9.1
  Mortgage, deed of trust, or other liens, gift exonerated from, 9.20
  Omitted heirs, transfers to
    Generally, 9.8
    Child, 9.24–9.25
    Manner of satisfying share of omitted spouse, registered domestic partner, or child, 9.25
    Registered domestic partner, 9.23, 9.25
    Spouse, 9.23, 9.25

Distributions—*cont.*
Preparing schedule, minimum
requirements for
Generally, 3.42
Carry value, accounting for
distributions using (see Carry
value, accounting for
distributions using, above)
Categorization of gifts (see
Categorization of gifts, above)
Principal and income
Generally, 9.26
Allocation of income after
decedent's death or after
income interest in trust ends
(see Allocation of income after
decedent's death or after
income interest in trust ends,
above)
Property not distributed by instrument,
9.15, 9.18
Proposed distributions
Generally, 11.5
Income beneficiary, distribution to,
11.6
Interest on bequests, gifts of
annuities, or gifts for
maintenance, 11.8
Sample, 1.50
Specifically devised property,
reporting on proposed
distribution schedule, 6.45,
8.25, 11.7
Residuary gifts, 9.15, 9.18–9.19
Rules of abatement
Generally, 9.9, 9.17
Property not disposed of by
instrument, 9.18
Remaining gifts, 9.19
Samples, 1.9, 1.21, 1.46, 1.50
Specific gifts
Abatement, 9.19–9.20
Debts and general expenses of
administration, 9.31
Defined, 9.10
Expenses and receipts attributable
to specific gifts (see Expenses
and receipts attributable to
specific gifts, above)
Taxes
Generally, 9.34

Taxes—*cont.*
Proration of estate and
generation-skipping taxes, 9.22
Termination of income interest (see
Allocation of income after
decedent's death or after
income interest in trust ends,
above)
UPAIA requirements (see Principal and
income, above)
Dividends
Purchase of bond and reinvestment of
dividends, sample spreadsheet,
11.19*f*
Receipts
Dividend reinvestment programs,
1.8, 6.44, 6.60*f*
Insurance company, reporting of
dividends paid by, 6.21, 6.26
Mutual funds, receipt of dividends
from, 6.11, 6.55*f*
Reinvestment of dividends
Generally, 3.13
Carry value, reinvestment of
dividends affecting, 11.19*f*
Purchases, 3.13, 3.45
Receipts, 6.44, 6.60*f*
Samples, 1.5, 1.8, 11.19*f*
Samples
Purchase of bond and reinvestment
of dividends, sample
spreadsheet, 11.19*f*
Reinvestment of dividends, 1.5, 1.8,
11.19*f*
DNI. See **Distributable Net Income (DNI)**
Domestic Partners
Omitted partners, distributions to, 9.23,
9.25
Domicile. See **Residence and Domicile**
Duties of Fiduciaries (Generally)
Account, duty to. See **Duty to
Account**
Agents under powers of attorney, 2.4
Attorneys. See **Attorneys**
Certified public accountants (CPAs).
See **Certified Public
Accountants (CPAs)**
Conservators. See **Conservators and
Conservatorships**
Engagement letter including duties of
accountant. See **Engagement
Letter**

Duties of Fiduciaries (Generally)—cont.
Guardians. See **Guardians and Guardianships**
Irrevocable trust, trustees of. See **Irrevocable Trusts, Trustees of**
Personal representatives, purpose of powers and duties of, 2.5
Private professional fiduciaries, duty to preserve confidences of clients, 2.70
Revocable trust, trustees of. See **Revocable Trusts, Trustees of**

Duty to Account
Generally, 14.22
Absconding guardian or conservator, attorney's duty to account in place of, 2.13
Absconding personal representative, court compelling attorney to account for, 2.36
Agents under power of attorney, no affirmative duty to account periodically, 2.4
Breach of duty to account, 2.70
Consultation with attorney, 14.25
Incapacity of beneficiary, trustee's duty to account to third party due to, 2.45
Irrevocable trusts, trustees of. See **Irrevocable Trusts, Trustees of**
Personal accountability of fiduciaries, 14.22
Revocable trusts, trustees of, 2.70
To whom accounting owed, 14.23

Elder Abuse
Allegation of financial elder abuse involving concurrent cases, 14.18

Eminent Domain
Receipts for property taken by eminent domain, 6.16

Encumbrances. See **Liens and Encumbrances**

Engagement Letter
Generally, 3.1, 15.2
Appraisal of assets, specifying responsibility for, 15.5
Deadlines, being realistic about, 15.7
Defined, 15.1
Deposit for future services, 15.11, 15.14
Fee structure
Flat-fee billing, 15.10
Hourly billing, 15.9
Hyperbole, avoiding, 15.4
Identifying parties to contract, 15.3
Principal and income provisions from will or trust document, engagement letter quoting, 15.6
Recordkeeping responsibilities
Fiduciary's responsibility, specifying, 15.6
List of records needed to prepare accounting, 15.8, 15.15, 15.28
Request for records, 15.8, 15.14
Retention of records, policy regarding, 15.12
Sample engagement letter, 15.27f
Scope of engagement, defining, 15.3, 15.6
Signature requirements, 15.14
Termination clause, 15.13

Escrow
Disbursements. See **Disbursements**
Original escrow closing statements filed by conservators and guardians, 2.23
Receipts in escrow, 1.28, 6.5

Estate Tax
Proration of estate tax, 9.22

Ethics. See **Legal Ethics**

Excess Income
Conservator's power to pay excess income to persons entitled to support from conservatee, 2.3

Execution of Documents. See **Signatures**

Executors. See **Personal Representatives**

Ex Parte Communications
Probate court matters, prohibition against ex parte communications in, 14.3

Expenses and Expenditures
See also **Costs; Fees**
Disbursements. See **Disbursements**
Funeral expenses, 1.30, 8.2
Irrevocable trusts, expenses for trustees of. See **Irrevocable Trusts, Trustees of**
Sales in which expenses paid in course of sale, 7.21f

Experts and Expert Witnesses
  Evid C §730, appointment of experts under, 14.26, 14.31
Extending and Shortening Time
  180-day statute of limitations on actions against trustee, trust instrument provision regarding, 2.58
Fees
  See also **Costs; Expenses and Expenditures**
  Attorney fees. See **Attorneys' Fees**
  Engagement letter, fee structure included in. See **Engagement Letter**
  Guardian ad litem, fees of, 2.70
  Personal representative's report instead of account including basis for determining statutory fees, 2.40
  Private judge, fees paid to, 14.29
  Referee fees, 14.28
  Trustee fees
    Disbursement, trustee fee as, 8.2
    Investigator appointed by court to assist with evaluation of trustee fees, 14.31
    Irrevocable trusts, fees for trustees of, 2.66
    Liability, trustee fee as, 1.12, 1.24, 1.49
Final Account
  Guardians and conservators, final accounting by, 2.15, 10.2
  Personal representatives
    Generally, 2.32, 10.3
    Waiver of final account, request for, 2.39–2.40
  Stub accounting, 2.15, 10.3–10.4
  Trustee, 10.4
Final Distribution, Petition for
  Summary of administration of decedent's estate included in petition, 2.32
  Waiver of account, court granting petitions for final distribution on, 2.39
Financial Statements
  Certified public accountants (CPAs) preparing financial statements. See **Certified Public Accountants (CPAs)**
  Defined, 15.22
  Gathering and organizing working papers to prepare fiduciary accounting, 3.2
  Guardians and conservators filing original account statements, 2.23
  Limited power of attorney allowing accountants to demand documents from financial institutions, 15.17
  Missing statements list, 3.2
  Personal representatives preparing inventory and appraisal using financial statements, 2.30
First Accounts
  Additional property received during period of account, 5.4
  Assets on hand at beginning of account period
    Generally, 4.9
    Carry value in first accounts, 4.13
    Court approval of accounts, 4.15
    Trustees, requirements for, 4.10
  Assets on hand at end of account period, carry value in first accounts, 10.1
  Local court rules governing, 2.11
Forests. See **Timberland**
Format of Trust Accounts
  Generally, 14.24
  Disclosures required, 2.72
  Minimum requirements, 2.71
  Schedules. See **Schedules**
Funeral Expenses
  Disbursement, payment of creditor's claim for funeral expenses as, 1.30, 8.2
Gains and Losses
  Appearance of schedule
    Gains on sales or other dispositions, 7.3
    Losses on sales or other dispositions, 7.4
  Asset-backed securities, 7.14
  Best practices for reporting sales, 7.7
  Carry value of property exchanged, transaction characterized as gain or loss based on gross fair market value of property received as greater or less than, 7.1

Gains and Losses—cont.
  Changes in form of assets without triggering gain or loss. See **Changes in Form of Assets**
  Common mistakes
    Calculating gain using net sales price, 7.17
    Calculating loss using net sales price, 7.18
    Interest, unnecessary payment of, 9.36
  Distinguishing gains from losses, 7.1
  Expenses paid in course of sale, 7.21*f*
  Gains on sales or other dispositions
    Generally, 7.2
    Appearance of schedule, 7.3
    Form, 7.19*f*
    Preparing schedule, minimum requirements for, 7.5
    Samples, 1.11, 1.18, 1.29, 1.43
  Income (see Principal and income, below)
  Insurance proceeds
    Life insurance proceeds, 6.25
    Property insurance proceeds, 6.23, 7.15, 7.20*f*
    Title insurance proceeds, 6.24
  Losses on sales or other dispositions
    Generally, 7.2
    Appearance of schedule, 7.4
    Expenses paid in course of sale, 7.21*f*
    Preparing schedule, minimum requirements for, 7.6
    Samples, 1.11, 1.20, 1.29, 1.45
  Marital deduction trusts, 7.16
  Mineral interests, sale of, 7.9
  Net sales price
    Calculating gain using net sales price, 7.17
    Calculating loss using net sales price, 7.18
  Obligation to pay money, sale, redemption, or other disposition of
    Generally, 7.10
    Obligations that mature in less than 1 year, 7.12
    Obligations that mature more than 1 year after acquisition, 7.11
  Options, 7.13
  Preparing schedules, 3.43, 7.5–7.6
  Principal and income
    Generally, 7.8
    Asset-backed securities, 7.14
    Insurance proceeds (see Insurance proceeds, above)
    Marital deduction trusts, 7.16
    Mineral interests, sale of, 7.9
    Obligation to pay money, sale, redemption, or other disposition of (see Obligation to pay money, sale, redemption, or other disposition of, above)
    Options, 7.13
    Timberland, sale of, 7.9
    Water interests, sale of, 7.9
  Receipt of short-term and long-term capital gains, 6.11, 6.55*f*
  Sales and condemnation proceeds, reporting, 6.16, 6.47–6.48
  Samples
    Gains on sales, 1.11, 1.18, 1.29, 1.43
    Losses on sales, 1.11, 1.20, 1.29, 1.45
    Sale without gain or loss, 1.31–1.32
  Separate schedules required for reporting of gains and losses, 7.2
  Timberland, sale of, 7.9
  Time considerations
    Obligations that mature in less than 1 year, 7.12
    Obligations that mature more than 1 year after acquisition, 7.11
  UPAIA requirements (see Principal and income, above)
  Water interests, sale of, 7.9

Generation-Skipping Transfer Tax
  Proration of generation-skipping transfer tax, 9.22

Gift, Bequest, or Devise
  Disbursements. See **Disbursements**
  Distributions. See **Distributions**
  Interest on bequests, gifts of annuities, or gifts for maintenance, 9.32, 9.36, 11.8
  Minor's estate created by gift, bequest, or devise, 2.2
  Receipts attributable to specifically gifted property, reporting, 6.45, 8.25, 11.7

Grantor Retained Annuity Trust (GRAT)
Creation of, 4.7
GRAT. See **Grantor Retained Annuity Trust (GRAT)**
Guardians Ad Litem
Appointment of guardian ad litem, 14.6, 14.30, 14.32
Conflict of interest issues, 14.32
Fees of, 2.70
Guardians and Guardianships
Generally, 2.2
Absconding guardian, effect of, 2.13
Appointment of guardian, generally, 2.2, 4.4
Approval of accounts
Auxiliary schedule of assets on hand at beginning and end of account period, guardian providing, 4.17, 11.2
Noticed hearing, obtaining approval of accounts at, 2.25
Petition for approval, 2.22
Assets on hand at beginning of account period. See **Assets on Hand at Beginning of Account Period**
Assets on hand at end of account period. See **Assets on Hand at End of Account Period**
Auxiliary schedules. See **Auxiliary Schedules**
Carry value, 4.12–4.13, 4.15–4.16
Court investigators, use of, 14.31
Death of guardian, effect of, 2.13
Death of ward, effect of, 2.31, 4.5, 10.2
Disbursements. See **Disbursements**
Distributions. See **Distributions**
Duties of guardian
Duration of guardian's duties, 2.2
Final accounting, 2.15, 10.2
Inventory and appraisal, duty to file. See **Inventory and Appraisal**
Periodic accounting. See **Periodic Accounting**
Final account, 2.15, 10.2
First accounts. See **First Accounts**
Gains and losses, reporting. See **Gains and Losses**
Hearing, notice of
Approval of accounts obtained at noticed hearing, 2.25

Hearing, notice of—*cont.*
Persons entitled to notice of hearing, 2.25
Inventory and appraisal. See **Inventory and Appraisal**
Legal entity, guardianships not constituting, 14.21
Notice
Failure to file accounting, notice of, 2.24
Hearing, notice of (see Hearing, notice of, above)
Objections to accounting, 2.25
Original account statements, filing of, 2.23
Penalties for late accounts, 2.24
Periodic accounting. See **Periodic Accounting**
Petition for approval of accounting, 2.22
Receipts. See **Receipts**
Release of guardian by ward, effect of, 2.27
Schedules, preparing. See **Schedules**
Second and subsequent accounts. See **Second and Subsequent Accounts**
Simplified accounting. See **Simplified Accounting**
Standard accounting. See **Standard Accounting**
Summary of account. See **Summary of Account**
Temporary guardians
Inventory and appraisal, filing requirements for, 2.10
Periodic accounting by, 2.14
Termination of guardianship, 10.2
Time. See **Time**
Waiver of account, 2.26
Handicapped Persons. See **Disabled Persons**
Hearings
Conservators and conservatorships. See **Conservators and Conservatorships**
Guardians and guardianships. See **Guardians and Guardianships**
Personal representative obtaining approval of accounts at noticed hearing, 2.41

Index

Historical Background
Trustees, 2.7

Incapacity
Beneficiary of irrevocable trust, capacity to grant release to trustee for disclosures made in accounting, 2.60–2.61
Conservators. See **Conservators and Conservatorships**
Encumbered property, effect of transferor's incapacity on gift of, 9.20
Guardian ad litem. See **Guardians Ad Litem**
Irrevocable trust, trustee's duty to account to third party due to beneficiary's incapacity, 2.45
Personal representative's incapacity, effect of, 2.35
Revocable trust, effect of incapacity of person holding power to revoke, 2.68–2.70

Income. See **Principal and Income**

Incompetence. See **Incapacity**

Indemnification
Trustees entitled to indemnification out of trust estate for expenses incurred in administration of trust, 2.57

Individual Retirement Accounts (IRAs)
Receipts from IRAs, rules governing, 6.28

Inferences. See **Presumptions and Inferences**

Inspection of Records
Agents under power of attorney, duty to make transaction records available for inspection by principal, 2.4
Beneficiary's right to inspect trustee's records, 14.9–14.10
Irrevocable trust records, inspection of, 2.53, 2.55
Personal representative's account, inspection and audit of supporting documents, 2.37

Insurance
Conservator's power to renew, modify, and terminate insurance for those entitled to support from conservatee, 2.3
Gains or loss schedules, reporting receipt of insurance proceeds on. See **Gains and Losses**
Life insurance. See **Life Insurance**
Property insurance proceeds, 6.23, 7.15, 7.20f
Receipts for insurance proceeds. See **Receipts**
Schedule used to report collection of insurance proceeds, determining, 6.22
Title insurance, 6.21, 6.24

Intent
Intestacy, presumption regarding settlor or testator's intent to avoid, 9.15
Public policy, protecting intent of settlor and testators as matter of, 9.8

Interest on Money
Assets on hand at beginning of account period. See **Assets on Hand at Beginning of Account Period**
Bequests, gifts of annuities, or gifts for maintenance, interest on, 9.32, 9.36, 11.8
Bonds
  Accrued interest, purchase of bond with, 1.7
  Receipts schedule, interest on bonds owed to trustee included on, 6.19, 6.58f
Distributions. See **Distributions**
Loans, interest payments on, 8.24, 8.33f
Receipts
  Bank account interest owed to trustee, 6.18, 6.57f, 11.14
  Bonds owed to trustee, interest on, 6.19, 6.58f

Interpretation of Statutory and Case Law. See **Construction and Interpretation**

Intestacy
Minor's estate as consequence of death of intestate decedent, 2.2
Presumption regarding settlor or testator's intent to avoid intestacy, 9.15

Index • 470

Inventory and Appraisal
Attorneys
    Role in preparing inventory and appraisal, 2.30
    Trustee's inventory and appraisal, attorney recommending deadline for, 4.10
Cash assets included on inventory and appraisal, 2.20
Conservators (see Guardians and conservators, below)
Date property inventoried included on inventory and appraisal, 2.20
Definition of professional appraiser, 6.10
Engagement letter specifying responsibility for appraisal of assets, 15.5
Failure to inventory asset, effect of, 4.23, 5.6, 10.7, 10.9
Guardians and conservators
    Date of appointment as date used to inventory guardianship and conservatorship estates, 4.4
    Deadline for filing inventory and appraisal, 2.9, 4.9
    Failure to inventory asset, effect of, 4.23, 5.6, 10.9
    First account, requirements for, 4.9
    Postdeath accounting requirements, 2.31
    Supplemental inventory, 5.6
    Temporary guardians and conservators, requirements for, 2.10
Personal representatives
    Attorney's role in preparing inventory and appraisal, 2.30
    Deadline for filing inventory and appraisal, 2.6, 2.30, 4.9
    Failure to inventory asset, effect of, 4.23, 5.6, 10.7, 10.9
    Filing requirements, generally, 2.30
    First account, requirements for, 4.9
    Guardianship or conservatorship, administration following, 2.31, 4.5
    Identification of property to be administered and statement of value of each item as of date of decedent's death, inventory including, 4.5

Personal representatives—*cont.*
    Partial inventory filed by personal representative, 2.30
    Supplemental inventory, 5.6
Supplemental inventory, preparation of, 5.6
Trustees
    Attorney recommending deadline for completion of inventory and appraisal, 4.10
    Carry value in accounts of trustees, appraising assets to determine, 4.14
    Supplemental inventory, 5.6
Investigations
Probate court appointing court investigator, 14.31
Investment Accounts. See Securities
Investment Companies
Receipts from entities including regulated investment companies. See **Receipts**
IRAs. See Individual Retirement Accounts (IRAs)
Irrevocable Trusts, Trustees of
See also **Revocable Trusts, Trustees of**
Account, duty to
    Contingent remainder beneficiaries, trust requiring trustee to account to, 2.45
    Current beneficiaries, duty owed to, 2.45
    Definition of beneficiary, 2.44
    Frequency of accountings, 2.50, 4.10
    Incapacity of beneficiary, duty to account to third party due to, 2.45
    Preliminary step to performance of other duties, accounting as, 2.56
    Remainder beneficiaries, no duty owed to, 2.46
    Waiver of duty to account (see Waiver of duty to account, below)
Agents hired by trustee, 2.65
Breach of trust. See **Breach of Trust**
Compensation of trustee, 2.65
Definition of beneficiary, 2.44

Irrevocable Trusts, Trustees of—*cont.*
Disclosures made in accounting
List of disclosures, 2.65
Release of liability for disclosures made in accounting (see Release of liability for disclosures made in accounting, below)
Duties
Account, duty to (see Account, duty to, above)
Adverse trusts, duty to avoid administration of, 2.48
Apply full extent of skills to administration of trust, duty to, 2.48
Commingling trust with other property, duty to avoid, 2.48, 2.55
Conflicts of interest, duty to avoid, 2.48
Defend trust against action resulting in loss to trust, duty to, 2.48
Delegate or to supervise delegates, duty not to, 2.48
Enforce trust's claim, duty to, 2.48
Impartiality, duty of, 2.48
Keep beneficiaries informed, affirmative duty to, 2.44, 2.48, 2.52
Loyalty, duty of, 2.48
Make trust property productive, duty to, 2.48
Persons to whom duties owed, determining, 2.43
Prudent Investor Act, duty to administer trust according to, 2.48
Report, duty to, 2.44, 2.51
Take control and preserve trust property, duty to, 2.48
Expenses
Indemnification out of trust estate for expenses incurred in administration of trust, trustees entitled to, 2.57
Reserves to cover expenses, maintaining, 2.63
Inspection of trust records, beneficiaries' rights, 2.53, 2.55
Liabilities of trust, statement of, 2.65

Net income, calculating, 2.56
Notice
Right to petition court to obtain court review of account and acts of trustee, notice of, 2.65
Statute of limitations, notice of, 2.65
Vested or contingent beneficiaries entitled to notice of trustee's petition for court approval of account, 2.66
Objections by beneficiaries, limits on, 2.59
Order compelling trustee to account, 2.50
Petitions
Compel report, petition to, 2.46, 2.51
Court approval of trustee's account, petition for, 2.59, 2.66
Notice of right to petition court to obtain court review of account and acts of trustee, 2.65
Recordkeeping requirements
Inspection rights of beneficiaries, 2.53, 2.55
List of trustee records to be retained, 2.54
Personal records of trustee who commingles, 2.55
Release of liability for disclosures made in accounting
Generally, 2.60
Capacity of beneficiary to grant release, 2.60–2.61
Full disclosure of rights and material facts, 2.60, 2.62
Improper conduct of trustee, ineffectiveness of release induced by, 2.63
Recant of release, 2.62
Unfair advantage, ineffectiveness of release obtained through, 2.64
Removal of trustee, 2.66
Schedules, preparing. See **Schedules**
Service of accounting, 2.65
Statute of limitations
Notice of statute of limitations, 2.65
180-day statute of limitations, trust instrument provision regarding, 2.58–2.59

Irrevocable Trusts, Trustees of—*cont.*
  Statute of limitations—*cont.*
    3-year statute of limitations on actions by beneficiaries against trustees for breach of trust, 2.57, 2.59
    Waiver of duty to account not triggering statute of limitations, 2.49, 2.57
  Successor trustees, 2.45
  Time. See **Time**
  Trustee of revocable trust distinguished, 2.43
  Waiver of duty to account
    Beneficiary's written waiver, effect of, 2.48
    Statute of limitations, waiver not triggering, 2.49, 2.57
    Trust instrument, waivers in, 2.47

Judges
  Private judge, 14.29

Judgments
  "One final judgment" rule, 14.17
  Probate court rulings as orders versus judgments, 14.15
  Substituted judgment. See **Substituted Judgment**
  Trust versus trustees, unenforceability of judgment against, 14.21

Jurisdiction
  Foreign jurisdiction, guardians and conservators accounting for real property located in, 2.9, 6.49, 11.10
  Probate cases, jurisdiction in, 14.11, 14.16, 14.18–14.19

Jury Trial, Right to, 14.20

Landlord and Tenant
  Rent. See **Rent**
  Security deposits. See **Security Deposits**

Late Acquired Assets. See **Additional Property Received During Period of Account**

Law and Fact, Questions of. See **Questions of Law and Fact**

Legal Ethics
  Capacity of principal or proposed conservatee, 14.5–14.6
  Conflicts of interest, 14.4–14.5
  Removal of attorney by court, unethical behavior resulting in, 14.4

Letters
  Conservatorships
    Personal representative using letters testamentary to distribute conservatorship estate assets after conservatee's death, 2.15
    Powers created by letters of conservatorship, 2.3
  Engagement letter. See **Engagement Letter**

Liabilities
  Generally, 12.7
  Assets on hand at beginning of account period, liabilities accounted for on separate auxiliary schedule, 4.22
  Borrowed money, obligation to repay money accounted for on liabilities schedule, 6.7
  Contents of schedule, 11.9
  Debt incurred during account period, reporting, 11.9, 11.22*f*
  Increase in liabilities during period of account, 11.9, 11.22*f*
  Mortgage, principal or missed payments on, 1.34, 1.49, 11.9, 11.22*f*
  Payment of liabilities. See **Disbursements**
  Sample spreadsheets
    Increase in liabilities, 11.9, 11.22*f*
    Tenant's security deposit, accounting for, 1.49, 11.9, 11.21*f*
  Statement of liabilities of trust, 2.65
  Tenant's security deposit, 1.27, 1.49, 11.9, 11.21*f*
  Trustee fee as liability, 1.12, 1.24, 1.49

Liens and Encumbrances
  Mortgages and deeds of trust. See **Mortgages and Deeds of Trust**
  Transferor's incapacity, effect on gift of encumbered property, 9.20

Life Insurance
  Additional property received during period of account, reporting life insurance proceeds on, 6.25
  Assets on hand at beginning of account period, schedule including life insurance proceeds, 4.18–4.19, 6.25

Life Insurance—*cont.*
 Changes in form of assets schedule, reporting life insurance proceeds on, 1.23, 6.25
 Gains and losses schedule, reporting life insurance proceeds on, 6.25
 Receipts, 6.21
 Statute governing accounting for life insurance, 4.18
Limitations of Actions. See Statutes of Limitations
Limited Liability Companies (LLCs)
 Phantom income, accounting for, 6.51
 Receipts from entities. See **Receipts**
Limited Partnerships
 Assets on hand at end of account period, sample schedule, 1.22, 10.12*f*
Liquidation
 Definitions
  Liquidating assets, 6.33
  Partial liquidations, 6.10
Litigation
 Generally, 14.1
 ADR. See **Alternative Dispute Resolution (ADR)**
 Appeal, probate court retaining jurisdiction during, 14.16
 Attorney-client privilege, effect of, 14.7, 14.10, 14.14
 Attorneys. See **Attorneys**
 Blended pleadings, 14.19
 Capacity of principal or proposed conservatee, effect of, 14.5–14.6, 14.30–14.31
 Concurrent cases, 14.18
 Conflicts of interest
  Attorneys, 14.4–14.5
  Fiduciaries, 14.7–14.8
  Guardians ad litem, 14.32
 Contempt, 14.37
 Court of general jurisdiction, court in proceedings under Probate Code as, 14.11
 Differences between probate court matters and other court proceedings
  Generally, 14.12
  Appeal, probate court retaining jurisdiction during, 14.16
  Blended pleadings, 14.19

 Differences between probate court matters and other court proceedings—*cont.*
  Case law applicable to all fiduciaries, 14.14
  Concurrent cases, 14.18
  Jury trial, right to, 14.20
  "One final judgment" rule, inapplicability of, 14.17
  Orders versus judgments, probate court rulings as, 14.15
  Terminology, 14.13
  Trust not constituting legal entity, 14.21
 Discovery. See **Discovery**
 Ex parte communications, prohibition against, 14.3
 Experts, appointment of, 14.26, 14.31
 Guardian ad litem, appointment of, 14.6, 14.30, 14.32
 Inspection of records by trust beneficiaries, 14.9–14.10
 Jurisdiction in probate cases, 14.11, 14.16, 14.18–14.19
 Jury trial, right to, 14.20
 Limiting powers of fiduciary, 14.33
 "One final judgment" rule, inapplicability of, 14.17
 Orders versus judgments, probate court rulings as, 14.15
 Protective role of probate court, generally, 14.2–14.3
 Remedies available to probate court
  Generally, 14.30
  Attorneys, appointment of, 14.32
  Contempt, 14.37
  Experts, appointment of, 14.26, 14.31
  Fees and costs, 14.40
  Guardian ad litem, appointment of, 14.6, 14.30, 14.32
  Limiting powers of fiduciary, 14.33
  Removal of fiduciary, 14.8, 14.35, 14.39
  Replacement fiduciary, appointment of, 14.33–14.34, 14.36
  Return of assets, 14.39
  Surcharging, 14.38
  Suspension of fiduciary, 10.3, 14.8, 14.33–14.34, 14.39

Litigation—*cont.*
  Removal of fiduciary, 14.8, 14.35, 14.39
  Replacement fiduciary, appointment of, 14.33–14.34, 14.36
  Return of assets, 14.39
  Special needs trusts, role of probate court in litigation involving, 14.2, 14.31
  Surcharging, 14.38
  Suspension of fiduciary, 10.3, 14.8, 14.33–14.34, 14.39
  Terminology, 14.13
  Trust not constituting legal entity, 14.21
LLCs. See **Limited Liability Companies (LLCs)**
Loans
  Interest payments on loans, 8.24, 8.33*f*
  Receipt, borrowed money accounted for as, 6.7
  Trustee's loans to trust, 1.37
Local Court Rules. See **Rules of Court**
Logging. See **Timberland**
Losses. See **Gains and Losses**
Maintenance. See **Repairs and Maintenance**
Malpractice
  Statute of limitations on fiduciary's malpractice claims against accountant, 15.12
Marital Deduction Trusts
  90:10 rule of Prob C §16361(c), effect of, 6.30
  Principal and income, adjustments between
    Generally, 13.10
    Income beneficiary compelling trustee to make trust property productive, 13.11
    Trustee's response to demand to make trust property productive, 13.12
    Unproductive assets, treatment of, 7.16
Marriage. See **Spouses**
Mediation, 14.27
Mineral Interests
  Receipts from. See **Receipts**
  Sale of mineral interests, 7.9
Minors
  Age of majority, 2.2
  Guardians. See **Guardians Ad Litem; Guardians and Guardianships**
  Omitted children, distributions to. See **Distributions**
  Posthumously-conceived child defined, 9.16
Modifications. See **Amendments and Modifications**
Mortgages and Deeds of Trust
  Gift exonerated from mortgage, deed of trust, or other lien, 9.20
  Principal or missed payments on mortgage, 1.34, 1.49, 11.9, 11.22*f*
Motions
  Application or motion to withdraw stipulation for appointment of temporary judge, 14.29
  Referee, stipulation or motion for order appointing, 14.28
Mutual Funds
  Assets on hand at end of account period, sample schedule, 1.22, 10.12*f*
Name Changes, 3.27
90:10 Rule, 6.30, 6.37
Notice and Notification
  Adjustments between principal and income, trustee's notice of proposed action before making, 13.9
  Conservators and conservatorships. See **Conservators and Conservatorships**
  Guardians and guardianships. See **Guardians and Guardianships**
  Irrevocable trust, trustees of. See **Irrevocable Trusts, Trustees of**
  Personal representative obtaining court approval of accounts at noticed hearing, 2.41
  Probate cases, jurisdiction depending on notice of hearing in, 14.18–14.19
Objections to Accounting
  Bad faith opposition to beneficiary's objection to account, fiduciary's payment of objector's attorney fees for, 8.7
  Beneficiaries' objections, limits on, 2.59

Objections to Accounting—*cont.*
   Persons who may object to accounting, 2.25
Omitted Heirs
   Distributions to omitted heirs. See **Distributions**
   Public policy considerations, 9.8
Options
   Gain or loss realized by trustee, allocation of, 7.13
   Receipts from options, accounting for, 6.12, 6.15, 6.42
Orders
   Compelling trustee to account, order, 2.50
   Conservator, order for appointment of, 2.3, 4.4
   Guardian, order for appointment of, 2.2, 4.4
   Probate court rulings as orders versus judgments, 14.15
   Referee, order appointing, 14.28
   Show cause orders. See **Show Cause Orders**
   Surcharge order, 14.38
Other States
   Real property located in foreign jurisdiction, guardians and conservators accounting for, 2.9, 6.49, 11.10
Partnerships
   Fiduciary relationship created by formation of partnership, 2.1
   Limited partnerships. See **Limited Partnerships**
   Phantom income, accounting for, 6.51
   Receipts from entities. See **Receipts**
Penalties
   See also **Sanctions**
   Contempt. See **Contempt**
   Guardians or conservators, penalties for failure to file accounting, 2.24
   Late accounts, penalties for, 2.24
   Personal representative's failure to account, penalties for, 2.38
Pension Plans. See **Retirement and Pension Plans**
Periodic Accounting
   Agents under power of attorney, no affirmative duty to account periodically, 2.4

Conservators (see Guardians and conservators, below)
Guardians and conservators
   Absconding guardian or conservator, effect of, 2.13
   Death of guardian or conservator, effect of, 2.13
   First account, local court rules governing, 2.11
   Frequency of accountings, 2.12
   Temporary guardians and conservators, 2.14
Personal representatives
   Generally, 2.32
   Mid-administration accounting, 2.33
   Petition for final distribution including summary of administration of decedent's estate, 2.32
Personal Injuries
   Minor's estate as consequence of personal injury suit, 2.2
Personal Property
   Assets on hand at end of account period, sample schedule, 1.22, 10.12f
   Gathering and organizing information regarding personal assets. See **Preparation of Fiduciary Accounting**
Personal Representatives
   Absconding personal representative, effect of, 2.36
   Approval of accounts
      Auxiliary schedule of assets on hand at beginning and end of account period, personal representative providing, 4.17, 11.2
      Noticed hearing, obtaining court approval of accounts at, 2.41
   Assets on hand at beginning of account period. See **Assets on Hand at Beginning of Account Period**
   Assets on hand at end of account period. See **Assets on Hand at End of Account Period**
   Auxiliary schedules. See **Auxiliary Schedules**
   Carry value, 4.12–4.13, 4.15–4.16

Personal Representatives—*cont.*
  Conservatorship estate, personal representative using letters testamentary to distribute assets after conservatee's death, 2.15
  Deceased or incapacitated personal representative, legal representative filing account for, 2.35
  Disbursements. See **Disbursements**
  Distributions. See **Distributions**
  Duties, purpose of, 2.5
  Failure to account
    Penalties for failure to account, 2.38
    Terminated personal representative, 2.34
  Final account. See **Final Account**
  First accounts. See **First Accounts**
  Gains and losses, reporting. See **Gains and Losses**
  Incapacitated or deceased personal representative, legal representative filing account for, 2.35
  Inspection and audit of supporting documents, 2.37
  Inventory and appraisal. See **Inventory and Appraisal**
  Nature of fiduciary relationship, 2.5
  Penalties for failure to account, 2.38
  Periodic accounting. See **Periodic Accounting**
  Personal and general personal representatives distinguished, 2.6
  Powers and duties of personal representative, purpose of, 2.5
  Public policy favoring speedy administration of decedent's estate, 2.5
  Receipts. See **Receipts**
  Report instead of account, 2.40
  Resignation or removal of personal representative, effect of, 2.34, 10.3
  Schedules, preparing. See **Schedules**
  Second and subsequent accounts. See **Second and Subsequent Accounts**
  Suspension of personal representative, effect of, 10.3
  Terminated personal representative, 2.34, 10.3
  Time. See **Time**
  Waiver of account, 2.39–2.40
Personal Residence. See **Residence and Domicile**
Petitions
  Approval of accounting. See **Approval of Accounting, Petition for**
  Final distribution. See **Final Distribution, Petition for**
  Guardian, petition for appointment of, 2.2
  Irrevocable trusts, trustees of. See **Irrevocable Trusts, Trustees of**
  Mid-administration accounting, petition by interested person for, 2.33
  Revocable trusts, trustees of, 2.70
Phantom Income
  Receipt, form 1099 phantom income not constituting, 6.51
Pleadings
  Blended pleadings in probate proceedings, 14.19
Powers of Attorney
  Generally, 2.4
  Court ordering accounting by agent, 2.4
  Definitions, 2.4
  Duties of agent, 2.4
  Financial records, accountants requesting under limited power of attorney, 15.17
  Legal entities, powers of attorney not constituting, 14.21
  Limits on agent's duty to account, 2.4
  Powers of agent, 2.4, 15.17
  Trustees distinguished from agents, 2.4
Preparation of Fiduciary Accounting
  Carry value (see Third pass: reconciling assets, below)
  Checking and savings accounts
    Description columns, 3.6
    Entering data into spreadsheet, generally, 3.5, 3.32
    Receipts and disbursements columns, 3.7
    Reconciliation, 3.9

Preparation of Fiduciary Accounting—*cont.*
Checking and savings accounts—*cont.*
    Sample completed spreadsheet, 3.51*f*
    Setting up spreadsheet, 3.4
    Transfers between accounts, 3.8
Definition of accountant, 15.1
Engagement letter. See **Engagement Letter**
Fifth pass: preparing schedules. See **Schedules**
Final review
    Cash reconciliation spreadsheets, 3.18
    Reconciling assets, 3.28
First pass: gathering and organizing working papers, 3.2
Format of trust accounts. See **Format of Trust Accounts**
Fourth pass: reconciling whole accounting
    Assets, entering data for, 3.34
    Brokerage cash accounts, entering data for, 3.33
    Cash accounts, entering data for, 3.32
    Checking spreadsheet, 3.36
    Goal of fourth pass, 3.30
    Sample completed spreadsheet, 3.56*f*
    Setting up spreadsheet, 3.31
    Special assets, entering data for, 3.35
Gathering and organizing working papers (first pass), 3.2
Goal of fiduciary accounting, 3.1
Investment accounts
    Accounts with no cash, 3.16
    Assets, 3.12
    Dividend reinvestments, 1.5, 1.8, 3.13, 3.45
    Entering data into spreadsheet, generally, 3.10–3.11, 3.33
    Money market funds, 3.15
    Reconciling cash, 3.14
    Sample completed spreadsheet, 3.52*f*
    Setting up spreadsheet, 3.4
Missing statements list, preparing, 3.2
Personal assets (see Real estate and personal assets, below)
Real estate and personal assets
    Entering data into spreadsheet, generally, 3.17
    Sample completed spreadsheet for personal property, 3.54*f*
    Sample completed spreadsheet for real property, 3.53*f*
    Setting up spreadsheet, 3.4
Reconciling assets (see Third pass: reconciling assets, below)
Reconciling cash in each account (see Second pass: reconciling cash, below)
Reconciling whole accounting (see Fourth pass: reconciling whole accounting, above)
Records. See **Records and Reports**
Refining accounting (see Sixth pass: refining accounting, below)
Sample spreadsheets
    Checking account, 3.51*f*
    Investment account, 3.52*f*
    Personal property, 3.54*f*
    Portion of asset sold, sample spreadsheet illustrating, 3.25
    Purchases and sales of same asset, sample spreadsheet illustrating, 3.26
    Purchases only, sample spreadsheet illustrating, 3.24
    Real property, 3.53*f*
    Summary of account, 3.57*f*
    Summary reconciliation spreadsheet, 3.56*f*
    Third pass spreadsheet, 3.55*f*
Savings accounts (see Checking and savings accounts, above)
Schedules, preparing. See **Schedules**
Second pass: reconciling cash
    Assets distinguished, 3.19
    Checking and savings accounts (see Checking and savings accounts, above)
    Final review, 3.18
    Goals and strategies, 3.3
    Investment accounts (see Investment accounts, above)
    Real estate and personal assets (see Real estate and personal assets, above)

Preparation of Fiduciary Accounting—*cont.*
Second pass: reconciling cash—*cont.*
  Setting up spreadsheets, 3.4
Setting up spreadsheets
  Checking and savings accounts, 3.4
  Investment accounts, 3.4
  Real estate and personal assets, 3.4
  Reconciling assets, 3.20
  Reconciling cash, 3.4
  Reconciling whole accounting, 3.31
Six passes
  Generally, 3.1
  Fifth pass: preparing schedules. See **Schedules**
  First pass: gathering and organizing working papers, 3.2
  Fourth pass: reconciling whole accounting (see Fourth pass: reconciling whole accounting, above)
  Second pass: reconciling cash (see Second pass: reconciling cash, above)
  Sixth pass: refining accounting (see Sixth pass: refining accounting, below)
  Third pass: reconciling assets (see Third pass: reconciling assets, below)
Sixth pass: refining accounting
  Allocating income and principal, 3.49
  Goal of sixth pass, 3.47
  Missing descriptions, 3.48
  Missing information, 3.50
Software used to prepare accountings. See **Computers and Computer Software**
Summary of account. See **Summary of Account**
Summary reconciliation (see Fourth pass: reconciling whole accounting, above)
Third pass: reconciling assets
  Generally, 3.22
  Assets with no activity, example, 3.27
  Cash, assets distinguished from, 3.19

Third pass: reconciling assets—*cont.*
  Entering data into spreadsheet, generally, 3.21, 3.34
  Final review, 3.28
  Goal of third pass, 3.19
  Portion of asset sold, example, 3.25
  Purchases and sales of same asset, example, 3.26
  Purchases only, example, 3.24
  Sample completed spreadsheet, 3.55*f*
  Setting up spreadsheet, 3.20
  Steps for reconciling assets, 3.23
  When account does not balance, 3.29
Transfers between accounts, 3.8, 3.27

Presumptions and Inferences
Intestacy, presumption regarding settlor or testator's intent to avoid, 9.15

Principal and Income
See also **Uniform Principal and Income Act (UPAIA)**
Additional property received during period of account, 1.6, 5.7
Adjustments between principal and income by trustee
  Generally, 8.22, 13.1, 13.5
  Factors for trustee to consider, 13.8
  Notice of proposed action, 13.9
  Shifting economic interests or tax benefits, adjustments to offset (see Shifting economic interests or tax benefits, adjustments to offset, below)
  Threshold criteria, 13.6
  When prohibited, 13.7
Allocation of receipts and disbursements between principal and income, 2.56, 3.49, 4.20, 11.4, 11.6, 15.29
Assets on hand at beginning of account period. See **Assets on Hand at Beginning of Account Period**
Assets on hand at end of account period. See **Assets on Hand at End of Account Period**

Principal and Income—*cont.*
    Changes in form of assets schedule, reporting payments of principal from debtor to trust on, 11.14, 11.18*f*
    Depreciation reserve. See **Appreciation and Depreciation**
    Disbursements of principal and income. See **Disbursements**
    Distributable net income (DNI), 14.10
    Distributions of principal and income. See **Distributions**
    Engagement letter quoting principal and income provisions of will or trust document, 15.6
    Excess income. See **Excess Income**
    Gains and losses. See **Gains and Losses**
    Marital deduction trusts. See **Marital Deduction Trusts**
    Net income, calculating, 2.56
    Receipts of principal and income. See **Receipts**
    Shifting economic interests or tax benefits, adjustments to offset
        Discretionary adjustment of Prob C §16375(a), 13.19
        Mandatory adjustment of Prob C §16375(b), 13.20
        Mandatory allocation of Prob C §16374, 13.18
    Trade or business owned by trust, accounting separately for. See **Trade or Business Owned by Trust, Accounting Separately for**
    Unitrust, conversion to, 7.16, 13.1
    UPAIA. See **Uniform Principal and Income Act (UPAIA)**

Private Professional Fiduciaries
    Duty to preserve confidences of clients, 2.70
    Original account statements, filing of, 2.23
    Website for Professional Fiduciary Association of California (PFAC), 2.70

Privileges
    Attorney-client privilege, 14.7, 14.10, 14.14
    Tax return privilege, 14.10
    Work-product privilege, 14.7

Probate Litigation. See **Litigation**

Professional Fiduciaries. See **Private Professional Fiduciaries**

Promissory Notes
    Sale for promissory note, 1.31

Proof. See **Burden of Proof**

Proposed Distributions. See **Distributions**

Prudent Investor Act
    Trustee's duty to administer trust according to, 2.48

Public Policy
    Intent of settlors and testators, protecting as matter of public policy, 9.8
    Omitted heirs, public policy considerations, 9.8
    Speedy administration of estate, public policy favoring, 2.5
    Trustee's duty to report, waiver in trust instrument void as against public policy, 2.51
    Waivers of duty to account void as against public policy, examples of, 2.47

QPRT. See **Qualified Personal Residence Trust (QPRT)**

QTIP Trust. See **Qualified Terminable Interest Property (QTIP) Trust**

Qualified Personal Residence Trust (QPRT)
    Date that residence becomes subject to trust, determining, 4.6

Qualified Terminable Interest Property (QTIP) Trust
    Adjustments between principal and income prohibited for QTIP trust, 13.7
    Income interest in QTIP trust, determining ending date for, 4.7
    Mandatory income interest, surviving spouse's interest in QTIP trust as, 4.21
    Successor trustee, bank as, 4.8

Questionnaires. See **Charts, Checklists, Questionnaires, and Tables**

Questions of Law and Fact
  Statute of limitations for actions against trustee for breach of duty, commencement date as triable issue of fact, 2.49

Real Estate Investment Trusts (REITs)
  Receipts from entities. See **Receipts**

Real Property
  Assets on hand at end of account period, sample schedule, 1.47, 10.11f
  Cancellation of indebtedness income, 1.36
  Disbursements. See **Disbursements**
  Distributions. See **Distributions**
  Foreign jurisdiction, guardians and conservators accounting for real property located in, 2.9, 6.49, 11.10
  Gathering and organizing information regarding real estate. See **Preparation of Fiduciary Accounting**
  Rent. See **Rent**
  Short sales, 1.32

Receipts
  See also **Disbursements**
  Generally, 6.1
  Additional property received during period of account, 1.6, 5.7
  Annuities, receipts from, 6.28
  Appearance of schedule, 6.2, 6.53f
  Asset-backed securities, receipts from, 6.12, 6.15, 6.42
  Assets on hand at beginning of account period
    Payor, grouping receipts by, 6.4
    Principal or income, allocation or apportionment of receipts to, 4.20, 11.4
    Refunds as asset on hand at beginning, 4.28
    Responsibility for collection of receivable, effect of fiduciary's failure to recognize, 4.28
  Bank account interest owed to trustee, 6.18, 6.57f, 11.14
  Bonds owed to trustee, interest on, 6.19, 6.58f
  Borrowed funds accounted for as receipt, 6.7
  Categories
    Generally, 6.4
    Judicial Council form for standard and simplified accounts, categories for receipts and disbursements on, 2.20
  Collateral-backed securities, 6.43
  Commingled funds
    Disclosing mistake, 6.6
    Failing to account for receipts from commingled funds, 6.50
  Common mistakes
    Commingled funds, mistakes involving, 6.6, 6.50
    Form 1099 phantom income, accounting for, 6.51
    Gross sales proceeds, accounting for, 6.48
    Late-received assets, reporting of, 6.46
    Sales proceeds, reporting of, 6.47–6.48
    Source of receipt, omitting, 6.49
    Transfers between accounts not constituting receipt, 3.8, 6.52
  Corporations (see Entities, receipts from, below)
  Decedent's estates and other trusts, receipts from, 6.12–6.13, 6.16
  Deferred compensation plans, receipts from, 6.28
  Defined, 6.1
  Derivatives, receipts from, 6.12, 6.15, 6.42
  Disclosure of mistakes, 6.6
  Dividend reinvestment programs, 1.8, 6.44, 6.60f
  Eminent domain, property taken by, 6.16
  Entities, receipts from
    Generally, 6.8
    Allocation to principal, 6.10
    Asset-backed securities, receipts from, 6.12, 6.15, 6.42
    Decedent's estates and other trusts, receipts from, 6.12–6.13, 6.16
    Definition of entity, 6.9
    Derivatives, receipts from, 6.12, 6.15, 6.42f
    Example, 6.54f

Receipts—*cont.*
  Entities, receipts from—*cont.*
    Mutual funds, receipts from, 6.11, 6.55*f*
    Options, receipts from, 6.12, 6.15, 6.42
    Trust-owned businesses for which trustee accounts separately, receipts from. See **Trade or Business Owned by Trust, Accounting Separately for**
  Environmental matters, amounts recovered from third parties to reimburse trust for disbursements related to, 6.16
  Escrow, receipts in, 1.28, 6.5
  Income (see Principal and income, receipts of, below)
  Insubstantial receipts, 6.27
  Insurance proceeds
    Allocation of insurance proceeds between income and principal, rules governing, 6.21
    Determining which schedule to use, 6.22
    Dividends paid by insurance companies, reporting of, 6.21, 6.26
    Life insurance, 6.21
    Property insurance, 6.23, 7.15, 7.20*f*
    Title insurance, 6.21, 6.24
  Investment companies (see Entities, receipts from, above)
  Limited liability companies (LLCs) (see Entities, receipts from, above)
  Liquidating assets, receipts from, 6.33
  Mineral, water, and natural resources
    Generally, 6.34
    90:10 rule, applicability of, 6.37
    Production payments under agreement that provides for interest or its equivalent, 6.36
    Receipts allocated 100 percent to income, 6.35
    Sale of mineral and water interests, 7.9
    Trust-owned interests acquired on or before January 1, 2000, 6.38
  Mutual funds, receipts from, 6.11, 6.55*f*
  Natural resources (see Mineral, water, and natural resources, above)
  90:10 rule
    Mineral and water interests, 6.37
    Trusts described in IRC §2056(b)(7) or IRC §2056(b)(5), effect of rule on, 6.30
  Options, receipts from, 6.12, 6.15, 6.42
  Partnerships (see Entities, receipts from, above)
  Preparing schedule, minimum requirements for
    Generally, 3.39, 6.3
    Borrowed funds, 6.7
    Categorizing receipts by payor, 6.4
    Disclosing mistakes, 6.6
    Escrow, receipts in, 1.28, 6.5
  Principal and income, receipts of
    Allocation of receipts and disbursements between principal and income, 2.56, 3.49, 4.20, 11.4, 11.6, 15.29
    Asset-backed securities, 6.12, 6.15, 6.42
    Bank account interest owed to trustee, 6.18, 6.57*f*, 11.14
    Bonds owed to trustee, interest on, 6.19, 6.58*f*
    Collateral-backed securities, 6.43
    Deferred compensation plans, 6.28
    Definition of income, 6.8
    Derivatives, 6.12, 6.15, 6.42
    Dividend reinvestment programs, 1.8, 6.44, 6.60*f*
    Entities, receipts from (see Entities, receipts from, above)
    Individual retirement accounts (IRAs), 6.28
    Insubstantial receipts, 6.27
    Insurance proceeds (see Insurance proceeds, above)
    Liquidating assets, 6.33
    Mineral interests (see Mineral, water, and natural resources, above)
    100 percent to income, receipts normally allocated, 6.8
    100 percent to principal, receipts normally allocated, 6.8, 6.10, 6.16
    Options, 6.12, 6.15, 6.42

Receipts—cont.
Principal and income, receipts of—cont.
Prob C §16357(c), special rules for assets listed in, 6.20, 6.59*f*
Qualified and non-qualified retirement plans, 6.28
Rental properties, receipts from, 1.27, 6.17, 6.56*f*, 13.2
Short-term and long-term capital gains, 6.11, 6.55*f*
Specifically gifted property, reporting receipts attributable to, 6.45, 8.25, 11.7
Timberland (see Timberland, below)
Trusts described in IRC §2056(b)(7) or IRC §2056(b)(5), 6.28, 6.30–6.32
Trusts not described in IRC §2056(b)(7) or IRC §2056(b)(5), 6.28–6.29
Water interests (see Mineral, water, and natural resources, above)
Prob C §16357(c), special rules for assets listed in, 6.20, 6.59*f*
Real estate investment trusts (REITs) (see Entities, receipts from, above)
Refunds as receipts
Generally, 4.28
Escrow, receipts in, 1.28, 6.5
Prepaid property tax, 6.5
Rental properties, receipts from, 1.27, 6.17, 6.56*f*, 13.2
Samples, 1.17, 1.27–1.28, 1.42
Specifically gifted property, reporting receipts attributable to, 6.45, 8.25, 11.7
Tax refunds (see Refunds as receipts, above)
Timberland
Generally, 6.39
Property acquired after January 1, 2000, 6.40
Property acquired on or before January 1, 2000, 6.41
Sale of timberland, 7.9
Transfers between accounts not constituting receipt, 3.8, 6.52
Trust-owned businesses for which trustee accounts separately, receipts from. See **Trade or Business Owned by Trust, Accounting Separately for**
UPAIA requirements (see Principal and income, above)
Water interests (see Mineral, water, and natural resources, above)

Receivables
Assets on hand at end of account period, sample schedule, 1.47, 10.11*f*

Records and Reports
Collection of records, accountant assisting fiduciary with, 15.15
Engagement letter specifying fiduciary's recordkeeping responsibilities. See **Engagement Letter**
Financial statements. See **Financial Statements**
Inspection of records. See **Inspection of Records**
Irrevocable trusts, trustees of
Duty to report, 2.44, 2.51
Recordkeeping requirements. See **Irrevocable Trusts, Trustees of**
List of records needed to prepare accounting, 15.8, 15.15, 15.28
Management-use-only reports, 15.24
Personal representative's report instead of account including basis for determining statutory fees, 2.40
Sensitive information, security measures to protect, 15.16
Suspended or removed fiduciary transferring all books and records to successor, 14.39

Reference (Appointment of Referee), 14.28–14.29

Refunds
Receipts, refunds as. See **Receipts**
Tax refunds. See **Tax Refunds**

Registered Domestic Partners. See **Domestic Partners**

Reimbursement
Attorney fees, reimbursement of, 14.40

Reimbursement—cont.
  Environmental matters, amounts recovered from third parties to reimburse trust for disbursements related to, 6.16
REITs. See **Real Estate Investment Trusts (REITs)**
Relatives
  Distributions, categorization of relatives for purposes of, 9.16
  Sample accountings, descriptions of settlor, family members, and assets in, 1.4, 1.26
Release
  Guardian, release of, 2.27
  Irrevocable trust, release of trustee's liability for disclosures made in accounting. See **Irrevocable Trusts, Trustees of**
Removal
  Attorney, removal of, 14.4
  Personal representative, effect of resignation or removal of, 2.34, 10.3
  Probate court's removal of fiduciary, 14.8, 14.35, 14.39
  Trustee, removal of, 2.66, 14.8
Rent
  Disbursements, rent payments accounted for as, 8.2, 8.6
  Receipts from rental properties, accounting for, 1.27, 6.17, 6.56f, 13.2
Repairs and Maintenance
  Conservator's powers regarding repair and maintenance of home or other dwelling, 2.3
  Sample illustrating treatment of repairs and capital improvements, 1.33
Reports. See **Records and Reports**
Residence and Domicile
  QPRT. See **Qualified Personal Residence Trust (QPRT)**
Retirement and Pension Plans
  Annuities. See **Annuities**
  Deferred compensation plans, accounting for receipts from, 6.28
  IRAs. See **Individual Retirement Accounts (IRAs)**
  Qualified and non-qualified retirement plans, accounting for receipts from, 6.28
Revocable Trusts, Trustees of
  See also **Irrevocable Trusts, Trustees of**
  Approval of account, petition for, 2.70
  Breach of trust, 2.70
  Disclosure to contingent beneficiaries, 2.70
  Duties
    Breach of duty to account, 2.70
    Distinguishing persons to whom duties owed with persons with standing, 2.69
    Persons to whom duties owed, determining, 2.43, 2.67
  Incapacity of person holding power to revoke, effect of, 2.68–2.70
  Petition for court approval of accounts, 2.70
  Safe practices, 2.70
  Schedules, preparing. See **Schedules**
  Standing to assert claims against trustee, persons with, 2.69
  Statute of limitations
    Incompetence of person with power to revoke, effect of, 2.70
    Trustee's liability to beneficiary, commencement of statute of limitations on, 2.68
  Time. See **Time**
  Trustee of irrevocable trust distinguished, 2.43
  Waiver of duty to account, 2.70
Rules of Court
  Periodic accounting by guardians and conservators, local court rules governing, 2.11
Salaries and Compensation
  Temporary conservator, compensation of, 2.24
  Trustee's compensation, disclosure of, 2.65
Sample Accountings
  Generally, 1.2
  April Cash Trust
    Generally, 1.3, 1.13
    Account beginning date bisecting settlement amount of securities purchase, 1.5
    Additions to trust, 1.16, 5.8f

Sample Accountings—*cont.*
April Cash Trust—*cont.*
   Assets on hand at beginning of account period, 1.15, 4.3
   Assets on hand at end of account period, 1.22
   Changes in form of assets, 1.23
   Descriptions of settlor, family members, and assets, 1.4
   Disbursements, 1.19
   Distributions, 1.9, 1.21
   Distributions in breach of trust, 1.9
   Dividend reinvestment, 1.8
   Gains on sales, 1.11, 1.18
   Late acquired assets, receipt from fiduciary accounting for principal and income, 1.6
   Liabilities, 1.24
   Losses on sales, 1.11, 1.20
   Miscellaneous and routine receipts and disbursements, 1.10
   Purchase of bond with accrued interest, 1.7
   Receipts, 1.17
   Sales and exchanges, 1.11
   Summary of account, 1.14
   Trustee fee as liability, 1.12, 1.24
Real estate trust
   Generally, 1.25, 1.39
   Absconding beneficiary and proposed distribution, 1.38
   Assets on hand at beginning of account period, 1.41, 4.3
   Assets on hand at end of account period, 1.47
   Cancellation of indebtedness income, 1.36
   Capital improvements and repairs, 1.33
   Changes in form of assets, 1.48
   Descriptions of settlor, family members, and assets, 1.26
   Disbursements, 1.35, 1.44, 8.5*f*
   Distributions, 1.46, 1.50
   Funeral expenses and debts of decedent, 1.30
   Gains and losses on sales, 1.29, 1.43, 1.45
   Liabilities, 1.27, 1.49
   Mortgage payments, 1.34, 1.49
   Promissory note, sale for, 1.31
   Proposed distributions, 1.50

Real estate trust—*cont.*
   Receipts, 1.27–1.28, 1.42
   Rents and security deposits, 1.27
   Repairs and capital improvements, 1.33
   Sale without gain or loss, 1.31
   Short sale, 1.32
   Summary of account, 1.40
   Trustee fee as liability, 1.49
   Trustee's loans to trust, 1.37
Sanctions
   See also **Penalties**
   Contempt for violation of probate court orders, sanctions for, 14.37
Savings Accounts, Gathering and Organizing Information Regarding. See **Preparation of Fiduciary Accounting**
Schedules
   Additional property received during period of account. See **Additional Property Received During Period of Account**
   Allocation of receipts and disbursements between principal and income, 2.56, 3.49, 4.20, 11.4, 11.6, 15.29
   Appearance of schedule. See **Appearance of Schedule**
   Assets on hand at beginning of account period. See **Assets on Hand at Beginning of Account Period**
   Assets on hand at end of account period. See **Assets on Hand at End of Account Period**
   Auxiliary schedules. See **Auxiliary Schedules**
   Caption, 3.38
   Changes in form of assets. See **Changes in Form of Asset**
   Disbursements. See **Disbursements**
   Distributions. See **Distributions**
   Gains and losses, schedules for reporting. See **Gains and Losses**
   Late acquired assets. See **Additional Property Received During Period of Account**
   Liabilities. See **Liabilities**
   Preparing schedules
      Generally, 3.37

Schedules—cont.
  Preparing schedules—cont.
    Additional property received during period of account, 3.40
    Assets on hand at beginning of account period. See **Assets on Hand at Beginning of Account Period**
    Assets on hand at end of account period. See **Assets on Hand at End of Account Period**
    Caption, 3.38
    Changes in form of assets, 3.45
    Disbursements, 3.41, 8.6
    Distributions. See **Distributions**
    Gains and losses, 3.43, 7.5–7.6
    Receipts. See **Receipts**
    Summary of account. See **Summary of Account**
    Proposed distributions. See **Distributions**
    Receipts. See **Receipts**
    Specifically devised property, 6.45, 8.25, 11.7
    Summary of account. See **Summary of Account**

S Corporations
  Phantom income, accounting for, 6.51

Second and Subsequent Accounts
  Additional property received during period of account, 5.5
  Assets on hand at beginning of account period, 4.11, 4.16
  Assets on hand at end of account period, carry value in second and subsequent account periods, 10.1

Securities
  Asset-backed securities
    Receipts from asset-backed securities, accounting for, 6.12, 6.15, 6.42
    Reporting requirements, 7.14
  Assets on hand at end of account period, sample schedule, 1.22, 10.12f
  Gathering and organizing information regarding investment accounts. See **Preparation of Fiduciary Accounting**
  Receipts
    Asset-backed securities, receipts from, 6.12, 6.15, 6.42
    Collateral-backed securities, receipts from, 6.43
  Separate assets, reporting contents of each account as, 4.32

Security Deposits
  Asset on hand at beginning of account period, scheduling security deposit as, 4.29
  Liabilities schedule, including tenant's security deposit on, 1.27, 1.49, 11.9, 11.21f

Service of Process and Papers
  Proof of service, 2.65
  Trustee's service of accounting, 2.65

Shortening Time. See **Extending and Shortening Time**

Show Cause Orders
  Personal representative ordered to appear and show cause for failure to file account, 2.38

Signatures
  Engagement letter, signature required for, 15.14
  Trustee obtaining signed proof of beneficiary's receipt of accounting, 2.65

Simplified Accounting
  See also **Standard Accounting**
  Generally, 2.16
  Judicial Council account forms, mandatory use of, 2.17, 2.21
  Permissible use of simplified accounting, 2.21
  Prob C §§1060-1063, guardian or conservator providing information required by, 2.22
  Receipts and disbursements, listing of, 2.20–2.21
  Standard accounting distinguished, 2.21
  Summary of account. See **Summary of Account**

Small Claims Court
  Advantages of using small claims court to resolve accounting disputes, 14.26

Software. See **Computers and Computer Software**

Special Administrators. See **Personal Representatives**
Special Needs Trusts, 14.2, 14.31
Specifically Devised Property, 6.45, 8.25, 11.7
Spouses
   Fiduciary relationship created by marriage, 2.1
   Marital deduction trusts. See **Marital Deduction Trusts**
   Omitted spouses, distributions to. See **Distributions**
Spreadsheets
   Advantages of using spreadsheet programs, 15.18
   Preparing fiduciary accounting, use of spreadsheets for. See **Preparation of Fiduciary Accounting**
   Sample spreadsheets
      Additions to trust, 1.16, 5.8*f*
      Assets on hand at beginning of account period, 1.15, 1.41, 4.3
      Assets on hand at end of account period. See **Assets on Hand at End of Account Period**
      Bonds. See **Bonds**
      Changes in form of assets. See **Changes in Form of Assets**
      Disbursements. See **Disbursements**
      Distributions, 1.9, 1.21, 1.46, 1.50
      Dividends. See **Dividends**
      Gains and losses. See **Gains and Losses**
      Liabilities. See **Liabilities**
      Preparing fiduciary accounting, sample spreadsheets for. See **Preparation of Fiduciary Accounting**
      Receipts, 1.17, 1.27–1.28, 1.42
      Summary of account, 1.14, 1.40, 3.57*f*, 12.2–12.3
   Summary of account
      Best practice, use of equals function on spreadsheet as, 12.4
      Sample spreadsheet, 1.14, 1.40, 3.57*f*, 12.2–12.3
Standard Accounting
   See also **Simplified Accounting**
   Generally, 2.16
   Judicial Council account forms, use of
      Generally, 2.17–2.18
      Summary of account. See **Summary of Account**
   Mandatory use of standard accounting, circumstances requiring, 2.18
   Prob C §§1060-1063, guardian or conservator providing information required by, 2.22
   Receipts and disbursements, categories for, 2.20
   Simplified accounting distinguished, 2.21
   Summary of account. See **Summary of Account**
Standing
   Revocable trusts, determining persons with standing to assert claims against trustees of, 2.69
Statutes of Limitations
   See also **Time**
   Disclosure of potential breaches of trust triggering running of statute of limitations, 8.6, 15.25
   Fiduciary's malpractice claims against accountant, statute of limitations on, 15.12
   Irrevocable trusts, trustees of. See **Irrevocable Trusts, Trustees of**
   Record retention, effect of statute of limitations on claims against trustee for actions taken during account period, 15.12
   Revocable trusts, trustees of. See **Revocable Trusts, Trustees of**
   Trustee's waiver of duty to account not triggering statute of limitations, 2.49, 2.57
Stipulations
   Private judge, stipulation to, 14.29
   Referee, stipulation or motion for order appointing, 14.28
Stocks. See **Securities**
Subsequent Accounts. See **Second and Subsequent Accounts**
Substituted Judgment
   Conservator's revocation of trust through substituted judgment, 2.70
Successor Trustees, 2.45
Summary of Account
   Generally, 12.1

Summary of Account—*cont.*
  Appearance of summary of account
    Format required by Probate Code, sample, 12.2
    Improved summary of account, sample, 12.3
  Best practices
    Charges equal credits, setting up equation in worksheet to confirm, 12.5
    Discrepancies in account, steps to address, 12.6
    Equals function on spreadsheet, use of, 12.4
  Carry value, use of, 12.7
  Charges equal credits, setting up equation in worksheet to confirm, 12.5
  Common mistakes, avoiding, 12.7
  Discrepancies in account, steps to address, 12.6
  Equals function on spreadsheet, use of, 12.4
  Judicial Council form for standard and simplified accounts
    Mandatory use of, 2.17, 2.19–2.21
    Receipts and disbursements, categories for, 2.20
  Preparing summary of account
    Generally, 3.46
    Sample spreadsheet, 3.57f
  Samples, 1.14, 1.40, 3.57f, 12.2–12.3
  Supporting schedules. See **Schedules**

Summary Reconciliation. See **Preparation of Fiduciary Accounting**

Suspension of Fiduciary, 10.3, 14.8, 14.33–14.34, 14.39

Tables. See **Charts, Checklists, Questionnaires, and Tables**

Taxes
  Disbursements. See **Disbursements**
  Distributions. See **Distributions**
  Estate tax. See **Estate Tax**
  Generation-skipping transfer tax. See **Generation-Skipping Transfer Tax**
  Property taxes, 6.5, 8.21
  Refunds. See **Tax Refunds**
  Returns. See **Tax Returns**

Tax Refunds
  Asset on hand at beginning of account period, reporting tax refund as, 4.28
  Receipts, refunds as. See **Receipts**

Tax Returns
  Privilege regarding tax returns, 14.10
  Trade or business, reporting net income or loss from (Schedule C or F), 2.20

Temporary Conservators. See **Conservators and Conservatorships**

Temporary Guardians. See **Guardians and Guardianships**

Tenant. See **Landlord and Tenant**

Third Parties
  Environmental matters, amounts recovered from third parties to reimburse trust for disbursements related to, 6.16
  Incapacity of beneficiary, trustee's duty to account to third party due to, 2.45
  Qualified personal residence trust (QPRT), effect of third-party trustee's written agreement to administer property, 4.6
  Settlor's death, effect of third party transferring assets to trustee due to, 4.6

Timberland
  Receipts from timberland. See **Receipts**
  Sale of timberland, 7.9

Time
  See also **Statutes of Limitations**
  Assets on hand at beginning of account period. See **Assets on Hand at Beginning of Account Period**
  Assets on hand at end of account period. See **Assets on Hand at End of Account Period**
  Conservators
    Assets on hand at beginning of account period. See **Assets on Hand at Beginning of Account Period**
    Assets on hand at end of account period. See **Assets on Hand at End of Account Period**

Time—*cont.*
  Conservators—*cont.*
    Duration of conservatorships, 2.3
    Inventory and appraisal, deadline to file, 2.9, 4.9
    Penalties for late accounts, 2.24
    Periodic accounting. See **Periodic Accounting**
  Engagement letter, deadlines addressed in, 15.7
  Extending. See **Extending and Shortening Time**
  Gains and losses, time considerations. See **Gains and Losses**
  Guardians
    Assets on hand at beginning of account period. See **Assets on Hand at Beginning of Account Period**
    Assets on hand at end of account period. See **Assets on Hand at End of Account Period**
    Duration of duties, 2.2
    Inventory and appraisal, deadline to file, 2.9, 4.9
    Penalties for late accounts, 2.24
    Periodic accounting. See **Periodic Accounting**
    Release of guardian by ward, effective date of, 2.27
  Irrevocable trusts, trustees of (see Trustees, below)
  Mid-administration accounting, time considerations for court-ordered, 2.33
  Periodic accounting. See **Periodic Accounting**
  Personal representatives
    Assets on hand at beginning of account period. See **Assets on Hand at Beginning of Account Period**
    Assets on hand at end of account period. See **Assets on Hand at End of Account Period**
    Deceased or incapacitated personal representative, legal representative timely filing account for, 2.35
    Inventory and appraisal, deadline to file, 2.6, 2.30, 4.9

Personal representatives—*cont.*
    Terminated personal representative, timely filing of account by, 2.34, 10.3
  Revocable trusts, trustees of (see Trustees, below)
  Shortening. See **Extending and Shortening Time**
  Trustees
    Assets on hand at beginning of account period. See **Assets on Hand at Beginning of Account Period**
    Assets on hand at end of account period. See **Assets on Hand at End of Account Period**
    Frequency of accountings by, 2.50, 4.10
    Inventory and appraisal, attorney recommending deadline for completion of, 4.10
    Objections to account by beneficiaries, limits on, 2.59
    Order compelling trustee to account, 2.50
    Petition to compel report, 2.51
Title and Title Companies
  Receipts, 6.21, 6.24
  Schedule for reporting title insurance proceeds, determining, 6.24
Trade or Business Owned by Trust, Accounting Separately for
  Generally, 13.2
  Disbursements, separate categories for each real property and business enterprise, 8.9, 8.29*f*
  Examples of activities for which trustees may account separately, 13.3
  Guidelines for accounting separately for activity, 13.4
  Receipts
    Generally, 6.12, 6.14, 13.2
    Rental properties, receipts from, 1.27, 6.17, 6.56*f*, 13.2
Trustees (Generally)
  Agents under powers of attorney distinguished, 2.4
  Assets on hand at beginning of account period. See **Assets on Hand at Beginning of Account Period**

Trustees (Generally)—*cont.*
    Assets on hand at end of account period. See **Assets on Hand at End of Account Period**
    Auxiliary schedules. See **Auxiliary Schedules**
    Breach of trust. See **Breach of Trust**
    Disbursements. See **Disbursements**
    Distributions. See **Distributions**
    Final account, 10.4
    First accounts. See **First Accounts**
    Gains and losses, reporting. See **Gains and Losses**
    Historical background, 2.7
    Inventory and appraisal. See **Inventory and Appraisal**
    Irrevocable trusts, accounts required of trustees of. See **Irrevocable Trusts, Trustees of**
    Loans by trustee to trust, 1.37
    Receipts. See **Receipts**
    Revocable trusts, accounts required of trustees of. See **Revocable Trusts, Trustees of**
    Schedules, preparing. See **Schedules**
    Second and subsequent accounts. See **Second and Subsequent Accounts**
    Successor trustees, 4.8
    Time. See **Time**
    Vacancy, trustee assuming office after, 4.8
    Waiver of account, trustee requesting, 2.39

Trusts
    Creation of trust, 2.7
    Definitions, 2.7
    Disaster clause, 14.23
    GRAT. See **Grantor Retained Annuity Trust (GRAT)**
    Irrevocable trusts, accounts required of trustees of. See **Irrevocable Trusts, Trustees of**
    Legal entity, trust not constituting, 14.21
    Marital deduction trusts. See **Marital Deduction Trusts**
    QPRT. See **Qualified Personal Residence Trust (QPRT)**
    Receipts. See **Receipts**
    REITs. See **Real Estate Investment Trusts (REITs)**
    Revocable trusts, accounts required of trustees of. See **Revocable Trusts, Trustees of**
    Special needs trusts, 14.2, 14.31
    Trade or business owned by trust, accounting separately for. See **Trade or Business Owned by Trust, Accounting Separately for**
    Trustees. See **Trustees (Generally)**
    Will-substitute trusts as tools for avoiding probate, 2.8

Types of Fiduciaries
    Generally, 2.1
    Administrators of estate. See **Personal Representatives**
    Agents under powers of attorney. See **Powers of Attorney**
    Conservators. See **Conservators and Conservatorships**
    Executors. See **Personal Representatives**
    Guardians ad litem. See **Guardians Ad Litem**
    Guardians. See **Guardians and Guardianships**
    Personal representatives. See **Personal Representatives**
    Private professional fiduciaries. See **Private Professional Fiduciaries**
    Special administrators. See **Personal Representatives**
    Trustees
        Generally. See **Trustees (Generally)**
        Irrevocable trusts. See **Irrevocable Trusts, Trustees of**
        Revocable trusts. See **Revocable Trusts, Trustees of**

Uniform Principal and Income Act (UPAIA)
    See also **Principal and Income**
    Generally, 1.1, 5.7
    Agents under power of attorney, limits on duties of, 2.4
    Chart, allocation of receipts and disbursements under California Uniform Principal and Income Act, 15.29
    Distributions, rules governing. See **Distributions**

Uniform Principal and Income Act (UPAIA) —*cont.*
Four components of UPAIA, 13.1
Gains and losses, requirements for reporting. See **Gains and Losses**
Receipts. See **Receipts**
Terminology
Accounting period, 2.56, 7.14
Estate trust, 13.7
Income, 2.56, 6.8, 13.1
Partial liquidations, 6.10
When an income interest begins, 4.6
When an income interest ends, 4.6

Unitrusts
Conversion to, 7.16, 13.1

Unproductive Assets
Marital deduction trusts, treatment of unproductive assets in, 7.16

UPAIA. See **Uniform Principal and Income Act (UPAIA)**

Valuation of Assets
Carry value. See **Carry Value**
Gross fair market value, 4.1

Void and Voidable Transactions
Trustee's duties
Duty to report, waiver in trust instrument void as against public policy, 2.51
Waivers of duty to account as void, examples of, 2.47

Waiver (Generally)
Account. See **Waiver of Account**
Confidentiality, waiver of, 14.5
Conflict of interest, waiver of, 14.5
Work-product privilege, waiver of, 14.7

Waiver of Account
Conservatorship, 2.26
Guardianship, 2.26
Irrevocable trust, waiver of trustee's duty to account. See **Irrevocable Trusts, Trustees of**
Personal representatives, 2.39–2.40
Revocable trust, waiver of trustee's duty to account, 2.70

Water Interests
Receipts from water interests. See **Receipts**
Sale of water interests, 7.9

Websites
Professional Fiduciary Association of California (PFAC), website for, 2.70

Wills
Administrator with will annexed defined, 2.6
Holographic wills, 9.15, 9.19
Intestacy, broad and liberal interpretation of will provision to avoid, 9.15
Will-substitute trusts as tools for avoiding probate, 2.8

Word and Phrases. See **Construction and Interpretation; Definitions**

Work-Product Privilege, 14.7

Writings
Beneficiary's written waiver, effect on trustee's duty to account, 2.48
Qualified personal residence trust (QPRT), writing requirements for establishing, 4.6
Release of trustee, writing requirement, 2.61

Make sure you are using the latest update

For your convenience, the following list identifies the most recent publication date of each CEB update (as of March 2015).

Update Title	Product Number	Publication Date
Advising California Common Interest Communities, 2d Edition	RE-30531	12/14
Advising California Employers and Employees	BU-33689	2/15
Advising California Nonprofit Corporations, 3d Edition	BU-33945	7/14
Advising California Partnerships, 3d Edition	BU-32887	2/15
Appeals and Writs in Criminal Cases, 2d Edition	CR-33667	6/14
Business Buy-Sell Agreements	BU-31495	7/14
Business Succession Planning: Strategies for California Estate Planners and Business Attorneys	ES-34034	8/14
California Administrative Hearing Practice, 2d Edition	CP-32679	10/14
California Administrative Mandamus, 3d Edition	CP-32892	5/14
California Attorney Fee Awards, 3d Edition	CP-34015	3/15
California Attorney's Guide to Damages, 2d Edition	CP-33552	12/14

Update Title	Product Number	Publication Date
California Automobile Insurance Law Guide, 2d Edition	TO-30201	10/14
California Basic Practice Handbook	MI-34272	10/14
California Business Litigation	BU-33572	6/14
California Child Custody Litigation and Practice	FA-31888	5/14
California Child and Spousal Support: Establishing, Modifying, and Enforcing	FA-33844	7/14
California Civil Appellate Practice, 3d Edition	CP-32439	5/14
California Civil Discovery Practice, 4th Edition	CP-32298	5/14
California Civil Litigation Forms Manual	CP-34477	10/14
California Civil Procedure Before Trial, 4th Edition	CP-31701	7/14
California Civil Writ Practice, 4th Edition	CP-33887	2/15
California Client Communications Manual: Sample Letters and Forms	MI-34263	3/15
California Conservatorship Practice	ES-33529	5/14
California Construction Contracts, Defects, and Litigation	RE-33797	11/14
California Criminal Law Forms Manual, 2d Edition	CR-33209	9/14
California Criminal Law Procedure and Practice, 2014	CR-32116	5/14
California Criminal Sentencing Enhancements 2014	CR-34163	4/14
California Decedent Estate Practice, 2d Ed V 1, 2, 3	ES-33045	7/14
California Domestic Partnerships and Same Sex Marriage	FA-30101	2/15

Update Title	Product Number	Publication Date
California Easements and Boundaries: Law and Litigation	RE-31506	7/14
California Elder Law Litigation: An Advocate's Guide	ES-33622	5/14
California Elder Law Resources, Benefits, and Planning: An Advocate's Guide	ES-33632	8/14
California Estate Planning	ES-33463	4/14
California Eviction Defense Manual, 2d Edition	RE-32083	6/14
California Expert Witness Guide, 2d Edition	CP-31685	3/14
California Franchise Law and Practice	BU-33822	3/13
California Government Tort Liability Practice, 4th Edition	TO-33137	2/15
California Guardianship Practice 2015	ES-33531	1/15
California Juvenile Dependency Practice 2015	CR-34125	2/15
California Land Use Practice	RE-33598	8/14
California Landlord-Tenant Practice, 2d Edition	RE-32698	4/14
California Law of Contracts	BU-33617	3/14
California Liability Insurance Practice: Claims & Litigation	CP-39265	9/14
California Local Probate Rules 2015	ES-39668	2/15
California Marital Settlements and Other Family Law Agreements, 3d Edition	FA-35519	3/14
California Mortgages, Deeds of Trust, and Foreclosure Litigation, 4th Edition	RE-33926	1/15
California Mechanics Liens and Related Construction Remedies, 4th Edition	RE-33092	10/14
California Personal Injury Proof	TO-34151	5/14

Update Title	Product Number	Publication Date
California Powers of Attorney and Health Care Directives	ES-33906	10/14
California Probate Code Annotated to CEB Publications 2015	ES-31198	1/15
California Probate Workflow Manual Revised	ES-31567	8/14
California Property Insurance: Law and Litigation	RE-34063	5/14
California Real Estate Bankruptcies: Law and Litigation	RE-34172	6/12
California Real Estate Brokers: Law and Litigation	RE-33865	7/14
California Real Estate Finance Practice: Strategies and Forms	RE-33186	1/15
California Real Property Practice Forms Manual	RE-30927	7/14
California Real Property Remedies and Damages, 2d Edition	RE-33444	8/14
California Real Property Sales Transactions, 4th Edition	RE-33698	2/15
California Subdivision Map Act, 2d Edition	RE-33255	8/14
California Title Insurance Practice, 2d Edition	RE-32623	5/14
California Summary Judgment 2014	CP-34084	6/14
California Tort Damages, 2d Edition	TO-33514	1/15
California Tort Guide, 3d Edition	TO-32541	2/15
California Trial Objections 2014	CP-32557	6/14
California Trial Practice: Civil Procedure During Trial, 3d Edition	CP-32191	4/14
California Trust Administration, 2d Edition	ES-33305	3/15
California Trust and Probate Litigation	ES-32857	3/15
California UCC Sales and Leases	BU-33474	12/14

Update Title	Product Number	Publication Date
California Uninsured Motorist Practice, 2d Edition	TO-33284	7/14
California Wage and Hour: Law and Litigation	BU-34145	1/15
California Will Drafting, 3d Edition	ES-30325	11/14
California Workers' Compensation Practice, 4th Edition	WC-33155	6/14
California Workers' Damages Practice, 2d Edition	WC-33295	9/14
CJER Benchbook: Domestic Violence Cases in Criminal Court, 2014	CR-33766	6/14
CJER Benchbook: Search & Seizure, 2d Edition	CR-33599	8/14
CJER Felony Sentencing Handbook 2015	CR-33151	3/15
CJER Mandatory Criminal Jury Instructions Handbook 2014	CR-33101	1/15
Complete Plans for Small and Mid-Size Estates	ES-32928	11/14
Condemnation Practice in California, 3d Edition	RE-31309	10/14
Counseling California Corporations, 3d Edition	BU-33816	4/14
Crossover Issues in Estate Planning and Family Law	ES-34233	8/14
Debt Collection Practice in California, 2d Edition	BU-32987	12/14
Dividing Pensions and Other Employee Benefits in California	FA-32387	7/14
Drafting Business Contracts: Principles, Techniques and Forms	BU-30802	1/14
Drafting California Irrevocable Trusts, 3d Edition	ES-32719	8/14
Drafting California Revocable Trusts, 4th Edition	ES-33612	9/14

Update Title	Product Number	Publication Date
Drafting Employment Documents for California Employees	BU-34243	11/14
Effective Direct & Cross Examination	CP-32331	11/04
Effective Introduction of Evidence, 2d Edition	CP-33236	12/14
Employment Damages and Remedies	CP-34252	4/14
Estate Planning for Special Assets	ES-33511	12/14
Family Law Financial Discovery	FA-33857	1/15
Fee Agreement Forms Manual, 2d Edition	MI-33248	9/14
Financing and Protecting California Businesses	BU-31899	2/15
Forming and Operating California Limited Liability Companies, 3d edition	BU-30021	12/14
Forming California Common Interest Developments	RE-33612	1/15
Ground Lease Practice, 2d Edition	RE-33083	6/13
Intellectual Property In Business Transactions	BU-33736	4/14
Internet Law & Practice in California	BU-33581	8/14
Jefferson's California Evidence Benchbook, 4th Edition	CP-33836	3/15
Neighbor Disputes and Remedies	RE-34071	4/14
Office Leasing: Drafting and Negotiating the Lease	RE-30891	12/14
Organizing Corporations in California, 3d Edition	BU-33425	3/15
Persuasive Opening Statements and Closing Arguments	CP-39653	10/03
Practice Under the California Environmental Quality Act, 2d Edition	RE-33787	3/15

Update Title	Product Number	Publication Date
Practice Under the California Family Code: Dissolution, Legal Separation, Nullity 2015	FA-31956	3/15
Practice Under the California Family Code: Case and Legislation Highlights 2015	FA-31956	3/15
Privacy Compliance and Litigation in California	BU-33936	9/14
Real Property Exchanges, 3d Edition	RE-33568	10/13
Retail Leasing: Drafting and Negotiating the Lease	RE-33577	11/14
Sales and Mergers of California Businesses	BU-33454	9/14
Scientific Evidence in California Criminal Cases	CR-32365	9/13
Secured Transactions in California Commercial Law Practice, 2d Edition	BU-33395	1/15
Selecting & Forming Business Entities, 2d Edition	BU-33317	4/14
Small Business Tax Deductions 2010	BU-31904	5/10
Special Needs Trusts: Planning, Drafting, and Administration	ES-33746	6/14
Trade Secrets Practice in California, 2d Edition	BU-32599	11/14
Trial Attorney's Evidence Code Notebook 2015	CP-31099	1/15
Wrongful Employment Termination Practice, 2d Edition	CP-32658	5/14

Not Yet Updated	**Product Number**
California Tort Forms From Expert Litigators	TO-3011*

To Order Forms on CD

Forms CDs include both Word and WordPerfect formats of the attorney-drafted forms in this book. You are not required to purchase the Forms CD when you buy the book but you must own the book in order to buy the Forms CD.

Book Title: _____

☐ Please send me the Forms CD for the above book for $54.95 plus applicable sales tax and shipping.

Ship to:
Name:

State Bar No.:

Firm:

Street:

City/State/Zip:

Telephone:

E-mail:

Purchase of this Forms CD makes you a CEB Automatic Update customer. Updates of Forms CDs will be sent to you automatically as they are released at a special discount price. You may cancel this service at any time.

Prices subject to change.

Call Toll-Free 1-800-232-3444   **Fax Toll-Free 1-800-640-6994**

Send This Coupon To:
CEB, Order Dept., 2100 Franklin Street, Suite 500
Oakland, CA 94612-3098

Priority Code 5391A

To Order OnLaw Titles

OnLAW® gives you online access to more than 140 of CEB's California practice guides. With OnLAW you can search the full text of CEB's publications to find the expert step-by-step guidance, legal analysis, and forms you will need to practice law in California.

If you already own the book, the OnLAW version can be purchased for only $95!

A subscription allows access by the user for one year and includes any updates or revisions during that year. Law firms, corporate legal departments, and public agencies may purchase additional user access to an OnLAW Library or title for a small fee. Additional users must claim a seat from the firm or agency to have access. OnLAW subscriptions are automatically renewed. Near the end of a subscription period, an invoice will be sent for the next year's subscription. Prompt payment of the renewal invoice will allow for uninterrupted access for the next year.

Call CEB Customer Service Toll-Free
1-800-232-3444

Priority Code 5391A
CD Order 6 x 9